IFIP Advances in Information and Communication Technology 681

IFIP Advances in Information and Communication Technology

The IFIP AICT series publishes state-of-the-art results in the sciences and technologies of information and communication. The scope of the series includes: foundations of computer science; software theory and practice; education; computer applications in technology; communication systems; systems modeling and optimization; information systems; ICT and society; computer systems technology; security and protection in information processing systems; artificial intelligence; and human-computer interaction.

Edited volumes and proceedings of refereed international conferences in computer science and interdisciplinary fields are featured. These results often precede journal publication and represent the most current research.

The principal aim of the IFIP AICT series is to encourage education and the dissemination and exchange of information about all aspects of computing.

More information about this series at https://link.springer.com/bookseries/6102

Ton van Kollenburg · Alinda Kokkinou ·
Olivia McDermott
Editors

Challenging the Future with Lean

9th IFIP WG 5.7
European Lean Educator Conference, ELEC 2023
's-Hertogenbosch, The Netherlands, October 24–26, 2023
Proceedings

Springer

Editors
Ton van Kollenburg
Avans University of Applied Science
Breda, The Netherlands

Alinda Kokkinou
Avans University of Applied Science
Breda, The Netherlands

Olivia McDermott
University of Galway
Galway, Ireland

ISSN 1868-4238 ISSN 1868-422X (electronic)
IFIP Advances in Information and Communication Technology
ISBN 978-3-031-63264-8 ISBN 978-3-031-63265-5 (eBook)
https://doi.org/10.1007/978-3-031-63265-5

This Springer imprint is published by the registered company Springer Nature Switzerland AG
The registered company address is: Gewerbestrasse 11, 6330 Cham, Switzerland

Preface

The 9th European Lean Educators Conference (ELEC 2023) aimed to encourage Lean practitioners, educators, and researchers to "Challenge the Future with Lean," examining how important societal issues such as war, healthcare, digitalization, and sustainability can be addressed through Lean thinking. The ELEC community views Lean thinking as a broad management and operations improvement philosophy, grounded in science and encompassing a wide range of methods, techniques, and tools. ELEC conferences therefore promote the exchange of knowledge both within academia, but more importantly, also between academic institutions and industry. True to this mission, ELEC 2023 provided a platform for educators, researchers, trainers, consultants, and practitioners to meet, share their knowledge, and learn from each other. ELEC 2023 was organized by the Centre of Expertise Wellbeing Economy and New Entrepreneurship and hosted by Avans University of Applied Sciences in 's-Hertogenbosch, the Netherlands from October 24–26, 2023. During the course of three intellectually stimulating days, a mix of keynotes, parallel sessions, and interactive workshops highlighted the challenges ahead, and equipped us with resources to deal with them.

On day one of the conference, Jaap van de Heuvel, Professor Emeritus of Healthcare Management, gave an inspiring keynote highlighting the challenges faced by healthcare, and demonstrating how he introduced Six Sigma in hospitals across the Netherlands, achieving significant improvements in operational performance. Later in his career he emphasized the role of Lean, focusing on people and leadership in communicating the vision, guiding the implementation, but also empowering employees in order to achieve more benefits. The second keynote was about the need for organizations to adopt a company-wide and multidisciplinary approach to digitalization. Alinda Kokkinou, associate lector at Avans University of Applied Sciences, used a bicycle wheel as a metaphor to explain how an organization's data analytic capability needs to be strongly linked to its strategy, and give equal importance to multiple implementation aspects, in order to be fit for purpose for the organization. The day was concluded with presentations in parallel sessions.

Day two of the conference started with a humbling yet optimistic keynote by Serhii Komberianov, President of Lean Institute Ukraine, who joined online from Ukraine to describe how Lean practices were successfully being applied in a situation of war, and the context of a devasted economy. One of the key findings was that Lean companies had fewer problems with relocation. Serhii emphasized the role of leadership in time of crisis and the importance of combining Lean and Agile to set small goals for overwhelmed teams. Some applications of Lean that were particularly helpful in a war situation included the rapid relocation of production facilities and increasing the speed of reconstruction. Joriene Beks, specialist in psychological safety, stressed its importance as a key enabler of better, performing teams. Through a combination of probing questions and empirical evidence, Joriene explained that better-performing teams report making more mistakes, and that this is due to team members experiencing clearer boundaries and more trust, thereby having the courage to speak up, self-reflect, and thus learn from mistakes. To create psychological safety it is important to try it and take small steps to improve it. After these two keynotes again presentations were given in parallel sessions.

In the afternoon of the second day, Michael Sanders, Grand Master in Quantum Lean, gave a provocative keynote on Quantum Lean, explaining that the only Key Performance Indicator that mattered was the time a product spent in the system. Focusing on improving this Key Performance Indicator would significantly simplify the methods, while concurrently improving other Key Performance Indicators such as inventory, costs, and lead time for customers. Mark Hijmans, Senior Manager Operational Excellence at ASML, followed by puzzling the audience with the statement that 100% of successful change programs had the right methodology as well as 98% of unsuccessful programs. Hijmans sees three barriers causing resistance to change: failure to see and feel the need for change, failure to move, and failure to finish.

Day three of the conference was about "Challenging the Future with Lean." Jim Lippens and Iris Hond joined forces to give an inspirational and moving keynote, highlighting the human aspects of any transformation. Jim Lippens, CEO of 4D Lean, emphasized the importance of passion and talent and stepping out of one's comfort zone. To illustrate this concept, Iris Hond relayed her personal story of overcoming difficulties and growing up to become a world-class musician. She concluded with three lessons that were important to her: we are all equal, create a culture of belonging, and make a real connection with others. Rose Heathcote, Senior Advisor at Thinking People, concluded the keynote lineup by challenging us to a more sustainable future with Lean, and reassuring us with a touch of humor that not all companies that make money are bad, and sustainability is a good thing for them too, because sustainable enterprises are competitive, resilient, and take care of the planet for future generations. We would like to thank all our keynote speakers and presenters for sharing their experiences, insights, and inspiration with us.

In this book, you will find the proceedings of ELEC 2023. We would like to thank the International Federation for Information Processing (IFIP) for sponsoring the conference for the 3rd time in its history. The conference was organized in close collaboration with the IFIP Working Group 5.7 Special Interest Group (SIG) on the Future of Lean Thinking and Practice. IFIP Working Group 5.7 also sponsored the publication of the proceedings. A total of 35 papers were submitted to the conference. After a rigorous double-blind peer review, 23 papers were included in the proceedings. Each paper was sent out to three reviewers. The average number of reviews per paper was 2.2. We also want to take this opportunity to thank our reviewers for their time and effort.

We hope that ELEC 2023 achieved its purpose to stimulate the exchange of research results and practical experiences, thereby enhancing the state of the art of Lean thinking and practice.

October 2023

Ton van Kollenburg
Alinda Kokkinou
Olivia McDermott

Organization

Conference Chair

Ton van Kollenburg	Avans University of Applied Sciences, The Netherlands

Program Chair

Ton van Kollenburg	Avans University of Applied Sciences, The Netherlands

Conference Co-chairs

Maurice Janssen	Organon, The Netherlands
Jeroen Kooijman	Avans University of Applied Sciences, The Netherlands

International Advisory Board

Arno Koch	Makigami.info, Belgium
Christian Groeneveld	B Lab, The Netherlands
Daryl John Powell	SINTEF Manufacturing, Norway
Helen Zak	Shingo Institute, USA
Eefke de Kam	Futureprove, The Netherlands
Jim Lippens	4D Lean, Belgium
Kjeld Aij	Erasmus Medical Center, The Netherlands
Leon van der Loo	Möbius Business Redesign, The Netherlands
Pascal Pollet	Sirris, Belgium
Patricia Verstappen	Maruna Continuous Improvement, The Netherlands
René Aernoudts	Lean Management Institute, The Netherlands
Edwin Drabbels	Triodin, The Netherlands

International Scientific Committee

Corné Dirne	Fontys University of Applied Sciences, The Netherlands
Christoph Roser	Karlsruhe University of Applied Sciences, Germany
Jannes Slomp	HAN University of Applied Sciences, The Netherlands
Dinis Carvalho	Universidade do Minho, Portugal
Monica Rossi	Politecnico di Milano, Italy
Dennis Gawlik	University of Bahrain, Bahrain
Peter Hines	Waterford Institute of Technology, Ireland

Contents

Sustainability

Social Lean Production

Education

Lean Concepts

Towards a Reappreciation of the Concept of Value in Sustainable and Circular Lean Thinking: A Proposal for an Ethically Based Lean Practice

Joop de Zwart(✉) and Ton van Kollenburg

AVANS University of Applied Sciences, Hogeschoollaan 1, Breda, The Netherlands
Jg.dezwart@avans.nl

Abstract. Lean thinking has been influenced by developments in the field of sustainability and circularity. This has led to the development of concepts like Lean-green and Circular Lean, and many have proposed alternative lists of wastes, to address the challenges that modern society faces. A concept that received little attention in these developments is the concept of value. In traditional Lean thinking, waste was defined as everything that does not contribute to customer value. It seems, however, that the increasing number of environmental and social wastes at least suggest that there has been a shift in the way value is conceived. This (conceptual) paper a) traces down the value shift underlying the increasing number of wastes and b) proposes a reappreciation of the concept in Lean practices.

Keywords: Lean Thinking · Ethics · Values · Sustainability

1 Introduction

Many scholars agree upon the idea that current economic development is destroying the planet [1]. As far back as 1972, the Club of Rome warned that economic growth would ultimately stretch beyond the capacities of the planet [2]. In the decades that followed, the body of knowledge on what would later be called sustainable development grew steadily. However, criticizing an existing system is one thing, changing it is quite a different story. More recently, Circular economy has become one of the ways to conceptualise both the destructive forces of traditional linear economy and showing along what lines change can be achieved [3].

The development from a linear towards a circular economy is a deeply profound one, which will not only require change at a superficial level, but rather changes on a systemic level [4]. To achieve such a transition, for example, the European Commission has introduced policies to stimulate the development towards a more (sustainable and) circular economy [5]. But also, at the level of individual corporations people are searching for ways to improve their practices. Next to attempts to radically change business models [6] or redesign products [7], a growing number of publications look for the necessary

Published by Springer Nature Switzerland AG 2024
T. van Kollenburg et al. (Eds.): ELEC 2023, IFIP AICT 681, pp. 3–11, 2024.
https://doi.org/10.1007/978-3-031-63265-5_1

change in Lean thinking and continuous improvement. Many contributions have been made to improve sustainability and circularity performance of corporations (e.g., Lean-green [8, 9]), combining Lean thinking and sustainability and, more recently, combining Lean thinking and circularity [10].

Combining the more radical ideas of new circular business models and redesigning products (be it as a service or not) with the more incremental approach of Lean thinking could improve business practices as a whole. In this paper we focus on the incremental approach of Lean thinking, in its different varieties as it seeks to "increase value of products by minimizing waste", as a literature study on Lean and the circular economy states [10]. Of course, there is nothing new about that, you can find it in all the classics on Lean thinking. What stands out if one reads on in this and other papers and books, is that most attention is given to the concept of *waste*, and much less (or close to none) to *value*.

The fact that truly little attention is paid to value (or values), does not mean that there has been no shift in what is of value. There has been an implicit shift from a narrow interpretation of value as customer value towards a wider conception of value. In other words, the ethics behind Lean thinking developed during the years, but is has not yet been acknowledged in the concept of value. *How can the concept of value be addressed in such a way that developments in the field of sustainability and circularity are adequately considered?*

In this conceptual paper we will first show how the concept of value has moved implicitly from a narrow perspective of customer value, toward a broader conception of value. What this broader conception of value means for an individual company is difficult to establish universally in a paper like this. Therefore, we suggest an approach that explicitly includes reflecting upon the company's value system by the stakeholders of the company. From that point onward, it should be easier (although not easy at all) to translate values into performance indicators and programs of continuous improvement.

2 The Concept of Waste and Value in Traditional Lean Thinking, Lean-Green and Circular Lean

'*Muda*. It is the one word of Japanese you really must know. It sounds awful as it rolls off your tongue and it should, because *muda* means "waste," specifically any human activity which absorbs resources but creates no value' [11]. These are the opening words of the introduction of *Lean Thinking*, by Womack and Jones. Thus, they place waste in the centre of attention of their work, next to the concept of value, which they use as the ultimate criterion to establish what adds value and what does not. Also, Liker [12] puts banishing waste at the heart of the Toyota Production System. Perhaps it is there, immediately, where a circle initiates, from which it is difficult to escape: 'Value can only be defined by the ultimate customer. And it is only meaningful when expressed in terms of a specific product (…) which meets the customer's needs at a specific price at a specific time' [11].

Although very brief, the first paragraph of this section does contain what both Womack and Jones and Liker consider to be at the heart of Lean thinking. From that point onward, wastes are defined to be everything that does not contribute to customer value.

Let us call this view on value and waste Traditional Lean (TL). TL has a narrow definition of value – only to be defined by the customer – and therefore, a narrow definition of waste. It must be said, however, that this definition still provides many companies with useful insights in their efficiency (or the lack of it). Many companies have only started to explore the benefits of this way of looking at their daily practices.

The choice for this approach to (customer value) is a normative one. It presupposes that the goal, the *raison d'être* of the corporation is the creation of customer value. That is as narrow as the view on which the shareholder value is the main goal of the corporation. To the question 'what is the responsibility of the corporation?' TL seems to have a simple answer: creating customer value by banishing waste. Again, that is just as narrow an answer as 'creating shareholders value' (by reducing costs).

To move towards a more sustainable future, therefore, the concept of waste needs to be widened. Arroyo and Gonzalez [13], for example, widen waste from within the context of lean construction. They wish to "update and rethink the concept of waste" in such a way, that it includes "environmental and social impacts". Starting with the seven wastes, distinguished by Ohno [14],[1] they (like others, such as Zokaei et al. [8]) add environmental waste. They state that "the difficulty in relating both Lean and environment is due to the fact that environmental waste is not the focus of improvement in traditional Lean management". Other authors have tried to do similar things: Schmitt et al. [15] elaborate mainly on circularity potential at different levels of the manufacturing system but does so without mentioning value. They verify the thought of Arroyo and Gonzalez [13] that Lean thinking should also incorporate environmental benefits, not just customer value, but criticise Lean-Green (see below), that "it primarily focuses on internal operations".

The same happens in another important branch of the Lean debate, which explicitly tries to connect Lean thinking with sustainability: the so-called *Lean-Green Manufacturing* (LGM), already mentioned once. This refinement of Lean thought aims specifically at the "reduction of the environmental footprint and minimisation of health risks throughout the entire product life cycle" [16]. Abualfaraa et al. mention another four (green) wastes: solid wastes, hazardous wastes, air emissions and wastewater discharges. Zokaei et al. [8] are even more specific in their list of green wastes: energy consumption, air emissions, water usage, physical waste, land contamination, discharge to water, noise and nuisance and lost people potential. Again, a group of eight wastes. Almeida Ribeiro [7] also comes up with eight wastes, not exactly similar, but comparable to the former.

What they have in common is a clear idea that waste in TL is too narrow a concept to deal with sustainability issues. What they also have in common is that they tend to jump from the hypothesis that the concept of waste in TL is not sufficient, to new lists of wastes. In that way, the approaches are not different from TL, except for a rare exception, to which we'll turn later.

The widening of the concept of waste already starts within TL. Liker [12], in his first of fourteen Toyota way principles, states that the purpose of the company should be to "create value for the customer, society, and the economy". Ecological issues and harm done to animals are still left out. The Toyota guiding principles, Liker refers to, at that time are not yet sustainability proof, so to say. The corporate citizenship that Toyota

[1] Overproduction, rework, material movement, processing, inventory, waiting and motion.

wants to pursue, in that example does not yet include the concepts of the Earth Charter (published in 1992 and mentioned in Zokaei [8]).

In the example of Liker, value is not limited to the customer, but extended to the community where the corporation is located. The examples from LGM and others share this idea and have further widened their scope towards ecological values. So, what all approaches have in common, is that they do not refine the concept of value, even though they all seem to implicitly move from a narrow interpretation of customer value towards a wider idea of value. The Toyota guiding principles and the Earth charter are beautiful examples of such an implicit value shift within Toyota. The customer value seems to be restrained by something else. First it is the value of respect for people, later it becomes the community, and later again climate impact.

Although the Circularity debate – let us call the Lean variety Circular Lean (CL) – has a specific place for the concept of value, it also tends to focus on wastes [among others, 17]. In the literature on Circular Economy, waste also plays a significant role, as does the reduction of it. This concept does not seem to start at the micro level of the company, but rather at a systems level. The urgency is defined from a macro level: it is the entire socio-economic system that has become stuck in a linear take – make – waste/dispose system. Initiatives are needed to transform that system to a circular, more regenerative system, where virgin resources are more or less left where they are, and pollution by emissions and landfill are to be reduced to an absolute minimum.

The idea that systems should in the future be regenerative (restorative and regenerative, to be more precise [18]), does imply a special place for the concept of value. Value should be maintained in a system that does not anymore need virgin resources and that does not anymore cause landfill and harmful emissions. That implies that we not only create value for whoever, without bothering about what comes next, but that this value should be maintained or easily transformed into new value. Loss of value, in this conception, means waste. Again, CL could mean that the list of wastes gets longer (or, worse, that a third list of eight – circular – wastes is added, and we end up with three lists). What would happen further if we, for example, would consider yet another concept like *wellbeing economy*? A fourth list?

It is in the field of CL that we found a rare example of a paper that dealt with the refinement of value [17]. It started with the same statement that we already saw before: "This limited view of value is the core contributor to the speedy depletion and scarcity of resources. Therefore, it would be best to redefine value while focussing on the lifecycle of a resource and not just the product alone." The authors even define value in a new way: "Any activity/output that utilises its required resources in a manner that maximises its utility at all stages of its lifecycle, including the afterlife, as well as to ensure the longevity of its lifecycle while satisfying the needs/demands of the stakeholders (people [present and future] and planet) and making impact for them." Although this is abstract and formulated in the form of an imperative (a 'commandment'), it is finally an example where value is explicitly addressed and expressed. Is this where one wants to finish? We think that there is more to be said about values.

3 Value: An Ethical Concept in Lean Thinking?

Is it because of the narrow focus of TL that value receives so little attention? Is this narrow focus, combined with our over-economized society a reason that we almost take the concept for granted? As we have seen above, it seems almost self-evident to jump immediately to that other concept, waste.

As we also have seen, underneath the surface of all the wastes lies hidden all kinds of implicit values: the very fact that people started adding wastes to the original list of seven, means that 'new' values are considered to become important. The eighth waste, for example, show how the human factor became more important and how the potential of every employee was considered valuable. The development of LGM could only take place because of the rise of different sustainability values (Zokaei et al. [8] take a lot of effort to convince their readers of the necessity of a greener approach), and the same can be said about circularity. Society has been changing and values have been doing so accordingly.

The value proposal of Nadeem et al. [17] has a lot of the modern values in it. It contains circularity principles (life cycle and after life), it contains the idea of sustainable development (people, present and future), so what could possibly be wrong with it? It has the form of an imperative, a commandment. Much of the proposals of Lean-green, in fact are of such an imperative nature: an author tries to convince the audience of the importance of sustainable and/or circular development and develops a number of wastes to fit the argument. In ethics that is called *prescriptive ethics*. If we read the definition mentioned before as a proposal, to be discussed further, we enter the realm of ethics as a reflection by the actors themselves. It is in that way, a proposal, that we want to read it, and by doing so we introduce ethics in Lean thinking. Too often, Lean thinking, in whatever variety, is a toolkit of improvement techniques. The reflective steps get too little attention, although it is the starting point for much of the Lean theories [9, 10].

In a complex society, where corporations are supposed to be responsible 'citizens' it may be of foremost importance to make ethical reflection just as much part of business practices as continuous improvement. Painter-Morland [19] criticized the lack of attention for ethics in everyday business life. If it is present in a company, she argues, it is often institutionalised and therefore at a distance from what in TL would be called the gemba.

Prescriptive ethics gives answers to questions, instead of questions that people can answer. Such a kind of ethics provides conclusions; an author analysed an ethical issue and confronts you with the result. However, philosophical ethics should help you to reflect by yourself. Perhaps the imperative of Nadeem et al. [17] can be used as a true north, but it needs to be specified by companies. A corporation must find out what values are relevant and worthwhile pursuing. Where Womack and Jones [11] start with "specify value" as "the critical starting point" for Lean thinking, they immediately narrow it down to customer value. We propose to keep the first step as it is, without restraining it immediately. Define the values of the corporation in a much wider sense. The definition of value is not an answer or an imperative. It should be a question, and this question should be a matter of the corporation as a whole. Further still, it should even be a question of the corporation and its environment. What is the impact of the corporation? Both positively and negatively.

The reflection upon the values of the corporation must not be a matter of a few wise people, somewhere in a sustainability or strategy department. Taking Painter-Morland seriously [19], but also taking Lean thinking itself seriously, one cannot let something crucial like values be left to a small number of people. Lean thinking has always taken people seriously, involving them actively in continuous improvement programs. Why not involving them in the process of value definition as well?

The complex nature of the modern corporation requires that we rethink the first step of Womack and Jones seriously. A responsible corporation should regularly reflect upon its values. These values are not straightforward, and they have never been straightforward. From an early point onward, too narrow values had to be constrained. Respect for people was a constraint that needed to protect employees. The earth charter was a constraint. In fact, they reflect different values that can be contradictory, that can cause dilemmas. Being explicit about the values that are to be pursued in a corporation can help tactical and operational practices. It can give a direction about the performance indicators to be chosen.

4 Conflicting Values: Stuck in the Middle?

In a 2022 paper [18], we argued that – according to Henry Ford – it would cause problems if one was not clear about what he mentioned 'service power'. In his case, he was very critical about the power of financial institutions and Ford stated that when financial objectives became dominant over the customer, then the service power of the company would diminish. We even called profit the ninth waste. How does that relate to the sections above?

If Ford is right, where does that leave the socially and environmentally responsible corporation? If one wants to consider environmental, social, circular principles, does that inevitably mean that one gets stuck between different goals, that are almost necessarily at odds with one another? The same Ford, in the same book [21], also showed some concern for sustainability issues, when he (chapter 11, Saving the Timber) argues that "there is wood enough in this country for everyone – when we learn how to use it". The advocate of service power of the corporation seemed very much aware that this concept could only be sustained if resources were used responsibly. Service power apparently was not meant to be a one stakeholder concept, which of course is also present in the way Ford treated the issue of wages.

The critical attitude towards dominant financial institutions is in fact consistent with a more sustainable view towards the corporation: the planning horizon of shareholders can be short term and thus stand in the way of what Liker calls a long-term philosophy (his first principle of the Toyota Way [12]). The value of short-term financial results is at odds with values that aim for the longer term.

To avoid becoming stuck in the middle, a long-term philosophy of a corporation should include a regular reflection upon the values of the company. If it is done thoroughly, conflicting values can be identified in the process and decisions on dilemmas can be made consciously.

5 Implications for Practitioners: Refining the Step of 'Value Definition'

To finish this brief reflection upon values in Lean thinking, we propose to take seriously the definition, mentioned earlier, but not as a conclusive imperative, but rather as a point of departure for an ongoing reflection upon the values the corporation wishes to embody.

Such an ongoing reflection should consist of several elements:

- A thorough stakeholders' analysis: who and what are beneficiaries of the company and who and what are damaged by the company's current activities? This should include the direct activities and the impacts later (and after) in the life cycle of the products and services. In one question: what is the harm done by the corporation and who is being harmed?
- What values are to be realised or pursued? To prevent a solely negative atmosphere that might arise from the first questions (what harm is done), it is important to think about the positive side of values as well. What does the corporation contribute to its stakeholders and how can this contribution be improved?
- How do different values align or conflict? When one starts a process of value definition, conflicts between values will be inevitable. The objective is not necessarily to resolve all issues; knowing the dilemmas is a good starting point for continuous improvement, also at an ethical level.
- How do these values translate into the current organisational practice? What is the gap between the desired values and the realized values. Can objectives be derived from these gaps?
- How do stakeholders see their position in the value system of the company and how can they be involved in the process?

Taking a thorough analysis of stakeholders seriously implies steps beyond traditional stakeholders' analysis. The 'who's harmed' question may be helpful, as well as the original imperative of sustainable development, including future generations: who gives voice to them? Who speaks on behalf of the landscape? Who of that of a monumental factory building? Involving children in your stakeholders' dialogues may give surprising depth to your process of value definition.

It is only after such an exercise that wastes (and continuous improvement projects) come into sight. According to us, complex societal challenges ask for companies to become ethical before they can become sustainable of circular. That is, if a company desires to be pro-active, instead of reactive. Many examples exist of companies who became heavily criticised for their practices, because they were unaware of the value shifts in society. A responsible corporation is a corporation that is ahead of such developments, a corporation that is intrinsically responsible [22]. Hollender and Breen insist that theirs will be the future of business.

6 Conclusion

Although many reflections upon a more sustainable and circular variety of Lean thinking exist, they tend to focus on the wastes inflicted on the environment of the corporation, and much less on the values that are hidden beneath the surface. Nevertheless, the shift towards more sustainable and circular Lean practices shows that Lean thinking has long gone far beyond the one-sided idea of customer value as the one and sacrosanct value.

As far as we are aware of, this is the first contribution to Lean thinking that proposes to include ethics – not as prescriptive ethics, but as reflective ethical practice – into the Lean body of knowledge. Where much of the literature on more sustainable and circular Lean thinking almost immediately turns to the concept of waste, we would rather see a practice where stakeholders are invited to reflect upon the values that a company creates and the values it destroys. We have put the concept of value in the spotlight, rather than the concept of waste.

The values that a corporation pursuits are not prescribed. It is rather a procedure that we would advise corporations to follow. A procedure that would take ethics to the gemba, and even beyond the walls of the company. The success of such a procedure would be a topic for further (empirical) research.

To conclude we would like to repeat the statement of Hollender and Breen [22]: the future belongs to intrinsically responsible businesses. Or more accurate and realistic: we hope for a future where ethics is part and parcel of business practices, and we want to contribute to such a future.

References

1. IPCC: Climate Change 2022: Impacts, Adaptation and Vulnerability. In: Pörtner, H.-O., Roberts, D.C., Tignor, M., Poloczanska, E.S., Mintenbeck, K., Alegría, A., Craig, M., Langsdorf, S., Löschke, S., Möller, V., Okem, A., Rama, B. (eds.). Contribution of Working Group II to the Sixth Assessment Report of the Intergovernmental Panel on Climate Change, p. 3056. Cambridge University Press. Cambridge University Press, Cambridge, UK and New York, NY, USA (2022). https://doi.org/10.1017/9781009325844
2. Meadows, D.H., Meadows, D.L., Randers, J., Behrens III, W.W.: Limits to Growth. A Report for the Club of Rome's Project on the Predicament of Mankind. Potomac Association Books, Washington (1972)
3. Ellen MacArthur Foundation: Towards the Circular Economy. Ellen MacArthur Foundation (2013)
4. Rotmans, J.: Omarm de chaos. De Geus (2021)
5. EU commission (2019). https://commission.europa.eu/strategy-and-policy/priorities-2019-2024/european-green-deal_en
6. Jonker, J., Faber, N., Haaker, T.: Circular Business Models. A study to classify existing and emerging forms of value retention and creation. Ministry of Economic Affairs and Climate Policy The Hague, The Netherlands (2022)
7. MacArthur, E.: Towards the circular economy. J. Ind. Ecol. **2**(1), 23–44 (2013)
8. Zokaei, K., Lovins, H., Wood, A., Hines, P.: Creating a Lean and Green Business System. CRC Press, Techniques for improving Profits and Sustainability (2013)
9. Almeida Ribeiro, T.B.: Analysis of the impact of Lean and Green Practices in manufacturing companies: an exploratory study. Thesis (2021)
10. Salibi, J.G.D.O.R., Rodrigues, A.L.D.S.M., Lima, P.A.B., de Souza, F.B.: Lean and the circular economy: A systematic literature review. Journal of Lean Systems **7**(4), 23–46 (2022)
11. Womack, J.P., Jones, D.T.: Lean Thinking. Simon & Schuster (1996)
12. Liker, J.: The Toyota Way. 14 Management Principles from the World's Greatest Manufacturer. McGraw-Hill (2004)

13. Arroyo, P., Gonzalez, V.: Rethinking Waste definition to account for environmental and social impacts. In: Proceedings of the 24th Annual Conference of the International Group for Lean Construction. Boston, MA, USA. P. 9 and 20–22 (2016)
14. Ohno, T.: Toyota Production System. CRC Press, Beyond Large-Scale Production (1988)
15. Schmitt, T., Wolf, C., Lennerfors, T.T., Okwir, S.: Beyond "Leanear" production: a multi-level approach for achieving circularity in a lean manufacturing context. J. Clean. Prod. **318**, 128531 (2021)
16. Abualfaraa, W., Salonitis, K., Al-Ashaab, A., Ala'raj, M.: Lean-green manufacturing practices and their link with sustainability: A critical review. Sustainability **12**(3), 981 (2020)
17. Nadeem, S.P., Garza-Reyes, J.A., Anosike, A.I., Kumar, V.: Coalescing the lean and circular economy. In: Proceedings of the 9th International Conference on Industrial Engineering and Operations Management (IEOM), pp. 1–12 (2019)
18. Morseletto, P.: Restorative and regenerative: exploring the concepts in the circular economy. J. Ind. Ecol. **24**(4), 763–773 (2020)
19. Painter-Morland, M.: Business Ethics as Practice. Cambridge University Press, Ethics as the Everyday Business of Business (2008)
20. De Zwart, J.: Is there such a thing as a lean philosophy? In: European Lean Educator Conference, pp. 3–13. Springer International Publishing, Cham (2022)
21. Ford, H.: 1926. BN Publishing, Today and Tomorrow (2012)
22. Hollender, J., Breen, B.: The Responsibility Revolution. Jossey-Bass, How the Next Generation of Businesses Will Win (2010)

The Culture and Climate for Agile Lean Thinking

Stuart Nelson and Olivia McDermott(✉)

College of Science and Engineering, University of Galway, Galway, Ireland
Olivia.McDermott@universityofgalway.ie

Abstract. The study aimed to investigate the impact of leadership style and psychological Safety on employee engagement. It further examined whether these variables differed in organisations that carried out initiatives such as Lean or Agile and their impact on the program's success. A self-selecting sample (N = 122) completed a series of questions, including the Multifactor Leadership Questionnaire Rater, the Utrecht Work Engagement Scale and Team Learning Psychological Safety instruments, and demographic information. A mixed design was used, part correlational and part cross-sectional. Results found that Transformational leadership style and Psychological Safety predicted Employee Engagement and that Quality Initiative organisations scored significantly higher on Transformational Leadership, Psychological Safety and Engagement. These factors also predicted the success of the Quality Initiative. This research demonstrated the importance of transformational Leadership and a psychologically safe environment to improve Engagement and that both can be learned.

Keywords: Leadership · Transformational Leadership · Engagement · Psychological Safety

1 Introduction

The economic conditions of the past decade have led to a radically changed landscape in which to do business. The global recession and the COVID-19 pandemic changed how employees interact with their jobs [1]. An organisation's ability to change quickly is critical for success in today's economic world; short-term fixes and resolving inefficiencies are essential to remain competitive and ensure growth [1]. Organisations are employing quality initiatives such as Lean to remove Non-Value add activities and do more with less [2] and are employing Agile to be more responsive to customer needs and changing market conditions [3]. Lean placed the customer and respect for the company's human element at its core, but not all adoptions have succeeded in this aspect, recognising more importance on cost reduction elements [4]. This failure negatively affects employees, demotivating them and damaging company loyalty [5].

Organisations now recognise that achieving full employee engagement can be as valuable as driving efficiencies and *Discretionary effort;* the difference between what

T. van Kollenburg et al. (Eds.): ELEC 2023, IFIP AICT 681, pp. 12–22, 2024.
https://doi.org/10.1007/978-3-031-63265-5_2

employees *can* and *must do* is valued at over 20% [6]. Discretionary effort comes from employees who are energetic and dedicated to their work, which has been linked with how engaged they are with their jobs [7]. *Psychological Safety* was introduced by Edmondson [8]. It is described as the belief within a team where individuals feel safe to comment, and this belief allows for greater team efficacy and learning. *Psychological Safety* creates an environment where information and knowledge are pooled and considered, moving from the *groupthink* model of conformity to what Manz & Neck [9].

(1995) called *Teamthink,* where open and frank discussions from diverging opinions within a team are considered in the decision process.

Creating engaged teams in a learning environment takes good Leadership with a clear vision. This research will assess leadership styles as perceived by the team members on a spectrum from *transformational* to *transactional* to *laissez-faire,* as described by Bass [10]. T*ransformational Leaders* inspire with a clear vision and lead positive change, while *Transactional* leaders manage by compliance with reward and punishment. A *Laissez-Faire* leader is hands-off and uninvolved, leaving followers to make the decisions. Furthermore, the research will gauge the impact of leadership style on the level of Engagement and the levels of psychological Safety while also assessing if differences exist with organisations engaged in quality initiatives. Engaged employees in a learning environment are more open to change; this research will demonstrate the effects of the Leader's behaviour on these constructs and identify if changes are needed at the Leadership and team levels. Thus, the aims of the study are:

Hypothesis 1: There will be a significant relationship between Transformational Leadership, Psychological Safety and Engagement.

Hypothesis 2: There will be a significant difference in Leadership style scores between organisations that have carried out quality initiatives and those that have not.

Hypothesis 3: There will be a significant difference between Psychological Safety scores for organisations that have carried out quality initiatives and those that have not.

Hypothesis 4: There will be a significant difference in Engagement scores between organisations who have carried out quality initiatives and those who have yet to.

Section 2 outlines the literature review, Sect. 3 the methodology, While Sects. 4, 5 and 6 summarise the Results, Discussion and Conclusion.

2 Literature Review

2.1 Leadership Types

Leadership differs for different people, and although much research has been carried out, more than one clear leader profile has been identified [11]. The superstar, headline-grabbing leaders are the exceptions, and this research will be grounded in the realities and practicalities of everyday Leadership: Transformational and Transactional. The benefits of this model of Leadership are that they are not distinct traits but more of a continuation along a spectrum, and effective leaders can use both techniques to get results [10]. Moreover, this hybrid nature of Leadership is not down to charisma but is a behavioural process that can be learned [12]. Bass [13, 14], a key guru in leadership research, was one of the first to put forward the transformational style of Leadership to replace transactional forms.

Transactional Leadership describes traditional managerial styles where managers promote compliance and improved performance by offering rewards or punishing bad or non-conformance results [14]. These styles are useful for steady-state situations but could be better for organisations undergoing rapid change or other unanticipated conditions; thus, a transformational style is required in these situations [14]. Transformational Leadership requires a clear and inspirational vision, garnering employee commitment and embedding organisational change in the culture [16]. Transactional Leadership is based on some transactions, such as exchanging money for work. This is modelled in 2 behaviours: Rewards Achievement and Monitors Deviations & Mistakes. Rewards Achievement is where leaders agree with followers on the tasks to be completed and articulate performance expectations in exchange for rewards [17]. Monitors Deviations and mistakes is a corrective form of Leadership and measures how a leader intervenes with the follower [18]. An active leader will seek out errors or issues in the output and then act, whereas a passive leader waits for things to go wrong before becoming active [19]. Bass and Avolio proposed a Full Range Leadership Model (FRLM) model as an approach to transformational leadership styles that covers low to high Engagement, leading to different leadership efficiency [20]. This is achieved by measuring 5 behaviours, the first of which is Transformational Leadership (which consists of building Trust, acting with Integrity, encouraging others, encouraging innovative thinking, and coaching and developing people [13]. The other four behaviours are Transactional Leadership (rewards achievement, monitors deviations and mistakes), Passive/Avoidant management (fights fires or avoids involvement) and Outcomes of Leadership (generates extra effort, is productive).

2.2 Employee Engagement

Kahn [21] was the earliest to discuss Engagement as the extent to which individuals invest themselves in their work performance. Engagement as a concept has become complicated, not because of its difficulty to comprehend, but because it is a construct that consulting firms have championed, and one they propose can be created and leveraged [22]. They are attempting to gain *Discretionary Effort,* which Katoma [23] defines as *"an unsolicited effort, which employees expend when certain work expectations are met"* and delivered freely when intrinsically motivated. It increases productivity by creating an environment where employees' expectations are met. Engagement is "a desirable condition, has an organisational purpose, and connotes involvement, commitment, passion, enthusiasm, focused effort, and energy, so it has both attitudinal and behavioural components" [22].

2.3 Psychological Safety

Edmondson [24] introduced the term *Psychological Safety* and described it as the belief within a team where individuals feel safe for interpersonal risk-taking, that is, to comment freely without fear of judgement, and this belief allows for greater team efficacy and learning. In a study, Carmeli et al. [25] put forward that psychological Safety is an important mediating mechanism through which transformational leadership results in enhanced employee involvement and creativity. *Psychological Safety* should not be confused with TrustTrust as it is a belief about a group norm, whereas TrustTrust is based on an individual relationship [26]. The benefit of *Psychological Safety* is that it facilitates team learning, ensuring all voices are heard and considered. Asch's [27] conformity studies showed that people go with the group dynamic, leading to bad decisions, so creating an environment where information and knowledge are shared, and dissenting opinions welcomed is valuable in modern organisations. This sharing environment can move from the *groupthink* model of conformity to what Manz & Neck [9] called Teamthink, where open and frank discussions from diverging opinions are welcomed.

3 Methodology

3.1 Introduction

Participation in this research was open to all currently employed; self-employment was excluded. A *self-selecting snowball* sampling technique was used, and the survey was promoted through social media networks, including LinkedIn and Facebook. To access organisations engaged in quality initiatives, links to the study were posted on specialist forums and groups on LinkedIn and directly on websites in the UK and USA. The survey was circulated to the Dublin Chamber of Commerce and Agile and Lean Enterprise Institutes in the UK and the US and shared among members.

A total of one hundred and twenty-two participants completed the survey. Participants were excluded if they selected anything other than employed for the first question and redirected to a closing page thanking them for participation [28]. Participants comprised 76 females and 46 males, ranging in age from twenty to sixty-eight years old ($M = 36.59$, $SD = 9.05$) and ranged in years at the current organisation from 0.2 to 30 years ($M = 6.23$, $SD = 6.07$. An example of the questions asked is listed in Table 1.

Table 1. Survey Questions

1.	Which employment status best describes you?
2.	Gender
3.	Age
4.	What is your nationality?
5.	What country do you work in?
6.	Which best describes the organisation in which you work?
7.	Approximately how long (years) have you worked at this organisation?

(*continued*)

Table 1. *(continued)*

8.	Which best describes your position in your organisation
9.	Has your company ever run a quality initiative such as Lean/ Agile/ Six Sigma/TQM?
10.	What quality initiative(s) program was it?
11.	Did the company receive grant funding from any bodies (Enterprise Ireland, Industrial Development Authority, Skillnet, etc.
12.	When did the program start?
13.	Is the program still running?
14.	If no, how long did it run for?
15.	At what levels of the organisation was the program applied?
16.	To what extent did the initiative positively change the organisational culture?

3.2 Design

This research is of mixed design, partly correlational and partly cross-sectional. It is primarily designed to explore the relationship between predictor variables (PV), leadership style, psychological Safety and criterion variable (CV) employee engagement. Furthermore, it looks for differences in leadership style psychological Safety and Engagement (DVs) scores between groups that have or have not engaged in quality initiatives (IVs).

This research is of mixed design, partly correlational and partly cross-sectional. It is primarily designed to explore the relationship between predictor variables (PV), Leadership style, Psychological Safety and Criterion Variable (CV) employee engagement. Furthermore, it looks for differences in leadership style Psychological Safety and Engagement (DVs) scores between groups that have or have not engaged in Quality initiatives (IVs).

A questionnaire was deployed with a range of demographic questions asked of participants, including age, gender and time with current employer. Three instruments were used to assess the research variables. These were the *Multifactor Leadership Questionnaire* [16], *the Utrecht Work Engagement Scale* [29] and the *Psychological Safety Survey* [24].

The Full Range Leadership model [15] was used to assess the observable leadership behaviours for this research, which evaluates Leadership on a spectrum rather than a type. This model gives us 9 leadership behaviours that can be measured, modelled, or avoided. Multifactor Leadership Questionnaire (MLQ): The MLQ (5X) is a 45-item survey that assesses three leadership styles across 3 scales, using 9 subscales.

The second instrument used in this research was Schaufeli and Bakker's Utrecht Work and Well-Being Survey [30], which assumes that Engagement is the opposite of burnout, as described by Maslach [31]. Schaufeli et al. describe Engagement as "a positive, fulfilling, work-related state of mind" (2002), made up of 3 components: Vigour, high energy levels and mental resilience while working, willingness to invest effort and persistence; Dedication, strong personal involvement in work, sense of enthusiasm and pride; and Absorption: happily, engrossed in work, time passes quickly and has difficulties separating work and personal life. The Utrecht Work Engagement Scale was developed by Schaufeli and Bakker [30] and assessed an overall scale of Engagement and three subscales of *Vigor, Dedication,* and *Absorption.*

The third instrument utilised was the Team Psychological Safety Scale, developed by Edmondson (1999) to examine team learning behaviours. Participants assess the accuracy of statements along a seven-point Likert scale from *very inaccurate* to *very accurate* [24].

4 Results

4.1 Descriptive Statistics

Descriptive statistics for variables were collected and are displayed in Table 2. A total of 122 valid participants were analysed for all variables. Participants were made up of 76 females and 46 males, ranging in age from twenty to sixty-eight years old (M = 36.59, SD = 9.05) and ranged in years at their current organisation from .2 to 30 years (M = 6.23. SD = 6.07). Leadership scores showed Transformational Leadership to be the highest (M = 2.25, SD = .88), followed by Transactional Leadership (M = 2.06, SD = .71) and then Laissez-faire leadership (M = 1.41, SD = .93). The scores for the other variables were Engagement (M = 3.83, SD = 1.18) and Psychological Safety (M = 3.99, SD = 1.06).

Table 2. Descriptive Statistics for Variables

Descriptive Statistics			
	N	Mean	Std. Deviation
Recommend your company as a place to work	122	6.73	2.59
Recommend your company's products or services	121	7.66	2.38
Transformational	121	2.24	.86
Transactional (EX-MBEP)	121	2.05	.70
Laissez-faire (+MBEP)	121	1.41	.92
Total Engagement	121	3.80	1.18
TOTAL PSYCH SAFETY	121	3.98	1.06
Valid N (listwise)	120		

4.2 Hypothesis Results

Hypothesis 1: Transformational Leadership, Psychological Safety and Engagement will have a significant relationship.

A multiple regression was used to test whether Transformational Leadership and Psychological Safety were predictors of Engagement (Table 3). The results of the regression indicated that two predictors explained 30.9% of the variance ($R^2 = .31$, $F(2, 118) = 27.80$, $p < .001$). It was found that Transformational leadership significantly predicted engagement ($\beta = .37$, $p < .001$, 95% CI = .279 to .739) as did Psychological Safety ($\beta = .29$, $p = .001$, 95% CI = .13 to .51). Hypothesis 1 was supported.

Hypothesis 2: There will be a significant difference in Leadership style scores between organisations that have carried out quality initiatives and those that have not.

A one-way analysis of variance showed that Transformational leadership scores differed significantly between the three groups ($F(2, 118) = 10.79$, $p < .001$). More specifically, Tukey HSD post hoc analyses highlighted that the Yes group (M = 2.75, SD = .77) scored significantly higher than the No group (M = 1.88, SD = .85, $p < .001$). Thus highlighting that carrying out quality initiatives leads to significantly higher scores in Transformational Leadership.

Hypothesis 3: There will be a significant difference between Psychological Safety scores for organisations that have carried out quality initiatives and those that have not.

A one-way analysis of variance showed that Psychological Safety scores differed significantly between the three groups ($F(2, 118) = 3.12$, $p = 0.48$). More specifically, Tukey HSD post hoc analyses highlighted that the Yes group (M = 4.34, SD = 1.13) scored significantly higher than the No group (M = 3.77, SD = 1.01, $p = .045$). Thus highlighting that carrying out quality initiatives leads to significantly higher scores in Psychological Safety.

Hypothesis 4: There will be a significant difference in Engagement scores between organisations who have carried out quality initiatives and those who have yet to.

A one-way analysis of variance showed that Engagement scores differed significantly between the three groups ($F(2, 118) = 4.37$, $p = .015$). More specifically, Tukey HSD post hoc analyses highlighted that the Yes group (M = 4.25, SD = 1.07) scored significantly higher than the Not Sure Group.

Table 3. Transformational - Engagement Correlations

Correlations								
		1	2	3	4	5	6	7
1. Transformational	Pearson Correlation	1						
	Sig. (2-tailed)							
	N	121						
Builds Trust	Pearson Correlation	.894**	1					
	Sig. (2-tailed)	.000						

(continued)

Table 3. (*continued*)

Correlations								
		1	2	3	4	5	6	7
	N	121	121					
2. Acts with Integrity	Pearson Correlation	.717**	.563**	1				
	Sig. (2-tailed)	.000	.000					
	N	121	121	121				
3. Encourages Others	Pearson Correlation	.868**	.733**	.576**	1			
	Sig. (2-tailed)	.000	.000	.000				
	N	121	121	121	121			
4. Encourage Innovative Thinking	Pearson Correlation	.884**	.726**	.507**	.680**	1		
	Sig. (2-tailed)	.000	.000	.000	.000			
	N	121	121	121	121	121		
5. Coaches and Develops People	Pearson Correlation	.911**	.798**	.530**	.713**	.818**	1	
	Sig. (2-tailed)	.000	.000	.000	.000	.000		
	N	121	121	121	121	121	121	
6. Total Engagement	Pearson Correlation	.505**	.468**	.443**	.474**	.372**	.425**	1
	Sig. (2-tailed)	.000	.000	.000	.000	.000	.000	
	N	121	121	121	121	121	121	121

**. Correlation is significant at the 0.01 level (2-tailed)

5 Discussion

Hypothesis 1 predicted that there would be a significant relationship between Transformational Leadership, Psychological Safety and Engagement. This was supported, demonstrating that Leadership behaviour and the team climate they created influenced and predicted the level of employee engagement. Much of the previous focus on Engagement has been on employee behaviour and interest in the role. Engagement cannot be trained, but leaders can create a climate and culture in which it can flourish. These results align with studies linking transformational Leadership with employees' psychological Safety and levels of engagement [32, 33].

Hypothesis 2,3, and 4 predicted that there would be a significant difference in Leadership styles, Psychological Safety, and Engagement between organisations that have carried out quality initiatives and those that have not. This was supported, demonstrating that Lean and Agile change initiatives require a culture and climate that fosters and encourages change from many levels: the Leader, the team, and the individual. Further analysis of the data showed that the perceived success of the Lean initiative was predicted positively by these 3 factors. Several studies by Laureani and Antony on the leadership role in operational excellence have highlighted the importance of Leadership in moulding and promoting an OpEx culture ([34–36]. Albliwi et al. [37] have also described in their study on CSFs for Lean Six Sigma deployment that Leadership and their role in transforming strategy, creating a safe culture and engaging in the program are important factors for success in Operational Excellence deployment.

Successful implementation of Lean and Agile requires more than just applying tools and techniques; the Leadership and teams must have a desire and a willingness to change. Great Leadership, team engagement, and a climate of learning are necessary to achieve this, factors that are often overlooked during Lean initiatives [38, 39].

6 Conclusion

This research has shown that investing in Lean or Agile cannot be just about tools; organisations must also create the culture and climate for sustainable change. This research identified 3 factors of behaviour, observable and measurable, which make the culture and climate for Agile & Lean organisations and the success of their initiatives: the Leader, the Team Relationship and the Individual Engagement. A limitation of this study is that most respondents were Irish-based; it would be interesting to expand the study to a larger global population.

This study has academic and managerial implications. Theoretically, this study extends the existing knowledge and literature on Engagement. Still, moreover, the antecedents measured are tangible constructs that, with effort, can be learned. From a managerial implication viewpoint, the Leadership attributes have been isolated to nine dimensions, and these can be developed in organisations by their leaders and managers.

Future research opportunities are to look at a more longitudinal study in an organisation and measure the transformational leadership journey in the context of an Operational Excellence journey. Also, an investigation into interventions in Leadership and psychologically safe environments could be carried out and Engagement measured before and after. The need for qualitative input is, and this also presents a further opportunity. It is essential that research, especially in the organisational psychology field, provides theory but also functional interventions.

References

1. Janssen, M., van der Voort, H.: Agile and adaptive governance in crisis response: Lessons from the COVID-19 pandemic. Int. J. Info. Manage. 102180 (2020). https://doi.org/10.1016/j.ijinfomgt.2020.102180

2. Snee, R.D.: Lean Six Sigma – getting better all the time. Int. J. Lean Six Sigma **1**, 9–29 (2010). https://doi.org/10.1108/20401461011033130
3. Coimbra, H., Cormican, K., McDermott, O., Antony, J.: Leading the transformation: agile success factors in an Irish manufacturing company. Total Quality Manage. Bus. Excell. 1–28 (2023)
4. McDermott, O., Antony, J., Sony, M., Looby, E.: A critical evaluation and measurement of organisational readiness and adoption for continuous improvement within a medical device manufacturer. Null. 1–11 (2022). https://doi.org/10.1080/17509653.2022.2073917
5. McDermott, O., Antony, J., Sony, M., Daly, S.: Barriers and Enablers for Continuous Improvement Methodologies within the Irish Pharmaceutical Industry. Processes 10, (2022). https://doi.org/10.3390/pr10010073
6. Harter, J.K., Schmidt, L.W.A., Killham, E.A.: The Relationship Between Engagement at Work and Organisational Outcomes. Presented at the (2009)
7. Bakker, A.B.: An evidence-based model of work engagement. Curr. Dir. Psychol. Sci. **20**, 265–269 (2011). https://doi.org/10.1177/0963721411414534
8. Edmondson, A.C., Roberto, M., Tucker, A.: Children's hospital and clinics. HBS case (2001)
9. Manz, C.C., Neck, C.P.: Teamthink: beyond the groupthink syndrome in self-managing work teams. J. Manag. Psychol. **10**, 7–15 (1995). https://doi.org/10.1108/02683949510075155
10. Bass, B.M., Bass Bernard, M.: Leadership and performance beyond expectations (1985)
11. George, B., Sims, P., McLean, A.N., Mayer, D.: Discovering your authentic Leadership. Harv Bus Rev. **85**, 129–130, 132–138 and 157 (2007)
12. Tichy, N.M., Devanna, M.A.: The transformational Leader. Train. Dev. J. **40**, 27–32 (1986)
13. Bass, B.M., Bass, R., Bass B.M: The Bass handbook of Leadership: theory, research, and managerial applications. Free Press, New York (2008)
14. Bass, B.M.: Bass & Stogdill's Handbook of Leadership: Theory, research, and managerial applications, 3rd edn. Free Press, New York, NY, US (1990)
15. Kirkbride, P.: Developing transformational leaders: the full range leadership model in action. Ind. Commer. Train. **38**, 23–32 (2006). https://doi.org/10.1108/00197850610646016
16. Avolio, B.J., Bass, B.M., Jung, D.I.: Re-examining the components of transformational and transactional leadership using the Multifactor Leadership. J. Occupant. Organisat. Psychol. **72**, 441–462 (1999)
17. Waldman, D.A., Bass, B.M., Yammarino, F.J.: Adding to contingent-reward behavior: the augmenting effect of charismatic leadership. Group & Organization Studies **15**, 381–394 (1990)
18. Willis, S., Clarke, S., O'Connor, E.: Contextualising leadership: transformational leadership and management-by-exception-active in safety-critical contexts. J. Occup. Organ. Psychol. **90**, 281–305 (2017)
19. Bono, J.E., Judge, T.A.: Personality and transformational and transactional leadership: a meta-analysis. J. Appl. Psychol. **89**, 901 (2004)
20. Salter, C.R., Harris, M.H., McCormack, J.: Bass & Avolio's full range leadership model and moral development. E-Leader Milan. **2008**, 28 (2014)
21. Kahn, W.A.: Psychological conditions of personal Engagement and disengagement at work. Acad. Manag. J. **33**, 692–724 (1990). https://doi.org/10.2307/256287
22. Macey, W.H., Schneider, B.: The meaning of employee engagement. Indus. Organisat. Psychol. **1**, 3–30 (2008). https://doi.org/10.1111/j.1754-9434.2007.0002.x
23. Katoma, V.: A framework for discretionary effort based on performance expectancies in integrated work environment (2011). https://open.uct.ac.za/handle/11427/30554
24. Edmondson, A.: Psychological safety and learning behavior in work teams. Adm. Sci. Q. **44**, 350–383 (1999). https://doi.org/10.2307/2666999

25. Carmeli, A., Sheaffer, Z., Binyamin, G., Reiter-Palmon, R., Shimoni, T.: Transformational leadership and creative problem-solving: The mediating role of psychological safety and reflexivity. The Journal of Creative Behavior **48**, 115–135 (2014)
26. Edmondson, A.C.: Speaking up in the operating room: how team leaders promote learning in interdisciplinary action teams. J. Manage. Stud. **40**, 1419–1452 (2003). https://doi.org/10.1111/1467-6486.00386
27. Asch, S.E.: Studies of independence and conformity: I. A minority of one against a unanimous majority. Psychological Monographs: General and Applied **70**, 1–70 (1956). https://doi.org/10.1037/h0093718
28. Evans, J.R., Mathur, A.: The value of online surveys: a look back and a look ahead. Internet Res. **28**, 854–887 (2018). https://doi.org/10.1108/IntR-03-2018-0089
29. Schaufeli, W.B., Bakker, A.B., Salanova, M.: Utrecht Work Engagement Scale-9 (2011). https://doi.org/10.1037/t05561-000
30. Schaufeli, W.B., Bakker, A.B., Salanova, M.: Utrecht work engagement scale-9. Educational and Psychological Measurement (2003)
31. Maslach, C.: Burnout, the cost of caring. Prentice-Hall, Englewood Cliffs, NJ (1982)
32. Vakira, E., Shereni, N.C., Ncube, C.M., Ndlovu, N.: The effect of inclusive Leadership on employee engagement, mediated by psychological safety in the hospitality industry. J. Hospit. Touri. Insig. **6**, 819–834 (2023)
33. Siyal, S.: Inclusive Leadership and work engagement: exploring the role of psychological safety and trust in Leader in multiple organisational context. Business Ethics, the Environment & Responsibility
34. Laureani, A., Antony, J.: Standards for Lean Six Sigma certification. Int. J. Product. Perform. Manag. **61**, 110–120 (2012). https://doi.org/10.1108/17410401211188560
35. Laureani, A., Antony, J.: Leadership characteristics for Lean Six Sigma. Total Qual. Manag. Bus. Excell. **28**, 405–426 (2017). https://doi.org/10.1080/14783363.2015.1090291
36. Laureani, A., Antony, J.: Leadership and Lean Six Sigma: a systematic literature review. Total Qual. Manag. Bus. Excell. **30**, 53–81 (2019). https://doi.org/10.1080/14783363.2017.1288565
37. Albliwi, S., Antony, J., Abdul Halim Lim, S., van der Wiele, T.: Critical failure factors of Lean Six Sigma: a systematic literature review. Int. J. Qual. Reliabil. Manage. **31**, 1012–1030 (2014). https://doi.org/10.1108/IJQRM-09-2013-0147
38. Antony, J., Gupta, S., Sunder M., V., Gijo, E.V.: Ten commandments of Lean Six Sigma: a practitioners' perspective. Int. J. Product. Perform. Manage. **67**, 1033–1044 (2018). https://doi.org/10.1108/IJPPM-07-2017-0170
39. Antony, J., et al.: An empirical study into the reasons for failure of sustaining operational excellence initiatives in organisations. The TQM Journal. Ahead-of-print (2022). https://doi.org/10.1108/TQM-05-2022-0176

A Confrontation Between Lean Thinking and Postmetaphysical Philosophy

Joop de Zwart(✉)

Avans University of Applied Science, Hogeschoollaan 1, Breda, The Netherlands
jg.dezwart@avans.nl

Abstract. In this conceptual paper, the philosophical concept of metaphysics is brought into Lean thinking to a) further examine the deeply felt reluctance towards Lean thinking many people have and the difficulty many organizations have to implement continuous improvement programs, and b) to explore what further insights this philosophical approach can provide about Lean thinking. Using the concept of *weak thought*, originally introduced by the Italian philosopher Gianni Vattimo, Lean thinking is revealed as possibly violent thought, threatening the principle of respect for people. Some proposals are made to reduce the violent potential.

Keywords: Lean Philosophy · Postmetaphysics · Conceptual Lean

1 Introduction

"Is there such a thing as Lean philosophy" was the title and central question of a paper, published in the ELEC proceedings of 2022. It contained a first exercise of a philosophical approach towards Lean thinking, with the aim of a better understanding of the *thinking behind Lean* [1]. This paper will further elaborate on a theme from the paper mentioned above: what makes Lean thinking so difficult to accept and maintain?

In last year's paper, Lean thinking was characterized as a dynamic form of thinking, while the tradition of western thought was considered to be more or less static, or – preferably – thought that prefers a static situation above one that is intrinsically dynamic. This argument was not thoroughly elaborated, and only briefly the underlying philosophical arguments were mentioned. In this paper the argument is examined more thoroughly, which at the same time is an example of what was called the outside-in philosophical approach towards Lean thinking: a philosophical concept is taken to examine an issue relevant to Lean practitioners and scholars and see what insights this may produce.

The paper is structured as follows: first the question is addressed why Lean thinking is not easily embraced by many. Then the philosophical 'school' that is primarily concerned with the same problem is being introduced: we'll specifically look at the line of thought that criticizes the metaphysical tradition of western thought, more in particular the concept of *weak thought*, introduced by the Italian philosopher Gianni Vattimo and which incorporates the thought of giants like Nietzsche and Heidegger. It reveals

Published by Springer Nature Switzerland AG 2024
T. van Kollenburg et al. (Eds.): ELEC 2023, IFIP AICT 681, pp. 23–34, 2024.
https://doi.org/10.1007/978-3-031-63265-5_3

something of the fundamental difficulty some (or many) people have in learning Lean thought. A final section examines the lessons learned from this philosophical approach towards Lean thinking.

2 Resistance to Lean: Rationale and Method

"I have seen firsthand not only resistance to continuous improvement (...) commitment to inefficiency is quite perplexing" [2]. There are all kinds of reasons why people are reluctant to continuous improvement programs. Korb and Ballard [3] link this reluctance to the Kuhnian concept of paradigm and thus show that the difference between what they call traditional thinkers and Lean thinkers is quite fundamental. They state that conformation bias is the main reason why people won't accept Lean thinking: the way the make sense of the world is so fundamentally different, that every argument 'pro Lean' is countered immediately.

Korb and Ballard refer to (construction) professionals in their paper, people of whom one could expect otherwise. Why would a highly educated professional object to the idea that processes should be analysed and that wastes should be reduced? Why is it that so many scientifically educated people object to methods that follow (applied) scientific methods, based upon facts and causalities?

In my own practice, working with bachelor students, who have not chosen for a Lean course, but are simply confronted with it as a part of their curriculum, there seems to be a natural division between 'believers' and 'non-believers' every year. A part of each group is open towards the arguments that support Lean thinking while another part of the group seems to simply reject everything you say. As an observer of other Lean trainers I witnessed exactly the same thing: part of the groups are almost hostile towards the concept of waste, and of customer value (almost programmed with the idea that profit is the ultimate goal of an enterprise).

Over the years, there have been several attempts to explain why so many Lean programs fail. Only two thirds or even less than that, depending on what research, of the Lean initiatives does not meet the expectations [4, 5]. Apparently, it is difficult to implement Lean thinking in an organization, as it is difficult to accept its principles for a large number of people.

The question remains why 'traditional' thinking is so fundamentally different, compared to Lean thinking. Why is this apparently simple idea of continuous improvement, which is by no means rocket science, so notoriously difficult to establish and maintain.

This paper elaborates on the hypothesis that Lean thinking challenges a key characteristic of western thought as it developed from the ancient Greek philosophers onward. A characteristic so fundamental and deeply rooted that the German philosopher Martin Heidegger thought it was impossible to escape from; in the interview with Der Spiegel, published after his death, he stated "only a God can save us" [6]. What he was talking about was *metaphysics*, and the next section will be dedicated to this rather specialized philosophical concept.

Following the outside-in approach, mentioned in the first section, implies more than the elaboration of a hypothesis. That would only be an in-depth explanation of the hypothesis. The outside-in approach, where the philosophical concept is used to gain new insights as well, also is a kind of adventure: does the exercise provide surprising new insights about Lean thinking?

3 Are We Trapped in Metaphysical Thinking?

The question of being trapped in a certain way of thinking and, more importantly, the question whether it is possible to be liberated from that, especially puzzled the Italian philosopher Gianni Vattimo (1936). His concept of *weak thought*, first introduced in 1983 [7], marked the end of a journey in search of liberation from the 'thinking trap', as well as the beginning of a journey to explore the further consequences of it.

The trap, *strong thought*, that keeps human thinking in a grip, so strong that it is almost impossible to be liberated from, is the trap of metaphysics. Is it this trap that explains the resistance or even hostility towards Lean thinking? And is a concept like *weak thought*, or – in the original language – *pensiero debole*, a possibility to help Lean professionals overcome the resistance?

Gianni Vattimo is heavily inspired by his giant predecessors Friedrich Nietzsche and Martin Heidegger, but remains dissatisfied by the way they think their way out of metaphysics. But what exactly is it that characterizes metaphysics? And why does Vattimo call it strong thought (and the alternative way of thinking weak thought)?

The strength of strong thought is not a positive quality, in the eyes of Vattimo. It is a way of thinking that is potentially violent [8]. In a text of 2007, he explicitly connects metaphysics and violence: "the problem of metaphysics and violence seem to me to be one of the central problems of philosophy" [9]. Metaphysics, and its most sublime manifestation of it, modernism [10] are considered to be a problem, precisely because of the violence that inherently comes with it.

What is meant by this all? Nietzsche, Heidegger and Vattimo consider western thought to be metaphysical, and modern thought as the latest phase of metaphysics. Welsch [11] summarizes the meaning of that in four elements:

1. Metaphysics is fundamentalist;
2. Metaphysics is a belief in progress;
3. Metaphysics is totalitarian;
4. Metaphysics has a tendency to objectify.

Each of the four elements sheds a slightly different light on what is meant by the violent potential of metaphysics.

Metaphysics as fundamentalism: as was also highlighted in the paper, mentioned at the beginning of the paper [1], western thought has an inclination to Truth (with a capital T). This means that from Plato onward, people searched for single principles [12], a foundation for everything. This was, after Plato, also the aim of Christian religion: thinking differently was not a virtue, but rather a vice that had to be strongly opposed. This immediately shows the potential violence that comes with foundationalism: if someone claims to have found such a foundation, it immediately excludes other possibilities, let alone the negation of a foundation.

But modern thought got rid of religious foundations, didn't it? Although in recent history fundamentalist religion seems to have become stronger again, didn't Enlightenment showed us different paths? Vattimo points at new claims of foundationalist thought, although sometimes cleverly disguised: the rigorous way that economic principles are implemented and considered to be 'the' truth. During the crisis following 2007, countries like Greece had to implement severe measures, including for example pension cuts. The economics behind it were considered to be almost sacrosanct, but relentlessly made individual pensioners suffer. Exactly that is what is meant by violence: the abstract Truth of economics, which consists of formulas and statistics, in reality makes real people suffer.

More recently, the same applied to the way science seemed to overrule all other disciplines, during the Covid pandemic. Many times, politicians (at least in the Netherlands) hid behind science: it seemed that they had almost no choices, because scientists advised... Because reality is very diffuse, and making one discipline dominant over all others almost inevitably will hurt people in real life situations.

The examples show how the application of rigid measures are almost inevitably painful to specific individuals, but at the same time – given the context at hand – can be necessary. Without actions taken, the damage will be even much greater to a huge number of individuals. The critique of Vattimo is that often minorities have almost no voice in the game and are crushed at the altar of that one (natural) law.

Metaphysics as belief in progress: in it's ultimate form, as modernism, metaphysics considers the modern, the novel to be almost by definition better than the existing. The optimist view towards progression has the characteristic of a belief. Karl Jaspers refers to that as scientific superstition [13]. An example of this positive attitude towards progression is the way that in many cases the way towards sustainability consists of ever more technology: we'll invent our way out of ecological disaster.

Can this belief in progress also be violent? Didn't technology give contribute to the positive development of a huge number of people? For example, sewage systems did a great lot to improve living conditions of millions and although fossil fuels are now causing climatological problems, it also brought unprecedented affluence.

However, what has been the collateral damage of all this? Still, many millions live in horrible conditions all over the world and the affluent society has been primarily affluent for human beings. If one takes into account other beings as well, human technological progress has been extremely violent, causing the extinction of many species and making large areas of the planet inhabitable (both on land as in the oceans).

From a cultural perspective, progress has also a violent aspect, when representatives of a certain culture consider themselves superior above others, because they haven't developed the way 'we' did. The violence becomes real when people are forced into developments.

Progress has brought a lot to a great number of people, but it also creates new borders between groups of people that can keep up with the pace and those who can't. During a debate on the future of Amsterdam national Airport in the Netherlands, it was quite bizarre that a member of a political party who is in favor of further growth of the airport called flying a basic right. Even within the Netherlands, a large group of people has no access to this 'right' and internationally that number is even much larger. Even something that has become as common as flying, is common for an elite only [14, 15].

Postmodern thought, like that of Vattimo, is nuanced and does not simply criticize progress with a call for its opposite. That would imply a new metaphysical position again. It is critical, and at the same time acknowledges that it cannot be simply be changed or done away with. Like many critical thinkers about technology (e.g. Jacques Ellul [16]) they seem to be aware of the ambiguous character of progress: it seems to be an inevitable part of our society. One cannot escape it, but that does not mean that one cannot be critical about it and see what is possible to reduce the collateral damage.

Metaphysics as totalitarian thought: following thinkers like Adorno and Horkheimer [17] Vattimo regularly expresses the modernist ideal of 'total organization' [18–20]. The two characteristics of metaphysics seem to be combined: progress moves towards total control. Is this a justified fear? Horkheimer and Adorno wrote their book years before the revolution of information technology, but after the horrors of the second world war. Vattimo wrote his Transparent Society in the eighties, so also before the revolution of the internet.

The developments in China, with face recognition technology in the public domain, but also in countries that consider themselves more free, show that technology is able to track and trace many of our movements and that it depends on governments and companies how this technological capacity is used. Even in a country like the Netherlands, which considers itself to be quite democratic, it is by no means self-evident that technology is used properly: for a number of years, the government used algorithms to trace fraud, which used ethnic profiling. Finding people who apparently abused the social security system (control) was more important than morality. Or can we say that *control becomes morality* (if you've got nothing to hide, you shouldn't have a problem with control systems).

Companies have a long tradition of control systems, and not many people seem to be bothered. The pursuit of productivity makes much technology allowed and in Lean thinking, with it's high value of measurable facts, the temptation to measure all kinds of human behavior must be enormous. In top sport, there seems to be no limit in what is allowed. The human body is almost completely and continuously monitored in order to push it to the limits. Of course, a sportsperson chooses to submit themselvesto total control. Or does it?

Metaphysics and objectification: the fourth and last characteristic of metaphysics is its tendency to objectify everything. Heidegger, in his *Question Concerning Technology* [21], uses the river Rhine to show what that means: the Rhine, rather than being a mysterious and mythical force, has become a resource: it is a logistical resource as a water way, a source of energy, of tourist industry et cetera. It has lost its mythical status, or, even its myths have also become a resource for the tourist industry (for city marketeers and place branding specialists).

What is typical for objectification is the desire to count and measure everything. If something has been objectified, the next step is that it becomes manageable. Objectification makes it possible to take control of the phenomenon that is objectified. A classic example from the antiquity is the story of the golden calf, written in the book Exodus in the Old Testament. The story tells about the God of the Hebrews, who remained somewhat abstract, by just being there as a cloud by day and a column of fire by night. The people demanded from the leaders, while Moses was away on the mountain to talk with God, that they should create a more tangible representation of a God. There, even the deity was reduced to an object. The people involved could not cope with an abstract idea of a god, but wanted something that could be carried with them. History, according to Heidegger, is full of examples of objectifications of being. In the modern era, the situation has become even more radical: even time has been objectified and it seems that every aspect of life must be controlled or managed. Scientific approaches to formerly subjective phenomena as happiness promise us to get control over our own lives (again).

Why should Lean practitioners bother with these reflections about metaphysics? What is the use (value added) of these abstract analyses? The former paragraphs summarized briefly what characterizes metaphysics. According to philosophers like Heidegger and Vattimo the entire western philosophical tradition can be analyzed along this concept: the history of western civilization is a history of the ongoing development of metaphysics. That means that our entire way of thinking and the language we use is drenched with metaphysics. In his Letter on Humanism [22], Heidegger writes that his planned third part of Being and Time couldn't be written, because he had no adequate vocabulary for it. And Vattimo: 'language is not just a system of grammatical rules, but (...) it also implies a hierarchical organization (...) the same world of concepts-words is a world of dominion and oppression' [18]. It seems like we're trapped in metaphysics and that would explain why thinking differently is so difficult.

The first characteristic of metaphysics is one that shows a preference for stable truths. Diversity means chaos and there must be one best way of organizing things. The dynamic approach that Lean thinking proposes is disturbing for many a metaphysical mind. Standards are to be developed and maintained. The Lean idea that a standard has to be developed in order to challenge it again is exhausting for the metaphysical mind.

A critical reader could counter that the third characteristic, that of progress, is exactly what Lean thinkers would want. If progress is part of metaphysics, than Lean thinking should not be a problem! Although the continuous strive for improvement could be interpreted as a metaphysical trait of Lean thinking (as I will show in the next section), the idea of progress in metaphysics is utopian. Scientists and technologists seem to believe that progress is necessary in civilization and technology has become a force by itself, totally outside the sphere of influence of the individual. Vattimo sees both threats and opportunities in the technological developments. His position is never a pessimist one.

Next to the idea that metaphysics makes it hard for people to cope with continuous change and challenge, the analysis of especially Vattimo shows that it has a violent potential. Especially the world of organization is a world of hierarchy, a world of structure and a world in which violence is always lurking. So perhaps, the Lean practitioner could be helped by the awareness of both aspects of metaphysics in daily practices: the difficulty of accepting an intrinsically dynamic concept like Lean thinking and the awareness of the violent character of concepts, also used in the Lean body of knowledge. In that way, the concept of *respect for people* could be given a more profound content. The next section will show a number of ways in which respect for people could be threatened by implicit violence that lies hidden in Lean thinking.

4 Lean Thinking as Metaphysical Thought

After this brief introduction of metaphysical thought the connection with Lean thinking can be made: if metaphysics is such a deeply rooted thinking habit, can we recognize elements of it in Lean thinking? After that (in the next section), we'll take a look at the way Gianni Vattimo perceived his weak thought and how that relates to Lean thinking.

If we take the four characteristics of metaphysics – foundationalist, progress, totalitarian and objectification – it seems that some of these are more easy to be recognized than others. Is Lean thinking foundationalist? In last year's paper it seemed that we argued the exact opposite. The hesitation or hostility towards Lean was linked to our thinking tradition, so that would make Lean thinking less suspicious.

It depends on how one looks at it. Although Lean thinking has some characteristics that are not necessarily metaphysical, there are some 'suspect' things in it as well. What about traditional Lean's occupation with customer value? In these sustainability times, it seems that this single principle can stand in the way of sustainability performance. If the customer value becomes the sacrosanct unique principle where companies should strive for, than the environment could pay a price. Lean Green literature tries to widen the scope a bit [23] but shows at the same time that traditional Lean needs adaptation.

The same goes for a Lean principle like 'flow'. If that gets an absolute status, a refraining principle like respect for people is needed to prevent it from becoming violent. And runs Lean thinking in itself the risk of becoming the one and only truth for business? As a 'believer' one can easily forget that other people are not that enthusiastic, or even afraid of what Lean thinking may bring them. Especially in companies that are driven by the profit motive, and which use Lean thinking to become even more profitable, fears for a next reorganization can be completely justified. Fears of Lean being used in a violent way.

The next example to finish this argument on foundationalism is the use of performance indicators. Even if profit is not the ultimate performance indicator for a company, the way one pursues performance indicators can become relentless. In sports, there are numerous examples. In Dutch gymnastics, in recent years a number of cases of unacceptable behavior by coaches towards their pupils were unveiled. Top sports have this huge pressure on performance and many misconducts were rationalized by saying that the way to the top is never easy [24]. Why should we suppose that in companies respect for people is always obeyed?

On the one hand, the dynamic character of Lean thinking is almost contradictory to the foundational aspect of metaphysics. But that doesn't mean that, at the other hand, Lean thinking is completely free from foundationalism.

What about the belief in progress? In the aforementioned I already discussed this briefly. Although Lean thought speaks about things like 'true north' and a 'long term philosophy' [25], that is different from the modern belief in progress. Lean thinking is – as far as I know – never utopian, rather pragmatic. There is no 'belief' in some kind of ideal society, like in metaphysical thought (from the Augustinian City of God, to the Marxist communist society, the fascist varieties like the third Reich, or the final capitalist globalized society that could develop after the fall of the Berlin wall [26].

Also, the belief in something like a theory of everything, which some scientist seem to pursue, has a certain utopian content. Science and technology could create a better or even perfect society (again Ellul with the inquiry in the 60's).

One of the reasons that many Lean programs seem to fail, is exactly the lack of a 'utopian' perspective. Continuous improvement is never finished and exactly that never ending 'perspectivelessness' seems to be an important reason why on the long run, it is very difficult to establish and maintain a Lean culture. It seems that people want something like a perspective, a finish line, a project rather than a never ending program.

On the other hand, Lean enthusiasts might be too pushy about change. Is it possible that Lean thinking can become a goal in itself? That continuous improvement becomes a goal in itself? Is that perhaps what could make it metaphysical? Perhaps these question could be a basis for empirical research.

Two characteristics of metaphysics remain, the first of which is totalitarianism. Lean thinking does not aim for societal reform, its focus is the level of the organization. The fear of a totalitarian society, therefore, seems to be ungrounded. But how is the situation on the level of the organization? Is there any freedom left for the employee of a company that is continuously seeking for more efficient processes? Is it possible that organizations become totalitarian?

Of course, there is the possibility that Lean thinking contributes to more favorable working conditions and a reduction of pressure and case load of employees [27]. In certain industries, cases are known where employees have to follow very strict procedures about the time they are allowed to spend on certain activities (cleaning companies, health care institutions). How far can organizations go in their quest for efficiency and customer value?

Organizations, although they have to obey laws, are not always democratic institutions. They are run by elites and often are structured in a highly hierarchical way. It is strange to see that people in the public debate talk about rights, like freedom of speech, while they, when at work, accept limitations of rights without any hesitation. How far may organizations go in their efforts to get all noses in the same direction?

The last characteristic of metaphysics was objectification of about everything. Here Lean thinking seems guilty even at first sight. Processes should be mapped and measured. Wastes must be analyzed and flow is the ultimate goal of each process. Isn't Lean thinking all about objectification? And is this endless pursuit of transparency in processes not also linked with the former point, that of totalitarianism? Is there any chance of freedom in Lean thinking?

Metaphysics, or strong thought, as Gianni Vattimo calls it, can be violent if the freedom of individuals is threatened. It is strong because people might get hurt by it. Lean thinking has that same potential, if it is not refrained by values like respect for people. If pursued relentlessly, Lean thought can have the violent potential of metaphysics.

In the paper about Lean philosophy [1] the main perspective was on the different way of thinking Lean thinking proposed ideally. That is a difficult way of thinking if one has an inclination to absolute truths (foundationalism). In this paper we have also been critical about the potential Lean thinking has if used metaphysically. The violent potential of Lean thinking can be yet another explanation of the reluctancy of many people towards Lean practices. But is there a way out of the metaphysical trap?

5 Weak Thought and Lean: An Escape from the Metaphysical Trap?

Although the German philosopher Martin Heidegger, at the end of his life, sighed that "only a God can save us", the Italian philosopher Gianni Vattimo was more positive about our possibilities to escape the metaphysical trap. He actually searched for that for a long time, but in a paper, published in 1983, he finally seemed to have found an answer with the concept of *weak thought*. In later work, he further elaborated on it.

It is difficult to summarize briefly what is actually quite a nuanced concept. It starts with an analysis of other attempts to overcome metaphysics in the 20th century. The problem with these attempts, according to Vattimo, is that they try to put forward a way of thinking opposite of metaphysics, which immediately becomes in itself metaphysical: a revolution can at first liberate from an oppressive force, but it is often a matter of one form of *strong thought* against another one [7].

Weak thought tries not to do away strong thought, but tries to accept the heritage and incorporate it. Vattimo uses a concept, *Verwindung*, again taken from Heidegger, although elaborated in an original way, to illustrate the resignation to metaphysics. It is the idea of an illness, that is overcome, but still scars remain. You cannot get rid of the metaphysical heritage of an entire civilization, but you can be aware of it's violent character.

When Vattimo discusses a text by Walter Benjamin, in which a work by Paul Klee is reflected upon, it becomes clearer what he means: the painting by Klee shows an angel, with at it's feet the remnants of history's victims (Benjamin was known for his statement that history is written by conquerors). The attention for the ones that were and are conquered and oppressed can be a start of the disarmament of metaphysics.

It almost is impossible to do justice to the concept of *weak thought*, and even Vattimo himself regularly states that we are just beginning to understand the consequences of the philosophies by Nietzsche and Heidegger. It has been a lifelong endeavor for him: at a certain point [28] he summarizes his philosophical project with the words "above all, I searched for freedom".

Can Lean thinking be thought of in a non-violent way? Is there a possibility of freedom within the Lean enterprise? The point of departure is the previous section, where the characteristics of metaphysics were summarized. This exercise in itself shows some aspects that can be considered to be *strong thought*. What *respect for people* implies can be deepened using these insights (which is at the same time an example of how philosophy can be used to renew ones perspective on Lean thinking).

Although Lean thinking questions the idea of foundationalism, by being intrinsically dynamic [1], it does have the potential to become foundationalist. Lean thinking does create some kind of (social) unity, and with that a border, between believers and non-believers. How much attention is paid to the people who cannot (yet) follow the implementation plans?

Something that I touched at years ago [8], but never was able to further elaborate on, was the absolute status of the corporation. How many times in Lean literature is the company itself considered to be waste? If there is one foundation in Lean thinking, it perhaps is the corporation in which Lean practices take place. Is there a point where that holy of holiest must be put into question? Is the existence of some companies absolutely necessary? Certainly, if one takes into consideration a broader view of corporate responsibility (where stakeholders value, rather than mere customer value is pursued), some organizations might be so wasteful that it is more efficient for society to liquidate them. As this paper is written, there is much rumor about a Chemours department in Dordrecht (the Netherlands), because of the huge amounts of poisonous waste they deposit in the surroundings of the factory. Again we turn to Nietzsche, when he argued that "it is a fallacy to think that something has a right to exist, simply because it exists" [29].

Lean thinking seems very much in line with the ideal of progress. Continuous improvement is all about progress, although we already saw that the metaphysical value of progress is not exactly the same. When continuous improvement becomes a utopian ideal, it can become violent, and the awareness of that could prevent companies of becoming divided between the winners and losers of the continuous improvement programs. Is the fear of such a division a possible reason for the hesitation people have to accept Len programs?

What can an organization do against the threat of totalitarianism? With digital tools being all-present and increasingly easy to implement, the possibility to control all aspects of organizational life increase as well. Is it possible to combine *respect for people* and *going to gemba*? Create a dialogue at all the layers of the organization to reflect upon values: what does respect for people mean for the people involved? Perhaps the time is right for a further elaboration of the concept of respect for people, or better still, both the concepts respect and people and the combination of the two.

Objectification was the last characteristic of metaphysics and very much linked to some of the ideals of Lean thinking. Standardization of processes, aiming for *poka yoke*, measuring all steps in processes... Objectification seems to be an inevitable part of Lean thinking. Combined with the other characteristics of metaphysics the question rises whether or not there is freedom left in an organization that aims for continuous improvement. Is continuous improvement a wolve in sheep's clothes?

In the aforementioned there seems to be a similar refrain between all the different paragraphs: whether or not Lean thinking becomes strong thought, depends on the implementation of it: what values lie beneath the surface? Is a continuous improvement program backed up by corporate values that are dominated by shareholder value, or does the corporation have other values at its core? How does the corporation apply the value of respect for people? Lean thinking can be 'weakened', starting with the awareness of the potential violence that lurks within it.

6 Conclusion

The idea to confront Lean thinking and Vattimo's reflections on metaphysics was originally triggered by the hesitation of many people towards Lean programs. For some people it is very difficult to accept a way of thinking that is so dynamic and without end. When one accepts that it is understandably so, because a more static way of thinking has been rule, rather than exception for many centuries, the Lean trainer acknowledges that sometimes Lean training requires a huge effort to slowly adapt to this way of thinking.

The theory about metaphysics can thus *explain* why some people are bothered by huge barriers before they can accept Lean thinking. The outside in approach, which takes a philosophical concept with the aim to reflect on Lean thinking, aims at more than just an explanation of a certain phenomenon. The question is whether or not the confrontation of Lean thinking and philosophy has a productive effect: does the confrontation generate new insights?

The first insight follows from the distinction between (metaphysical) strong thought and weak thought. Can Lean thinking be strong thought, and therefore be violent? Can Lean practices be violent? Especially when Lean thinking is applied as a set of tools, and the underlying corporate values are not consistent with the principles of respect for people, Lean practices can be relentless for employees. Especially when companies – despite perhaps all kind of beautiful CSR promises – still are driven by the desire to maximize shareholders value, Lean thinking will have the violent potential of strong thought.

Weak thought desires to reduce the violent potential of metaphysics. Weak Lean thinking does not only aim for reduction of waste, but also at the reduction of violence. This would require further research into the principle of respect for people. What does this concept mean if one takes into consideration the violence of strong thought? And shouldn't the principle of respect for people be extended to other stakeholders that may be affected by the violence of the corporation's activities? Biodiversity, ecology, water quality… What other values should be respected by the company?

A second insight is the concept of the company itself. Despite all the critical elements of Lean thinking, that seems to put all the company's processes under critique, one issue never is criticized: the company itself. What if the corporation itself has become 'waste'? What would happen if one dares to ask the question whether or not the existence of a corporation ads value? This may be too much asked from Lean practitioners, and this requires further reflection.

Of course, this view towards metaphysics and modernism is quite specific for a certain current in philosophy. Vattimo belongs to what is often called postmodernism, and philosophy is much richer than this one concept. Last year's paper was a first exercise of the inside out approach, while this one is a first exercise in the outside in approach. Who knows what insights can be further obtained.

References

1. Zwart, J.G. de: Is There such a thing as a lean philosophy? In: McDermott, O. (ed.) European lean educators conference, pp. 3–13. Springer, Heidelberg (2022)
2. Ortiz, C.A.: The psychology of lean improvements: why organizations must overcome resistance and change the culture. CRC Press (2012)
3. Korb, S., Ballard, H.G.: Believing is seeing: paradigms as a focal point in the lean discourse. In: Gonzalez, V.A. (ed.) 26TH Annual Conference of the International Group for Lean Construction (IGLC). IGLC.net (2018)
4. McLean, R., Antony, J.: Why continuous improvement initiatives fail in manufacturing environments? a systematic review of the evidence. Int. J. Product. Perform. Manage. **63**(3), 370–376 (2014)
5. Basin, S., Burcher, P.: Lean viewed as a lean philosophy. J. Manufact. Manage. Emerald, Leeds (2006)
6. Heidegger, M.: Spiegel-Gespräch mit Martin Heidegger. Vittorio Klostermann, Frankfurt am Main (2000)

7. Vattimo, G.: Dialectics, Difference, Weak Thought. In: Vattimo, G., Rovatti, P.A. (eds.) Weak Thought. SUNY, New York (2012)
8. De Zwart, J.G.: Corporate Social Responsibility, an interpretative practice. Rediscovering CSR through the hermeneutic philosophy of Gianni Vattimo. Ridderprint, Ridderkerk (2016)
9. Vattimo, G.: Conclusion: metaphysics and violence. In: Zabala, S. (ed.) Essays in honour of Gianni Vattimo. McGill-Queen's University Press, Montreal & Kingston (2007)
10. Vattimo, G.: The End of Modernity. Johns Hopkins University Press, Baltimore (1988)
11. Welsch, W.: Unsere postmoderne Moderne. Akademie Verlag, Berlin (2008)
12. Vattimo, G.: The Adventure of Difference. Polity Press, Oxford (1993)
13. Jaspers, K.: Der Philosophische Glaube Angesichts der Offenbarung. Piper, Munich (1962)
14. BNNVARA: https://www.bnnvara.nl/artikelen/wat-is-de-impact-van-jouw-vlieggedrag-op-het-klimaat. Last accessed 16 September 2023
15. CNBC: https://www.cnbc.com/2017/12/07/boeing-ceo-80-percent-of-people-never-flown-for-us-that-means-growth.html. Last accessed 16 September 2023
16. Ellul, J.: The Technological Society. Vintage Books, New York (1964)
17. Horkheimer, M., Adorno, T.W.: Dialektik der Aufklärung, 15th edn. Fischer, Frankfurt am Main (2004)
18. Vattimo, G.: Il Soggetto e la maschera. Bompiani, Milan (1974)
19. Vattimo, G.: La società trasparente. Garzanti, Milan (1989)
20. Vattimo, G.: Addio alla verità. Meltemi, Rome (2009)
21. Heidegger, M.: Die Frage nach der Technik. Klett-Cotta, Stuttgart (2007)
22. Heidegger, M.: Over het Humanisme. Damon, Budel (2005)
23. Zokaei, K., Lovins, H., Wood, A., Hines, P.: Creating a Lean and Green Business System. CRC Press, Techniques for Improving Profits and Sustainability (2013)
24. NOS : https://nos.nl/artikel/2470012-trainen-met-botbreuken-niet-ongewoon-ruim-acht-ton-aan-tegemoetkoming-gymsporters. Last accessed 16 September 2023
25. Liker, J.: The Toyota Way. McGraw-Hill, New York (2004)
26. Vattimo, G.: Hermeneutic Communism. Columbia University Press, New York (2011)
27. IVALUEIMPROVEMENT: https://www.ivalueimprovement.com/blog/lees-nu-het-artikel-kan-continu-verbeteren-werkdruk-voorkomen/
28. Vattimo, G., Paterlini, P.: Non essere Dio. Aliberti, Reggio Emilia (2006)
29. Nietzsche, F.: Menselijk, al te menselijk. De Arbeiderspers, Amsterdam/Antwerp (2000)

Digitalization

Barriers and Enablers of Lean Industry 4.0

Peter Hines[1(✉)] and Guilherme Luz Tortorella[2]

[1] South East Technological University, Waterford, Ireland
peter@enterpriseexcellencenetwork.com
[2] The University of Melbourne, Melbourne, Australia

Abstract. This paper provides the result of a global qualitative open-question survey into the barriers and enablers of Lean Industry 4.0. The key barrier identified were financial constraints and the key enabler was the various Industry 4.0 technologies. However, outside this, the barriers and enablers are mainly concerned with people, management and change management.

The paper also examines how these factors change for respondents from organizations with different levels of maturity in Lean and Industry 4.0. It was found that financial resources were the most important barriers for advanced Lean and Industry 4.0 organizations with change management more important for high Lean, low Industry 4.0 firms and engagement and alignment for low Lean, high Industry 4.0 firms. The use of the various Industry 4.0 technologies was the most important enabler for the most advanced Lean and Industry 4.0 organizations, with high Lean, low Industry 4.0 more unsure of the most important enabler and for low Lean, high Industry 4.0, engagement and alignment was the most cited enabler.

These findings provide both academia, industry and third party providers such as government agencies and Universities the most detailed and scaled insights into barriers and enablers within Lean Industry 4.0. It also shows the linkage between the two and provides insights into the higher level of importance of change management, people resources and the role of leaders than had been cited in earlier work.

Keywords: Lean Industry 4.0 · Enablers · Inhibitors

1 Introduction

Over the last 30 years Lean has been the primary improvement approach attracting academic and industrial interest [1]. However, this position has been challenged by the rise of Industry 4.0 (I4) over the last decade leading to discussion about the future role of Lean [2, 3]. Much of the literature suggests a synergistic relationship [4] leading to the use of the term Lean Industry 4.0 (LI4) [5]. This approach is seen as combining the process and people perspective of Lean with the technological perspective of Industry 4.0 [6].

Published by Springer Nature Switzerland AG 2024
T. van Kollenburg et al. (Eds.): ELEC 2023, IFIP AICT 681, pp. 37–51, 2024.
https://doi.org/10.1007/978-3-031-63265-5_4

There has been an intensive recent discussion of how this marriage might be brought about [5, 7] as there is still much confusion in industry [8]. Although the topic of LI4 has attracted a great deal of recent attention there many gaps in the literature including: the inputs required, the enabler, the inhibitors as well as maturity assessments and roadmaps [9]. This paper seeks to address the area of the barriers and enablers of LI4 as this is such a formative element of LI4. We also consider whether these depending on the maturity of Lean and I4 within organisations.

Much of the previous research is based on limited geographical quantitative surveys [10], case studies [6] or literature reviews [11] resulting in a lack of both depth and/or breadth of empirical evidence. This paper seeks to address this gap by drilling deep into the evidence from a qualitative global industry survey [9].

2 Literature Review

The literature typically talks about enablers and barriers of change [12]. We will follow this convention in the literature review. However, as some of the enablers are responses to the barriers, we will discuss barriers before enablers in our results.

The literature on enablers to LI4 is scarce and so we will start by reviewing the coverage of this area within I4. Twenty-three references have recently been summarized by Guerrero et al. [12]. They divided the factors into: strategic; operational; human resources; technological; economic; political, legal & social and environmental. The enabler factors where they found three or more references are shown in Table 1. The most cited factors are technological and refer mostly to specific technologies whilst two strategic factors and one environmental factor were popular. This review gives us an insight into what is most cited but not their relative importance.

The literature on LI4 demonstrates a similar finding, typified by Kashyap et al. who identifying eight technological factors as well as professional training and development, the weakest of their driver [25]. Indeed, Moraes et al. (pp. 11), in a review of reviews, found "very little input ... in issues such as leadership, people, and cultural management, integration (downstream and upstream) in the value chain, innovation and design, and problem solving" [11]. An exception to this is the call by Komkowski et al. for Lean management as a precursor including areas such as transformation strategy, design, delivery, governance, and leadership [26]. In this respect Rossi et al. also point to the importance of people as the center for innovation in a sustainable way [27]. In a more rounded perspective Macias-Aguayo et al. point to a group of enabling technologies as well as the importance of investment in training, the involvement of employees and stakeholders and the support and commitment of top management [28].

Table 1. Top Cited Enablers of Industry 4.0 [12]

Enabler	Areas	Cited By
Coordination & collaboration among supply chain members	Strategic	[13–17]
Big Data and analytics	Technological	[17–21]
Cloud computing and manufacturing	Technological	[17–21]]
Collaborative robots, automated guided vehicles	Technological	[17, 19–21]
Waste recovery, reduction and pollution monitoring and control	Environmental	[13, 16, 17, 22]
Effective facility planning, infrastructure buildings and standardization	Strategic	[13, 15, 19]
To integrate digital and physical systems	Technological	[17, 20, 23]
To digitize supply chain activities	Technological	[18, 23, 24]
Cybersecurity	Technological	[20, 21, 24]

Again, the literature on barriers to LI4 is scarce, but on L4 more plentiful. A similar review of the I4 barriers was undertaken by Guerrero et al. using the same classification [12]. The most cited barriers are shown in Table 2 with the cost and access to capital most referenced. Most of the other enablers are around human resources, specifical management, change management and employee engagement and training. Government support and resource and infrastructure quality also receive attention.

Macias-Aguayo et al., in summarizing the recent literature, identify barriers within LI4 as falling into four areas: cultural suitability (CS), financial plausibility (FP), operational viability (OV) and technological feasibility (TF) [31]. Within this they closely mirror the findings of Guerrero et al. in finding the key factors as: high implementation costs (FP), technology incompatibility (TF), long learning curve (OV), insufficient IT design and infrastructure (TF) and resistance to change (CS).

Table 2. Top Cited Barriers to Industry 4.0 [12]

Barriers	Areas	Cited By
High cost of sustainability adoption/difficulty to access credit/lack of access to capital for I4.0	Economic	[17, 20, 23, 24, 28–30]
Lack of understanding the importance of I4.0 at top management levels	Human resources	[20, 22–24, 29, 30]
Ineffective employee training for sustainability, lack of skilled workforce	Human resources	[22, 23, 28, 29]

(continued)

Table 2. (*continued*)

Barriers	Areas	Cited By
Poor team management and lack of cross function team. Lack of inter-departmental communication. Contradictory interest	Human resources	[23, 28–30]
Lack of government policy frameworks/support	Political, legal, and social	[20, 22, 24, 30]
Resistance of culture change, lack of digital culture	Human resources	[22, 23, 30]
Lack of effective employee engagement and empowerment. Resistance to change by employees and middle managers	Human resources	[23, 28, 30]
Poor resource / infrastructure quality or utilization	Technology	[22, 29, 30]

3 Methodology

The approach taken involved the use of a 1030 response qualitative survey from 6 continents and 66 countries which allows for clear and comprehensive responses and unforeseen answers [32]. The survey This involved 26 mostly open questions (42 including sub-questions) with a global coverage that provides the potential to capture a diversity of perspectives, experiences, and sense-making [33]. The authors was supported by 31 other academics and 6 partners in distributing the survey to a purposive sample of individuals in companies who were familiar with Lean and/or I4.[1] Full details of the methodology can be found in the summary paper by Hines et al. [9]. Here we extracted the detailed data from 305 complete responses where full data was available about the level of maturity of the organizations that the respondents worked in.

4 Results

4.1 Barriers to LI4

The respondents identified a very wide range of primary barriers to LI4 with no one factor predominating. We clustered the 305 responses into 36 groups (Fig. 1). Highest ranked was financial constraints with most respondents suggesting this mainly due to

[1] The authors would like to thank Jiju Antony, David Romero, Aidan Walsh, Darrin Taylor, Anabela Carvalho Alves, Massimo Bertolini, Rodrigo Caiado, José Carvalho, Krisztina Demeter, Luis Ferreira, Diego Fettermann, Moacir Godinho Filho, Paolo Gaiardelli, Graham Howe, Guvan Gurkan Inan, Maneesh Kumar, Hieu Chi Le, Florian Magnani, Juan Manuel Maqeira Marin, Josefa Mula, Michael Packianather, Paolo Peças, Maria Teresa Ribeiro Pereira, Daryl Powell, Anupama Prashar, Masood Ur Rehman, José Carlos Vieira De Sá, Henrik Saabye, Erol Selim, Leonor Teixeira, Helen Zak, Enterprise Ireland, HKPO, ICBE, Lean Forum, Shingo Institute and UnoPro. We would also like to thank Renan Silva Santos for data analysis support.

the lack of availability of a budget, although justifying expenditure and demonstrating returns were also mentioned. The next three clusters were all people related, namely: change, culture, and engagement & involvement. The change area concerned change management, as well as the adaptability and flexibility to make the change successful. The cultural area included culture of the organisation and in particular the mindset of employees at all levels as well as their openness to buy in to LI4. This links to the engagement and involvement which relates to whether people were happy to take up the new approach and actively get involved and become committed.

Another important barrier was competence which included the skill and competence level of existing employees and the problems associated with their training and development. The technical areas of I4 was only the 6th most mentioned area and included the areas of data acquisition and management, automation, digitization as well as keeping up with new technologies. Barriers were also seen in the strategy area particularly around the development of a vision, in setting direction and in deciding upon priorities. For many, knowledge was also a barrier as LI4 is not only a broad area but one that includes many recent new developments particularly in the technology area. The last major set of barriers were people related, particularly the accessibility of new recruits and the availability of existing employees who had competing priorities.

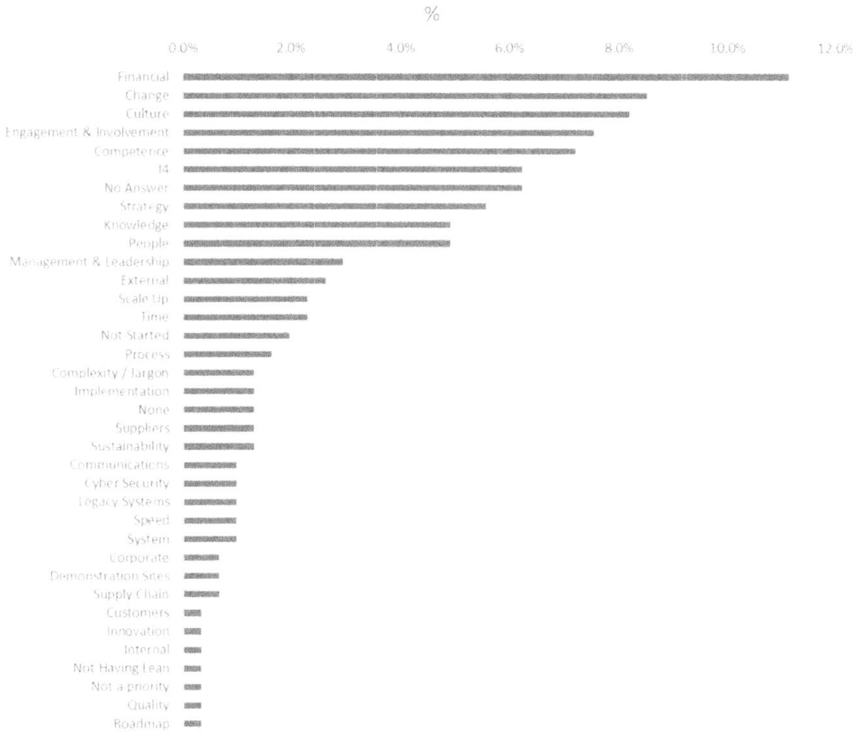

Fig. 1. Barriers to LI4

Barriers by Level of Maturity

Next, we considered whether some of these barriers were more or less important for organisations with differing maturity levels. It has become popular to develop combined maturity assessments for LI4 [34]. However, as there is some doubt as to whether LI4 is yet a coherent phenomenon [9], we followed Tortorella & Fettermann [10] preferring to look at the maturity of Lean and I4 independently. To do this we adopted two existing nine-point frameworks that represented the socio-technical nature of Lean (people and process) as well as the technological perspective of I4 (respectively Chiera et al. [35] and Tortorella et al. [36]). In both cases a coding score was assigned to each of these with dimensions ranging from 1–5 where 1 is none, 2 is early stage, 3 is partial, 4 is high and 5 is advanced. From this we were able to calculate the mean scores for Lean and I4 and segment our sample into firms: 90 as Early Stage (below average Lean and I4), 55 as I4 (below average Lean, above average I4), 67 as Lean (above average Lean, below average I4) and 93 as LI4 (above average Lean and I4). We then tested the categorical data non-parametrically using chi-squared test and considered their significance associations with adjusted residual values larger than 1.60, 1.96 and 2.58, corresponding a significance level of 0.10, 0.05 and 0.01, respectively [37] as shown in Table 3.

Table 3. Significant Barriers by Level of Maturity Using Chi-Square Test (Significant only)

Barrier	LI4 Adjusted Residual	LI4 Frequency 93	L Adjusted Residual	L Frequency 67	I4 Adjusted Residual	I4 Frequency 55	Early Adjusted Residual	Early Frequency 90
Change					–2.0**	1		
Engagement & Alignment					2.2**	8	–1.8*	3
Knowledge					1.6*	5		
People	2.0**	8						
Management & Leadership			–1.6*	0	3.0***	5		
External			1.9**	4				
Time							1.6*	4
Scale Up	–1.8*	0					2.5**	5
Process	3.4***	5						
Speed					2.2**	2		
Internal					2.1**	1		
Not Having Lean					2.1**	1		
Quality			1.9**	1				
Not a Priority			1.9**	1				

* Significant at 10%, ** Significant at 5%, *** Significant at 1%

Table 4 shows a collation of the top 10 ranking for barriers for the total sample and respondents in the LI4, Lean, I4 and Early Stages. Many of the same clusters feature in each column although there are some significant differences. In Table 4 we only see clusters that are similar or those that are significantly higher in bold. None of the significantly lower clusters shown in Table 3 fell within the top 10 of any firm maturity type.

With regards to LI4 firms the shortage of people and the barriers in the process area stand out as more significant. The process cluster includes the understanding and standardization of processes. For Lean firms, change management and I4 technologies were seen to be the biggest barriers with a significant increase in importance of external drivers such as changes in customer requirements and market competition. Respondents from I4 firms identified the engagement & involvement as the #1 cluster, with knowledge and management & leadership also significantly higher. For Early Stage firms the position as broadly similar to the total population although there was greater concerns about the scale up of early Lean implementation or I4 use cases, and well as a shortage of time.

Table 4. Top Barriers to Lean Industry 4.0

Rank	Total Sample	Lean Industry 4.0	Lean	Industry 4.0	Early Stage
1	Financial	Financial	Change	**Engagement & Involvement****	Financial
2	Change	Change	Industry 4.0	Financial	Change
3	Culture	**People****	No Answer	Culture	Culture
4	Engagement & Involvement	Culture	Competence	Strategy	Competence
5	Competence	Engagement &Involvement	Engagement & Alignment	**Knowledge***	Industry 4.0
6	Industry 4.0	Competence	Culture	**Management & Leadership*****	Strategy
7	No Answer	**Process*****	Financial	Competence	Knowledge
8	Strategy	No Answer	Strategy	Industry 4.0	No Answer
9	Knowledge	Industry 4.0	**External****	No Answer	**Scale Up****
10	People	Time	Not Started	People	**Time***

Bold = Positive Significance for Higher Position. *Italics* = Negative Significance for Higher Position. * Significant at 10%, ** Significant at 5%, *** Significant at 1%

4.2 Enablers of LI4

The enablers of LI4 were considered in a similar way to the barriers (Fig. 2). The highest ranked enabler was the various I4 technologies focusing particularly on data visibility, collection and management, the use of big data, connectivity as well as automation and digitization. Again, several human-related clustered scored highly including engagement & involvement, culture, and management & leadership. Particularly important was the role of management in being committed and sponsoring LI4 and engaging the wider workforce within a positive, blame-free attitude. It was noticeable that there was a high number of no answers and people who were unsure suggesting that people were often not able to clearly see what they needed to do to proceed successfully. People and change management were also seen as important as well as having a Lean foundation.

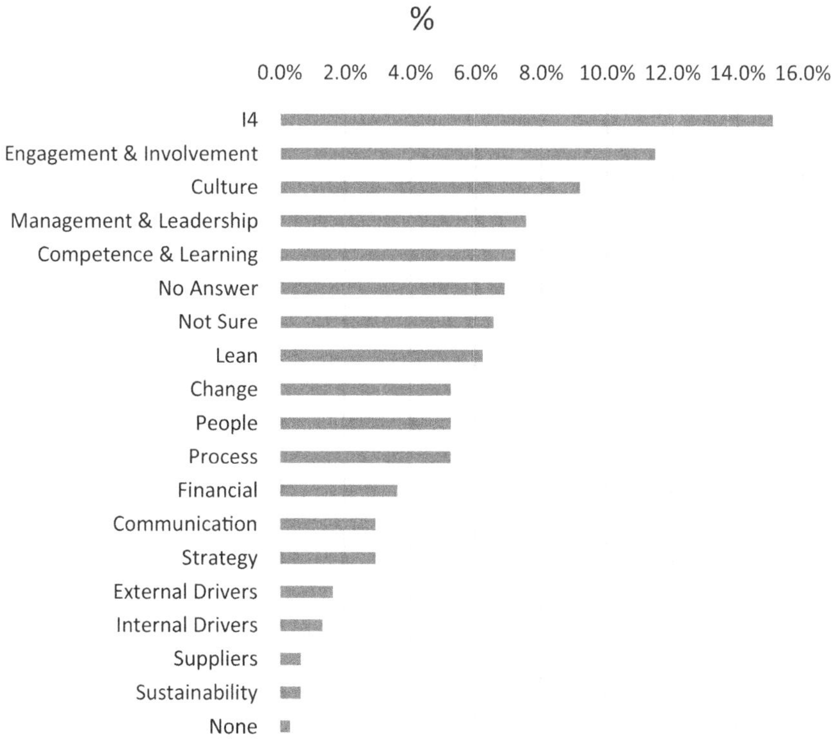

Fig. 2. Enablers of LI4

Enablers by Level of Maturity

The same method was used to consider enablers for LI4, Lean, I4 and Early Stage organizations with the significant differences from the total population shown in Table 5. Table 6 shows a collation the top 10 ranking for enablers for the total sample and respondents from the four types of organization. As with the barriers, many of the main clusters appear for each firm type but with some significant differences. The most striking difference for LI4 firms is the higher rating for the various LI4 technologies suggesting that they see as the key to their future. For Lean firms there was a significantly higher no answer as well as also a high ranking for I4 technologies. This perhaps suggests a split with some Lean firms being happy on their Lean journey and not seeing I4 as important and others who see I4 as their next enabling step. Management and leadership were seen as significantly less importance suggesting that this area had already been addressed within their past Lean activity.

Table 5. Significant Enablers by Level of Maturity Using Chi-Square Test (Significant only)

Enabler	LI4 Adjusted. Residual	LI4 Frequency 93	L Adjusted. Residual	L Frequency 67	I4 Adjusted. Residual	I4 Frequency 55	Early Adjusted. Residual	Early Frequency 90
I4	2.1**	20			−1.8*	4		
Management & Leadership			−1.6*	2				
Competence & Learning					−2.3**	0		
No Answer			2.4**	9			−2.1**	2
Not Sure	−2.1**	2					1.6*	9
Lean					1.6*	6		
People	−1.6*	2			2.1**	6		
Financial							1.9**	6
Strategy			−1.6*	0				
Internal							2.0**	3
None			1.9**	1				

* Significant at 10%, ** Significant at 5%, *** Significant at 1%

Table 6. Top Enablers for Lean Industry 4.0

Rank	Total Sample	Lean Industry 4.0	Lean	Industry 4.0	Early Stage
1	Industry 4.0	**Industry 4.0****	**No Answer****	Engagement & Involvement	Industry 4.0
2	Engagement & Involvement	Engagement & Involvement	Industry 4.0	**Lean***	Engagement & Involvement
3	Culture	Culture	Engagement & Involvement	**People****	Culture
4	Management & Leadership	Competence & Learning	Culture	Management & Leadership	**Not Sure***
5	Competence & Learning	Management & Leadership	Competence & Learning	No Answer	Management & Leadership
6	No Answer	Process	Change	*Industry 4.0*	Competence & Learning

(continued)

Table 6. (*continued*)

Rank	Total Sample	Lean Industry 4.0	Lean	Industry 4.0	Early Stage
7	Not Sure	Lean	Not Sure	Culture	**Financial****
8	Lean	No Answer	Lean	Not Sure	People
9	Change	Strategy	People	Process	Change
10	People	Change	*Management & Leadership**	Strategy	Process

Bold = Positive Significance for Higher Position. *Italics* = Negative Significance for Higher Position. * Significant at 10%, ** Significant at 5%, *** Significant at 1%

The main differences from the total population for I4 firms is the greater importance of Lean as a foundation and well the importance of people and in particular their engagement and involvement. The I4 technologies were seen as less important as an enabler as these firms were already advanced in these areas. Lastly the Early Stage firms had a broadly similar pattern to the total population but with a significantly higher number of respondents not sure of the key enabler, perhaps due to the lack of knowledge and management expertise. These organisations also saw that finance was a key enabler and in particular the cost of applying Lean and I4 as well as getting a good return on investment.

5 Discussion

5.1 Barriers

We identified a very wide range of barriers to LI4 which we clustered in 36 groups (Fig. 1). Financial and human related issues ranked highest. Our results were broadly similar to the barriers to I4 collated by Guerrero et al. [12]. They are particularly close to the earlier detailed summaries on I4 barriers by Yadav et al. [23] and Gadge et al. [30]. Each of these point out the importance of the high cost of implementation, a lack of knowledge about the importance of I4 by senior management, cultural issues and employee engagement. However, the literature of I4 barriers pays little attention to the importance of change management, strategy and scarce human resources found in this study. The finding about a change management and scarce human resources can be explained as they rank highly in our LI4 organization sample but not in I4 firms. This suggests that there may be an explainable difference in these two areas between LI4 and I4 organizations. However, the strategy finding is more surprising as this ranks highly in our I4 sample but not the LI4 one. This suggest there may be a gap in the I4 literature in this area.

When compared with the literature on barriers in LI4 we find many commonalities with the findings of Macias-Aguayo et al. [31]. The literature has however underestimated the impact of cultural factors, in particular the engagement and alignment of people and change management. These areas are rarely mentioned with the exception of Gupta et al. [38], Raut et al. [39] and Ghobadian et al. [40]. We also found that the role of management was key both in terms of their knowledge and in including LI4 within their strategy. This area again seems, with the exception of Vinodh [41], to be largely ignored in the literature. We also found that there was considerable concern about a lack of skilled human resources, an area receiving scant previous attention. In contrast, we found that the frequent concerns expressed in the literature around data privacy, loss and security were not reflected in our respondents [31].

5.2 Enablers

We found a wide range of enablers which we clustered into 19 groups (Fig. 2). Foremost among these was various I4 technologies, which showed a good alignment with the literature on I4 enablers [12]. We did however find that 85% of our responses pointed to other factors. The extant literature seems highly polarized on I4 technologies as enablers with other factors rarely mentioned [12]. This would appear to be a major problem as we found that issues concerning engagement, culture, management and leadership were all very important enablers. There was however some limited mention in the I4 literature of competence and learning an area we found to be important [14, 17]. This myopic attention on technological enablers is all the more surprising as our I4 group had a significantly lower focus on this area than the remainder of the sample and indeed I4 technologies was the number one factor in LI4 firms. This lack of focus is perhaps driven by the literature in I4 being dominated by people from engineering backgrounds [42].

There is a similar heavy focus on technological enablers in most of the LI4 enabler literature [25]. The main exception to this is the inter-disciplinary work of Komkowski et al. [26] as well as a focus on Lean being an enabler of LI4 [43]. Our findings support the fact that Lean is an enabler of LI4 but would suggest that other factors are far more important, notably the engagement and involvement of the workforce, culture, management and leadership, and competence and learning. Indeed, our findings would suggest that the clusters for enablers closely mirror the barrier clusters. This would of course seem to be highly likely. Surprisingly, this is not what the literature on I4 [12] or LI4 enablers [31] would suggest.

6 Conclusions

This paper has addressed the issue of barriers and enablers of LI4 based on a global survey. LI4 has received considerable attention over the last few years but, an area that has little attention is that of the barriers and enablers [42]. The existing literature has typically identified a small number of factors based on case research or literature reviews. These previous findings are limited either by their small research population or due to being summaries of past works. Although they can provide useful insights, the only way these tend to be gauged for importance is by adding up the number of times the factors are cited by other researchers [12, 31]. In this work we have taken a global sample of 305 respondents and asked about the main barrier and enabler to LI4. By analyzing the findings, we have been able to not only understand the differing factors but also their relative importance to industry. In addition, we have been able to segment our sample into whether the firms represented had advanced Lean or not and advanced I4 or not. We segmented the organisations as LI4, Lean, I4 and Early Stage organisations using this information.

What we found was that there were a wide range of factors involved for both barriers and enablers. The most important barrier was financial in terms of access to funds, or overcoming internal barriers to releasing funds. Apart from this, the most important barriers were human related with change management, culture, engagement and alignment, and competence most important. Many of the findings on barriers validate previous research although we have additionally identified the importance of change management, strategy and scarce human resources.

In terms of enablers, we have established that these are in large way responses to the barriers, surprising a finding not discussed in the literature where results are often presented as enablers and barriers missing the important flow of enablers being the response to barriers. We found the most important enabler to be a range of I4 technologies, notably in the area of data visibility, collection and management, the use of big data, connectivity as well as automation and digitization. However, in contrast to the literature we found that 85% of the responses were in other areas mainly concerned with people, leadership and change.

As yet the literature has not compared the barriers to firms at different levels of maturity of Lean and I4 with the implicit assumption that the factors must similar. We have found that there are some significant differences with financial barriers being most cited for LI4 firms whereas change management is highest for Lean organizations and engagement and involvement for I4 firms. Compared to the total sample population, the shortage of skilled people and the process area were higher for LI4 organizations.

In a similar way there is no known literature comparing the enablers to firms at different levels of Lean and I4 maturity. We have filled this gap and found that the most important enabler within such advanced Lean and I4 firms is the various I4 technologies, whereas there was more uncertainty in what was the most important enabler in Lean firms and again engagement and involvement being most important for I4 firms.

In terms of our contribution to industry, we would highlight that organizations might review the barriers that we have summarized to check whether they have considered them as well as reviewing barriers that other organizations have encountered at later maturity stages. They may then develop an appropriate set of countermeasures. This may involve some of the enablers that we have also summarized. This may also help them to identify appropriate sources of outside support from governmental agencies, consultancies and universities [9]. The work also provides a detailed insight that might be useful for these third party providers in reviewing their existing offers, as well developing and providing better support for organizations at differing levels of maturity.

This paper has a number of limitations. First, it is only a snapshot in time and does not provide a dynamic view of barriers and enablers. Second, although the sample size of 305 is much larger than in previous research, it is still only a limited number. The open-question qualitative data has however provided a richness of information hence enabling us to provide far more depth than more limited quantitative or closed-question surveys. We would like to suggest three areas of future research which can take this work further. First, would be to survey the same respondents to see how barriers and enablers change over time. Second, would be to interview a sample of the respondents to gain greater insight to the reasons for the barriers and enablers and find out how successfully they have managed them. Third, it will of interest to see how contingent these barriers and enablers by industry, country or size of firm.

References

1. Womack, J., Jones, D., Roos, D.: The Machine that Changed the World. HarperCollins, New York (1991)
2. Netland, T.: Industry 4.0: where does it leave lean? Lean Manag. J. **5**(3), 22–23 (2015)
3. Sanders, A., Elangeswaran, C., Wulfsberg, J.: Industry 4.0 implies lean manufacturing: research activities in Industry 4.0. J. Ind. Eng. Manag. **9**(3), 811–833 (2016)
4. Buer, S.-V., Semini, M., Strandhagen, J., Sgarbossa, F.: The complementary effect of lean manufacturing and digitalisation on operational performance. Int. J. Prod. Res. **59**, 1–17 (2020)
5. Ejsmont, K., Gladysz, B., Corti, D., Castaño, F.: Towards 'Lean Industry 4.0′ – Current trends and future perspectives. Cogent Bus. Manag. **7**(1), 1781995 (2020)
6. Ciano, M., Dallasega, P., Orzes, G., Rossi, T.: One-to-one relationships between Industry 4.0 technologies and Lean production techniques: a multiple case study. Int. J. Product. Res. **59**(5), 1386–1410 (2021)
7. Nedjwa, E., Bertrand, R., Sassi Boudemagh, S.: Impacts of Industry 4.0 technologies on Lean management tools: a bibliometric analysis. Int. J. Interact. Des. Manuf. **16**(1), 135–150 (2021). https://doi.org/10.1007/s12008-021-00795-9
8. Tortorella, G., Saurin, T., Hines, P., Antony, J., Samson, D.: Myths and facts of Industry 4.0. Int. J. Product. Econ. **255**, 108660 (2023). https://doi.org/10.1016/j.ijpe.2022.108660108660
9. Hines, P., Tortorella, G., Antony, J., Romero, D., Walsh, A., Taylor, D. et al., Global industrial perspective on Lean Industry 4.0: a qualitative wide-angle lens approach, under review
10. Tortorella, G.L., Fettermann, D.: Implementation of Industry 4.0 and lean production in Brazilian manufacturing companies. Int. J. Product. Res. **56**(8), 2975–2987 (2018)
11. Moraes, A., Carvalho, A., Sampaio, P.: Lean and Industry 4.0: a review of the relationship, its limitations, and the path ahead with Industry 5.0. Machines **11**, 443 (2023)
12. Guerrero, B., Mula, J., Tormo, G.: Enablers and barriers to Industry 4.0. In: Izquierdo, L., Santos, J., Lavios, J., Ahedo, V. (eds.) Industry 4.0: The Power of Data. Lecture Notes in Management and Industrial Engineering, pp. 303–315. Springer, Cham (2023)
13. Ghadimi, P., O'Neill, S., Wang. C., Sutherland, J.: Analysis of enablers on the successful implementation of green manufacturing for Irish SMEs. J. Manuf. Technol. Manag. 85–109 (2020)
14. Pessot, E., Zangiacomi, A., Battistella, C., Rocchi, V., Sala, A., Sacco, M.: What matters in implementing the factory of the future: insights from a survey in European manufacturing regions. J. Manuf. Technol. Manag. **32**(3), 795–819 (2020)
15. Veile, J., Kiel, D., Müller, J., Voigt, K.-I.: Lessons learned from Industry 4.0 implementation in the German manufacturing industry. J. Manuf. Technol. Manag. **31**(5), 977–997 (2019)
16. Hong, J., Zhang, Y., Ding, M.: Sustainable supply chain management practices, supply chain dynamic capabilities, and enterprise performance. J. Clean. Prod. **172**, 3508–3519 (2018)
17. Rajput, S., Singh, S.: Connecting circular economy and Industry 4.0. Int. J. Inform. Manag. **49**, 98–113 (2019)
18. Chiarini, A., Belvedere, V., Grando, A.: Industry 4.0 strategies and technological developments. an exploratory research from Italian manufacturing companies. Product. Plann. Control **31**(16), 1385–1398 (2020)
19. Makris, D., Hansen, Z., Khan, O.: Adapting to supply chain 4.0: an explorative study of multinational companies. Supply Chain Forum Int. J. **20**(2), 116–131 (2019)

20. Ivanov, D., Tang, C., Dolgui, A., Battini, D., Das, A.: Researchers' perspective on Industry 4.0: multi-disciplinary analysis and opportunities for operations management. Int. J. Product. Res. **59**(7), 2055–2078 (2021)
21. Ramirez-Peña, M., Fraga, F., Salguero, J., Batista, M.: Assessing sustainability in the shipbuilding supply chain 4.0: a systematic review. Sustain. Switzerland **12**(6), 6373 (2020)
22. Kumar, P., Singh, R., Kumar, V.: Managing supply chains for sustainable operations in the era of Industry 4.0 and circular economy: analysis of barriers. Resour. Conserv. Recycl. **164**, 105215 (2021)
23. Yadav, G., Luthra, S., Jakhar, S., Mangla, S., Rai, D.: A framework to overcome sustainable supply chain challenges through solution measures of Industry 4.0 and circular economy: an automotive case. J. Cleaner Product. **254**, 120112 (2020)
24. Khanzode, A., Sarma, P., Mangla, S., Yuan, H.: Modeling the Industry 4.0 adoption for sustainable production in micro, small & medium enterprises. J. Cleaner Product. **279**, 123489 (2021)
25. Kashyap, A., Yadav, A., Vatsa, Y., Chandaka, T., Shukla, O.: Investigation of the critical success factors in the implementation of the Lean Industry 4.0 in manufacturing supply chain: an ISM approach. Manag. Env. Qual. An Int. J. **34**(4), 981–996 (2023)
26. Komkowski, T., Antony, J., Garza-Reyes, J., Tortorella, G., Pongboonchai-Empl, T.: The integration of Industry 4.0 and Lean management: a systematic review and constituting elements perspective. Total Quality Manag. Bus. Excellence **34**(7–8), 1052–1069 (2023)
27. Rossi, A., et al.: Lean tools in the context of Industry 4.0: literature review, implementation and trends. Sustainability **14**, 12295 (2022)
28. Horváth, D., Szabó, R.: Driving forces and barriers of Industry 4.0: do multinational and small and medium-sized companies have equal opportunities? Technol. Forecast. Soc. Change **146**, 119–132 (2019)
29. Kumar, S., Luthra, S., Govindan, K., Kumar, N., Haleem, A.: Barriers in green lean six sigma product development process: an ISM approach. Product. Plann. Control **27**(7–8), 604–620 (2016)
30. Ghadge, A., Er Kara, M., Moradlou, H., Goswami, M.: The impact of Industry 4.0 implementation on supply chains. J. Manuf. Technol. Manag. **31**(4), 669–686 (2020). https://doi.org/10.1108/JMTM-10-2019-0368
31. Macias-Aguayo, J., Garcia-Castro., L., Barcia, K., Mcfarlane, D., Abad-Moran, J.: Industry 40 and Lean Six Sigma Integration: a systematic review of barriers and enablers. Appl. Sci. **12**(22), 11321 (2022)
32. Creswell, J.: Education Research: Conducing and evaluating quantitative and qualitative research. Pearson, Chandler (2014)
33. Braun, V., Clarke, V., Boulton, E., Davey, L., McEvoy, C.: The online survey as a qualitative research tool. Int. J. Soc. Res. Methodol. **24**(6), 641–654 (2021). https://doi.org/10.1080/13645579.2020.1805550
34. Treviño-Elizondo, B., García-Reyes, H., Peimbert-García, R.: A maturity model to become a smart organization based on lean and industry 4.0 synergy. Sustainability **15**(17), 13151 (2023)
35. Chiera, M., Lupi, F., Rossi, A., Lanzetta, M.: Lean maturity assessment in ETO scenario. Appl. Sci. **11**(3833), 1–20 (2021)
36. Tortorella, G., Saurin, T., Hines, P., Antony, J., Samson, J.: Myths and facts of industry 4.0. Int. J. Product. Econ. **255**, 108660 (2023)
37. Tabachnick, B., Fidell, L.: Using Multivariate Statistics. Pearson, Upper Saddle River, NJ
38. Gupta, S., Modgil, S., Gunasekaran, A.: Big data in lean six sigma: a review and further research directions. Int. J. Product. Res. **58**, 947–969 (2020)

39. Raut, R., Mangla, S., Narwane, V., Dora, M., Liu, M.: Big data analytics as a mediator in Lean, Agile, Resilient, and Green (LARG) practices effects on sustainable supply chains. Transport. Res. Part E: Logist. Transport. Rev. **145**, 102170 (2021)
40. Ghobadian, A., Talavera, I., Bhattacharya, A., Kumar, A., Garza-Reyes, J., O'Regan, N.: Examining legitimatisation of additive manufacturing in the interplay between innovation, lean manufacturing and sustainability. Int. J. Product. Econ. **219**, 457–468 (2020)
41. Vinodh, V.: Development of a structural model based on ISM for analysis of barriers to integration of lean with industry 4.0. TQM J. **33**(6), 1201–1221 (2021)
42. Hines, P., Tortorella, G.L., Antony, J., Romero, D.: Lean Industry 4.0: past, present, and future. Qual. Manag. J. **30**(1), 64–88 (2023)
43. Powell, D., Morgan, R., Howe, G.: Lean first ... then digitalize: a standard approach for Industry 4.0 implementation in SMEs. In: Dolgui, A., Bernard, A., Lemoine, D., von Cieminski, G., Romero, D. (eds.) Advances in Production Management Systems. IFIP Advances in Information and Communication Technology, vol. 631, pp. 31–39 (2021)

How Organizations Can Harness Continuous Improvement Practices to Develop Their Data Analytic Capability: A Conceptual Paper

Alinda Kokkinou[1,2(✉)]

[1] Breda University of Applied Sciences, Mgr. Hopmanstraat 1, Breda, The Netherlands
kokkinou.a@buas.nl

[2] AVANS University of Applied Sciences, Hogeschoollaan 1, Breda, The Netherlands

Abstract. In pursuit of competitive advantage in an increasingly globalized and complex environment, organizations are turning to continuous improvement and digitalization to achieve operational excellence. Viewed through the lens of Dynamic Capabilities Theory, the similarities complementarities, and synergies of continuous improvement capability and data analytic capability are examined. Bridging the gap between theory and practice, continuous improvement routines and practices that can be harnessed to accelerate the implementation of data analytical capability are identified. These include Hoshin Kanri to link digitalization projects to organizational strategic, training to develop organizational knowledge of digitalization, problem solving teams to break knowledge silos, and the use of PDCA-type processes for adopting and monitoring the performance of digital technologies.

Keywords: Continuous improvement · Lean · Digitalization · Data analytic capability · Organizational change · Hoshin Kanri

1 Introduction

Organizations are under increasing pressure from both supply and demand side to improve their operational performance. Supply chains, fueled by global competition, are becoming increasingly complex and vulnerable to disruptions [1]. Customers, spurred by technological trends, are becoming increasingly demanding in terms of product quality and innovation, and timeliness of delivery [2]. Competition is also intensifying from organizations who are quicker to take advantage of these concurrent trends of globalization and digitalization to better meet customer demand. Organizations are therefore increasingly (re)turning to continuous improvement methodologies, discovering the possibilities of digitalization, or combining both as a way to compete in this increasingly globalized and competitive world [3].

Organizations invest in continuous improvement (CI) methodologies such as Lean, Six Sigma, Lean Six Sigma (LSS), and/or Total Quality Management (TQM) to improve their processes, enhance the quality of their products and/or services, thereby achieving

Published by Springer Nature Switzerland AG 2024
T. van Kollenburg et al. (Eds.): ELEC 2023, IFIP AICT 681, pp. 52–69, 2024.
https://doi.org/10.1007/978-3-031-63265-5_5

operational excellence [4–8]. CI is the *"organized effort where all members of an organization work together on an ongoing basis, improving processes and reducing errors to improve overall performance for the customer"* [9] and has been adopted both in manufacturing and service industries alike [5]. Applications of CI have been documented in numerous sectors such as automotive [10, 11], aerospace [12], education [13], and healthcare [14, 15].

A different approach for organizations to improve their processes (for example manufacturing processes and product development processes) or to improve value for customers and other stakeholders (for example through better and more sophisticated products and services) is through digitalization [16]. Digitalization, defined as *"the use of the technologies and data to improve and transform the business processes"* [17] has taken different forms across industries and disciplines, leading to the related concepts of Industry 4.0 [18]and smart manufacturing [19] smart tourism and smart hospitality [20], and big data analytics [21]. All these concepts focus on the application of technologies such as Internet of Things (IoT), robotics, Machine Learning (ML), and Artificial Intelligence (AI) to improve outcomes on an geographical, industry, and/or organizational level [22]. The scope of the present paper is organizational performance.

Previous studies examining CI and digitalization have found them to have a positive effect on organizational performance both individually and in combination [23–26]. In the context of manufacturing, the application of digital technologies to lean production has been termed Lean Automation [27, 28] or Digital Lean Cyber-Physical Production Systems [29]. By combining CI methodologies (e.g. lean and six sigma) and digitalization, organizations have been found to reduce costs and waste, increase system flexibility, and improve quality [28, 29], however the mechanisms explaining these synergistic effects remain unclear [30]. Nevertheless, studies in this line of research have typically viewed CI and digitalization as (combinations of) tools and methods [28, 31].

Yet both CI and digitalization can be viewed as more than an amalgamation of tools, namely as dynamic capabilities. Dynamic capabilities allow organizations to *"integrate, build, and reconfigure internal and external competencies to address rapidly changing environments"* [32]. This is achieved by means of organizational routines, namely processes used to alter an organizations' resource base [33]. These processes are unique to each organization, having evolved as a function of the organization's unique combination of learning mechanisms, past mistakes, and context. When viewed from the lens of dynamic capabilities, CI capability is the organizational ability to consistently improve current processes and learn new ones [34] and has been defined as the *"organization-wide process of focused and sustained incremental innovation"* [35]. Similarly, digitalization has enabled the development of Data Analytic Capability (DAC), a capability that enables organizations to sense and seize opportunities, and reconfigure and transform in response to them [36, 37].

DAC is defined as *"an organization's capability to deploy data, technology and people to quickly access and analyze information to support complex decision-making"* [38]. The successful development of DAC enables organizations to increase their information processing capacity, thereby generating insights that allow them to improve production processes and achieve the corresponding product and service improvements and cost reductions [39], improve supply chain agility [40, 41], increase supply chain resilience and robustness [42], and increase productivity and competitiveness [43]. Yet, to develop DAC in such way as to create competitive advantage, organizations need to navigate a complex socio-technical process that requires the orchestration of organization's assets such as IT infrastructure, human talent, and data assets [44–46].

Previous research has identified numerous enablers and inhibitors of DAC, including senior management and leadership commitment, alignment with strategy, and organizational learning [46, 47]. Guidance for organizations is currently primarily available in the form of maturity models stemming from Capability Maturity Model (CMM), such as the Business Analytics CMM (BACMM) [48], the Data Science CMM (DSCMM) [49], the Advanced Data Analytics CMM (ADACMM) [50] and the Advanced Analytics CMM [51]. While these models provide some guidance to practitioners looking to develop the DAC of their organization, they have several limitations. First, they lack actionability due to their complexity [52, 53]. Furthermore, these models have been developed from the perspective of a single discipline (e.g. information systems, data science) and thus lack a comprehensive approach to develop DAC [53]. Such a comprehensive approach includes tangible, intangible, and human aspects [45, 47, 54].

From the context of Dynamic Capabilities Theory, the purpose of this conceptual paper is to formulate as a theoretical framework linking CI capability and DAC, thereby explaining their synergistic effect. Bridging the gap between theory and practice, the framework is used to propose tangible ways in which organizations can harness CI practices to develop their DAC. This study thereby contributes to the body of research investigating the synergistic effects of lean and digitalization [30].

2 Review of the Literature

2.1 Dynamic Capabilities Theory

Dynamic Capabilities Theory (DCT) is an extension of the Resource Based View (RBV) of the firm [33]. According to RBV, organizations can achieve sustained competitive advantage by having resources that are valuable, rare, inimitable, and non-substitutable [33, 55]. Resources can be divided into assets and capabilities, where assets are not organization-specific and can thus be traded [56]. Examples of such assets are physical assets, financial assets, knowledge assets (e.g. patents and licenses) and human capital. Capabilities are organization-specific, mostly intangible, and thus not tradeable. They consist of organization-specific processes used to deploy combinations of assets in such a way as to achieve a specified objective. A common criticism of RBV is that it considers assets and capabilities to be static, and ignores the need for organizations to evolve their assets and capabilities in response to the dynamics of the market in which they operate [33, 57]. DCT evolved to address this limitation.

DCT is an appropriate framework to examine how organizations evolve by reconfiguring their assets and capabilities to keep up with rapidly changing markets, and thereby acquire or maintain competitive advantage [32, 58]. The processes or routines by which they achieve this are called dynamic capabilities, defined as their "ability to integrate, build, and reconfigure internal and external competencies to address rapidly changing environments" [32]. Dynamic capabilities are distinct from ordinary capabilities. Ordinary capabilities, also known as operational capabilities, enable organizations to generate value right at a specific moment [59, 60]. Wang and Ahmed [57] further distinguish "first order capabilities" which they define as "the ability to deploy resources to attain a desired goal" and "second-order" or "core capabilities" which are capabilities that are strategically important to the organization's competitive advantage at this specific moment in time. Dynamic capabilities, termed by Wang and Ahmed [57] as "third-order" capabilities, are those that are needed to modify the ordinary capabilities to sense and seize new business opportunities [59].

Three functions of dynamic capabilities have been specified, namely sensing, seizing, and reconfiguring and transforming capabilities [36, 37]. Organizations *sense* opportunities (or threats) in their environment by using a mix of analytical and managerial acumen to pick up and interpret signals from their competitors, market and suppliers [61]. Organizations *seize* these opportunities (or neutralize these threats) by developing new business models. These investments require the development of decision-making procedures to invest and allocate resources in new technologies and innovations, and make appropriate changes to the organization [61, 62]. Organizations also need to reconfigure and transform their assets and capabilities to ensure that their assets and capabilities remain in congruence with their evolving environment, and in line with changes in technology and market conditions [36, 61]. Both CI [63] and DAC [54, 58] have been conceptualized as dynamic capabilities.

2.2 Continuous Improvement as a Dynamic Capability

CI's origins are subject to debate, with some authors attributing them to the introduction of mass production and scientific management during the Second Industrial Revolution and the corresponding encouragement of employees to participate in product and process improvements [64]. Others authors attribute it to Shewhart's [65] introduction of statistical process control, while yet others credit it to the Japanese "Kaizen" [66]. CI has evolved from its early documented applications which have involved mostly tools and process innovations at the project level [5], towards a comprehensive customer-centric organization-wide business philosophy [67]. Several distinct methodologies have been developed, each with their own tools and principles. Lean, said to have originated in Japan in the 1950s, focused on the elimination of waste and non-value added activities through tools such as line balancing, Single Minute Exchange of Dies (SMED), and visual management [68]. Six Sigma, first introduced by Motorola in 1986, and made popular by GE's successes in the late 1990s [69], was defined as a "*organized and systematic approach for strategic process improvement and new product and service development that relies on statistical methods and the scientific method to make dramatic reductions in the customer defined defect rates*" [70]. Contrasting with Six Sigma's focus on hard tools and statistical methods, TQM puts a greater emphasis on soft tools [71, 72]. TQM was since its inception a more integrated and company-wide approach with less emphasis on hard tools [73]. Early studies documenting applications of CI have mostly focused on the tools and process innovations, and thus viewed CI implementation at the project level [5] and distinguished between the various CI practices and methodologies, treating them as distinct [74]. However, in the past ten years, CI practices and methodologies have been increasingly treated as interchangeable or complementary [9, 75]. This study adopts this perspective, treating CI as the umbrella for CI practices and methodologies including Lean, Six Sigma, LSS, TQM, etc.

While CI can be viewed as a collection of tools and techniques that organizations engage to improve their processes (e.g. EFQM and 5S) [8], it has also been conceptualized as an organization-wide sustained process of improving performance through focused incremental changes [35, 76]. Anand et al. [63] argue that the difference between the first (ad-hoc projects using tools and techniques) and the latter (sustained process) is the establishment of a CI infrastructure to coordinate and support CI activities and in particular those related to organizational learning (e.g. selection of projects, preserving lessons learned, training, and motivating employees to participate in CI). Similarly. Knol et al. [77] distinguished between lean operating routines and CI routines, where lean operating routines are necessary for the implementation of lean production (e.g. by enabling the creation of flow and pull, and the use of Kanban). CI routines were those enabling the initiation and execution of the improvement of the operating routines (e.g. mapping a current situation and finding ways to improve it). Like Anand et al. [63], Knol et al. [77] argue that organizational routines interact with organizational structures, which they refer to artefacts. Artefacts can be physical (e.g. machines, raw materials, products) or intangible (e.g. software, standard operating procedures). Seen from the perspective of RBV and DCT, Anand et al.'s CI infrastructure [63] and Knol et al.'s artefacts [77] can be likened to assets [56] and first-order capabilities in that they are physical or intangible structures that enable the enactment of operational and CI routines (artefacts and ordinary routines in Fig. 1).

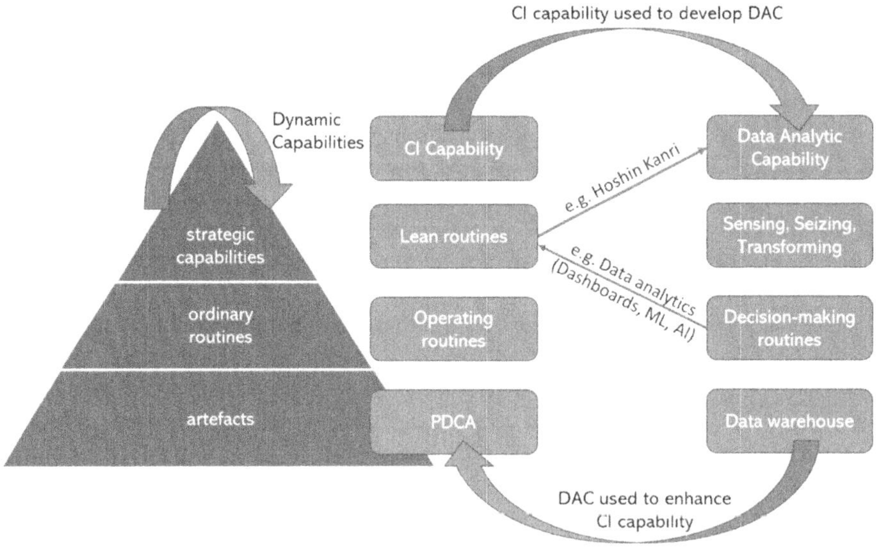

Fig. 1. Conceptual Framework of the synergistic effects of Continuous Improvement Capability and Data Analytic Capability.

Organizations' lean operating routines and CI routines can be likened to core capabilities and dynamic capabilities respectively, as described by Wang and Ahmed [57]. For organizations pursuing CI to achieve competitive advantage, the enactment of lean routines is of strategic importance and can thus be qualified as core capabilities (strategic routines in Fig. 1). In the context of CI implementation, operational and lean operating routines are improved through structured activities that promote employee and organizational learning [77, 78]. When CI implementation is mature, reaching the stage of the learning organization as defined by Bessant and Francis [35], it enables the organization to pursue incremental and radical innovation, and thus reconfigure or transform the organization to ensure its assets and capabilities remain in congruence with its organizational context (dynamic capability in Fig. 1).

2.3 Data Analytic Capability as a Dynamic Capability

For this study, a distinction is made between (Big) Data Analytics (BDA) and DAC. BDA refers to the "*the application of advanced statistics to any kind of stored electronic communication, which may include – but is not limited to – messages, updates, and images posted to social networks, readings from sensors, and GPS signals from cell phones*" [79, 80] and is thus an amalgamation of tools and techniques to deal with data and technology. DAC is a broader concept, that also encompasses organizational aspects (e.g. people, structure, and organizational culture) in addition to the data and technology aspects [38, 81]. Unlike BDA, which is viewed as a practice or methodology, DAC is viewed as a dynamic capability.

Viewed from the lens of DCT, DAC is considered a dynamic capability because it allows organizations to identify new patterns (e.g., in consumer behavior, customer requirements, supplier behavior), thus *sensing* their environments [82]. By enabling organizations to use data-driven decision-making to assess business opportunities and potential investment opportunities, DAC facilitates organizations in *seizing* these opportunities. Finally, the changes in organization culture towards a more data-driven culture that DAC supports help organizations make progress towards *transforming and reconfiguring* their activities, also by promoting a culture of organizational learning. DAC can also be viewed as a enabler of other dynamic capabilities [83] such as supply chain agility [40, 41, 84], process innovation capability [85], and sustainable innovation capability [86, 87].

Little is known still about the mechanisms by which DAC contributes to competitive performance gains beyond enabling other dynamic capabilities. Mikalef et al. [81] proposed that DAC affects two distinct operating capabilities, namely marketing capability and technological capability. In their study, marketing operating capability consisted of ways to build privileged relationships with customers and suppliers, market knowledge, control over distribution channels, and strong "installed" customer base [81, 88]. Technological operating capability consisted of an efficient production department, technological capabilities and infrastructure, and economies of scale and technical experience. Artefacts supporting these operating capabilities include data standards, databases and data platforms (e.g. Customer Relationship Management systems) [89].

Similar to CI [90], the development of DAC is considered a complex socio-technical process involving people and processes. Also like CI, DAC has received extensive academic attention, albeit from diverse disciplines including information systems, business, manufacturing, operations research, and supply chain. This has led to fragmentation in the research addressing the enablers and inhibitors of DAC. The information systems literature takes a relatively narrow view of DAC as primarily IT resources [91]. Wamba et al. [92] broadened this view by also considering management and employee resources. A more comprehensive view is that of Gupta and George [54] who viewed DAC as a combination of tangible (e.g. tradeable resources such as time, financial, data and technology), intangible (e.g. organization-specific resources such as data-driven culture and organizational learning), and human resources (e.g. management and technical skills that need to be acquired or developed). Using a combination of literature and empirical research, Kokkinou et al. [46] identified six categories of assets and resources needed for the development of DAC, including management, knowledge and skills, data, data analytics, technology, and structure and processes, emphasizing the need to view these as interlinked.

2.4 Digitalization and Continuous Improvement

Digitalization and CI have been found to have a synergistic effect on operational performance [93], however this is still an emerging area of research with the number of studies steadily increasing since 2015 [23, 26–29, 31, 93, 94]. This area of study focused on identifying the causal relationships between CI and digitalization, concluding that CI acted as an enabler of digitalization. However, the underlying mechanisms explaining how CI enables digitalization remain under-explored. [26, 28, 93]. Furthermore, studies examining CI and digitalization have not adopted DCT as a theoretical framework.

Studies examining digitalization and CI have typically viewed them as combinations of tools and practices [28, 31]. For example, Yilmaz et al. [95] reviewed case studies detailing the sequence in which lean tools and digitalization tools were implemented and identified operational benefits (e.g. increased throughput, productivity, quality and reliability and decreased cost, inventory, and lead time), and the potential for environmental benefits (decrease in resource consumption and defects), and social benefits (decrease in accidents and labor intensive work, and improved communication and decision-making). Tortorella et al. [28] used a survey approach for the same purpose and found that a sequential implementation approach of first lean management practices to create a robust basis, followed by Industry 4.0 technologies, yielded the greatest gains in operational performance. Pongboonchai-Empl et al. [24] reviewed the literature on how Industry 4.0 technologies could be integrated in LSS and found that BDA tools and techniques (including Machine Learning, Data Mining, Process Mining) and Internet of Things (IoT) show potential in supporting LSS practices such as data analysis, simulation, poka yoke and root cause analysis. The integration of CI and digitalization on a project level is a promising way for organizations to achieve benefits on an operational and tactical level, however combining them on a strategic level can provide greater and more sustained benefits.

Achieving synergies between CI capability and DAC on a strategic level would entail that organizations can harness their CI capability to further develop their DAC. Specifically, we propose several ways in which organizations can use CI routines, practices, and artifacts to accelerate their implementation of DAC (see Fig. 1).

3 Proposed Interventions

The development of DAC is a complex socio-technical process requiring the consideration of both technical and organizational aspects. Enablers and inhibitors of DAC that have been identified include alignment with strategic objectives, management and leadership commitment, employee knowledge and skills, changes in structure and processes, and organizational learning [46, 47]. These enablers closely resemble those of CI capability [90, 96], supporting the notion that CI routines and artefacts could provide a suitable avenue to further develop DAC. The following section proposes three such CI routines and corresponding artefacts.

3.1 Using Hoshin Kanri to Link Digitalization Objectives to Strategy

An important enabler of DAC is the alignment of digitalization projects with the organizational strategy [46, 47]. This is also an important success factor for CI implementation [13, 90]. A best practice in the context of CI implementation for communicating and aligning strategy to projects is Hoshin Kanri, or policy deployment. Hoshin Kanri is meant to strengthen the connection between strategy and annual planning cycle [97] and is "*a methodology for strategic planning that communicates the strategic vision of an organization throughout the organization*" [98]. It is commonly perceived to originate from Hoshin, meaning compass, course, plan or aim; and Kanri, meaning management control [99]. Central to Hoshin Kanri is the process of catchball, a two-way communication process that occurs top-down and bottom-up to achieve consensus between the various layers of organization on how strategic goals will be operationalized and achieved [99, 100]. The catchball process is implemented through the X-Matrix, a structured framework linking strategic objectives, goals, tactics, KPIs and stakeholders/ actors [101].

Hoshin Kanri synergizes well with DAC, as it similarly aims to identify opportunities for change and necessary actions to achieve them [102] (illustrated in Fig. 1). Previous research has shown that an inhibitor of DAC development is senior leadership and management struggling to link digitalization projects to the organizational strategy and make the corresponding resource allocation decisions. The catchball process, facilitated by the X-Matrix could be modified to explicitly link digitalization projects to the organization's strategic objectives and engage different levels of the organization in this dialogue and resource allocation process. The X-Matrix is a distillation of a four-phase cycle consisting of the (1) focus, (2) alignment, (3) integrate, and (4) review phases [97, 99, 101] that can be amended as follows. *Focus* phase: management should concentrate on a few strategic priorities and explicitly state how digitalization can contribute to them. *Alignment* phase: available resources should be linked through (newly developed) policies to these strategic priorities in a participatory manner. *Integrate* phase: policies should be integrated in operational activities (e.g. through implementation plans). *Review* phase: assessment of policies and their results.

3.2 Training as a Dual Mechanism for Organization Learning and Change

The lack of management and employee knowledge and skills regarding digitalization has been found to be an important inhibitor of DAC [46, 47, 81]. Senior leadership and management need knowledge of digital technologies and their possibilities to envision how they can contribute to the organizational strategy, make appropriate resource allocation decisions, and more generally initiate the necessary organizational culture change. Employees need knowledge of data analytics to enact these changes in the organization. One way for managers and employees to acquire this knowledge is through training.

Training can be used to develop individuals' explicit knowledge about a topic and is a recognized enabler of CI implementation [103]. In the context of CI implementation, three distinct approaches to training were identified that can be used for the development of DAC. A first, more common approach of blanket training for all employees was seen as an appropriate way to introduce a CI initiative or programme and link it to the organizational strategy, in the process (re)acquainting employees with the organizational strategy [104, 105]. This approach to initiating organizational change through training is suitable for the development of DAC. However, such training needs to focus on the "why" of the programme, and not go into depth in the tools.

A second approach revolved around training as a mechanism for knowledge transfer. This consisted of training employees in the primary process on the needed knowledge and skills and ensuring that their achievements were shared with the rest of the organization to increase visibility of the change [106]. This bottom-up approach of giving employees room to experiment with the technology and allowing their knowledge to organically expand to the rest of the organization is particularly appropriate for the development of DAC and has been recognized as a best practice [107]. From this perspective, training is also an avenue for organizational learning as the individuals' explicit knowledge is transferred to the organization [108].

A third approach consisted of training senior leadership and managers to enable them to model the desired behavior [103]. This approach was deemed for suitable for organizations with low levels of employee empowerment and/or operating in high power distance cultures. Drawing on the CI literature shows that training contributes to organizational change in two distinct ways. First, training contributes to the acquisition, creation and assimilation of new knowledge regarding digitalization. Second, training enables the organization to transform and exploit this new knowledge towards the organizational change needed for the implementation of DAC [109].

3.3 Problem Solving Teams as a Mechanism for Organizational Learning

A particular challenge when implementing CI bottom-up [90] that also been recognized in the context of DAC development is that much of the knowledge remains in organizational silos [46]. This is an important inhibitor of DAC in organizations when training and experimentation are taking place at the departmental level with little coordination.

A CI operating routine that can contribute to this issue is the use of cross-functional problem-solving teams. Problem solving teams are described as a human-related and soft lean practice in conducting continuous improvement [110]. As the name indicates, small group/cross-functional/problem-solving teams consist of employees and/or managers from different departments or entities of the organization, bringing different expertise, to solving a common objective. The origin of problem solving teams can be found in the "Quality Circles" introduced by Toyota in the 1950s [7] but their use is widespread in CI [111]. Even though the way in which organizations set up these teams differs, a formal structure or process is needed to facilitate them. This typically requires senior leadership and management commitment to coordinate the initiative by ensuring the employees are appointed to the team, a goal or objective is formulated, and team members have the opportunity to meet. Furthermore, resources (time, finance, and training) are needed.

In the context of DAC development, cross functional teams are particularly appropriate to transfer the learnings regarding digitalization from one organizational silo to another, contributing to organizational learning. Furthermore, cross functional teams can provide valuable information to IT departments regarding data needs across the organization. For organizations deciding to employ dedicated data scientists, cross functional teams are a mechanism to develop the domain knowledge of data scientists and conversely, develop the technical knowledge of domain experts. When organizations decide to employ consultants, cross-functional teams can ensure that these consultants receive input in a coordinated way. This cross-functional team CI operating routine can thereby contribute to the development of DAC.

3.4 Adapting the PDCA Cycle to Adopt and Implement Digitalization Tools

While CI capability can contribute to the development of DAC, DAC can contribute to the further development of CI capability. A feature of CI capability is the deliberate process improvement achieved through the application of Plan-Do-Check-Act (PDCA) or other equivalent (e.g. Define – Measure – Analyze – Improve – Control). In the course of applying these steps, organizations can use the data insights made possible by the application of digitalization tools and DAC to improve their decision-making [24, 107] (illustrated in Fig. 1). From this perspective, CI capability and DAC synergize to allow organizations to create the data insights needed to make more data-driven decisions about how to invest and allocate resources in new technologies and innovations [61, 62].

4 Discussion

Previous research found digitalization and CI to synergize well [23–26], in reducing costs and waste, increasing system flexibility, and improving quality [28, 29]. Nevertheless, the mechanisms underlying these processes remained unclear [30]. While previous studies in this area viewed CI and digitalization as (combinations of) tools and methods [28, 31], the present study viewed CI and digitalization through the lens of DCT as dynamic capabilities [63, 77] and proposed a conceptual framework showing how the artefacts (e.g. PDCA), ordinary routines (problem solving), and strategic routines (e.g.

policy deployment) developed as part of CI implementation could accelerate the development of DAC. Conversely, the sensing and seizing capabilities enabled by DAC enable organizations to make more data-driven decisions instead of relying only on intuition when making decisions about technology investments [39, 107].

4.1 Implications for Practice

The present conceptual study presents some tangible ways in which CI infrastructure can be used by organizations in the process of developing their digitalization and more specifically DAC. Organizations that have relatively mature CI implementations will have adopted tools and practices such as the PDCA cycle, policy deployment, and problem solving teams which they can harness to accelerate the adoption of digitalization technologies and tools.

5 Conclusion and Further Research

The present study viewed CI and DAC from the perspective of DCT. By distinguishing between dynamic capabilities, strategic capabilities, ordinary routines and artefacts, a conceptual framework proposing ways in which CI and DAC complement each other and thus synergize was formulated (see Fig. 1). The study thereby contributes to the body of research investigating the synergistic effects of lean and digitalization by identifying specific mechanisms by which CI implementation contributes to the development of DAC. Four ways were proposed to harness the infrastructure developed in the context of CI capabilities and use it to institutionalize organizational learning about digitalization. These included using Hoshin Kanri to link digitalization objectives to strategy, using training to concurrently introduce new knowledge and prompt organizational change in the organization, organizing problem solving teams to ensure organizational learning beyond organizational silos, and adapting the PDCA cycle to both use and introduce digitalization tools.

The conceptual framework was used to bridge the gap between theory and practice and propose tangible ways in which organizations can use CI operational routines and artefacts to further develop their DAC. Conversely, the study also proposed ways in which operating routines developed in the context of DAC can be used by organizations to enhance their decision-making ability by incorporating data insights. Future research should examine the proposed interventions empirically, e.g., through action research.

Acknowledgements. We would like to acknowledge funding received from the Dutch Taskforce for Applied Research (SIA). This publication is part of the project *A roadmap for developing Data Analytic Capability for Digital Transformation* (project number KIEM.K23.01.081) funded by the Taskforce for Applied Research (SIA) and the Dutch Research Council (NWO).

References

1. Bozarth, C.C., Warsing, D.P., Flynn, B.B., Flynn, E.J.: The impact of supply chain complexity on manufacturing plant performance. J. Oper. Manag. **27**, 78–93 (2009). https://doi.org/10.1016/j.jom.2008.07.003

2. Lim, S.F.W.T., Jin, X., Srai, J.S.: Consumer-driven e-commerce: A literature review, design framework, and research agenda on last-mile logistics models. IJPDLM. **48**, 308–332 (2018). https://doi.org/10.1108/IJPDLM-02-2017-0081
3. Hess, T., Matt, C., Benlian, A., Wiesböck, F.: Options for formulating a digital transformation strategy. MIS Q. Executive **15** (2016)
4. Jasti, N.V.K., Kodali, R.: Lean production: literature review and trends. Int. J. Prod. Res. **53**, 867–885 (2015). https://doi.org/10.1080/00207543.2014.937508
5. Li, J., Papadopoulos, C.T., Zhang, L.: Continuous improvement in manufacturing and service systems. Int. J. Prod. Res. **54**, 6281–6284 (2016). https://doi.org/10.1080/00207543.2016.1228235
6. Savolainen, T.I.: Cycles of continuous improvement: realizing competitive advantages through quality. Int. J. Oper. Prod. Manag. **19**, 1203–1222 (1999)
7. Bhuiyan, N., Baghel, A.: An overview of continuous improvement: from the past to the present. Manag. Decis. **43**, 761–771 (2005). https://doi.org/10.1108/00251740510597761
8. Rijnders, S., Boer, H.: A typology of continuous improvement implementation processes. Knowl. Process Mgmt. **11**, 283–296 (2004). https://doi.org/10.1002/kpm.208
9. Vijaya Sunder, M., Prashar, A.: Empirical examination of critical failure factors of continuous improvement deployments: stage-wise results and a contingency theory perspective. Int. J. Prod. Res. **58**(16), 4894–4915 (2020). https://doi.org/10.1080/00207543.2020.1727044
10. Saurin, T.A., Marodin, G.A., Ribeiro, J.L.D.: A framework for assessing the use of lean production practices in manufacturing cells. Int. J. Prod. Res. **49**, 3211–3230 (2011). https://doi.org/10.1080/00207543.2010.482567
11. Thun, J.-H., Drüke, M., Hoenig, D.: Managing uncertainty – an empirical analysis of supply chain risk management in small and medium-sized enterprises. Int. J. Prod. Res. **49**, 5511–5525 (2011). https://doi.org/10.1080/00207543.2011.563901
12. Chakravorty, S.S., Hales, D.N.: Sustainability of process improvements: an application of the experiential learning model (ELM). Int. J. Prod. Res. **55**, 4931–4947 (2017). https://doi.org/10.1080/00207543.2016.1277278
13. Kokkinou, A., van Kollenburg, T.: Critical success factors of Lean in Higher Education: an international perspective. IJLSS (2022). https://doi.org/10.1108/IJLSS-04-2022-0076
14. Henrique, D.B., Filho, M.G., Marodin, G., de Sousa Jabbour, A.B.L., Chiappetta Jabbour, C.J.: A framework to assess sustaining continuous improvement in lean healthcare. Int. J. Product. Res. **59**(10), 2885–2904 (2021). https://doi.org/10.1080/00207543.2020.1743892
15. Knapp, S.: Lean Six Sigma implementation and organizational culture. Int. J. Health Care QA **28**, 855–863 (2015). https://doi.org/10.1108/IJHCQA-06-2015-0079
16. Björkdahl, J.: Strategies for digitalization in manufacturing firms. Calif. Manage. Rev. **62**, 17–36 (2020). https://doi.org/10.1177/0008125620920349
17. Machado, C.G., Winroth, M., Carlsson, D., Almström, P., Centerholt, V., Hallin, M.: Industry 4.0 readiness in manufacturing companies: challenges and enablers towards increased digitalization. Procedia CIRP **81**, 1113–1118 (2019). https://doi.org/10.1016/j.procir.2019.03.262
18. Kagermann, H., Hellinger, A., Wahlster, W.: Recommendations for Implementing the Strategic Initiative Industrie 4.0: Securing the Future of German Manufacturing Industry. Communication Promoters Group of the Industry-Science Research Alliance, Frankfurt, Germany (2013)
19. Rosin, F., Forget, P., Lamouri, S., Pellerin, R.: Impacts of Industry 4.0 technologies on Lean principles. Int. J. Product. Res. **58**(6), 1644–1661 (2020). https://doi.org/10.1080/00207543.2019.1672902
20. Law, R., Ye, H., Chan, I.C.C.: A critical review of smart hospitality and tourism research. Int. J. Contemp. Hosp. Manag. **34**, 623–641 (2022). https://doi.org/10.1108/IJCHM-08-2021-0986

21. Fosso Wamba, S., Gunasekaran, A., Dubey, R., Ngai, E.W.T.: Big data analytics in operations and supply chain management. Ann. Oper. Res. **270**(1–2), 1–4 (2018). https://doi.org/10.1007/s10479-018-3024-7
22. Nayernia, H., Bahemia, H., Papagiannidis, S.: A systematic review of the implementation of industry 4.0 from the organisational perspective. Int. J. Product. Res. **60**(14), 4365–4396 (2022). https://doi.org/10.1080/00207543.2021.2002964
23. Buer, S.-V., Strandhagen, J.O., Chan, F.T.S.: The link between Industry 4.0 and lean manufacturing: mapping current research and establishing a research agenda. Int. J. Product. Res. **56**(8), 2924–2940 (2018). https://doi.org/10.1080/00207543.2018.1442945
24. Pongboonchai-Empl, T., Antony, J., Garza-Reyes, J.A., Komkowski, T., Tortorella, G.L.: Integration of Industry 4.0 technologies into Lean Six Sigma DMAIC: a systematic review. Product. Plann. Control (2023). https://doi.org/10.1080/09537287.2023.2188496
25. Sanders, A., Elangeswaran, C., Wulfsberg, J.: Industry 4.0 implies lean manufacturing: Research activities in industry 4.0 function as enablers for lean manufacturing. J. Ind. Eng. Manag. **9**(3), 811 (2016). https://doi.org/10.3926/jiem.1940
26. Buer, S.-V., Semini, M., Strandhagen, J.O., Sgarbossa, F.: The complementary effect of lean manufacturing and digitalisation on operational performance. Int. J. Prod. Res. **59**, 1976–1992 (2021). https://doi.org/10.1080/00207543.2020.1790684
27. Kolberg, D., Knobloch, J., Zühlke, D.: Towards a lean automation interface for workstations. Int. J. Prod. Res. **55**, 2845–2856 (2017). https://doi.org/10.1080/00207543.2016.1223384
28. Tortorella, G.L., Narayanamurthy, G., Thurer, M.: Identifying pathways to a high-performing lean automation implementation: an empirical study in the manufacturing industry. Int. J. Prod. Econ. **231**, 107918 (2021). https://doi.org/10.1016/j.ijpe.2020.107918
29. Powell, D., Romero, D., Gaiardelli, P., Cimini, C., Cavalieri, S.: Towards digital lean cyber-physical production systems: industry 4.0 technologies as enablers of leaner production. In: Moon, I., Lee, G.M., Park, J., Kiritsis, D., von Cieminski, G. (eds.) Advances in Production Management Systems. Smart Manufacturing for Industry 4.0: IFIP WG 5.7 International Conference, APMS 2018, Seoul, Korea, August 26-30, 2018, Proceedings, Part II, pp. 353–362. Springer International Publishing, Cham (2018). https://doi.org/10.1007/978-3-319-99707-0_44
30. Bokhorst, J.A.C., Knol, W., Slomp, J., Bortolotti, T.: Assessing to what extent smart manufacturing builds on lean principles. Int. J. Prod. Econ. **253**, 108599 (2022). https://doi.org/10.1016/j.ijpe.2022.108599
31. Elafri, N., Tappert, J., Rose, B., Yassine, M.: Lean 4.0: synergies between lean management tools and industry 4.0 technologies. IFAC-PapersOnLine **55**(10), 2060–2066 (2022)
32. Teece, D.J., Pisano, G., Shuen, A.: Dynamic capabilities and strategic management. Strat. Mgmt. J. **18**, 509–533 (1997). https://doi.org/10.1002/(SICI)1097-0266(199708)18:7%3c509::AID-SMJ882%3e3.0.CO;2-Z
33. Eisenhardt, K.M., Martin, J.A.: Dynamic capabilities: what are they? Strateg. Manag. J. **21**, 1105–1121 (2000)
34. Ittner, C.D., Larcker, D.F.: Quality strategy, strategic control systems, and organizational performance. Acc. Organ. Soc. **22**, 293–314 (1997)
35. Bessant, J., Francis, D.: Developing strategic continuous improvement capability. Int. J. Oper. Prod. Manag. **19**, 1106–1119 (1999). https://doi.org/10.1108/01443579910291032
36. Helfat, C.E., Raubitschek, R.S.: Dynamic and integrative capabilities for profiting from innovation in digital platform-based ecosystems. Res. Policy **47**, 1391–1399 (2018). https://doi.org/10.1016/j.respol.2018.01.019
37. Kähkönen, A.-K., Evangelista, P., Hallikas, J., Immonen, M., Lintukangas, K.: COVID-19 as a trigger for dynamic capability development and supply chain resilience improvement. Int. J. Prod. Res. **61**, 2696–2715 (2023). https://doi.org/10.1080/00207543.2021.2009588

38. Yu, W., Wong, C.Y., Chavez, R., Jacobs, M.A.: Integrating big data analytics into supply chain finance: the roles of information processing and data-driven culture. Int. J. Prod. Econ. **236**, 108135 (2021). https://doi.org/10.1016/j.ijpe.2021.108135
39. Sestino, A., Prete, M.I., Piper, L., Guido, G.: Internet of Things and Big Data as enablers for business digitalization strategies. Technovation **98**, 102173 (2020). https://doi.org/10.1016/j.technovation.2020.102173
40. Dubey, R., Gunasekaran, A., Childe, S.J.: Big data analytics capability in supply chain agility: the moderating effect of organizational flexibility. Manag. Decis. **57**, 2092–2112 (2019). https://doi.org/10.1108/MD-01-2018-0119
41. Ghasemaghaei, M., Hassanein, K., Turel, O.: Increasing firm agility through the use of data analytics: the role of fit. Decis. Support Syst. **101**, 95–105 (2017). https://doi.org/10.1016/j.dss.2017.06.004
42. Kokkinou, A., Mandemakers, A., Mitas, O.: Developing resilient and robust supply chains through data analytic capability. Continuity Resilience Rev. **5**, 320–342 (2023). https://doi.org/10.1108/CRR-07-2023-0013
43. Fosso Wamba, S., Akter, S., Edwards, A., Chopin, G., Gnanzou, D.: How 'big data' can make big impact: findings from a systematic review and a longitudinal case study. Int. J. Prod. Econ. **165**, 234–246 (2015). https://doi.org/10.1016/j.ijpe.2014.12.031
44. Garmaki, M., Boughzala, I., Wamba, S.F.: The effect of Big Data Analytics Capability on Firm Performance. Presented at the PACIS (2016)
45. Mikalef, P., Pappas, I.O., Krogstie, J., Giannakos, M.: Big data analytics capabilities: a systematic literature review and research agenda. Inf Syst E-Bus Manage. **16**, 547–578 (2018). https://doi.org/10.1007/s10257-017-0362-y
46. Kokkinou, A., van Kollenburg, T., Mandemakers, A.: Development of data analytic capability in organizations. In: Presented at the 2023 EUROMA Conference, Leuven, Belgium (2023)
47. Kokkinou, A., van Kollenburg, T., Mandemakers, A., Hopstaken, E., van Elderen, J.: The Data Analytic Capability Wheel: an implementation framework for digitalization. In: Pucihar, A., Kljajić Borštnar, M., Bons, R., Ongena, G., Heikkilä, M., and Vidmar, D. (eds.) Proceeedings of the 36th Bled eConference Digital Economy and Society: balancing act for digital innovation in times of instability: June 25–28. Univerza v Mariboru, Univerzitetna založba, Bled, Slovenia (2023)
48. Cosic, R., Shanks, G., Maynard, S.: Towards a business analytics capability maturity modeln (2012)
49. Gökalp, M.O., Gökalp, E., Kayabay, K., Koçyiğit, A., Eren, P.E.: The development of the data science capability maturity model: a survey-based research. Online Inform. Rev. **46**, 547–567 (2022). https://doi.org/10.1108/OIR-10-2020-0469
50. Korsten, G., Aysolmaz, B., Turetken, O., Edel, D., Ozkan, B.: ADA-CMM: A Capability Maturity Model for Advanced Data Analytics. Presented at the Hawaii International Conference on System Sciences (2022). https://doi.org/10.24251/HICSS.2022.032
51. Social Security Administration Analytics Center of Excellence: Advanced Analytics Capability Maturity Model (A2CM2)
52. Barton, D., Court, D.: Making advanced analytics work for you. Harv. Bus. Rev. **90**, 78–83 (2012)
53. Hein-Pensel, F., et al.: Maturity assessment for Industry 5.0: a review of existing maturity models. J. Manuf. Syst. **66**, 200–210 (2023). https://doi.org/10.1016/j.jmsy.2022.12.009
54. Gupta, M., George, J.F.: Toward the development of a big data analytics capability. Inform. Manag. **53**, 1049–1064 (2016). https://doi.org/10.1016/j.im.2016.07.004
55. Barney, J.: Firm resources and sustained competitive advantage. J. Manag. **17**, 99–120 (1991). https://doi.org/10.1177/014920639101700108

56. Amit, R., Schoemaker, P.J.H.: Strategic assets and organizational rent: strategic assets. Strat. Mgmt. J. **14**, 33–46 (1993). https://doi.org/10.1002/smj.4250140105
57. Wang, C.L., Ahmed, P.K.: Dynamic capabilities: a review and research agenda. Int. J. Manag. Rev. **9**, 31–51 (2007). https://doi.org/10.1111/j.1468-2370.2007.00201.x
58. van de Wetering, R., Mikalef, P., Krogstie, J.: Strategic value creation through big data analytics capabilities: a configurational approach. In: 2019 IEEE 21st Conference on Business Informatics (CBI), pp. 268–275. IEEE, Moscow, Russia (2019). https://doi.org/10.1109/CBI.2019.00037
59. Laaksonen, O., Peltoniemi, M.: The essence of dynamic capabilities and their measurement. Int. J. Manag. Rev. **20**, 184–205 (2018)
60. Denford, J.S.: Building knowledge: developing a knowledge-based dynamic capabilities typology. J. Knowl. Manag. **17**, 175–194 (2013). https://doi.org/10.1108/13673271311315150
61. Teece, D.J.: Explicating dynamic capabilities: the nature and microfoundations of (sustainable) enterprise performance. Strat. Mgmt. J. **28**, 1319–1350 (2007). https://doi.org/10.1002/smj.640
62. Ellström, D., Holtström, J., Berg, E., Josefsson, C.: Dynamic capabilities for digital transformation. JSMA **15**, 272–286 (2022). https://doi.org/10.1108/JSMA-04-2021-0089
63. Anand, G., Ward, P.T., Tatikonda, M.V., Schilling, D.A.: Dynamic capabilities through continuous improvement infrastructure. J. Oper. Manag. **27**, 444–461 (2009). https://doi.org/10.1016/j.jom.2009.02.002
64. Singh, J., Singh, H.: Continuous improvement philosophy – literature review and directions. Benchmark.: Int. J. **22**(1), 75–119 (2015). https://doi.org/10.1108/BIJ-06-2012-0038
65. Shewhart, W.A.: Statistical method from an engineering viewpoint. J. Am. Stat. Assoc. **26**, 262–269 (1931). https://doi.org/10.1080/01621459.1931.10502545
66. Imai, M.: Kaizen: The Key to Japanese Success. Random House, New York, NY (1986)
67. Hines, P., Holweg, M., Rich, N.: Learning to evolve: a review of contemporary lean thinking. Int. J. Oper. Prod. Manag. **24**, 994–1011 (2004). https://doi.org/10.1108/01443570410558049
68. Koning, H.D., Does, R.J.M.M., Bisgaard, S.: Lean Six Sigma in financial services. Int. J. Six Sigma Competitive Adv. (2008). https://doi.org/10.1504/IJSSCA.2008.018417
69. Chakraborty, A., Chuan Tan, K.: Case study analysis of Six Sigma implementation in service organisations. Bus. Process. Mgmt. J. **18**, 992–1019 (2012). https://doi.org/10.1108/14637151211283384
70. Linderman, K., Schroeder, R.G., Zaheer, S., Choo, A.S.: Six Sigma: a goal-theoretic perspective. J. Oper. Manag. **21**, 193–203 (2003). https://doi.org/10.1016/S0272-6963(02)00087-6
71. Calvo-Mora, A., Picón, A., Ruiz, C., Cauzo, L.: The relationships between soft-hard TQM factors and key business results. Int. J. Oper. Prod. Manag. **34**, 115–143 (2013). https://doi.org/10.1108/IJOPM-09-2012-0355
72. Yusof, S.M., Aspinwall, E.: TQM implementation issues: review and case study. Int. J. Oper. Prod. Manag. **20**, 634–655 (2000). https://doi.org/10.1108/01443570010321595
73. Hietschold, N., Reinhardt, R., Gurtner, S.: Measuring critical success factors of TQM implementation successfully – a systematic literature review. Int. J. Prod. Res. **52**, 6254–6272 (2014). https://doi.org/10.1080/00207543.2014.918288
74. Marodin, G.A., Saurin, T.A.: Implementing lean production systems: research areas and opportunities for future studies. Int. J. Prod. Res. **51**, 6663–6680 (2013). https://doi.org/10.1080/00207543.2013.826831
75. Vijaya, S.M., Ganesh, L.S., Marathe, R.R.: A morphological analysis of research literature on Lean Six Sigma for services. Int. J. Operat. Product. Manag. **38**(1), 149–182 (2018). https://doi.org/10.1108/IJOPM-05-2016-0273

76. Wu, C.W., Chen, C.L.: An integrated structural model toward successful continuous improvement activity. Technovation **26**, 697–707 (2006). https://doi.org/10.1016/j.technovation.2005.05.002
77. Knol, W.H., Lauche, K., Schouteten, R.L.J., Slomp, J.: Establishing the interplay between lean operating and continuous improvement routines: a process view. IJOPM. **42**, 243–273 (2022). https://doi.org/10.1108/IJOPM-06-2020-0334
78. Knol, W.H., Lauche, K., Schouteten, R., Slomp, J.: The duality of lean: organizational learning for sustained development. Proceedings. **2019**, 10594 (2019). https://doi.org/10.5465/AMBPP.2019.10594abstract
79. Kache, F., Seuring, S.: Challenges and opportunities of digital information at the intersection of Big Data Analytics and supply chain management. Int. J. Operat. Product. Manag. **37**, 10–36 (2017). https://doi.org/10.1108/IJOPM-02-2015-0078
80. McAfee, A., Brynjolfsson, E., Davenport, T.H., Patil, D., Barton, D.: Big data: the management revolution. Harv. Bus. Rev. **90**, 60–68 (2012)
81. Mikalef, P., Krogstie, J., Pappas, I.O., Pavlou, P.: Exploring the relationship between big data analytics capability and competitive performance: the mediating roles of dynamic and operational capabilities. Inform. Manag. **57**, 103169 (2020). https://doi.org/10.1016/j.im.2019.05.004
82. Mikalef, P., Van de Wetering, R., Krogstie, J.: From Big Data Analytics to Dynamic Capabilities: The Effect of Organizational Inertia. Presented at the Pacific Asia Conference on Information Systems (2019)
83. Helfat, C.E., Peteraf, M.A.: Understanding dynamic capabilities: progress along a developmental path. Strateg. Organ. **7**, 91–102 (2009). https://doi.org/10.1177/1476127008100133
84. Cadden, T., et al.: Unlocking supply chain agility and supply chain performance through the development of intangible supply chain analytical capabilities. Int. J. Operat. Product. Manag. **42**, 1329–1355 (2022). https://doi.org/10.1108/IJOPM-06-2021-0383
85. Mikalef, P., Krogstie, J.: Examining the interplay between big data analytics and contextual factors in driving process innovation capabilities. Eur. J. Inf. Syst. **29**, 260–287 (2020). https://doi.org/10.1080/0960085X.2020.1740618
86. Yu, D., Tao, S., Hanan, A., Ong, T.S., Latif, B., Ali, M.: Fostering green innovation adoption through green dynamic capability: the moderating role of environmental dynamism and big data analytic capability. IJERPH **19**, 10336 (2022). https://doi.org/10.3390/ijerph191610336
87. Al-Khatib, A.W.: Big data analytics capabilities and green supply chain performance: investigating the moderated mediation model for green innovation and technological intensity. BPMJ **28**, 1446–1471 (2022). https://doi.org/10.1108/BPMJ-07-2022-0332
88. Spanos, Y.E., Lioukas, S.: An examination into the causal logic of rent generation: contrasting Porter's competitive strategy framework and the resource-based perspective. Strat. Mgmt. J. **22**, 907–934 (2001). https://doi.org/10.1002/smj.174
89. Ashaari, M.A., Singh, K.S.D., Abbasi, G.A., Amran, A., Liebana-Cabanillas, F.J.: Big data analytics capability for improved performance of higher education institutions in the Era of IR 4.0: a multi-analytical SEM & ANN perspective. Technol. Forecast. Soc. Change **173**, 121119 (2021). https://doi.org/10.1016/j.techfore.2021.121119
90. Kokkinou, A., van Kollenburg, T., Touw, P.: The road to operational excellence is scenic: tales of continuous improvement journeys. In: Presented at the 2022 EurOMA Conference. Berlin (2022)
91. Kim, G., Shin, B., Kim, K., Lee, H.: IT Capabilities, Process-Oriented Dynamic Capabilities, and Firm Financial Performance. J. Assoc. Inform. Syst. **12**(7), 487–517 (2011). https://doi.org/10.17705/1jais.00270

92. Wamba, S.F., Gunasekaran, A., Akter, S., Ren, S.J., Dubey, R., Childe, S.J.: Big data analytics and firm performance: effects of dynamic capabilities. J. Bus. Res. **70**, 356–365 (2017). https://doi.org/10.1016/j.jbusres.2016.08.009
93. Rossini, M., Costa, F., Tortorella, G.L., Valvo, A., Portioli-Staudacher, A.: Lean Production and Industry 4.0 integration: how Lean Automation is emerging in manufacturing industry. Int. J. Product. Res. **60**(21), 6430–6450 (2022). https://doi.org/10.1080/00207543.2021.1992031
94. Kolberg, D., Zühlke, D.: Lean automation enabled by industry 4.0 technologies. IFAC-PapersOnLine **48**(3), 1870–1875 (2015)
95. Yilmaz, A., Dora, M., Hezarkhani, B., Kumar, M.: Lean and industry 4.0: mapping determinants and barriers from a social, environmental, and operational perspective. Technol. Forecast. Soc/ Change **175**, 121320 (2022). https://doi.org/10.1016/j.techfore.2021.121320
96. Banuelas Coronado, R., Antony, J.: Critical success factors for the successful implementation of six sigma projects in organisations. TQM Mag. **14**, 92–99 (2002). https://doi.org/10.1108/09544780210416702
97. Tennant, C., Roberts, P.: Hoshin Kanri: implementing the catchball process. Long Range Plan. **34**, 287–308 (2001). https://doi.org/10.1016/S0024-6301(01)00039-5
98. Wilson, R., Cudney, E.A., Marley, R.J.: Current status of Hoshin Kanri. TQM (2023). https://doi.org/10.1108/TQM-07-2022-0216
99. Jolayemi, J.K.: Hoshin kanri and hoshin process: a review and literature survey. Total Qual. Manag. Bus. Excell. **19**, 295–320 (2008). https://doi.org/10.1080/14783360701601868
100. Chiarini, A.: Corporate social responsibility strategies using the TQM: Hoshin kanri as an alternative system to the balanced scorecard. The TQM J. **28**, 360–376 (2016). https://doi.org/10.1108/TQM-03-2014-0035
101. Barnabè, F., Giorgino, M.C.: Practicing Lean strategy: Hoshin Kanri and X-Matrix in a healthcare-centered simulation. TQM. **29**, 590–609 (2017). https://doi.org/10.1108/TQM-07-2016-0057
102. Roberts, P., Tennant, C.: Application of the *Hoshin Kanri* methodology at a higher education establishment in the UK. TQM Mag. **15**, 82–87 (2003). https://doi.org/10.1108/09544780310461080
103. Kokkinou, A., van Kollenburg, T., Touw, P.: The Role of Training in the Implementation of Lean Six Sigma. In: Presented at the 2021 EurOMA Conference, Berlin (2021)
104. Desai, D.A., Antony, J., Patel, M.B.: An assessment of the critical success factors for Six Sigma implementation in Indian industries. Int. J. Prod. Perf Mgmt. **61**, 426–444 (2012). https://doi.org/10.1108/17410401211212670
105. Manville, G., Greatbanks, R., Krishnasamy, R., Parker, D.W.: Critical success factors for Lean Six Sigma programmes: a view from middle management. Int. J. Qual. Reliability Mgmt. **29**, 7–20 (2012). https://doi.org/10.1108/02656711211190846
106. Oliveira, J., Sá, J.C., Fernandes, A.: Continuous improvement through "Lean Tools": an application in a mechanical company. Procedia Manuf. **13**, 1082–1089 (2017). https://doi.org/10.1016/j.promfg.2017.09.139
107. Kokkinou, A., van Kollenburg, T., Mathijssen, G., Vissers, E., van Doren, S.: Enablers and inhibitors of digitalization as part of continuous improvement. IJLSS (2024). https://doi.org/10.1108/IJLSS-08-2023-0146
108. Nonaka, I.: A dynamic theory of organizational knowledge creation. Organ. Sci. **5**, 14–37 (1994)
109. Neirotti, P., Paolucci, E.: Why do firms train? Empirical evidence on the relationship between training and technological and organizational change: Relationship between training and technological and organizational change. Int. J. Train. Dev. **17**, 93–115 (2013). https://doi.org/10.1111/ijtd.12003

110. Bortolotti, T., Boscari, S., Danese, P.: Successful lean implementation: Organizational culture and soft lean practices. Int. J. Prod. Econ. **160**, 182–201 (2015). https://doi.org/10.1016/j.ijpe.2014.10.013
111. Gutierrez-Gutierrez, L., De Leeuw, S., Dubbers, R.: Logistics services and Lean Six Sigma implementation: a case study. IJLSS. **7**, 324–342 (2016). https://doi.org/10.1108/IJLSS-05-2015-0019

Introducing DACAR: A Process Mapping Tool to Uncover Robotization Implications in Manufacturing

Peter Schuurhuis[1](✉), Ronald van den Hoek[2], Milan Wolffgramm[2,3], and Mitchell van Roij[4]

[1] Windesheim University of Applied Sciences, Campus 2-6, 8017 CA Zwolle, The Netherlands
P.SCHUURHUIS@WINDESHEIM.NL

[2] Saxion University of Applied Sciences, M.H. Tromplaan 30, 7513 AB Enschede, The Netherlands

[3] University of Groningen, Broerstraat 5, 9712 CP Groningen, The Netherlands

[4] HAN University of Applied Sciences, Ruitenberglaan 29, 6826 CC Arnhem, The Netherlands

Abstract. To prepare a robot implementation, it is of key importance to have an overview of the technical and non-technical implications. Process modeling techniques could be used for mapping relevant implications related to robot implementation in today's manufacturing. However, we argue that existing process mapping tools lack an in-depth perspective, making it potentially difficult for manufacturers to comprehensively and efficiently prepare their robotization project. In an attempt to enrich existing process mapping methodology, we introduce our newly developed process mapping tool in this contribution: the DACAR model. The DACAR model allows the identification of relevant technical and non-technical implications related to integrating a robot solution into a manufacturing process. In this contribution, we elaborate on DACAR's theoretical and methodological underpinnings and present a research agenda comprising various fruitful opportunities for DACAR-related research.

Keywords: Robotics · Lean · Industry 4.0 · Process Modelling · Automation

1 Process Mapping Tools in Today's Manufacturing

Industrial manufacturers in the Netherlands face economic and demographic challenges that jeopardize the continuity of their production systems. Increasing customer demand for customized products in small batches, coupled with personalized services, necessitates greater flexibility in production systems [34]. Historically, manufacturers could enhance flexibility by employing additional temporary production workers [27]. However, the availability of production labor is diminishing throughout Europe, including the Netherlands [17]. Recent data reveals a labor shortage of approximately 31,000 individuals in the Dutch industry [9, 10]. Moreover, due to an aging workforce, insufficient labor replacement, high absenteeism rates in the industry, and declining birth rates, the

Published by Springer Nature Switzerland AG 2024
T. van Kollenburg et al. (Eds.): ELEC 2023, IFIP AICT 681, pp. 70–85, 2024.
https://doi.org/10.1007/978-3-031-63265-5_6

labor shortage is expected to escalate over time [7, 8, 11, 12]. These demographic developments, combined with considerable labor shortages in other sectors [9], could make it increasingly difficult for manufacturers to hire new workers and produce more flexibly. Nonetheless, manufacturers do have alternative strategies at their disposal to increase production system flexibility. One of these strategies is directed towards the robotization of production tasks.

As a production automation technique, robotization offers a potential solution to manufacturers that want to enhance production flexibility with fewer staff. The application of industrial robots has been common practice for many years. One could think of robot applications at large manufacturers in the automotive sector [3]. Industrial robots could enhance production system flexibility by taking over particular human tasks, either allowing the production worker to focus on tasks that require more human interference or making the production worker more capable of handling complex tasks through supporting human-robot interaction. In addition to its promising contribution to production system flexibility, industrial robots have become increasingly accessible.

Due to technological developments, economy of scale, and competition amongst suppliers, industrial robotics is becoming easier to operate, more widely applicable, and affordable [25]. These developments make industrial robots no longer exclusively available to larger and resourceful manufacturers. Instead, industrial robots become increasingly accessible to small- and medium-sized manufacturers with fewer resources [21]. However, buying a robot is one thing, but extracting its technical potential is another. In line with Wilson [40], we argue that the contribution of industrial robots strongly depends on how they are implemented.

A suboptimal robot implementation comes with considerable problems that threaten the production system's output and continuity [32]. To illustrate, Steinbauer [36] classified four technical problem categories related to robot implementation. First, a suboptimal interaction between the robot, the production worker, and the surroundings. Second, problematic algorithms that capture faulty methods and build-ups. Third, poor software that comes with one or more design mistakes, programming flaws, or integration errors with other software systems. Fourth, defective hardware being technically incapable of executing the envisioned tasks over time. Each of these problem categories could undermine the product flow and deteriorate performance. Moreover, the quality of production labor could be affected by suboptimal human-robot task divisions and poor work (re)design. Such human capital problems make it difficult for operators to remain employable and sustain the production system over time [30]. To avoid a suboptimal robot implementation, manufacturers could benefit from an integral overview of relevant robotic, production system, and human capital implications prior to their robot implementation.

Adopting an integral approach towards robot implementation, this contribution highlights the relevance of understanding how production management (i.e., input, throughput, output), workplace design, and human capital are affected by robot-induced implications [22]. To obtain such an understanding, a process mapping tool is required that allows a thorough identification of these technical and non-technical implications – from this point, we use the term 'situational characteristics' when referring to technical and non-technical implications. Process mapping tools can help to create sufficient understanding of relevant situational characteristics. In line with Hunt [20], visualizing processes by using a process mapping technique, for instance, is often one of the first steps to take when starting process improvement efforts. Production engineering literature offers plenty of tested process mapping tools.

An outstanding example of a process mapping tool is the Value Stream Map [31], which focuses on the entirety of value-adding processes within a production system and maps both product and information flows. Another process mapping tool is Makigami [14], intended to analyze and subdivide a series of activities in a process, revealing the interaction amongst actors and highlighting process metrics [1]. In this respect, there are many more process mapping tools to mention. A comprehensive overview can be found in Lunau et al. [23]. Acknowledging the amount of process mapping tools and their reputation, we do argue that current process mapping tools often fall short when it comes to providing in-depth insight into relevant situational characteristics specifically related to robotization in production.

To illustrate our argument, the Value Stream Map gives a good overview of the production system but does not provide plenty of detail due to its broad scope. The Makigami, on the other hand, tends to ignore relevant data and information, such as setup times or failures of machines [14]. Moreover, and in line with Braglia et al. [5], process mapping tools are often relatively time-consuming to fill out in detail. This is particularly problematic in production systems that change frequently (i.e., more flexible production). In such systems, manufacturers run the risk of investing in process mapping activities that, due to their long-lasting execution, cannot keep up with the production system's dynamics, resulting in structurally inaccurate information. Therefore, we argue that manufacturers could benefit from an additional in-depth process mapping tool allowing an efficient, yet thorough, preparation of robotization projects in production systems. We effectuated our argument by constructing a process mapping tool ourselves, called DACAR. The goal of this contribution is to provide a detailed explanation of DACAR's theoretical underpinnings and method. In our view, DACAR is not a substitute for existing process mapping tools. Instead, DACAR should enrich available process mapping tools and stimulate robotization in modern manufacturing.

In the next section, we elaborate on DACAR's theoretical underpinnings. Subsequently, a methodological section follows describing how to organize and run a DACAR exercise. We finalize this contribution with a DACAR research agenda.

2 DACAR's Theoretical Underpinnings

DACAR is an innovative three-stage process mapping tool specifically designed by the authors to support projects aimed at implementing robots in manufacturing. The acronym stands for: Data stream, Arrival (infeed), Critical-to-quality, Away (outfeed), Requirements – originally DAKAR in Dutch: Datastroom, Aanvoer, Kwaliteitscontrole, Afvoer, Randvoorwaarden. As suboptimal interaction between robot, production worker, and the surroundings is an important problem category for robotization [36], the goal of DACAR is to serve as an in-depth process mapping tool aimed at creating an understanding of the situational characteristics relevant to integrating a robot into an existing process. In essence and as illustrated in Fig. 1, DACAR provides a detailed description of tasks and steps embedded in a pre-selected part of the production process, thereby providing a robust foundation for designing an optimal interaction of the robot with its surroundings.

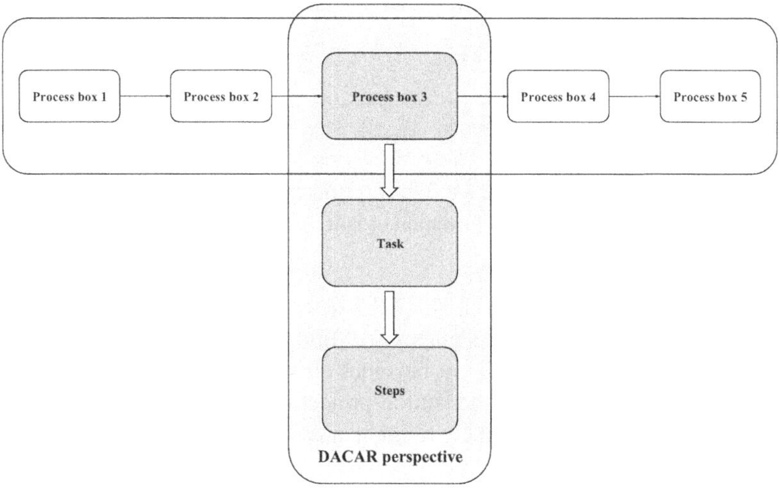

Fig. 1. Illustration of DACAR's in-depth perspective

Ultimately, DACAR was developed to enrich process mapping methodology by complementing two well-established process mapping tools, namely: the Value Stream Map and the Makigami. To achieve complementarity and to contribute to process mapping methodology, DACAR's theoretical underpinnings are based on established Value Stream Mapping and Makigami literature. To illustrate, the Value Stream Map originates from Lean Manufacturing and is intended to describe relatively stable and high-volume production processes for a specific product family in order to identify waste [31]. Makigami, on the other hand, aims at describing transactional office processes including those individuals who are involved in executing the process steps [14]. Even though it originates from Lean Office, Makigami can also be used for mapping manufacturing processes [15] (for an example, see [13]).

When it comes to their scoping and method, both the Value Stream Map and the Makigami adapt a high-level perspective on process mapping [2]. By grouping task sequences into process boxes, describing the process performance per box, and declaring added value, waste, and other outcomes, both the current and future state of the production system become visible [31]. These findings are rather abstract. Therefore, and as stressed in the previous section, there is reason to assume that manufacturers and their operators could also benefit from having a more in-depth understanding about how situational characteristics are affected by the robot implementation. Consequently, DACAR has been constructed to make situational characteristics tangible by specifying the general process descriptions generated by the Value Stream Map and the Makigami.

As illustrated in Fig. 2, DACAR comprises three sequential stages. These stages are inspired by the current state and future state embedded in the Value Stream Map [14]. The *first DACAR stage* is intended to identify the goal(s) of the robotization project. Particular (process) problems are highlighted that must be addressed by implementing a robot. Considerable attention goes out to identifying which (manual) tasks are performed within the process.

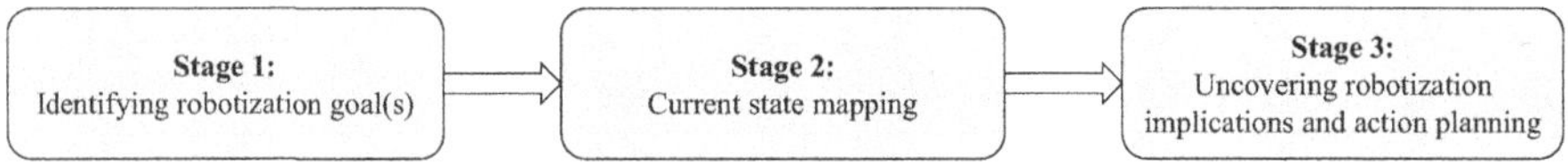

Fig. 2. Illustration of DACAR's Stages

are performed within the process. This helps determining which of these tasks should be robotized and directs the process mapping efforts to a specific part of the production system. Moreover, in this first stage, it becomes clear if all relevant stakeholders agree on the motives for the specific robotization project at hand. In case the stakeholders' opinions diverge majorly, this is likely to ignite a situation of ambiguity, hampering the project's success [6, 37].

The *second DACAR stage* focuses on creating a detailed, comprehensive, and dynamic map of the production system's current state. Similar to the Value Stream Map, the process is analyzed by using process boxes. However, DACAR limits the modeled production system to three distinct process boxes, namely: (1) infeed, (2) tasks to be automated, and (3) outfeed. For each of these three boxes, descriptions are written down chronologically, from top to bottom, about the tasks being performed. To increase the description's richness, seven information boxes were added, requiring specific details about the modeled production system. These information boxes, ideally, make situational characteristics tangible.

The seven information boxes cover the following implications: (1) product specifications (e.g., weight, dimensions and material type of the infeed), (2) instructions for production workers (e.g., means of communication of work instructions), (3) communication about internal logistics of the infeed (e.g., information on who communicates how about the arrival of new supplies), (4) process specifications (e.g., information on how the infeed is being packed, presented and in which amounts), (5) quality control (e.g., information on what is being checked; where and by whom), (6) communication about internal logistics of the outfeed (e.g., information about whether the outfeed is being presented to the next station in bulk or in a structured manner) and (7) performance indicators (e.g., cycle time, changeover time and first time through). Figure 3 illustrates a single DACAR process box. Additionally, Appendix A captures a worksheet, inspired by the work of Bouchard [4] and Malik and Bilberg [24], for filling out a DACAR process box.

The *third DACAR stage* is aimed at uncovering robotization implications by meticulously analyzing the current state of the modeled production system. In the Value Stream Map, the use of Kaizen bursts is a common practice to express key points of attention [31]. In DACAR, each challenge identified is written down as a Kaizen burst and added to the process map of the current state. Each Kaizen burst should be positioned near the process or information box it concerns, signaling key implications for realizing the robotic solution in practice. Finally, for each Kaizen burst, a concise action plan is to be defined, indicating how this particular implication can be accounted for. For this purpose, we use the action-oriented questions of De Witte and Jonker [16]: why is an action plan needed, what action should be taken, who should act, and how and when should we act? Appendix B visualizes a completed DACAR process map.

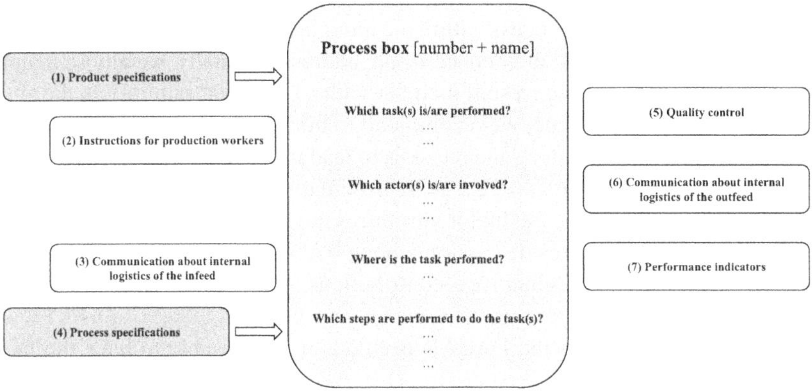

Fig. 3. Schematic representation of the DACAR process box and information boxes

3 Organizing and Running a DACAR Exercise

This chapter explains the methodology for executing the DACAR model and the conditions that should be met to get the envisioned result. This result is an in-depth insight into robotization implications, to be used as a starting point for designing and successfully deploying a fitting robot solution in the modelled production system. We will describe which organizing practices are required before executing a DACAR exercise and how to run each of the three DACAR stages.

Prior to executing a DACAR exercise, it is of key importance to carefully sort out at which place in the production system applying a robot is expected to have a major positive impact on productivity, cost reduction, quality of labor, and so forth. The Value Stream Map and the Makigami hold the potential to make points of improvement in the current state salient and could indicate which part of the production system benefits most from robotization. Therefore, we advise to start with modelling the current state of the production system using a Value Stream Map or Makigami – a description on how to execute these process mapping tools can be found [14] and [31].

Moreover, we strongly advise to apply DACAR in a multidisciplinary focus group. Robotizing is complex due to its large impact on different levels, departments and personnel within the organization. Therefore – following Oakland and Tanner [29] – it is important to invite representatives from different layers of the company, both office- and production-related, to capture the multiplicity of views about the goals, current and future state of the to-be-robotized process within the manufacturing company. Furthermore, to assure all representatives and their concerns are addressed equally, we advise to appoint an independent facilitator (e.g., a staff member with a Lean belt training). In the absence of a suitable internal candidate, we recommend to hire an external facilitator, such as a Lean consultant. The facilitator's main task is to lead the focus group, guide the process during the three stages of DACAR, ensure representatives' participation, and reach consensus. More specifically, the facilitator introduces the DACAR model, ensures DACAR is used as intended, stimulates discussion amongst representatives by asking follow-up questions, summarizes representatives' contributions, makes notes, keeps track of time, and interrupts when discussions go off topic.

In addition to managing the DACAR exercise, it is advisable to have the facilitator prepare various materials. First are the DACAR worksheets. These worksheets are embedded in Appendix A. By printing these on A0 paper (84 × 118.8 cm) and by hanging them on the wall, the worksheets become a central and visual part of the DACAR exercise. Moreover, by organizing sticky notes and pencils, it becomes possible for representatives to actively write down their input and stick it to the hanging worksheets during the DACAR exercise. This way, relevant robotization implications could become visible for all representatives and, since these insights would be written down on sticky notes, these inputs remain easy to move across the worksheets.

The execution of the DACAR exercise is structured chronologically according to the three stages of the DACAR model. In the following paragraphs, each stage will be elaborated upon. Running the entire DACAR is expected to take approximately half a working day.

During the *first DACAR stage*, the main goal of robotizing a particular process step is determined. Determining the main goal of robotizing is important for two reasons. First, the nature of the goal can have a major impact on the design of the robot solution. For example, while a main goal of increasing the output through 24/7 production leads to a design with automated infeed and outfeed of the robot, a main goal of increasing product quality leads to a design focused on 'first time right' production. Second, discussing the goal will reveal whether the representatives have a commonly shared view on what should be achieved through robotization. To facilitate the group discussion, we have developed a categorization which stimulates a broad perspective on which robotization implications are relevant when determining the goal. As such, the categorization is a supporting tool for the facilitator to guide the discussion and group the input provided. Inspired by Slack and Brandon-Jones [33], Ferdows and De Meyer [19], Faber [18] and Morgeson and Humphrey [28], we propose the following goal categories: Efficiency, Costs, Speed, Flexibility, Reliability, Product and Process Quality, Quality of Labor, and Innovation. To ensure that each representative has the opportunity to come up with unbiased input, to eliminate the potential risk for conflicts among members potentially disrupting the DACAR execution, and to avoid the possibility of one or more members dominating the discussion, it is advisable to start the first stage with a brainwriting pool. In line with VanGundy [38], a brainwriting pool comes down to a situation where individuals are writing down their thoughts, ideas, and suggestions about a particular topic. Thereafter, all individual input is gathered and grouped using the aforementioned goal categorization. All findings are discussed by the representatives in order to establish a common view on the most important (category of) goal(s) to be achieved through robotization, finalizing DACAR stage 1.

The *second DACAR stage* starts with writing down chronologically, from top to bottom, which tasks are being performed during the infeed, the to-be-robotized step(s), and the outfeed. The facilitator guides this conversation, paying particular attention to the input of representatives responsible for executing these three steps of the process, and writes down the result using the three process boxes on the hardcopy DACAR worksheets: (1) infeed, (2) tasks to be automated, and (3) outfeed. Next, the facilitator guides a conversation aimed at filling out the seven information boxes, one-by-one, to acquire as much detailed information about the situational characteristics as possible. A key element of DACAR is that it makes implicit process knowledge explicit, which is key for successfully integrating a robot solution. For example, while an employee's job description prescribes *packaging finished products for shipment* as its sole task (i.e., explicit process knowledge), the employee might in practice also automatically perform an additional quality check to prevent the customer from receiving damaged goods (i.e., implicit process knowledge). Ideally, the procedure used in the first DACAR stage is applied in this second DACAR stage too. However, replicating the first stage's procedure could potentially drain the representatives' energy. Alternatively, the facilitator could fill out the information boxes by using input from the group as a whole, write these findings down on sticky notes and add them to the hardcopy DACAR worksheets. When applying this alternative procedure, the facilitator needs to put additional effort into ensuring that each representative has the opportunity to provide unbiased input and mitigate the potential dominance of particular representatives during the discussions.

To be able to identify robotization implications in the next stage, we feel that it is important to continuously keep the following questions in mind while discussing the contents of the information boxes: what are the (unique) capabilities of a human and a robot with respect to this box and which tasks are easy for a human and hard for a robot and vice versa? To highlight the importance of this discussion and the potential multiplicity of views, we have added two exemplary questions for two information boxes. Example 1, concerning the information box on quality control: which quality checks are performed, is it easy for a robot to do these checks, do we want to automate these quality checks or is there an alternative to perform a check to ensure quality? Example 2, concerning the information box on process specifications: how are the products supplied to the robot, is the supply structured, should we structure the supply, or should we design the robot solution to cope with unstructured supplies? The second DACAR stage has been completed when all information boxes are fully discussed and described, and when the representatives agree that all relevant information for identifying potential robotization implications has been gathered.

The *third DACAR stage* focuses on identifying the most important robotization implications that arise from the DACAR process map and resonates in specific action plans. To achieve such outcome, the facilitator ignites a group discussion based on the output of the first and second DACAR stage. The purpose of this discussion is to uncover which situational characteristics of the current state do not fit the needs of the envisioned robotized future state. These implications, requiring a significant change compared to the current state, are written down on Kaizen burst-shaped sticky notes and attached to the hardcopy DACAR worksheet – these notes should be positioned close to those process or information boxes they concern. Once finalized, for each Kaizen burst, the representatives formulate a concise plan of action that accounts for the situational characteristic(s) encountered. These plans of actions should answer the four following questions: why is an action plan needed, what action should be taken, who should act, and when should be acted? However, for situational characteristics with a high level of complexity, it is likely that, due to a lack of time, limited expertise or both, the representatives are unable to produce a complete and practical plan of action. At the end of this third DACAR stage, the facilitator will assess the plan of action's status and list the information or other resources representatives need to finalize the plan of action at a later time. Together with the representatives, the facilitator summarizes and prioritizes the formulated actions by using a multi-voting technique [39]. Based on group voting, formulated actions are being prioritized in terms of urgency. Once prioritized, the third DACAR stage has been completed.

To conclude the DACAR exercise, firstly, the facilitator will evaluate with the representatives if all relevant robotization implications were identified. Any additional information will be administered. Secondly, the facilitator and representatives will plan a follow-up meeting to review and, if necessary, specify the DACAR outcomes. Finally, the facilitator will assure that specific arrangements are formulated that relate to the design and deployment of the robot solution.

4 Research Agenda

In this contribution, we elaborated upon the relevance of an integral approach towards the robotization of production systems. Having insight into both technical and non-technical implications, and understanding of how to manage these implications, is expected to increase industrial manufacturers' potential to come to relevant robot applications. Production engineering provides fruitful and empirically validated process mapping tools to identify such situational characteristics. Two of these comprehensive process mapping tools, the Value Stream Map and the Makigami, were elaborated upon extensively. We argued that these process mapping tools are relevant for manufacturers to understand the build-up of their production systems. However, due to their broad scoping, the

Value Stream Map and the Makigami do not describe situational characteristics in-depth. Motivated to fill this methodological gap, we developed a complementary DACAR process mapping tool. The main contribution of DACAR is that it allows a specification of insights generated by the Value Steam Map and the Makigami. In addition to DACAR's theoretical underpinnings, we attempted to provide a comprehensive methodological description on how to organize and run a DACAR exercise.

Having DACAR introduced in this contribution, we reached the point where DACAR's robustness is to be validated empirically. Striving for a relevant and evidence-based enrichment of existing process mapping tools, we direct our DACAR research agenda towards the achievement of three goals: 1) assessing DACAR's applicability, 2) laying an empirical foundation for DACAR, and 3) reinforcing the use of DACAR in robot implementation trajectories. How we, together with the Lean community, intend to achieve these three goals will be briefly elaborated upon in the following paragraphs.

Firstly, to validate DACAR's applicability, we plan to conduct a multiple case study in the Dutch manufacturing industry. This validation focusses on the methodological execution of DACAR. Particular attention goes out to the procedure's achievability, the supplementary materials' usability, the dynamics amongst representatives, and the mediating role of the facilitator. To determine the extent to which DACAR can be applied in different contexts, we favor a multiple case study over a single case study [35]. Ideally, this multiple case study includes different production architypes, ranging from mass production to more customized production. To allow any sort of comparability between cases, we will include at least two cases per production architype. Once the multiple case study has been completed, we will reflect upon DACAR's applicability. We will not hesitate to methodologically improve DACAR if its applicability turns out to be suboptimal or in case DACAR's application requires a more tailored approach across production architypes.

Secondly, to lay an empirical foundation, deliberate attention should go out to the richness of the data collection and the obtained results. DACAR has been created to generate detailed results about a wide range of situational characteristics. Various methodological suggestions were proposed to obtain such results, such as: a multidisciplinary focus group, a capable facilitator, and opportunities for representatives to provide individual input. By conducting the multiple case study as mentioned in the previous paragraph, we are likely able to gather a considerable amount of relevant and rich data. Based on measures commonly used in qualitative research [26], we will deeply reflect on the richness of the results. Moreover, to assess the findings' applicability, we plan to involve external robot system designers to determine whether they are able to draft a first design based on the obtained results. Methodological points of improvement will be formulated if the obtained results turn out to be too abstract or incomplete.

Thirdly, to reinforce the application of DACAR in robotization trajectories, we will study the integration between the Value Stream Map, the Makigami, and DACAR. In this contribution, DACAR has been positioned as complementary to the mainstream Value Stream Map and the frequently used Makigami. Ideally, DACAR guides the selection of and deep dive into the most relevant data generated through Value Stream Map or Makigami exercises. We, therefore, deliberately argue in favor of an integrated application that starts with the Value Stream Map or the Makigami, followed by DACAR. Any inefficiency or misfit between these process mapping tools are to be identified and translated into methodological points of improvement.

Being able to make considerable progress on our DACAR research agenda on the short term, we expect to have a follow-up contribution available soon. The Lean community, manufacturing professionals, and other robotization enthusiasts are warmly invited to accompany us in our DACAR pursuit. Opportunities for collaboration can be explored by contacting the first author.

Acknowledgements. This contribution originated from research project "Robotizing Integrally" (in Dutch: Integraal Robotiseren), financially supported by the Dutch national funding agency SIA (Dutch Research Council). The authors would like to express their gratitude to Vincent Wiegel (HAN University of Applied Sciences), Aart Schoonderbeek (Windesheim University of Applied Sciences), and Rik Grasmeijer (Fieldlab Industrial Robotics) for their valuable contributions and support. The authors would like to extend their appreciation to Luuk Collou (Saxion University of Applied Sciences) for reviewing earlier versions of this contribution. His constructive feedback improved the textual quality.

Appendix A

This appendix contains the standard worksheet to describe the situational characteristics of the to-be-robotized part of a production process (see Fig. 4). Depending on the specific context of a company being studied, it might be required to add additional items or justified to skip particular items from the standard worksheet.

Data streams			Arrival (infeed)	Critical-to-quality	Away (outfeed)	Requirements
[1] Product specifications	[2] Instructions for production workers	[3] Communication about internal logistics of the infeed	[4] Process specifications	[5] Quality control	[6] Communication about internal logistics of the outfeed	[7] Performance indicators
Product description (e.g. different parts, etc.)	Information carrier (e.g. drawing, work instruction, oral instruction, training)	Signalling of new infeed to production worker (digital,oral, etc.)	Type of infeed carrier (crate, bin, pallet, bag, on a table etc.)	Does this part of the process contain a quality check as a task? If yes, who performs this check?	Signalling of new infeed to production worker (digital,oral, etc.)	How much time is available for the task(s)? What is the uptime and downtime?
Dimensions	Medium of information carrier (e.g.screen, printed paper, sound)	Medium of signal (ERP system, kanban, etc.)	How does the infeed arrive?(individually, as a group, stacked on top of each other, etc.)	Description of the type of quality check	Medium of signal (ERP system, kanban, etc.)	Changeover required? If yes, how much time does this take?
Type of material(s)	Goal of the task(s)	Recipient(s) (who orders new infeed?)	Moving or static infeed? (e.g. by a conveyor belt)	Where and when is the quality check performed?	Recipient(s) (who orders new infeed?)	First time through-% / data about number of accepted and rejected products
Weight		Sender (who sends new infeed?)	Number of products delivered at infeed	Which steps are performed during the quality check task?	Sender (who sends new infeed?)	Value-added time of the task compared to time available
			Bulk or structured infeed? (fixed or random position of products)		Bulk or structured outfeed? (fixed or random position of products)	Are many customer-specific steps required? (e.g.regarding different dimensions, batch sizes, parts, etc.)

Fig. 4. Worksheet used to fill a DACAR process box (part 1 and part 2).

Appendix B

This appendix contains an illustration of a completed DACAR process map (see Fig. 5). The model contains a series of three process boxes for (1) infeed, (2) to-be automated (manual) tasks within the manufacturing process and (3) outfeed. Each process box is complemented by seven information boxes regarding the situational characteristics. Kaizen bursts, recognizable by the black explosion icons, are added to indicate any implications with regard to implementing a robot in the modelled production system.

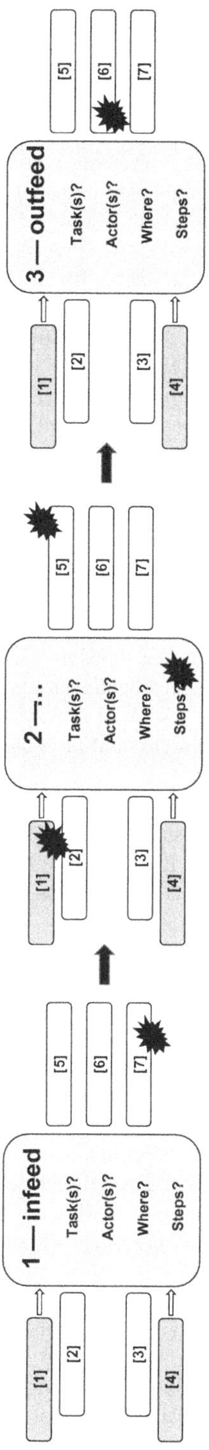

Fig. 5. Visualization of completed DACAR process map.

References

1. Aij, K.H., Simons, F.E., Visse, M., Widdershoven, G.A.: A focus on throughput: lean improvement of nurse scheduling in the operating theatre. Glob. J. Manag. Bus. Res. **14**(1), 75–82 (2014)
2. Aij, K.H.: Lean Leadership Health Care: enhancing peri-operative processes in a hospital (PhD thesis). Free University of Amsterdam, Amsterdam, NL (2015)
3. Bartoš, M., Bulej, V., Bohušík, M., Stanček, J., Ivanov, V., Macek, P.: An overview of robot applications in automotive industry. Transport. Res Procedia **55**, 837–844 (2021)
4. Bouchard, S.: Lean Robotics: A Guide to Making Robots Work in your Factory. Bouchard (2017)
5. Braglia, M., Carmignani, G., Zammori, F.: A new value stream mapping approach for complex production systems. Int. J. Prod. Res. **44**(18–19), 3929–3952 (2006)
6. Brugnach, M., Dewulf, A.R.P.J., Henriksen, H.J., Van der Keur, P.: More is not always better: coping with ambiguity in natural resources management. J. Environ. Manage. **92**(1), 78–84 (2011)
7. CBS Stateline: Birth: https://www.cbs.nl/en-gb/visualisations/dashboard-population/population-dynamics/birth. Last accessed 29 June 2023a
8. CBS Stateline: Elderly people: https://www.cbs.nl/en-gb/visualisations/dashboard-population/age/elderly-people. Last accessed 29 June 2023b
9. CBS Stateline: Vacaturegraad naar bedrijfstak. https://www.cbs.nl/nl-nl/visualisaties/dashboard-arbeidsmarkt/vacatures/vacaturegraad-naar-bedrijfstak. Last accessed 29 June 2023c
10. CBS Stateline: Werkgelegenheid structuur. https://www.cbs.nl/nl-nl/visualisaties/dashboard-arbeidsmarkt/banen-werkgelegenheid/toelichtingen/werkgelegenheidsstructuur. Last accessed 29 June 2023d
11. CBS Stateline: Werklozen. https://www.cbs.nl/nl-nl/visualisaties/dashboard-arbeidsmarkt/werklozen. Last accessed 29 June 2023e
12. CBS Stateline: Ziekteverzuim. https://www.cbs.nl/nl-nl/visualisaties/dashboard-arbeidsmarkt/werkenden/ziekteverzuim. Last accessed 29 June 2023f
13. Chakraborty, S., Kumar, B., Malguri, A.: Reducing the truck turnaround time inside a heavy manufacturing industry through Makigami Analysis. Int. J. Adv. Inform. Sci. Technol. **5**(9), 39 (2016)
14. Chiarini, A., Gabberi, P.: Comparing the VSM and Makigami tools in a transactional office environment: exploratory research from an Italian manufacturing company. Total Qual. Manag. Bus. Excell. **33**(1–2), 127–145 (2022)
15. Chiarini, A.: Lean organization: from the Tools of the Toyota Production System to Lean Office, vol. 3. Springer Science & Business Media, Berlin, DE (2012)
16. De Witte, M., Jonker, J.: De kunst van veranderen. Kluwer, The Hague, the Netherlands (2013)
17. Commission, E.: Towards a Sustainable, Human-Centric and Resilient European Industry. Publications Office of the European Union, Brussels, BE (2021)
18. Faber, M.: Robots and reshoring: evidence from Mexican labor markets. J. Int. Econ. **127**, 103384 (2020)
19. Ferdows, K., De Meyer, A.: Lasting improvements in manufacturing performance: in search of a new theory. J. Oper. Manag. **9**(2), 168–184 (1990)
20. Hunt, V.D.: Process mapping: How to Reengineer your Business Processes. John Wiley & Sons, Hoboken, NJ, USA (1996)
21. International Federation of Robotics Press Release World Robotics 2022. https://ifr.org/downloads/press2018/2022_WR_extended_version.pdf. Last accessed 21 June 2023

22. Kragic, D., Sandamirskaya, Y.: Effective and natural human-robot interaction requires multidisciplinary research. Scie Robot. **6**(58), eabl7022 (2021)
23. Lunau, S., et al.: Design for Six Sigma+Lean Toolset. Springer-Gabler, Frankfurt/Main, DE (2013)
24. Malik, A.A., Bilberg, A.: Framework to implement collaborative robots in manual assembly: a lean automation approach. In: Katalinic, B. (ed.) Proceedings of the 28th International DAAAM Symposium 2017, pp. 1151–1160. DAAAM International Vienna (2017). https://doi.org/10.2507/28th.daaam.proceedings.160
25. Matheson, E., Minto, R., Zampieri, E.G., Faccio, M., Rosati, G.: Human–robot collaboration in manufacturing applications: a review. Robotics **8**(4), 100 (2019)
26. Mays, N., Pope, C.: Assessing quality in qualitative research. Bmj **320**(7226), 50–52 (2000)
27. Michie, J., Sheehan, M.: Business strategy, human resources, labour market flexibility and competitive advantage. Int. J. Hum. Res. Manag. **16**(3), 445–464 (2005)
28. Morgeson, F.P., Humphrey, S.E.: The Work Design Questionnaire (WDQ): developing and validating a comprehensive measure for assessing job design and the nature of work. J. Appl. Psychol. **91**(6), 1321 (2006)
29. Oakland, J.S., Tanner, S.: Successful change management. Total Qual. Manag. Bus. Excell. **18**(1–2), 1–19 (2007)
30. Parker, S.K., Andrei, D.M., Van den Broeck, A.: Poor work design begets poor work design: capacity and willingness antecedents of individual work design behavior. J. Appl. Psychol. **104**(7), 907 (2019)
31. Rother, M., Shook, J.: Learning to See: Value Stream Mapping to Add Value and Eliminate Muda. Lean enterprise institute, London, UK (2003)
32. Sheridan, T.B.: Human–robot interaction: status and challenges. Hum. Factors **58**(4), 525–532 (2016)
33. Slack, N., Brandon-Jones, A.: Operations Management, 9th edn. Pearson, Harlow, UK (2019)
34. Smart Industry: Implementation Agenda 2018–2021: Dutch Industry Fit for the Future. Peters Publicatie (2018)
35. Stake, R.E.: Multiple Case Study Analysis. Guilford, New York, USA (2006)
36. Steinbauer, G.: A Survey about Faults of Robots Used in RoboCup. In: Van der Zant, T., Chen, X., Stone, P., Sucar, L.E. (eds.) Lecture Notes in Computer Science, vol. 7500. Springer, Berlin, DE (2013)
37. Van den Hoek, R.E., Brugnach, M., Hoekstra, A.Y.: Shifting to ecological engineering in flood management: Introducing new uncertainties in the development of a building with nature pilot project. Environ. Sci. Policy **22**, 85–99 (2012)
38. VanGundy, A.B.: Brain writing for new product ideas: an alternative to brainstorming. J. Consum. Mark. **1**(2), 67–74 (1984)
39. Voehl, F., Harrington, H.J., Mignosa, C., Charron, R.: The lean six sigma black belt handbook: tools and methods for process acceleration. CRC Press, Florida, US (2013)
40. Wilson, M.: Implementation of Robot Systems: An Introduction to Robotics, Automation, and Successful Systems Integration in Manufacturing. Butterworth-Heinemann, Oxford, UK (2014)

Toward 1+1 = 3 with Lean Robotics: The Introduction of a Human-Centered Robotization Method

Milan R. Wolffgramm[1,2,3](✉), Stephan Corporaal[1,2], Aard J. Groen[3], and Mitchell J. P. A. M. van Roij[4]

[1] Saxion University of Applied Sciences, M. H. Tromplaan 28, 7513 AB Enschede, The Netherlands
m.r.wolffgramm@saxion.nl

[2] Centre of Expertise for Technology Education TechYourFuture, M.H. Tromplaan 28, 7513 AB Enschede, The Netherlands

[3] University of Groningen, Broerstraat 5, 9712 CP Groningen, The Netherlands

[4] HAN University of Applied Sciences, Ruitenberglaan 31, 6826 CC Arnhem, The Netherlands

Abstract. Industrial robotics and Lean Manufacturing are becoming increasingly intertwined with one another. Lean Robotics aims to synergize process, machine, and human capital challenges by pursuing a human-centered design approach. In this contribution, we argued that, despite its promising virtues, Lean Robotics' human-centered design approach lacks a methodological bases and runs the risk of becoming overshadowed by technical issues. To preserve Lean Robotics' human-centered design approach, the goal of this contribution was to introduce a suitable human-centered robotization method. Building further upon work from the field of Human-Robot Interaction, a robotization method on human-robot interdependence optimization was brought forward and reviewed extensively. To unite this method with the guiding principles of Lean Robotics, a human-centered extension was developed. This human-centered extension, referred to as the Interdependence Scoring Method, is ready to test and comes with a step-by-step explanation and various illustrations. Lean educators, scholars, and professionals have been encouraged to test the Interdependence Scoring Method in a wide variety of class, lab, and field settings. Moreover, these Lean experts are urged to bundle their strengths and, collectively, challenge the future of manufacturing with Lean Robotics.

Keywords: Lean Manufacturing · Lean Robotics · Human-Robot Interaction · Interdependence · Human-Centered Design · Design Methodology

1 Introduction

Automation plays a core role in Lean Manufacturing. By deploying advanced machinery, production processes can be streamlined, become less susceptible to human error, and produce less waste [1]. Industrial (collaborative) robots can be considered a particular type or subset of automation. With their multifunctionality, user interface, and interaction

Published by Springer Nature Switzerland AG 2024
T. van Kollenburg et al. (Eds.): ELEC 2023, IFIP AICT 681, pp. 86–99, 2024.
https://doi.org/10.1007/978-3-031-63265-5_7

with individual operators, these mechanical manipulators distinguish themselves from other traditional machines, such as CNC or welding machines [2]. The role of industrial robotics in Lean Manufacturing is of such growing importance that part of the Lean community is drawing attention to a new extension within their field of expertise. This extension is being referred to as Lean Robotics.

The most comprehensive definition of Lean Robotics we encountered has been provided by Bjurstöm and Jackson [3]. They stated that "Lean Robotics would mean automation which supports an ongoing and distributed problem-solving activity with a strong emphasis on the knowledge and competence of the company's human resources" (p. 211). Jasarevic and Colomo-Palacios [4] described how Lean Robotics, as a design method, can be characterized by four guiding principles: 1) safe and operable robot applications, 2) robotic performance that satisfies internal client needs, 3) eliminating system error and human underutilization, and 4) improving the robot application. They showed how these guiding principles partially relate to Lean Manufacturing, such as eliminating waste and continuous improvement. However, in contrast to Lean Manufacturing, Lean Robotics pursues a human-centered design approach by tailoring robot applications to the operators working with them. Jasarevic et al. [4] illustrated this by stating that Lean Robotics is rather internally oriented (i.e., robot applications designed to support the operator), focuses on human demands (i.e., operator needs and requirements), and pays considerably more attention to the interaction between operator and robot (i.e., safe and constructive working conditions).

With its human-centered design approach, Lean Robotics could potentially contribute to the establishment of not only high-performing but also sustainable robot applications. In line with neighboring design streams, such as Socio-Technical Systems [5] and Workplace Innovation [6], by paying close attention to the wants of the individual operator, robot applications could be established that extend the operator beyond its own human capabilities and make working conditions more sustainable. But despite its considerable potential, we argue that Lean Robotics requires methodological attention.

The reason why we argue that Lean Robotics requires methodological attention has to do with the fact that scholarly work on Lean Robotics is highly conceptual. As illustrated in [4], Lean Robotics literature finds itself in an early stage of development. While considerable attention has been paid to definitions and guiding principles [7, 8], there is no Lean Robotics methodology available that prescribes how to design a human-centered robot application. We argue that without such design methodology, human factors in Lean Robotics could become overshadowed by more technical factors. We base ourselves upon recent developments in the field of Human-Robot Interaction.

As stated in [9], the field of Human-Robot Interaction is concerned with "the design, understanding, and evaluation of robotic systems, which involve humans and robots interacting through communication" (p. 85). Similar to Lean Robotics, the field of Human-Robot Interaction is striving toward the creation of functional work systems that encompass at least one robotic manipulator and an operator. However, instead of eliminating waste, Human-Robot Interaction focuses on optimizing human-robot task allocations by dividing system autonomy and control. Bartneck et al. [10] stressed how Human-Robot Interaction research should be considered an interdisciplinary endeavor, uniting human factors, technological implications, and system (re)configuration. Such scoping, inherently, requires Human-Robot Interaction scholars to pay considerable attention to each of these three aspects. However, various Human-Robot Interaction scholars reported an alarming disbalance.

Recent work by Jahanmahin et al. [11] showed how the majority of Human-Robot Interaction research in industrial contexts is robot-centered, paying more attention to hardware and software implications than human factors. Prati et al. [12] echoed a similar message, stating that recent work on Human-Robot Interaction is "strongly 'robot centered', focusing mainly on technical issues and technological solutions, without reasoning on the human perspective" (p. 2). Moreover, Sheridan [13] urged for a stronger focus on human factors in Human-Robot Interaction research, predicting significant human safety and acceptance challenges coming with modern, interactive robotics. Finally, Coronado et al. [14] stated that Human-Robot Interaction research has been rather machine-centered and performance-oriented. They urged fellow scholars to include more human-centricity in their Human-Robot Interaction research by awarding more attention to human factors. These illustrations underline that human factors are prone to being overshadowed by technical factors. Moreover, considerable efforts are required to call attention to human factors once these are lost out of sight.

Given its prematurity and similar scoping, there is a considerable risk that the field of Lean Robotics will undergo the same fate as the field of Human-Robot Interaction. To avoid that Lean Robotics is unable to pursue its human-centered design approach, the goal of this contribution is to develop a human-centered robotization method that captures the guiding principles of Lean Robotics [4]. Despite its aforementioned challenges, the field of Human-Robot Interaction provides an extensive array of empirically validated design methodologies. Particularly promising are methodologies on optimizing the mutual reliance, or interdependence, between operator and robot since they provide fruitful opportunities for a human-centered design approach.

In the remainder of this contribution, we will elaborate on the concept of human-robot interdependence, review an interdependence optimization method, and develop a human-centered extension for this method. We finalize our contribution with a discussion and a call to action.

2 Literature

Machines and operators possess unique and complementary capabilities. According to Fitts [15], machines will surpass workers in terms of speed, power, and computation. These capabilities underline the operational excellence of industrial machinery. Operators, on the other hand, are more creative and flexible. These capabilities are essential to swiftly cope with sudden change and handle tasks too costly to automate. Despite all the technological developments that were introduced since the introduction of the Fitts' List in the 1950s, the characterization of machine and operator capabilities remained relevant [16]. Nonetheless, placing a robot and an operator in one workspace and dividing tasks does not automatically lead to a full extraction of their capabilities and joint value creation. Instead, the interaction between the operator and the robot requires considerable attention and decision-making.

In essence, each robot and operator represents an autonomous actor that can function in a certain work system to the extent of its capabilities. This implies that their functioning is bound to physical, mental, or technical constraints. Consequently, in case the system requirements are too demanding, such as a high-strain or unpredictable production system, an autonomous operator or robot cannot function properly on its own. However, when the operator and the robot rely on each other's capabilities, potentially, production units can be created that are more capable than the sum of its parts. For instance, an operator could benefit from the robot's operational excellence in demanding circumstances while the robot could be sustained by the operator's flexibility and remain operable in highly dynamic circumstances. According to Clark [17], in such situations, where one party depends on what another party does (and vice versa), there is 'interdependence'.

Since the 1970s, various frameworks have been developed for designing interdependent human-machine systems. Two prominent frameworks are those of the Levels of Automation [18] and Adaptive Automation [19]. In addition to the Levels of Automation and Adaptive Automation frameworks, a widespread of concurrent frameworks were created over time. A recent and extensive overview of Human-Robot Interaction frameworks can be found in [20]. But despite all these frameworks and their relatedness to human-robot interdependence, Human-Robot Interaction scholar Matthew Johnson argued that these frameworks were falling short considerably.

2.1 Johnson's Coactive Design Method

In his dissertation, Johnson [21] wrote a chapter about what he called "The Fallacy of Autonomy" (pp. 28–42). In the chapter, he stressed how Human-Robot Interaction frameworks are relying too excessively on the levels of automation, resulting in oversimplification and insufficient context sensitivity. From his viewpoint, the design process is being narrowed down to a static distribution of tasks with too little explicit attention to interdependence. Using these frameworks could result in problematic design practices and outcomes in the case of dynamic and complex systems. Furthermore, Johnson [21] underlined that various frameworks are biased toward autonomous system applications (i.e., systems that can function without human interference). He argued that autonomous system applications are a myth since they will always require certain human interference (e.g., prompts, maintenance, and troubleshooting). Moreover, aiming for optimized machine autonomy would minimize interdependence and remove the operator and as its human capabilities from the system. Such removal opposes a threat to the system's robustness. To prevent the design of rigid human-robot systems, Johnson [21] built on the human-machine design frameworks, resulting in his Coactive Design Method.

In essence, the Coactive Design Method helps designers determine if and how the task performance of the most capable actor (i.e., the performer) can be extended, improved, or reinforced by an assisting actor (i.e., the supporter). Task-extending interdependencies are referred to as hard interdependencies given their unlocking character (i.e., the performer cannot execute these tasks without the supporter's assistance). Reliability- and efficiency-enhancing interdependencies are coined soft interdependencies due to their upgrading character. The Coactive Design Method could be used as a human-centered robotization method since the performer role could be ascribed to the operator, concentrating all design efforts on what the operator needs to perform more, better, and faster.

The theoretical and methodological underpinnings of the Coactive Design Method can be found in [21].

To show the Coactive Design Method in action and underline its benefits, Johnson [21] tested his method in multiple studies. In both studies, the Coactive Design Method did, however, not result in excellent performance. On the contrary, subtask execution often took longer and was less successful than concurrent design approaches. Nevertheless, Johnson [21], and later Johnson et al. [22], stressed how the Coactive Design Method generated flexible and resilient design and high development efficiency. The method allowed designers to explore possible interdependencies and their required development efforts. Consequently, not only the most potential but also alternative human-robot designs surfaced. In case of unforeseen situations, designers could shift rapidly from one design to another, allowing their human-robot design to handle the unexpectedness and make the production system more robust. Johnson's [21] method and findings laid a fundament for future research.

In the decade that followed, designers applied the Coactive Design Method in different contexts. For instance, the method has been used for satellite navigation in cars [23] humanoid robots [24] team cognitive walkthroughs [25] (un)manned aerial vehicles [26–30] unmanned ground vehicles [31], and air battle management [32]. Scholars who used the Coactive Design Method echoed [21] and [22], stating that the Coactive Design Method helped to ignite, structure, and visualize design options and make adequate design decisions accordingly.

Its wide application and methodological maturity make the Coactive Design Method a relevant robotization method for the field of Lean Robotics. However, the Coactive Design Method has various shortcomings when it comes to human-centric design. We applied the method in two design studies involving collaborative robotics – both studies are to be reviewed – and faced five shortcomings related to the method's interdependence analysis. Firstly, how to systematically determine the performer and supporter capabilities is unclear. Secondly, the performer and supporter capabilities are treated too statically, leaving no room for fluctuation. Thirdly, scenarios in which the supporter provides reliability- and efficiency-enhancing assistance to the performer are insufficiently taken into consideration. Fourthly, interdependencies that are harmful to the performer, also known as negative interdependencies [33], are overlooked. Fifthly, quantifying the strength of human-robot interdependencies and comparing these between designs is problematic. In the next section, we propose a human-centered extension that addresses all five shortcomings.

3 Human-Centered Extension

To find a methodological solution for the human-centered shortcomings encountered in the Coactive Design Method [21], we analyzed scholarly work that advanced the Coactive Design Method, such as [23, 27] and [34]. Since these advancements only addressed the negative interdependencies and scoring shortcomings, additional inspiration was derived from literature related to the unaddressed shortcomings (e.g., capability assessment techniques [35]). Based on these insights, a step-by-step guide was created that could address each of the encountered shortcomings. This laid the foundation for a human-centered extension of the Coactive Design Method [21].

This human-centered extension, referred to as the Interdependence Scoring Method, focuses on the interdependence analysis of the Coactive Design Method [21]. The Interdependence Scoring Method aims at fulfilling two methodological functions. Firstly, it aims at structuring the design processes by providing robot application designers with detailed instructions on how to optimize the interdependence between the operator and the robot. Secondly, it aims to improve these designers' decision-making by incorporating the concept of negative interdependence and by introducing a more sophisticated scoring approach. Moreover, the buildup of the Interdependence Scoring Method is closely in line with the guiding principles of Lean Robotics [4]. To illustrate this, the Interdependence Scoring Method fosters a human-centered design approach by treating the operator as the performer and the robot as the supporter. Furthermore, the Interdependence Scoring Method accounts for the operator's needs from a capability point of view and allows the incorporation of additional needs (e.g., work preferences). Finally, the Interdependence Scoring Method fosters the design and redesign of constructive human-robot interdependencies by making helpful, redundant, and harmful human-robot interactions salient.

The Interdependence Scoring Method will be explained using three main steps and one optional step. Following the first three steps will result in a total interdependence score. This score represents the overall strength of the human-robot interdependencies embedded in a robot application. The optional step allows designers to determine the leveraged interdependence ratio. This ratio captures the result of a comparison between the interdependence score of a robot application and a pre-determined optimum.

Step 1: Determine Subtask Boundary and Reliability Standards

In line with the Coactive Design Method [21], designers should conduct a hierarchical task analysis prior to the interdependence analysis – consult [36] for a step-by-step method for conducting a hierarchical task analysis. Such an analysis is relevant for listing the tasks and subtasks under study and their requirements. To determine whether the performer requires enabling or reliability-enhancing support in Step 2, designers should formulate a boundary standard and a reliability standard for each subtask. The boundary standard is an absolute, measurable threshold the performer should meet to complete the subtask. Boundary standards could be related to particular actions that must have taken place, such as filling in a form or realizing a certain product modification. Moreover, boundary standards could be related to performance standards, such as not exceeding a certain subtask cycle time or waste limit. Additionally, designers should obtain or decide when a subtask is being executed reliably. Reliability standards could, for instance, be related to particular product features being actualized or certain quality measures being met. As with the boundary standards, the reliability standards should be formulated as specific thresholds.

Step 2: Assess Performer and Supporter Capabilities

Again, in line with the Coactive Design Method [21], after listing the subtasks, designers should determine per subtask to which extent the performer is capable of executing the subtask and how the supporter is capable of assisting the performer. However, different from the Coactive Design Method, designers using the Interdependence Scoring

Method are encouraged to systematically assess the maximum capabilities of the performer and the supporter by, for instance: conducting direct observations, backtracking performance logs, running simulations, or through calculations and estimations. Insights from these exercises are used to create an overview that shows per subtask and for both the performer and the supporter whether the subtask could be executed and, if possible, at what reliability and efficiency. It is important to note that designers should assess the supporter's capacity to assist across all subtasks.

Step 3: Find, Code, and Score Interdependencies

Once the capabilities have been assessed, designers should find the interdependencies. Starting with the hard and soft interdependencies (i.e., positive interdependencies). Hard interdependencies apply when, on the one hand, the performer fails to meet the boundary standards and, on the other hand, the supporter is capable of assisting. Soft interdependencies apply to subtasks being executed more reliably and/or efficiently when the supporter provides assistance. Negative interdependencies are related to subtasks that cannot be executed anymore or do not get executed more reliably and/or more efficiently when the supporter assists. Finally, we added that designers have the possibility to cancel particular interdependencies by deciding which subtasks will not or cannot be assisted by the supporter. Once the positive, negative, and canceled interdependencies have been found, designers are recommended to color code the interdependencies. We adapted and extended the color codes embedded in the Coactive Design Method [21] and in [34]. A color code overview has been presented in Table 1.

Table 1. Color Codes Interdependence Scoring Method.

Color Code	Meaning:
Blue	Reliability- and efficiency-enhancing interdependence
Green	Efficiency-enhancing interdependence
Yellow	Reliability-enhancing interdependence
Orange	Hard interdependence
Light Grey	Supporter's assistance is not used
Dark Grey	Interdependence cannot take place
Red	Negative interdependence

After color coding, the interdependencies should be awarded a score. A standardized overview of scores and when they should be applied has been summarized in Table 2. These scores range from –1.0 to 1.0. A –1.0 score applies to interdependencies that do not contribute to or reduce the performer's subtask reliability and efficiency – interdependencies that do not contribute to the performer's subtask execution are considered negative since they burden the performer with an additional, yet unnecessary or wasteful, dependency. A 0.0 score applies to subtasks that cannot be assisted by the supporter or in case the supporter's assistance has been canceled. Soft interdependencies receive either a

.5 score or a 1.0 score. A .5 score applies to interdependencies that either improve the performer's subtask reliability or efficiency. A 1.0 score applies to hard interdependencies and interdependencies that enhance both the performer's reliability and efficiency – hard interdependencies receive a 1.0 score since subtask execution becomes possible due to the supporter's assistance, likely stimulating the performer's subtask reliability and efficiency.

Table 2. Standardized Interdependence Scoring Approach.

Score	Applies to:
–1	Interdependencies hindering performer's reliability and efficiency
–1	Interdependencies equaling performer's reliability and efficiency
0	Supporter cannot assist
0	Supporter's assistance is/was not used
.5	Reliability- or efficiency-enhancing interdependencies
1	Reliability- and efficiency-enhancing interdependencies
1	Hard interdependencies

It is important to note that designers can prioritize particular interdependencies over others by adding weight to the scores in Table 2. Such priority could, for instance, be relevant in case of high subtask requirements, safety risks, or costliness. Moreover, designers could further increase the Interdependence Scoring Method's human-centric design approach by deliberately accounting for the operator's work preferences. In such instances, the weights would be higher or lower depending on whether the operator perceives the subtasks as important, pleasant, difficult, or dull.

To calculate a total interdependence score, all awarded scores must be multiplied by their weight factors and totaled. The higher the total interdependence score, the more symbiotic the robot application. A total interdependence score higher than zero shows that, across all subtasks, the supporter's assistance allows the performer to execute more tasks, execute task tasks more reliably, execute tasks more efficiently, or a combination of these three. A total interdependence score equal to zero means that the supporter's assistance is either absent or does, overall, not contribute to the performer's subtask execution. A total interdependence score smaller than zero implies that the supporter's assistance, overall, is harmful to the performer's subtask execution (i.e., the performer is better off without assistance). Figure 1 illustrates a total interdependence score calculation using equal weights (example 1) and differentiated weights (example 2).

Example 1: Unweighted Subtasks

Task	Subtasks	Boundary Condition	Reliability Condition	Performer Reliable	Performer Duration	Supporter Reliable	Supporter Duration	Interdependence	Score	Weight	Weighted Score
Assembling Part A	Picking part A	Part was collected	Collected part is A	100%	15 sec.	100%	5 sec.	Efficiency-enhancing	.5	1	.5
	Picking ten B screws	Ten screws collected	All collected screws are B	60%	3 sec.	Cannot assist		Cannot take place	0	1	0
	Inserting B screws in Part A	Screwing positions are filled with a screw	Screwing positions are filled with a B screw	60%	5 sec.	90%	15 sec.	Reliability-enhancing	.5	1	.5
	Tightening screw	B screws are tightened	B screws are fixated in Part A	20%	15 sec.	90%	10 sec.	Efficiency- and reliability-enhancing	1	1	1
	Inspecting part	Inspection conducted	All errors are spotted	Boundary condition was not met		Can assist		Hard interdependence	1	1	1
	Stacking part	Part A is stacked in 30 sec.	Part A is stacked on pile C	100%	10 sec.	100%	20 sec.	Negative interdependence	-1	1	-1
										Total interdependence score	2

Example 2: Weighted Subtasks

Task	Subtasks	Boundary Condition	Reliability Condition	Performer Reliable	Performer Duration	Supporter Reliable	Supporter Duration	Interdependence	Score	Weight	Weighted Score
Assembling Part A	Picking part A	Part was collected	Collected part is A	100%	15 sec.	100%	5 sec.	Efficiency-enhancing	.5	.5	.25
	Picking ten B screws	Ten screws collected	All collected screws are B	60%	3 sec.	Cannot assist		Cannot take place	0	.25	0
	Inserting B screws in Part A	Screwing positions are filled with a screw	Screwing positions are filled with a B screw	60%	5 sec.	90%	15 sec.	Reliability-enhancing	.5	2	1
	Tightening screw	B screws are tightened	B screws are fixated in Part A	20%	15 sec.	90%	10 sec.	Efficiency- and reliability-enhancing	1	1	1
	Inspecting part	Inspection conducted	All errors are spotted	Boundary condition was not met		Can assist		Hard interdependence	1	2	2
	Stacking part	Part A is stacked in 30 sec.	Part A is stacked on pile C	100%	10 sec.	100%	20 sec.	Negative interdependence	-1	3	-3
										Total interdependence score	1.25

Fig. 1. Examples of Total Interdependence Score Calculations.

Optional: Calculating a Leveraged Interdependence Ratio.
As mentioned at the start of this section, designers can, in addition to determining a total interdependence score, also calculate a leveraged interdependence ratio. To obtain such a ratio, designers must first determine the potential interdependence score and the realized interdependence score. The potential interdependence score is an accumulation of all presumed positive interdependencies the robot application could come with. It is important to acknowledge that there are scenarios thinkable where positive interdependencies are accompanied by or 'tied with' negative interdependencies (e.g., if interdependence A will be realized then interdependence B will also be realized). In such instances, only the positive interdependencies that could outweigh their tied negative interdependencies are to be included in the potential interdependence score. The realized interdependence score captures all hard, soft, canceled, and negative interdependencies achieved with the robot application. To determine the realized interdependence score, the aforementioned step 1, step 2, and step 3 are to be followed.

In order to calculate the leveraged interdependence ratio, the realized interdependence score should be divided by the potential interdependence score. This would result in a ratio ranging from negative infinity up to 1.0. The closer to 1.0, the more interdependence potential has been realized. A leveraged interdependence ratio of 0 indicates that the supporter has not assisted or contributed. A negative ratio shows that, in the realized interdependence score, the negative interdependencies outweigh the positive interdependencies. The farther below zero, the more negative interdependencies, as a proportion of the potential interdependence score, have been realized. An example of a leveraged interdependence ratio calculation has been presented in Fig. 2.

Potential Interdependencies

Task	Subtasks	Boundary Condition	Reliability Condition	Performer		Supporter		Interdependence	Score	Weight	Weighted Score
				Reliable	Duration	Reliable	Duration				
Machine Handling Part Y	Collecting part Y	Part Y is Collected	Part does not fall on floor	100%	15 sec.	100%	10 sec.	Efficiency-enhancing	.5	1	.5
	Opening machine door	Door is opened in 20 sec.	Door is fully opened	85%	10 sec.	100%	5 sec.	Efficiency- and reliability-enhancing	1	1	1
	Inserting part Y	Part Y is stuck in clamp	Part does not fall in machine	100%	15 sec.	95%	30 sec.	Negative interdependence	-1	1	-1
	Closing machine door	Door is closed in 5 sec.	Door is fully closed	90%	5 sec.	100%	5 sec.	Reliability-enhancing	.5	1	.5
	Activating machine	Machine is activated in 30 sec.	Program selection is first time right	100%	20 sec.	100%	10 sec.	Efficiency-enhancing	.5	1	.5
	Opening machine door	Door is opened in 20 sec.	Door is fully opened	50%	20 sec.	100%	5 sec.	Efficiency- and reliability-enhancing	1	1	1
	Removing part Y	Part Y is removed from clamp	Part does not fall in machine	80%	10 sec.	100%	20 sec.	Reliability-enhancing	.5	1	.5
	Measuring part Y	Measure conducted	80% of errors are spotted	70%	55 sec.	Cannot assist		Cannot take place	0	1	0
	Discarding part Y	Part Y is discarded in 30 sec.	Part Y is discarded in box Z	Boundary condition was not met		Can assist		Hard interdependence	1	1	1
										Potential interdependence score	5

Realized Interdependencies

Task	Subtasks	Boundary Condition	Reliability Condition	Performer		Supporter		Interdependence	Score	Weight	Weighted Score
				Reliable	Duration	Reliable	Duration				
Machine Handling Part Y	Collecting part Y	Part Y is Collected	Part does not fall on floor	100%	15 sec.	100%	10 sec.	Not used	0	1	0
	Opening machine door	Door is opened in 20 sec.	Door is fully opened	85%	10 sec.	100%	5 sec.	Efficiency- and reliability-enhancing	1	1	1
	Inserting part Y	Part Y is stuck in clamp	Part does not fall in machine	100%	15 sec.	95%	30 sec.	Negative interdependence	-1	1	-1
	Closing machine door	Door is closed in 5 sec.	Door is fully closed	90%	5 sec.	100%	5 sec.	Reliability-enhancing	.5	1	.5
	Activating machine	Machine is activated in 30 sec.	Program selection is first time right	100%	20 sec.	100%	10 sec.	Efficiency-enhancing	.5	1	.5
	Opening machine door	Door is opened in 20 sec.	Door is fully opened	50%	20 sec.	100%	5 sec.	Not used	0	1	0
	Removing part Y	Part Y is removed from clamp	Part does not fall in machine	80%	10 sec.	100%	20 sec.	Reliability-enhancing	.5	1	.5
	Measuring part Y	Measure conducted	80% of errors are spotted	70%	55 sec.	Cannot assist		Cannot take place	0	1	0
	Discarding part Y	Part Y is discarded in 30 sec.	Part Y is discarded in box Z	Boundary condition was not met		Can assist		Hard interdependence	1	1	1
										Realized interdependence score	2.5

Realized interdependence score	2.5
Potential interdependence score	5
Leveraged interdependence ratio	.5

Fig. 2. Example Leveraged Interdependence Ratio Calculation.

4 Discussion and Call to Action

Given the rising amount of robot installations [37], the technical limitations of robots to function fully autonomous [38] and the increasing labor shortage in Western industries [39], the development of robot applications that thoroughly support the individual operator has become increasingly important to sustain production systems. Lean Robotics advocates such a human-centered design approach but lacks the methodology to translate this approach to the development of robot applications. Therefore, the goal of this contribution was to introduce a human-centered robotization method that captures the guiding principles of Lean Robotics [4]. To achieve this goal, we reviewed the Coactive Design Method [21] and developed a human-centered extension, the Interdependence Scoring Method, to methodologically enrich the field of Lean Robotics. This human-centered robotization method, integrating the Interdependence Scoring Method with the remainder of the Coactive Design Method, has the potential to provide a wide audience of Lean experts with a specific guideline on how to pursue human-centered design through Lean practices. Nonetheless, there is still considerable work to be done in order to produce this guideline. The first step is to extensively test the Interdependence Scoring Method. Therefore, in the upcoming paragraphs, we call Lean educators, Lean scholars, and Lean practitioners to action and accompany us, both individually and collectively, by testing the human-robot interdependence method.

Lean educators are encouraged to introduce the content of this contribution in their classes on Lean management. This contribution provides the latest insights on Lean Robotics and its relation to Lean Manufacturing. Moreover, students could be educated about the relevance of human-centricity when designing robot-equipped production systems and the buildup of the Interdependence Scoring Method. Finally, Lean educators could test the Interdependence Scoring Method by providing students with field-inspired case assignments or by connecting students to research initiatives devoted to the testing of the Interdependence Scoring Method.

Lean scholars are encouraged to incorporate the Interdependence Scoring Method into their research agenda. The Interdependence Scoring Method has to be tested empirically in both lab and field settings. Lean scholars could conduct studies on how leveraged interdependence ratios develop over time. Particularly interesting is adhering to the growing urge for end-user involvement in design (e.g., [40]) by focusing on exploring a relationship between end-user involvement and human-robot interdependence. Finally, Lean scholars could study how the weights of interdependence scores are affected by the work preferences of individual operators [41]. Each of these research endeavors contributes to the validation and methodological robustness of the Interdependence Scoring Method.

Lean professionals are encouraged to test the Interdependence Scoring Method in their manufacturing facility. The method, potentially, determines the interdependence of existing human-robot interactions in production. Furthermore, Lean professionals can test the Interdependence Scoring Method when designing new robot applications. Despite its practical application, there is yet no peer-reviewed evidence available supporting the Interdependence Scoring Method's functionality. We used the method in two design studies and expect to have our empirical and methodological findings published soon. Given the method's scoping and the complexity of production systems, Lean professionals are encouraged to first use the Interdependence Scoring Method in a predictable part of their production system, such as a workstation known for its task simplicity and routine, and move toward more complex production contexts over time.

Finally, the Interdependence Scoring Method allows Lean scholars, Lean professionals, and Lean educators to bundle their strengths and test the method collectively. To illustrate, Lean scholars can share their latest findings on the Interdependence Scoring Method with Lean educators and Lean professionals and secure opportunities for future in-class or in-company research. Lean professionals can incorporate the latest findings from class and scientific exercises into their design processes and provide Lean educators and Lean scholars with business intelligence and access to the manufacturing facility. Finally, Lean educators can use the findings from Lean scholars and the business intelligence provided by Lean professionals to actualize their education materials and, in return, offer a testing ground for student-related research and exercises.

While testing the Interdependence Scoring Method is a considerable exercise, it is a first step. Once validated, the next step would be to test the Interdependence Scoring Method together with the remainder of the Coactive Design Method [21] and work towards an integrated human-centered robotization method. The method's compatibility with Lean Manufacturing methodology, such as the Value Stream Map [42], should not be overlooked since this creates fruitful opportunities for acquiring a notable position in the Lean landscape.

References

1. Kolberg, D., Zühlke, D.: Lean automation enabled by industry 4.0 technologies. IFAC-PapersOnLine **48**(3), 1870–1875 (2015)
2. Singh, B., Sellappan, N., Kumaradhas, P.: Evolution of industrial robots and their applications. Int. J. Emerg. Technol. Adv. Eng. **3**(5), 763–768 (2013)
3. Bjurström, E., Jackson, M.: Lean robotics for industrial renewal. In: Segelod, E., (eds.) Studies In Industrial Renewal. Coping with changing Contexts, pp. 201–214. Mälardalen University, Eskilstuna (2011)
4. Jasarevic, A., Colomo-Palacios, R.: Lean robotics: a multivocal literature review. In: Computational Science and Its Applications–ICCSA 2022 Workshops, pp. 436–446. Springer International Publishing, Cham (2022)
5. De Sitter, L.U., Den Hertog, J.F., Dankbaar, B.: From complex organizations with simple jobs to simple organizations with complex jobs. Hum. Relat. **50**(5), 497–534 (1997)
6. Oeij, P., Rus, D., Pot, F.: Workplace Innovation: Theory Research and Practice. Springer International Publishing, Cham (2017)
7. Bouchard, S.: Lean Robotics: A Guide to Making Robots Work in Your Factory. Samuel Bouchard (2017)
8. Sobaszek, Ł: A lean robotics approach to the scheduling of robotic adhesive dispensing process. Adv. Sci. Technol. Res. J. **16**(5), 136–146 (2022)
9. Murphy, R.R., Nomura, T., Billard, A., Burke, J.L.: Human–robot interaction. IEEE Robot. Autom. Mag. **17**(2), 85–89 (2010)
10. Bartneck, C., Belpaeme, T., Eyssel, F., Kanda, T., Keijsers, M., Šabanović, S.: Human-Robot Interaction: An Introduction. Cambridge University Press, Cambridge (2020)
11. Jahanmahin, R., Masoud, S., Rickli, J., Djuric, A.: Human-robot interactions in manufacturing: a survey of human behavior modeling. Robot. Comp.-Integr. Manuf. **78**, 102404 (2022)
12. Prati, E., Peruzzini, M., Pellicciari, M., Raffaeli, R.: How to include user experience in the design of human-robot interaction. Robot. Comp.-Integr. Manuf. **68**, 102072 (2021)
13. Sheridan, T.B.: Human–robot interaction: status and challenges. Hum. Factors **58**(4), 525–532 (2016)
14. Coronado, E., Kiyokawa, T., Ricardez, G.A.G., Ramirez-Alpizar, I.G., Venture, G., Yamanobe, N.: Evaluating quality in human-robot interaction: a systematic search and classification of performance and human-centered factors, measures and metrics towards an industry 5.0. J. Manuf. Syst. **63**, 392–410 (2022)
15. Fitts, P.M.: Human Engineering for an Effective Air-Navigation and Traffic-Control System. National Research Council, Washington (1951)
16. De Winter, J.C., Dodou, D.: Why the Fitts list has persisted throughout the history of function allocation. Cogn. Technol. Work **16**, 1–11 (2014)

17. Clark, H.H.: Using Language. Cambridge University Press, Cambridge (1996)
18. Sheridan, T.B., Verplank, W.L.: Human and Computer Control of Undersea Teleoperators. Massachusetts Inst of Tech Cambridge Man-Machine Systems Lab, Cambridge (1978)
19. Parasuraman, R., Bahri, T., Deaton, J.E., Morrison, J.G., Barnes, M.: Theory and Design of Adaptive Automation in Aviation Systems. Naval Air Development Center, Warminster (1992)
20. Onnasch, L., Roesler, E.: A taxonomy to structure and analyze human-robot interaction. Int. J. Soc. Robot. **13**, 833–849 (2020)
21. Johnson, M.: Designing Support for Interdependence in Human-Robot Teamwork (Dissertation). Matthew Jonson (2014)
22. Johnson, M., et al.: Team IHMC's lessons learned from the DARPA Robotics Challenge: finding data in the rubble. J. Field Robot. **34**(2), 241–261 (2016)
23. Baber, C., Vance, C.: Design of human-machine teams using a modified CoActive design. Method. In: Charles, R, Golightly, D. (eds.) Contemporary Ergonomics and Human Factors. CIEHF, Warwickshire (2019)
24. Calvert, D., Mishra, B., McCrory, S., Bertrand, S., Griffin, R., Pratt, J.: A fast, autonomous, bipedal walking behavior over rapid regions. In: 2022 IEEE-RAS 21st International Conference on Humanoid Robots (Humanoids), pp. 24–31. IEEE, Manhattan (2022)
25. Lee, K.H., Chua, K.W.L., Koh, D.S.M., Tan, A.L.S.: Team cognitive walkthrough: fusing creativity and effectiveness for a novel operation. In: Proceedings of the 20th Congress of the International Ergonomics Association (IEA 2018) Volume VII: Ergonomics in Design, Design for All, Activity Theories for Work Analysis and Design, Affective Design 20, pp. 117–126, Springer International Publishing, Cham (2019)
26. Wang, C., Wen, X., Niu, Y., Wu, L., Yin, D., Li, J.: Dynamic task allocation for heterogeneous manned-unmanned aerial vehicle teamwork. In: 2018 Chinese Automation Congress (CAC), pp. 3345–3349. IEEE, Manhattan (2018)
27. Wang, Z., Wu, L., Wang, C., Wen, X., Niu, Y., Yin, D.: Coactive design of human-machine collaborative damage assessment using UAV images and decision trees. In: 2018 Chinese Automation Congress (CAC), pp. 1140–1145. IEEE, Manhattan (2018)
28. Wang, C., Wu, L., Yan, C., Wang, Z., Long, H., Yu, C.: Coactive design of explainable agent-based task planning and deep reinforcement learning for human-UAVs teamwork. Chinese Soc. Aeronaut. **33**(11), 2930–2945 (2020)
29. Wang, Z., Wang, C., Niu, Y.: Mixed-initiative manned-unmanned teamwork using coactive design and graph neural network. In: 2020 3rd International Conference on Unmanned Systems (ICUS), pp. 538–543. IEEE, Manhattan (2020)
30. Johnson, B., et al.: A human-machine teaming approach for future marine corps hybrid operations: manned helicopters and air-launched unmanned aerial vehicles. Nav. Eng. J. **135**(1), 127–139 (2023)
31. Li, B., Wang, C., Tang, J., Liu, Y.: Coactive design of human-UGV teamwork using augmented reality. In: Proceedings of 2022 International Conference on Autonomous Unmanned Systems (ICAUS 2022), pp. 411–421. Springer Nature, Singapore (2023)
32. Peterson, J.E., McGuirl, J.M., Miller, M.E., Bales, D., Sternitzky, B.: Viewing air battle management through the lens of interdependence. In: 74th International Symposium on Aviation Psychology, pp. 184–189. Wright State University, Dayton (2021)
33. Tjosvold, D.: The dynamics of interdependence in organizations. Hum. Relat. **39**(6), 517–540 (1986)
34. Johnson, M., Vignati, M, Duran, D.: Understanding Human Autonomy Teaming through Interdependence Analysis. Social Psychological Implications, pp. 1–20 (2019)
35. Freeze, R., Kulkarni, U.: Knowledge management capability assessment: validating a knowledge assets measurement instrument. In: Proceedings of the 38th Annual Hawaii International Conference on System Sciences, p. 251a. IEEE, Manhattan (2022)

36. Annett, J., Stanton, N.A. (eds.): Task Analysis. Taylor & Francis, London (2000)
37. International Federation of Robotics Press Release World Robotics (2022). https://ifr.org/downloads/press2018/2022_WR_extended_version.pdf. Last accessed 27 Sep 2023
38. Inkulu, A.K., Bahubalendruni, M.V.A.R., Dara, A.K.S.: Challenges and opportunities in human robot collaboration context of Industry 4.0 – a state of the art review. Industr Robot **49**(2), 226–239 (2022)
39. Causa, O., Abendschein, M., Luu, N., Soldani, E., Soriolo, C.: The Post-COVID-19 Rise in Labour Shortages. OECD, Paris (2022)
40. Bano, M., Zowghi, D.: A systematic review on the relationship between user involvement and system success. Inf. Softw. Technol. **58**, 148–169 (2015)
41. Parker, S.K., Boeing, A.A.: Workplace innovation in the digital era: a role for SMART work design. In: Oeij, P., Dhondt, S., McMurray, A. (eds.) A Research Agenda for Workplace Innovation. Edward Elgar Publishing Limited, Cheltenham (2023)
42. Rother, M., Shook, J.: Learning to See: Value Stream Mapping to Add Value and Eliminate MUDA. Lean Enterprise Institute, London (2003)

Digital Tools Supporting Lean Program in a Multinational Enterprise

Stefano Frecassetti(✉), Matteo Ferrazzi, and Alberto Portioli Staudacher

Department of Management, Economics, and Industrial Engineering, Politecnico di Milano, Piazza Leonardo da Vinci 32, 20133 Milan, Italy
stefano.frecassetti@polimi.it

Abstract. Researchers have increasingly explored the intricate interplay between Lean methodologies and digital technologies in recent years, shedding light on synergistic effects and potential integration strategies. However, scarce attention has been given to the practical application of digital tools in supporting Lean programs and associated challenges. This paper presents a case study of a multinational company's utilization of digital tools to bolster its corporate Lean program. The findings showed a positive mutual relationship wherein digital tools augment the efficacy of Lean practices. The positive outcomes underscore the potential of digital technologies to enhance and streamline Lean initiatives. Nevertheless, the research also underscores significant challenges encountered during and after digitalization. In particular, the paramount importance of individuals in the digitalization journey has emerged. Their empowerment and active involvement emerge as fundamental factors throughout the entire process. The findings underscore that being Lean before digitalization is crucial, as it creates an environment and a change-oriented culture that is more receptive to incorporating technologies.

Keywords: Lean Production · Industry 4.0 · Digitalization

1 Introduction

Manufacturing firms have embraced lean production during the last decades [1], recognizing its ability to improve various aspects of performance, such as waste reduction [2], setup time, lead time, employee satisfaction, engagement, communication, and decision-making [1, 3]. By implementing lean production principles, companies can gain advantages through cost reduction and increased customer satisfaction. However, with today's complex systems and massive data generation, new solutions are required to maximize the potential of information and communication technology. It is time to embrace the future and shift the focus to Industry 4.0. With the fourth industrial revolution upon us, several opportunities can be exploited.

Industry 4.0 leverages technologies to create intelligent processes to enable autonomous data collection, analysis, and internet-based interaction [3]. By integrating these technologies into their processes, companies can experience improvements

Published by Springer Nature Switzerland AG 2024
T. van Kollenburg et al. (Eds.): ELEC 2023, IFIP AICT 681, pp. 100–108, 2024.
https://doi.org/10.1007/978-3-031-63265-5_8

in flexibility, productivity, delivery time, cost efficiency, and product quality [4]. Integrating factory systems, sensors, and Internet of Things (IoT) devices, Industry 4.0 also facilitates the implementation of lean production practices and enhances their powerfulness. Thanks to digital technologies, tools such as Kanban or VSM can be digitalized, and activities such as waste detection or data collection can be automated and improved [5–7]. Industry 4.0 can also help solve the issues and barriers beyond implementing lean production [5, 21] and vice-versa [19, 22].

This means that Lean will survive in the Industry 4.0 paradigms, and more than that, integrating both domains will be fundamental to survive [20]. Literature acknowledges a significant interdependency between the two paradigms [4, 6, 8].

While lean production and Industry 4.0 are interdependent, there is still a need to understand how they complement each other. It is essential to explore how lean business practices can accelerate digital development and the adoption of Industry 4.0 technologies and how digital technologies support the effectiveness of these practices.

This paper significantly contributes to the theory and practice by analyzing one case study from a multinational company that uses both paradigms. The article starts with a thorough review of literature that delves into lean production and Industry 4.0. It then outlines the research methodology and describes the company under analysis. The article concludes by presenting and discussing the key findings, addressing any limitations encountered, and proposing some research directions for future studies.

2 Literature Review

2.1 Lean Production

Since competitive market dynamics are more complex, the organization's competitiveness has adjusted to supply and demand factors [9]. Businesses must identify consumers' value demands and utilize effective management and production strategies to improve their performance. Lean Production was a key organizational and entrepreneurial business revolution of the second half of the 20th century and continues to improve. At first, "The Machine That Changed the World" [10] exposed Western companies to "lean" and the Japanese industry's achievements, notably Toyota, the "cradle" of lean production. It "uses less of everything," including labour, time to create new products, stockpiles and waste. Lean Production encompasses different principles, such as the five defined by [10] – defining value, mapping the value stream, establishing flow, employing a pull system, and chasing perfection. Lean Production has also evolved over the years, being integrated with recent technologies and, in many sectors, different from manufacturing.

2.2 Industry 4.0

Industry 4.0 has many meanings [12], and since it was born in 2011 as the fourth industrial revolution, it has brought several innovative technologies to manufacturing firms' shop floors. Rüßmann et al. [13] and Culot et al. [14] identified nine technological "pillars" of Industry 4.0, which are autonomous robots, simulation, horizontal and vertical integration, IoT, cybersecurity, cloud, additive manufacturing, augmented reality, big data, and analytics are emerging technologies. When implemented properly, these technologies can substantially benefit firms' performance. Shafiq et al. [15] note Industry 4.0's growing complexity and potential. They highlight the ability to provide unique industry-specific solutions and customize products to meet customers' needs, even in low production volumes. Nevertheless, implementing these technologies to exploit their benefits is not easy, especially when they must be implemented in a non-standardized environment [22]. Many firms are trying to merge this paradigm with existing managerial ones, such as Lean management [20, 22].

2.3 Linking Industry 4.0 and Lean Manufacturing

Mrugalska and Wyrwicka [11] say Lean Production and Industry 4.0 can work together. Sanders et al. [4] claim that Industry 4.0 can help companies overcome lean implementation barriers. Despite lean management's popularity, few studies have examined its relationship with Industry 4.0 [16]. This relationship is dual, meaning that Lean can facilitate the implementation of digital technologies, but also digital technologies can boost Lean practices. On one hand, Sanders et al. [4] suggest more research to understand this link and how it affects operational effectiveness. On the other hand, a literature review found that Lean Production is still difficult to implement in many firms [17]. Some studies suggested that Digital technologies can help fix this [17, 21].

Knowing all these facts makes it clear how Lean Production and Industry 4.0 play an interconnected role and can help companies improve their performance and cope with the changing market conditions. Nevertheless, there is still a lack at an operative level in understanding how practically Lean Production can be supported by digital technologies and vice-versa, thus meaning how these two domains can be integrated to obtain the most from the two and the benefits of doing that.

3 Methodology

To properly answer the research question and fill the highlighted gap, the authors decided to use the case study methodology, given the qualitative dimension of the study. The authors decided to use a single case study approach, an empirical investigation that examines a contemporary phenomenon in depth and its real context [18]. With this methodology, the authors analyzed a multinational company operating in italy and working in the renewable energy field, which extensively used Lean Production and Industry 4.0. Our research methodology included interviews and direct observation to collect data and structure our findings.

3.1 Digital Lean Program

The company implemented Lean Production several years ago and was crucial in turning its fortunes around. The company uses lean manufacturing principles for Safety, Quality, Delivery, and Cost (SQDC), achieving significant success through waste reduction and pull-based production. The company started integrating their lean production program with the most recent digital technologies in recent years. In that way, the company enhanced the performance of both paradigms even more. However, strong support was needed for the company to manage this new concept. With this aim, the company decided to support this integration with two main software, which could support them in this transition and after, but also exploit the benefits of both Lean Production and Industry 4.0 technologies. The two software will be described below.

Lean Suite. The company has developed the lean suite to digitalize conventional lean production tools. The Lean Suite software enables remote administration, generates reports, and facilitates collaboration among different departments within the company. It encompasses six essential functions that bolster production site operations: eAndon, TAKT, Practice Sharing, Factory 360, OS, and Ideas.

eAndon. Andon is a visual alert tool used in lean manufacturing to identify and address potential problems immediately. It reduces defects and downtime, improves transparency and product quality, and empowers the workforce. Eandon offers real-time alerts, notifications, and customizable sla groups for safety, productivity, efficiency, and minimal downtime. Users can define and edit alert types, add alarm sounds, and manage open alerts through the dashboard menu.

TAKT. Users can view an overview of selected lines and stations, identifying issues and comparing progress to the target. The view shows completed units, demand, and progress. There is also a weekly summary and colour-coded stations, and it is possible to highlight specific data related to selected lines or machines.

Practice Sharing. Sharing best practices is vital for organizational success. It enables knowledge exchange, enhances efficiency, and fosters leadership. Successful sharing requires a collaborative culture, effective communication, absorptive capacity for change, and a history of sharing successes. This part of the suite provides real-time best practices sharing for the users, keeping track of the historical changes. The benefits include a learning environment, talent attraction, better strategies, increased productivity, innovation, faster decision-making, time optimization, a supportive community, a knowledge base, reduced knowledge loss, and cost savings.

Factory360. This part is an app that allows creating and managing dashboards with data from different sources. It is possible to customize the layout using a drag-and-drop feature. It also allows creating and managing reports by choosing from sources like eAndon or any company cloud storage system.

OS. The OS supports establishing a common operating framework across manufacturing sites. Moreover, it enables visual management of key cell and plant metrics, captures historical data for trends, and provides a framework for operators' engagement and continuous improvement. Using this, the teams can improve on-time delivery, cycle time, and COQ. The system includes a control centre, status card, 5S audit schedule, and issue creation.

Ideas. Ideas lets all-suite users share interesting ideas to improve the business continuously. Users pick from categories like cost, quality and safety; they submit their ideas, which are then evaluated and scored by other members. If the desired score is reached, the idea can be standardized and sent to the Practice Sharing function to be shared among all the plants and, in case of success, to other plants.

Virtual Management Software. The company also has real-time software for the virtual and visual management of the factory. This software's name is Virtual Management Software, which helps industrial manufacturing areas improve connectivity, data enrichment, analytics and legacy assets. It captures, analyzes, and visualizes data to increase productivity and profitability. Virtual Management Software uses standardized protocols to connect to devices and software, identifying areas for targeted interventions to improve efficiency. It evaluates device efficiency and productivity, detecting production, standby, setup, downtime, and shutdown based on device events. Virtual Management Software categorizes device downtime by device profile, identifying standby devices ready to make parts and plant-wide or device-specific shutdowns. It is divided into five main bundles.

Dashboards. Real-time dashboards make monitoring production events and disruptions easier. They offer an overview of equipment utilization, part production, workforce productivity, and asset health. Assessing downtime and process parameter anomalies is crucial for effective production planning and identifying potential issues.

Alerts. Virtual Management Software alerts stakeholders when process parameters exceed limits, allowing for swift action and performance control. Alerts can be customized for maintenance, MES (Manufacturing Execution System), and operators based on device data or calculated metrics. Trigger alerts include device idle time, machine tool failure, emergency stops, feed rate override changes, and excessive spindle loads.

Operator Panel. Operator Panels on the shop floor improve employee communication and engagement. They allow access to automatic and manual cycles, a digital logbook for troubleshooting, and the ability to input part information and log machine work.

Tickets. A ticketing system lets users report plant issues easily, leading to faster problem-solving. Teams are alerted via email based on rules the Virtual Management Software Administrator sets for prompt resolution.

Reports. Virtual Management Software uses AI and Machine learning-based analytics to optimize manufacturing efficiency. The customizable reports provide valuable insights on downtime, performance variations, waste elimination, and OEE metrics for benchmarking.

4 Results and Discussion

After having seen the detailed description of the digitalized Lean program, the benefits of this are presented here. The results after the interviews with key personnel, including assembly operators, production supervisor, Lean leader, and quality manager.

4.1 Results

Digitalization Advantages
According to the respondents, digitization brings benefits across the board. It improves the foundation on which the firms' Lean program is built: identifying waste and problem-solving. In fact, thanks to these systems, the data quality has been significantly improved as the easiness of gathering them, thus leading to faster and more precise problem-solving and decision-making. Further, thanks to the shared platform, the data is reliable and easy to reach by everyone. Hence, everyone can be informed in real time about what is happening in the company. Also, the availability of these databases facilitates the sharing of information, thus leading to increased awareness and involvement. Furtherly, the management of the improvement projects, monitoring their progress and informing high-level managers about that becomes more straightforward and clear.

Lastly, from the interviews, it was clear how having a solid and long-lasting Lean Program was fundamental to managing the change brought by digitalization. In fact, the fundamental role of the Lean culture has been stressed as it favours teamwork and creates an environment more prone to change. In fact, engaging all project participants can be challenging, but it is still fundamental for a successful digitalization project. The ways in which the stakeholders could be involved vary from the hierarchical level in the company. For instance, it was clear that the Lean culture plays a huge role in involving operators by providing them with adequate training, explaining the benefits of digitalization and involving them. Furthermore, the study highlights the role of Lean Production in clarifying the strategies and benefits of digital improvement projects. Understanding these strategies and benefits becomes instrumental in engaging stakeholders, explaining methodologies, and involving top management, which are the other success factors in pursuing a digitalization project successfully.

Digitalization Challenges
While plant digitization offers advantages, it also faces challenges. User training and familiarization are key factors to consider since some operators unfamiliar with monitors and keyboards must learn to use digital tools. In this sense, relying on appropriate training becomes fundamental. If this is not carried out, there is a huge risk of detachment from operators, while through appropriate training, operators can be more involved than before and their empowerment, too. Also, from the respondents, it was clear that digitalization can be considered a change, as any improvement project. Thus, understanding the proper steps for introducing digital tools is crucial to effectively identifying and addressing potential issues. Thus, managers are critical in strategically evaluating, guiding, and promoting digitalization while managing a team.

They must also ensure proper software maintenance, launch, and long-term sustainability as dedicated people responsible for their management.

For successful implementation, managers must think long-term and convince operators of the benefits of the software; thus, their commitment becomes fundamental.

Lastly, a huge risk is getting "distance from the field", which is a risk that managers particularly stressed during the interviews. In fact, having instant and reliable information could lead people to forget the principle of "go and see"; thus, they could be discouraged from adopting this strategy and relying only on the collected data. In this sense, managers should spur people to keep this principle and use digital tools as a supportive tool, more than the only source of information to rely on.

4.2 Discussion

The integration of Lean and Digital tools has certainly created benefits for the company, and each other are strictly related since they boost the benefits of each other. On the one hand, the digitalization of the program magnifies some components of Lean's soft part, such as collaboration among supervisors, operators, or different departments.

On the other hand, leveraging Lean principles before digitalization is fundamental since it simplifies empowerment training, lowers barriers and creates an environment "ready to the change". Thus, integrating these two paradigms creates new opportunities and facilitates the management of production facilities.

Nevertheless, companies should be aware that, even with digitalization, there is the need to keep field observation, data collection, and analysis through Genchi Genbutsu. In fact, errors can occur without proper Gemba observation when relying on. Gaining a thorough understanding of the production site requires on-site observation to achieve a complete overview and fairly solve production problems.

Thus, this study confirms how digital technologies can help firms improve their Lean programs and boost the effectiveness of their tools [21]. However, it is also clear how being Lean before digitalizing is fundamental to coping with barriers and creating an environment ready for change [20, 22].

The findings also showed that when combined together, Lean and digital tools get the best out of each other, showing a high degree of synergy and improving the firm's capability even more.

Thus, combining Lean Production and digitalization enables organizations to improve processes more rapidly, achieve greater efficiency, and make data-driven decisions. In today's rapidly evolving business environment, adopting both approaches and leveraging their synergies is essential for success. However, addressing challenges such as user training, integration, and information overload is crucial. Managers are pivotal in guiding the digitalization process, supporting operators, and effectively communicating the benefits.

5 Conclusion and Limitations

This case study has shown how a multinational company have integrated its Lean program with digital technologies. The outcomes from this paper are many, some directly related to the technologies the company used while others related to the factors influencing a successful digital transformation project and the role of Lean in this process.

Firstly, the study uncovered intriguing insights into the business challenges of selecting digital software. Also, this study provided all the functionalities of each of the software, clearly showing how beneficial it is to have a suite where the company's Lean the program can be digitalized. Secondly, this case study delves into the interconnectedness of Lean Production and digitalization within a production site. The findings underscore the importance of educating workers about the benefits of digital systems, promoting stakeholder involvement, and leveraging lean methodologies to drive successful digitization efforts. Implementing a Lean system facilitates digital tools implementation through stakeholder empowerment, appropriate training, and top management involvement. Lean production also fosters collaboration across departments through horizontal communication, teamwork, and cooperation, thus facilitating cross-functional digitalization projects. Also, overcoming barriers to change is essential in digital transformation projects since digitalization can be seen as an improvement project where changes are needed, and Lean Production could play a fundamental role. Ultimately, the study highlights the compatibility between Lean Production and digital implementation, with the integration of digital tools being essential for improvement projects to exploit both paradigms and to bring firms' Lean programs to an improved level. This study has certain limitations that should be acknowledged. Firstly, the findings were derived from a single case study, which may introduce the influence of context-specific circumstances and limit generalizability, such as the company dimension. Nevertheless, these observations provide valuable insights that can guide further research. To enhance the robustness of the study's framework, it is recommended to conduct empirical testing using a larger sample size with additional case studies conducted in companies having different peculiarities. Further, this study only looked at one multinational manufacturing company, which can be facilitated to proceed as a first-mover towards innovative solutions. Thus, this solution's validity should also be investigated considering companies with other dimensions, such as small-medium enterprises.

References

1. Ciano, M.P., Pozzi, R., Rossi, T., Strozzi, F.: How IJPR has addressed 'lean': a literature review using bibliometric tools. Int. J. Prod. Res. **57**(15–16), 5284–5317 (2019). https://doi.org/10.1080/00207543.2019.1566667
2. Sancha, C., Wiengarten, F., Longoni, A., Pagell, M.: The moderating role of temporary work on the performance of lean manufacturing systems. Int. J. Prod. Res. **58**(14), 4285–4305 (2019). https://doi.org/10.1080/00207543.2019.1651458
3. Jasti, N.V.K., Kodali, R.: Lean production: literature review and trends. Int. J. Prod. Res. **53**(3), 867–885 (2014). https://doi.org/10.1080/00207543.2014.937508
4. Sanders, A., Elangeswaran, C., Wulfsberg, J.: Industry 4.0 implies lean manufacturing: research activities in industry 4.0 function as enablers for lean manufacturing. J. Ind. Eng. Manag. **9**(3), 811 (2016). https://doi.org/10.3926/jiem.1940
5. Kolberg, D., Zühlke, D.: Lean automation enabled by Industry 4.0 Technologies. IFAC-PapersOnLine **48**(3), 1870–1875 (2015). https://doi.org/10.1016/j.ifacol.2015.06.359
6. Buer, S.V., Strandhagen, J.O., Chan, F.T.S.: The link between Industry 4.0 and lean manufacturing: mapping current research and establishing a research agenda. Int. J. Prod. Res. **56**(8), 2924–2940 (2018). Available at: https://doi.org/10.1080/00207543.2018.1442945
7. Yin, Y., Stecke, K.E., Li, D.: The evolution of production systems from Industry 2.0 through Industry 4.0. Int. J. Prod. Res. **56**(1–2), 848–861 (2017). https://doi.org/10.1080/00207543.2017.1403664
8. Rossini, M., Costa, F., Tortorella, G.L., Portioli-Staudacher, A.: The interrelation between Industry 4.0 and lean production: an empirical study on European manufacturers. Int. J. Adv. Manuf. Technol. **102**(9–12), 3963–3976 (2019). https://doi.org/10.1007/s00170-019-03441-7

9. Alkhoraif, A., Rashid, H., McLaughlin, P.: Lean implementation in small and medium enterprises: literature review. Oper. Res. Perspect. **6**(100089) (2019). https://doi.org/10.1016/j.orp.2018.100089
10. Womack, J.P.: Lean Thinking: "Banish Waste And Create Wealth In Your Corporation", 1st edn, Hardcover. Productivity Press (1996)
11. Wyrwicka, K., Mrugalska, B.: Barriers to eliminating waste in production system. In: Proceedings of the 2015 (6th) International Conference on Engineering, Project, and Production Management (2015). https://doi.org/10.32738/ceppm.201509.0035
12. Moghaddam, M., Cadavid, M.N., Kenley, C.R., Deshmukh, A.V.: Reference architectures for smart manufacturing: a critical review. J. Manuf. Syst. **49**, 215–225 (2018). https://doi.org/10.1016/j.jmsy.2018.10.006
13. Rüßmann, M., et al.: Industry 4.0: The Future of Productivity and Growth in Manufacturing Industries April 09. Boston Consulting Group (2015). https://inovasyon.org/images/Haberler/bcgperspectives_Industry40_2015.pdf
14. Culot, G., Nassimbeni, G., Orzes, G., Sartor, M.: Behind the definition of Industry 4.0: analysis and open questions. Int. J. Prod. Econ. **226**, 107617 (2020). https://doi.org/10.1016/j.ijpe.2020.107617
15. Shafiq, S.I., Sanin, C., Szczerbicki, E., Toro, C.: Virtual engineering object/virtual engineering process: a specialized form of cyber physical system for Industrie 4.0. Proc. Comp. Sci. **60**, 1146–1155 (2015)
16. Nedjwa, E., Bertrand, R., Sassi Boudemagh, S.: Impacts of Industry 4.0 technologies on Lean management tools: a bibliometric analysis. Int. J. Interact. Des. Manuf. **16**(1), 135–150 (2022). https://doi.org/10.1007/s12008-021-00795-9
17. Cagnetti, C., Gallo, T., Silvestri, C., Ruggieri, A. (2021). Lean production and Industry 4.0: Strategy/management or technique/implementation? A systematic literature review. Procedia Computer Science, 180, 404–413. Available at: https://doi.org/10.1016/j.procs.2021.01.256
18. Yin, R.K.: Case Study Research Design and Methods, 5th edn. Sage, Thousand Oaks, CA. Can. J. Prog. Eval. (2014). https://doi.org/10.3138/cjpe.30.1.108
19. Frecassetti, S., Presciuttini, A., Rossini, M., Portioli-Staudacher, A.: Lean and digital strategy role in achieving a successful digital transformation. In: Alfnes, E., Romsdal, A., Strandhagen, J.O., von Cieminski, G., Romero, D. (eds) Advances in Production Management Systems (2023)
20. Ghobakhloo, M., Fathi, M.: Corporate survival in Industry 4.0 era: the enabling role of lean-digitized manufacturing. J. Manuf. Technol. Manag. **31**(1), 1–30 (2020). https://doi.org/10.1108/JMTM-11-2018-0417
21. Frecassetti, S., Kassem, B., Kundu, K., Ferrazzi, M., Staudacher, A.P.: Introducing Lean practices through simulation: a case study in an Italian SME. Qual. Manag. J. **30**(2), 90–104 (2023)
22. Frecassetti, S., Ferrazzi, M., Portioli-Staudacher, A.: Lean as a facilitator for AGVs implementation: a case study. In: McDermott, O., Rosa, A., Sá, J.C., Toner, A. (eds) Lean, Green and Sustainability (2023)

Lean Planning & Control in a High-Variety/Low-Volume Environment

Jannes Slomp[1(✉)] and Jatinder N. D. Gupta[2]

[1] HAN University of Applied Sciences, Arnhem, The Netherlands
jannes.slomp@han.nl
[2] University of Alabama in Huntsville, Huntsville, AL, USA
guptaj@uah.edu

Abstract. This paper illustrates the need for a systematic methodology in the design of a lean planning & control system in flexible automated high-variety/low-volume environments. The paper presents a bottom-up methodology building on the work of Bertrand, Wortmann and Wijngaard (1990). A case is presented to illustrate the need to carefully divide planning tasks among planning and work floor level. Visualization tools as well as smart algorithms and a digital twin concept might be helpful to cope with the complexities of flexible automated manufacturing systems. The extended methodology has to be added to the lean toolbox: the complexity and opportunities of new technologies and digital tools necessitates this extension.

1 Introduction

Many companies make nowadays use of Flexible Manufacturing Cells. A typical FMC consists of one or few automated machining centers connected by means of a pallet transportation system and, sometimes, served by a common tool magazine, next to the tool magazines at each machining center. A pallet pool serves as a buffer between the load/unload station(s) and the machining center. The pallet pool also enables unpersonned periods. This type of cells, as well as other Flexible Manufacturing Systems, enables high quality, efficient manufacturing in a high-mix/low-volume environment.

Unfortunately, the benefits of a flexible manufacturing cell are accompanied by additional complexities for planning, scheduling and controlling orders on the cell. Constraints on fixturing resources, the size of tool magazines and the absence of operators on an unpersonned shift require intelligence in job allocation and timing. Several authors in scientific papers have developed advanced algorithms and methods, but these solutions usually solve only part of the complexity and leaves practice with often too general, too simple, and not-appropriate solutions of software providers. Many manufacturing companies struggle with their planning, scheduling and control system.

Slomp and Gupta (1992) describe an interactive tool to be used in scheduling orders on an FMC. They also indicate how the tool fits in the company's planning hierarchy. The tool and the planning hierarchy have been used in the company for several years. Yet there were some limitations: the possibility of manufacturing in an unpersonned

Published by Springer Nature Switzerland AG 2024
T. van Kollenburg et al. (Eds.): ELEC 2023, IFIP AICT 681, pp. 109–117, 2024.
https://doi.org/10.1007/978-3-031-63265-5_9

period was not included the scheduling methodology. Furthermore, the interactive tool relied on the users' knowledge and experience with the orders on the FMC. They had to decide for a sequence of jobs on the machines. The tool only visualized and explored the feasibility of the outcomes. In case of unfeasibility, the user had to create another sequence. This paper shows how the shortcomings of the scheduling methodology can be remedied, using lean principles and current digital capabilities. Moreover, this paper indicates how the FMC can be integrated in the planning & control of a manufacturing company.

This paper is organized as follows. In Sect. 2, we shortly describe a general bottom-up methodology for developing a planning & control system for a manufacturing department. We will emphasize the importance of specifying relatively autonomous production units within the manufacturing department. In the following sections, we apply the methodology for a manufacturing situation with Flexible Manufacturing Cells. Section 3 describes a typical Flexible Manufacturing Cell and the complexities which have to be considered in a planning & control system. Section 4 concerns the design of the planning & control hierarchy, following the steps of the methodology. Useful tools and algorithms are described in Sect. 5. We will show how the decision tool developed by Slomp and Gupta (1992) serves the workfloor and how a digital twin concept may support planning & control. Section 6 concerns the conclusions of this study.

2 A Bottom-Up Methodology for Developing a Planning, Scheduling and Control System

A proper design of a planning, scheduling and control system is crucial to gain an effective and efficient manufacturing department. This section presents shortly a design-oriented approach for developing such a system. The proposed methodology comes from the work of Bertrand et al. (1990). A case study where this methodology is used is presented by Slomp and Ruel (2001). They also indicate how sociotechnical principles play a role in using the methodology. We will use the methodology in this paper to clarify choices for the integration of the FMC in a manufacturing department and in the planning, scheduling and control system of a company.

Figure 1 gives a schematic overview of the approach. First, operations are defined based on the company's means of production. These operations can be regarded as the smallest possible units in a manufacturing department which can be controlled independently. In practice an operation comprises a group of processes which each having little autonomy with respect to the moment of release. The processes of an operation are carried out in a fixed, logical sequence. An assembly line, for example, can be seen as an operation. The next step is to identify those stages in the goods flow requiring central control. At this point the so-called Goods Flow Controlled (GFC) items are established; these involve the materials, half-products, and end-products that are generated during the goods flow and need to be controlled by the central production control, or planning department in order to create controllability at the work floor. Deviations from scheduled times and quantities of GFC-items will have an impact on the whole goods flow and can only be dealt with at the central production control level. Elements which determine the selection of GFC-items are, for instance, fluctuations and uncertainty in demand and supply of items, the product structure (i.e. the need of having all components present before assembly can start), and presence of capacity bottlenecks.

In the next step, production units (PU) are specified. The PUs are defined in such a way that they are relatively independent of each other in the short term and responsible for the production of a specific set of half-products/end products. A PU can be regarded as a set of operations. Ideally, GFC-items determine the boundaries of the production units (PUs).

After this, the operational characteristics of the PUs need to be carefully defined, first in qualitative terms. In general four operational characteristics can be distinguished: (i) batch quantity constraints; (ii) sequence constraints; (iii) workload constraints; and (iv) capacity constraints. The quantification of these characteristics determines which lead times of jobs can be realized on each PU. These lead times are an important input for the planning & control (ERP) system of the company. In most cases, customers ask for short lead times.

The planning & control system consists of a decision hierarchy which determines what has to be decided in which sequence (e.g. aggregate production planning, workload control, material coordination and work order release), an organization hierarchy which determines who will take the decisions, and the information flow and decision support tools.

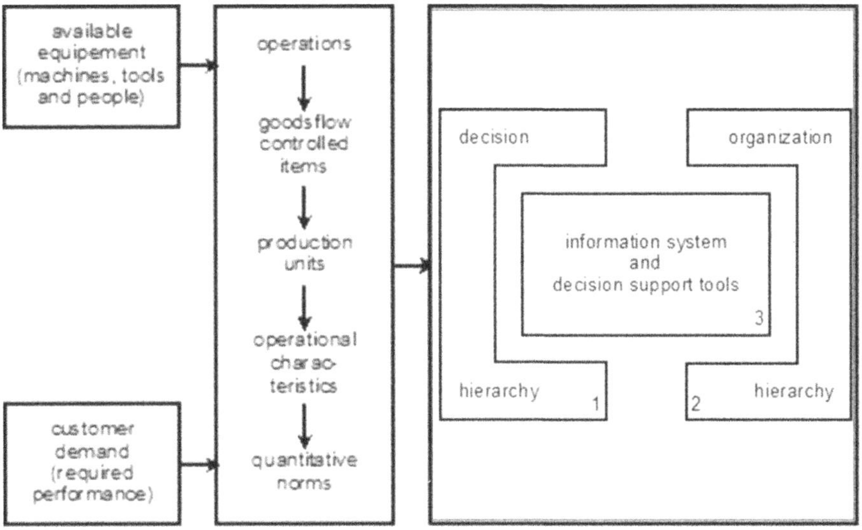

Fig. 1. Bottom-up methodology for developing a planning, scheduling and control system for manufacturing departments.

3 A Typical Manufacturing Cell (FMC)

Many companies make use of Flexible Manufacturing Cells in their manufacturing Department. A typical cell is depicted in Fig. 2. This cell consists of two identical machining centers (M1 and M2) linked together with an automatic material handling system. A pallet pool, which has a limited capacity (eight pallets, in the case of Fig. 2), is integrated with the material handling system. Each of the two machines can house a maximum of tools in the tool magazine (T). The changing of tools in the tool magazines is done manually, as is the clamping and unclamping of the components on the pallets. Two load/unload stations (L/U) are integrated in the system. Jobs, released to the cell, may vary with respect to lot sizes, processing times and required cutting tools and fixtures (to hold parts on pallets).

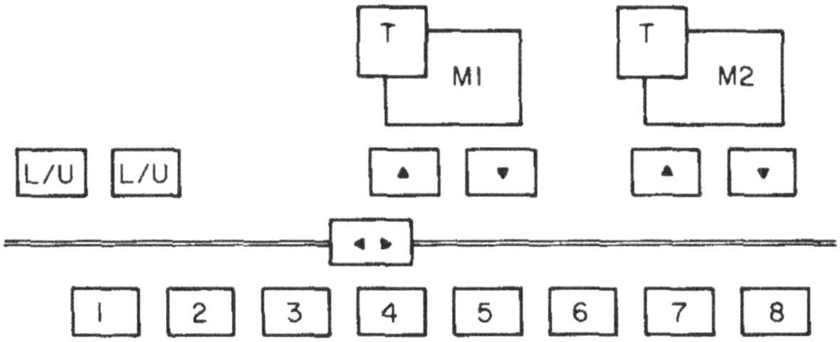

Fig. 2. Schematic presentation of a small Flexible Manufacturing Cell

A typical Flexible Manufacturing Cell is able to manufacture different product types in a random sequence without loss of production time (if it is operated properly, see below). The number of different product types that can be produced on the FMC depends on the available cutting tools, fixtures and machining programs. A product-type may require more than one operation on the FMC for which re-fixturing is needed.

Before manufacturing of a job can start on an FMC, an operator has to prepare the required pallet(s)/fixture(s), load the tool magazines with the appropriate tools (if they are not yet in the tool magazine), and instruct the FMC-computer. After this, one or more items of a job can be clamped on a pallet/fixture. This is done at a load/unload station. The automated material handling system transports the palletized items either to the pallet pool or directly to a machining center. After machining, the automated material handling system transports the palletized items either to the pallet pool or directly to a load/unload station. On this load/unload station the items are replaced by new items (of the same job). The refilled pallet/fixture continues its way through the system. The items on which an operation is performed may wait for their next operation.

In many practical cases, work in the manufacturing department is done in two manned shifts with a partial third unmanned shift (for the FMC). The size of the pallet pool limits the realizable production time in the unmanned shift.

Several aspects complicate the scheduling of operations on the FMC:

- Each operation of a job is assigned to just one pallet/fixture. All the products of the job need this pallet/fixture. To avoid idle time of the machining centers, caused by the time needed for unclamping and clamping of a pallet, operations are processed in an operation-mix on each of the machines.
- To avoid tool changes during the processing of a mix of operations, it is desirable that the number of cutting tools needed for a mix is less than or equal to the capacity of the tool magazine.
- A unique cutting tool cannot be used simultaneously on both machining centers.
- A unique fixture cannot be used simultaneously for more than one job.
- To utilize the unmanned shift as much as possible, it is desirable to have enough operations (at least eight!) to fill the pallet pool. As far as possible, operations with long processing times should be assigned to the unmanned shift.
- Operations to be processed by this FMS should be scheduled in such a manner that preceding and succeeding operations can be done within the time assigned by planning system.

4 Towards a Planning and Control Hierarchy

This section describes the considerations which lead to a specification of a planning and control hierarchy to be used for a manufacturing department which applies a Flexible Manufacturing Cell. The considerations are organized according the methodology presented in Sect. 2 of this paper.

In the first step of the methodology, operations are specified. Because of the integration of the elements in the system, we consider the FMC as one operation. The machines are integrated and do not need to be controlled separately from planning. In the second step of the methodology, the goods flow controlled (GFC) items must be specified. An expensive machine, like an FMC, is often a bottleneck in the goods flow of a company. To control the throughput times of products, or orders, it is important to carefully perform the planning of the items in front of the FMC. Because of the complexity of the FMC (see Sect. 3), it may even be wise to perform scheduling of products/orders on the FMC at the planning level. The outcome of the scheduling helps operators to start production of products/orders on time, in the right mix. In doing the scheduling, the planning level has to assure that subsequent operations can also be carried out in a timely manner. The scheduling of the FMC, can be seen as a GFC-item. This means that the planning level is responsible for a correct loading of the FMC. The third step of the methodology concerns the specification of so-called Production Units (PUs). Ideally, GFC-items indicate boarders of the PUs. So, the FMC should be the boarder of a Production Unit, which is a semi-autonomous cell. This ensures that the planning department does not interfere with the organization within the whole cell. It may be that the PU consists of more machines than only the FMC (as has been the case in the company, see Fig. 3). A PU can be a completely independent cell as defined in Group Technology and Cellular Manufacturing (see e.g. Suresh and Kay, 1998). A PU can also be a POLCA-type of cell where jobs need to visit a number of cells (see e.g. Suri, 2018). In the fourth step of the methodology, the key planning characteristics of each PU are specified. Most characteristics of the FMC relate to the constraints mentioned in Sect. 3 of this paper. Important characteristics concern:

a) The output uncertainty because of the dependency of this output on the particular products to be produced during the night and the fluctuating status at the end of the working day, i.e. which products are still running at the end of the day and for how long.
b) The fact that products to be produced in the unpersonned night shift need their own fixtures/pallets to be loaded before the night shift starts.
c) Working in an operation-mix increases the throughput time of jobs on the FMC.
d) The constraints with respect to cutting tools, tool magazines and fixtures (see Sect. 3)
e) Most jobs to be performed on the FMC need subsequent processes on other work centers.

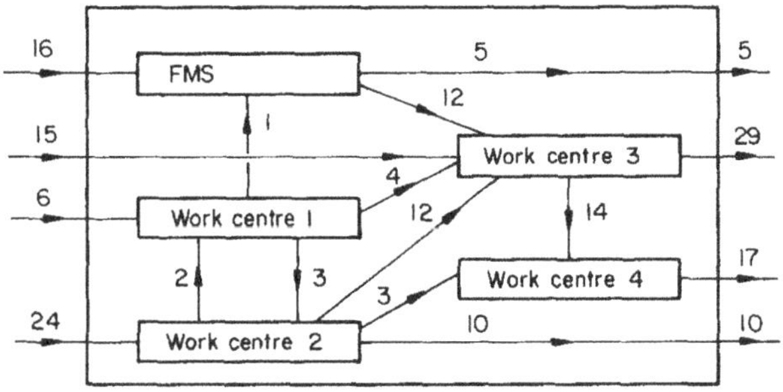

Fig. 3. Schematic representation of the PU in which the FMC (FMS) is the bottleneck (the number indicate the number of product types in the goods flow of the cell)

In the fifth step, quantitative norms have to be set as an input for the planning & control system, which is in most cases an MRP/ERP system. Based upon the required demand of the customers and the operational characteristics of the PU, some key decisions have to be made:

1. The lead times of the products/jobs entering the production unit and the capacity (output per period) which can be realized by the FMC and the PU. Related to this, also batch sizes of the products/jobs have to be set.
2. Which products will be manufactured in the unmanned night shift. Ideally, products with long processing times are selected for the night shift. These products are ideally make-to-stock products. The products in the unmanned night shift do not need to be produced batch wise.
3. Which criticality with respect to tools and fixtures are acceptable in order to realize the lead time targets by the autonomous PU? Either the limitations can be dealt with by the planning and scheduling tools, or additional tools and/or fixtures need to be purchased and integrated in the system to relax the various constraints.

The sixth step of the methodology concerns the integration of these decisions in the planning & control decision hierarchy. For this purpose, most companies apply an MRP/ERP system. We will not discuss this integration in this paper.

In the next section, we will present some tools which can be used in setting quantitative norms to be used in the planning & control system. These tools can also be used in the daily tasks of planners and operators.

5 Tools and Algorithms

This section describes shortly three main tools which can be used in the planning & control system of our case company. It is likely that the tools can be used in more situations. The first tool concerns a visualization tool which presents the scheduling of jobs/products to be produced on the FMC. This tool can be used at the planning level. The second tool concerns the suggestion to apply a sequencing algorithm, in combination with a simulation of the FMC. This tool helps the planner to make a good schedule of jobs on the FMC. This tool also supports the setting of quantitative norms for the lead time of jobs on the FMC. The third tool concerns the selection of products for the unmanned shift. We suggest to select Make-to-Stock products with long processing times.

5.1 A Visualization Tool

The design of a useful interactive scheduling tool for the FMC is presented by Slomp and Gupta (1992). Figure 4 illustrates how the outcome of the scheduling can be presented in a clear way. It show, for instance, that day 4 starts with jobs I1 en I2 on machining center 1 and jobs B1 and B2 on machine center 2. Jobs B1 and B2 will be finished in day 5. The operators have to prepare the FMC (fixtures, tools) for producing C1 and C2 at the end of day 5. As described in the introduction of this paper, the planner can build the schedule in an interactive way. Feasibility can be easily checked by the scheduling system: e.g. it is not acceptable if the number of tools to be used by simultaneously produced jobs is more that the capacity of the tool magazine.

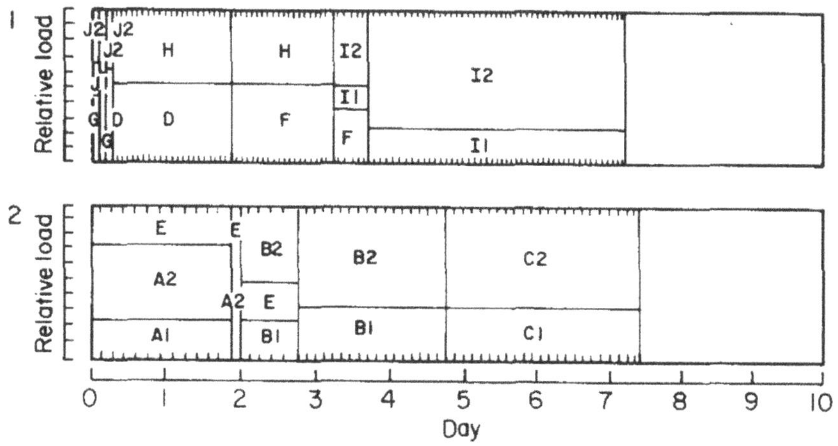

Fig. 4. Scheduling result.

5.2 Using an Algorithm and Discrete Simulation – Step Towards Digital Twin Control

It may be hard for a planner to make a good schedule, especially in case of several and severe constraints (see Sect. 3). A simple heuristic based on the NEH-sequencing heuristic (see Nawaz et al., 1983) can be applied to develop a schedule. The NEH heuristic can be easily adapted to a particular situation and is also a starting point for improvements (see e.g. Sauvey and Sauer, 2020). Discrete simulation can be used to calculate the performance after each iteration in the NEH algorithm. This simulation can be performed by means of standard simulation software. However, since these software packages are not easy available for many companies, it is our thought that the simulation can be easily programmed in Python or C++. Final outcomes can be visualized as described in Sect. 5.1.

A major advantage of using simulation concerns the future opportunity to implement Digital Twin Control. By automatically and continuously comparing the real and the planned situation of the FMC, real time decisions to alter the schedule can be made in case of a deviation which frustrates the performance of the planned sequence. See Wang and Wu, 2020.

5.3 Selecting Products for the Unpersonned Shift

Flexible manufacturing cells are often able to produce some hours in an unpersonned shift. A careful selection of products to be produced during the unpersonned shift may increase the utilization of the manufacturing cell substantially. It is important to select products with long processing times which also do not ask for a substantial number of tool changes. We suggest the planning level to create a set of Make-to-Stock products which can be made in the unpersonned shift. The product to be produced in the unpersonned shift may differ each day because of the different mixes of jobs at the end of the personned shifts and, therefore, the presence of different cutting tools in the tool magazine. Selecting, the products which can be produced on a machining center without the need of intermediate tool changes can probably be done manually. Otherwise, a heuristic algorithm may be developed. A more advanced methodology for using the unpersonned shift as good as possible, while also minimizing the need to perform many tool changes during day shift (at beginning and end of day shifts), is presented by Slomp and Stecke (2012).

6 Conclusion

Planning, scheduling and control is a challenge for many manufacturing companies. Their flexible automated machines enable high quality and efficient processes. They take care of short lead times because of the integration of several manufacturing steps. However, several constraints and characteristics of the flexible machinery ask for a careful design of the planning & control system. Also new digital options for planning & control, e.g. digital twin control, need to be considered to realize a better performance of a manufacturing department.

The case presented in this paper intends to make clear that a more structural approach to planning & control issues need to be added to the lean toolbox. The methodology of Bertrand et al. (1990) offers a good starting point because of its bottom-up (gemba) approach. Visualization issues and the opportunities presented by new digital capabilities should also be considered to become part of the lean toolbox.

References

Bertrand, J.W.M., Wortmann, J.C., Wijngaard, J.: Production Control, a Structural and Design Oriented Approach. Elsevier, Amsterdam (1990)

Nawaz, M., Enscore, E.E.J., Ham, I.: A heuristic algorithm for the m-machine, n-job flowshop sequencing problem. OmegaInt. J. Manag. Sci. **11**, 91–95 (1983)

Sauvey, C., Sauer, N.: Two NEH heuristic improvements for flowshop scheduling problem with makespan criterion. Algorithms. **13**(5), 112 (2020)

Slomp, J., Gupta, J.N.D.: Interactive tool for scheduling jobs in a flexible manufacturing environment". Computer-Integrated Manufacturing Systems **5**(4), 291–299 (1992)

Slomp, J., Ruel, G.C.: A Socio-Technical Approach for the Design of a Production Control System: Towards Controllable Production Units, Chapter 18 in: Human Performance in Planning and Scheduling: Fieldwork Studies, Edited by B.L. MacCarthy and J.R. Wilson, Taylor & Francis, London and New York, pp. 383–409 (2001)

Slomp, J., Stecke, K.E.: Changes in Production Control Required for Untended Operation of a Flexible Manufacturing Cell. Production Planning & Control **23**(9), 674–693 (2012)

Suresh, N.C., Kay, J.M.: Group technology and cellular manufacturing. Springer (1998)

Suri, R.: The Practitioner's Guide to POLCA. CRC Press, New York (2018)

Wang, Y., Wu, Z.: Model construction of planning and scheduling system based on digital twin. The Inter national Journal of Advanced Manufacturing Technology **109**, 2189–2203 (2020)

Sustainability

Sustainability Struggles: Investigating the Interactions of Lean Practices and Barriers to Environmental Performance in Manufacturing

Matteo Ferrazzi(✉), Stefano Frecassetti, and Alberto Portioli-Staudacher

Department of Management, Economics and Industrial Engineering, Politecnico di Milano, Milan, Italy
matteo.ferrazzi@polimi.it

Abstract. Nowadays, companies are struggling to improve their environmental impact. In this sense, using Lean Manufacturing practices helps companies have a reduced environmental impact, thus leading to improved environmental performance. However, having this improvement takes a lot of work, and the journey is long and full of hurdles. The goal of this paper is to identify the barriers that hamper the improvement of environmental performance and which are the Lean Manufacturing practices which help companies reach an enhanced level of environmental performance. Through two systematic literature reviews, this paper aims to highlight both barriers and practices and provides future research directions.

Keywords: Lean · Sustainability · Green · Barriers · Manufacturing

1 Theoretical Background

1.1 Introduction

In recent years, sustainability has evolved into a fundamental imperative within business. Companies must seamlessly integrate sustainable practices into their operations to survive and thrive in the contemporary competitive landscape. This entails the timely delivery of products and services at competitive prices, all while delivering value to customers without causing harm to the environment. This imperative is especially pronounced for manufacturing companies, as they are responsible for minimizing their ecological footprint. Embracing sustainability allows them to reduce their environmental impact, enhance operational efficiency, and bolster long-term profitability. Facing this challenge, Lean Management positions itself as a catalyst for achieving a heightened level of sustainability [65,67]. Its growing prominence is due to its ability to tackle challenges and improve environmental performance. The current literature shows evidence of how a Lean approach can help manufacturing firms address environmental performance issues [65–67].

Published by Springer Nature Switzerland AG 2024
T. van Kollenburg et al. (Eds.): ELEC 2023, IFIP AICT 681, pp. 121–137, 2024.
https://doi.org/10.1007/978-3-031-63265-5_10

1.2 Current Manufacturing Firms' Issues

Manufacturing companies increasingly recognize the significance of attaining sustainability standards within their operations, given the inherent importance of reconciling economic growth with environmental stewardship to foster a more sustainable and equitable future [67]. Towards this end, numerous strategies and initiatives have been identified, including implementing waste management practices, promoting responsible sourcing, and strategically applying technology and innovation [68]. These measures are instrumental in propelling manufacturing companies towards their sustainability objectives. However, it is imperative to acknowledge and address the challenges accompanying these pursuits to realize the potential of sustainability in manufacturing fully. One of the foremost challenges [68] lies in the financial implications of embracing sustainable practices. Upgrading machinery, investing in renewable energy sources, and establishing waste management systems necessitate substantial financial commitments. Thus, companies must judiciously assess the balance between upfront costs and the potential long-term benefits and savings resulting from sustainable practices. A second noteworthy challenge pertains to the intricacies of global supply chains, especially in industries characterized by multiple tiers of suppliers. Ensuring sustainability throughout the entire supply chain can be intricate, requiring the establishment of clear expectations, regular audits, and extensive support to facilitate supplier compliance with sustainability standards. Furthermore, the need for more transparency within supply chains poses hurdles [72], impeding the verification of sustainability claims made by suppliers or the tracing of raw material origins. The availability and affordability of sustainable materials and technologies represent a third challenge. While progress has been made in developing eco-friendly materials and energy-efficient technologies, cost constraints or limited availability can hinder their widespread adoption. Additionally, resistance to change from stakeholders who prioritize short-term financial gains over long-term sustainability can present obstacles. This resistance may emanate from employees, shareholders, or customers who might need to be more amenable to paying a premium for sustainable products. Consistent and clear sustainability standards and regulations across regions and industries add complexity to the compliance landscape, necessitating companies to navigate varying requirements and align their sustainability efforts with global best practices [70,71]. One of the major hurdles is the complexity of their operations. Manufacturing processes involve multiple stages, machinery, and materials, making tracking and managing environmental impacts difficult. Companies often operate in highly competitive markets, where cost reduction and productivity take precedence over environmental concerns. Another challenge is the need for more awareness and understanding of environmental issues [70]. Many manufacturing companies may need to fully grasp the potential impact of their operations on the environment or the benefits of sustainable practices. This lack of awareness can hinder the implementation of environmentally friendly measures. Lastly, resistance to change and lack of employee engagement can impede improving environmental performance [69]. Employees may resist new practices or technologies due to fear of job displacement or unfamiliarity with the changes. Overcoming this resistance and fostering employee buy-in is crucial for successfully implementing sustainable practices. To address these challenges effectively, manufacturing companies can foster collaboration and partnerships with stakeholders. Investing in research and development can facilitate the advancement of sustainable solutions while advocating for stronger sustainability regulations and standards that promote uniformity and clarity across the industry. Significant opportunities and challenges mark the journey towards achieving sustainability standards in manufacturing. While implementing pertinent strategies and initiatives is crucial, it is equally vital to acknowledge, address, and surmount the obstacles hindering progress. Manufacturing companies can make substantial strides towards their sustainability objectives through concerted commitment, collaboration, and strategic investments, contributing to a more sustainable and resilient global economy.

1.3 Lean and Environmental Performance

Environmental performances encompass a comprehensive and systematic evaluation of an entity's environmental impact, entailing the measurement and quantification of diverse ecological parameters. This assessment seeks to elucidate how an organization's activities, products, or services contribute to environmental degradation or conservation [66]. By delving into the intricate web of interactions between human endeavours and the environment, environmental performances yield critical insights concerning the overall sustainability of an entity's operations. Through this analytical lens, the intricate ecological consequences of an entity's actions are elucidated, allowing for informed decision-making and a greater understanding of the ramifications of human activities on the environment. In recent decades, heightened awareness of the ramifications of human activities on the natural environment has underscored the significance of environmental performances as a pivotal concept in the pursuit of sustainability. As a response to these challenges, environmental performances have emerged as a comprehensive framework to evaluate, quantify, and manage the ecological impacts of diverse entities, aiming to foster a more sustainable and resilient future. Lean Production is recognized for its persistent goal of banishing waste from the industrial shop floors to service providers. Present-day challenges require highly productive and responsive production systems and sustainable ones that provide more value with lower environmental impacts. This must be achieved without raising the production costs, with no hidden external environmental consequences in the short and the long run, so that sustainability is genuinely pursued and truly accomplished [73]. Uncovering the synergetic relationship between the Lean and Sustainable approaches, normally [59], is an imperious endeavour. The literature is rich in publications on Lean, sustainability, and eco-efficiency. However, still, there needs to be a research gap in the literature on the synergy between Lean and environmental performances [60]. Lean management represents a methodical approach centred on waste elimination and process optimization to bolster efficiency and productivity within manufacturing companies. Its prominence has surged in recent years owing to its capacity to tackle an array of challenges these enterprises face, particularly in advancing their environmental performance.

1.4 Research Objective

The manufacturing industry plays a crucial role in the global economy but also faces mounting pressure to improve its environmental sustainability. Governments, communities, and businesses regard environmental degradation as one of the critical concerns of the contemporary world. Manufacturing industries contribute significantly to this serious global challenge [61]. Furthermore, as resources decrease and the problems associated with the environment increase, manufacturers of developing countries face considerable pressure from the rest of the world to promote sustainable alternatives integrated into manufacturing and subsequently enhance their environmental and economic performance [62]. As sustainability concerns grow, manufacturing companies encounter various barriers hindering their efforts to enhance sustainable performance. These barriers can range from different aspects, and they generally include organizational constraints, economic constraints, human-related constraints, economic constraints, environmental constraints, and technological constraints. Overcoming these barriers is essential for manufacturing companies to transition towards more sustainable practices successfully. In this context, lean management tools have emerged as a potential solution to mitigate these barriers and drive sustainable transformation in the manufacturing sector. Lean management practices offer a systematic approach to improving efficiency, eliminating waste, and fostering a culture of continuous improvement. However, the extent to which lean management tools can effectively mitigate the barriers manufacturing companies face in pursuing sustainable performance remains a topic of investigation. Therefore, it is crucial to explore and analyze the specific barriers that manufacturing companies face and investigate how lean management tools can be leveraged to overcome these barriers and drive sustainable transformation [63]. The primary objective of this research is to identify and examine the barriers that manufacturing companies face in improving their sustainable performance and to investigate how lean management tools can help mitigate these barriers. Mainly, the study aims to: - RQ1: Identify the key barriers that manufacturing companies face in their efforts to improve sustainability performances. - RQ2: Identify the lean practices that the manufacturing companies can use to mitigate barriers to improve environmental performance. In the following section, a literature review will be proposed to answer the research question. In particular, in the discussion section, the current literature will be critically analyzed to understand the barriers the manufacturing firms face when trying to improve their environmental performance and which is Lean's role in this sense.

2 Research Methodology

Two different literature reviews have been structured to answer the two research questions. The authors relied on a systematic literature review protocol, which is divided into three main parts, starting with the identification phase, where possible articles (records) identified in the selected database (s) are isolated into a smaller database; the screening phase, where those isolated records are filtered according to certain requirements in order to identify the last and final database to be used. The last phase includes the articles in the final pool of records.

2.1 Literature Search for RQ1

Starting with the RQ1, aiming to identify articles that include the challenges manufacturing companies face when they strive to improve their environmental performance. For the RQ1, a query containing keywords that can gather the complete significance and meaning of the question of research. The used words were "barriers", "sustainable manufacturing", and "challenges". All of them were used in the manufacturing context, as many companies from different sectors may also face barriers to improving their environmental performance. Moreover, included filters for the research were set to articles related to Engineering, Business Management and Accounting fields, as it is the closest area to the manufacturing Industry. Identified articles following the previous queue were screened according to the information they provided; this information is related to the barriers that manufacturing companies face, including a clear description of the context and possible conclusions of the mentioned barrier. The main reasons found to exclude reports in the screening part are the Industry of Application for the described barriers and the Description of the related barriers. The final list of papers analyzed for RQ1 is provided in Fig. 1.

2.2 Literature Search for RQ2

The next research question (RQ2) focused on lean management practices in the context of manufacturing companies trying to overcome the barriers to improve environmental performance. The focus is the how lean management applications are currently helping the companies address these challenges and how they use them to become more sustainable, so how lean management will mitigate potential barriers. The setting of the query parameters for the identification of articles included words such as "lean tools", which refers to the practices or techniques based on theory and application, "benefits", and "sustainability", focusing on Engineering and Business Management and Accounting with the language of origin fixed to English were some records were excluded due to misalignments with the content. After identifying the potential articles, they were screened according to the methodology's second step and analyzed to look for the articles that provided the information needed for the analysis. The main reason found to exclude reports in the screening part is the Description of the lean practice: some described practices in academic articles are just mentioned but need to be fully detailed. The final list of papers analyzed for RQ2 is provided in Fig. 2.

ID	Document Title	Authors	Year
1	Barriers to a sustainability transformation of meat production practices - An industry actor perspective.	[29]	2022
2	Analysis of Barriers to Green Manufacturing Using Hybrid Approach: An Investigatory Case Study on Indian Automotive Industry.	[30]	2021
3	Paving the way for a green transition through mitigation of green manufacturing challenges: A systematic literature review.	[31]	2022
4	Refocusing the barriers to sustainability for small and medium-sized manufacturers.	[32]	2022
5	Main challenges involved in the adoption of sustainable manufacturing in Uruguayan small and medium sized companies.	[33]	2021
6	Enablers for Improving Environmental Performance of Manufacturing Operations.	[34]	2019
7	Analyzing the barriers to green apparel manufacturing implementation.	[35]	2023
8	Analyse the Critical Success Factor of Green Manufacturing for Achieving Sustainability in Automotive Sector.	[36]	2022
9	Green Supply Chain Management practices and impact on firm performance: The moderating effect of collaborative capability.	[37]	2021
10	Analysis of Industry 4.0 and circular economy enablers: A step towards resilient sustainable operations management.	[38]	2021
11	Analysing the Barriers for Implementation of Lean-led Sustainable Manufacturing and Potential of Blockchain Technology to Overcome these Barriers: A Conceptual Framework.	[39]	2022
12	Critical success factors-based strategy to facilitate green manufacturing for responsible business: An application experience in Indian context	[40]	2022
13	Assessment of Drivers and Barriers of Green Manufacturing Practices in Indian Manufacturing Companies	[41]	2023
14	The adoption of operational environmental sustainability approaches in the Thai manufacturing sector	[42]	2019
15	A new way of environmentally sustainable manufacturing with assessing transformation through the green deployment of Lean Six Sigma projects	[43]	2022
16	Total Quality Environmental Management: Adoption Status in the Chinese Manufacturing Sector	[44]	2017
17	Assessment of the current state of sustainability in a manufacturing firm.	[45]	2021
18	Organizational barriers to the sustainable manufacturing system: A literature review	[46]	2022
19	Developing a framework for adopting environmental manufacturing practices: learning from breweries.	[47]	2022
20	Prioritization of sustainable manufacturing barriers using Best Worst Method.	[48]	2019
21	Remanufacture for sustainability: Barriers and solutions to promote automotive remanufacturing.	[49]	2020
22	Enablers and Barriers of Sustainable Manufacturing: Results from a Survey of Researchers and Industry Professionals.	[50]	2015
23	Green quality circle: Achieving sustainable manufacturing with low investment.	[51]	2022
24	Barriers Analysis for Reverse Logistics Implementation in Indian Electronics Industry using Fuzzy Analytic Hierarchy Process.	[52]	2015
25	Prioritizing drivers for green manufacturing: Environmental, social and economic perspectives.	[53]	2014
26	Lean-Green models for eco-efficient and sustainable production.	[54]	2017
27	An investigation on lean-green implementation practices in Indian SMEs using analytical hierarchy process (AHP) approach	[55]	2016
28	Two-way assessment of barriers to Lean–Green Manufacturing System: insights from India	[56]	2016
29	Development of a model of barriers to environmentally conscious manufacturing implementation	[57]	2014
30	Drivers and barriers analysis for green manufacturing practices in Malaysian SMEs: A preliminary findings	[58]	2020

Fig. 1. Literature Search for RQ1

ID	Document Title	Authors	Year
1	Sustainable manufacturing-greening processes using specific Lean Production tools: an empirical observation from European motorcycle component manufacturers.	[1]	2014
2	Lean production systems, social sustainability performance and green competitiveness: the mediating roles of green technology adoption and green product innovation.	[2]	2021
3	Exploring the role of lean thinking in sustainable business practice: A systematic literature review.	[3]	2017
4	Managing construction and demolition waste using lean tools to achieve environmental sustainability: an Indian perspective.	[4]	2023
5	Implementation of green, lean and six sigma operations for sustainable manufacturing. A Review.	[5]	2022
6	Lean Implementation Framework: A Case of Performance Improvement of Casting Process.	[6]	2022
7	Relationship between lean manufacturing tools and their sustainable economic benefits.	[7]	2022
8	The relationship between lean and environmental performance: Practices and measures.	[8]	2019
9	Lean/Green integration focused on waste reduction techniques.	[9]	2016
10	The integration of lean manufacturing, Six Sigma and sustainability: A literature review and future research directions for developing a specific model.	[10]	2016
11	Lean and green combine to impact environmental and operational performance.	[11]	2018
12	Sustainable manufacturing: Exploring antecedents and influence of Total Productive Maintenance and lean manufacturing.	[12]	2019
13	Impact of Lean Manufacturing Practices on Firms' Sustainable Performance: Lean Culture as a Moderator.	[13]	2019
14	Lean manufacturing practices, ISO 14001, and environmental performance in Malaysian automotive suppliers.	[14]	2017
15	Lean practices and their effect on performance: a literature review.	[15]	2016
16	Operational practices of lean manufacturing: Potentiating environmental improvements.	[16]	2017
17	Evaluating the impact of lean practices on environmental performance: evidence from five manufacturing companies.	[17]	2020
18	The effect of lean methods and tools on the environmental performance of manufacturing organizations.	[18]	2018
19	Toolkit for simultaneously improving production and environmental efficiencies.	[19]	2021
20	Applying lean tools and principles to reduce cost of waste management: An empirical research in Vietnam.	[20]	2019
21	DMAIC-based approach to sustainable value stream mapping: towards a sustainable manufacturing system.	[21]	2020
22	Cleaner production implementation in an E-Waste recovery plant by using the Value Stream Mapping.	[22]	2018
23	Integration of lean and green supply chain - Impact on manufacturing firms in improving environmental efficiencies.	[23]	2011
24	A case study of lean, sustainable manufacturing.	[24]	2010
25	Evaluating Environmental Impacts of Construction Operation Before and After the Implementation of Lean Tools.	[25]	2016
26	Lean Manufacturing Benefits in a Pharmaceutical Production Plant.	[26]	2014
27	Review the influence of Lean tools and its performance against the index of manufacturing sustainability.	[27]	2015
28	An integrated lean and green approach for improving sustainability performance: a case study of a packaging manufacturing SME in the U.K.	[28]	2019

Fig. 2. Literature Search for RQ2

3 Findings and Discussion

3.1 RQ1

Based on the final set of articles gathered after performing the research methodology, an analysis and identification of the challenges that manufacturing companies encounter while enhancing their environmental performance. Every barrier found in the literature was systematically allocated to a specific macro category. The ultimate categories identified are as follows: Organizational and Managerial, Financial and Economic, Governmental, Environmental, Social and Human Resource, Technological and Informational.

1. Organizational and Managerial
   The Organizational and Managerial macro category mainly indicates the flow of information, awareness regarding the inclusion of sustainability in manufacturing operations, and the general management in industries. The microcategories involve competencies that are developed and retained, competence, culture, hierarchical structure, and support, which link to organizational design, work systems, and reward systems.
2. Financial and Economic
   This macro category delineates economic challenges, encompassing funding challenges and the prevailing association of concessional outcomes with sustainability investments. This linkage is frequently exacerbated by deficient decision criteria, exemplified by indicators like payback period and the need for more engagement of stakeholders well-versed in comprehending environmental opportunity costs, such as utility managers. Moreover, the Financial and Economic considerations domain extends to encompass facets encompassing financial risk and potential economic outcomes. These factors are of great importance to the attention of manufacturing enterprises to ensure competitiveness within the market landscape while simultaneously delivering value to their shareholders.
3. Governmental
   The governmental category refers to the absence of governmental protection, which could be seen as a lack of protection and instructions provided by the legislative authorities. Furthermore, this encompasses an insufficiency of industrial self-regulation mechanisms pertinent to applying sustainable practices within the Manufacturing Industry. This domain is further characterized by needing more clarity in formulating specific legislation, regulations, and policies related to various aspects, such as Green Practices and Manufacturing goods. The government's supportive role is also a constituent of this macro category, encapsulating provisions like the availability of loans, credits, and tax benefits designed to foster sustainability initiatives.
4. Environmental
   The Environmental category is related to the performance that manufacturing companies need to follow in certain countries and, in some cases, to sustain a

benefit when an improvement in terms of sustainability needs to be addressed. They are addressing the absence of regulatory frameworks and legal structures governing the production of goods within the manufacturing sector. Aspects such as market demand, which might exhibit varying dependencies across industries, come into play. Furthermore, the overarching market policies exert a notable influence over this encompassing category. Within this view, the environmental macro category is interconnected with the performance benchmarks that manufacturing entities must adhere to within specific factors. This dimension comes to the forefront, particularly when companies seek to enhance sustainability. In certain scenarios, the pursuit of sustainability improvements requires certain approaches, often dictated by a given country's regulatory and socio-economic landscape.

5. Social (Cultural) and Human Resource
   Deals with the lack of collective social responsibility, weak public pressure, customer and supplier unawareness of alternatives moreover barriers are also related to the lack of training and knowledge by the workforce regarding sustainable technologies. Human Resources commitment and enforcement resulted in being a cornerstone in the macro category, as the labour force directly impacts a manufacturing company's performance.
6. Technological and Informational
   The following category includes barriers related to the resources that manufacturing organizations need to improve their sustainable performances; those resources include technology-related, such as equipment, tools and methodologies. The informational side is related to the data availability and processing required to improve their sustainable performance. In addition, infrastructure and technology 'lock in' also appear as common challenges in the literature. Furthermore, the complexity and form of the information are also impacting some industries, as nowadays, companies face processing problems rather than gathering the information. To address these issues, technologies such as Big Data and Data Analytics emerge as potential mitigators. A recap of all the categories is provided in Fig. 3.

3.2 RQ2

After identifying the final database of articles related to lean manufacturing practices, a classification of the identified practices was performed to visualize systematically all the selected techniques. This classification was performed according to specific typologies introduced and utilized in the literature [64].

The lean manufacturing practices displayed in Fig. 4 appear in the selected literature as manufacturing companies utilize them for environmental performance. From the literature, it is clear how the Lean Manufacturing practices previously mentioned positively impact environmental performance. On the other hand, how these practices can mitigate the barriers identified before is still being determined. Consequently, we can only suppose from a theoretical perspective that Lean Manufacturing practices could have a mitigating effect on the barriers

Macro category	Micro category
Organizational and Managerial	Lack of top management committee & commitment
	Lack of management support
	Lack of organizational structure
	Lack of competences skills, tools, and expertise
	Lack of sustainable product design and development
	Managerial Factors
Financial and Economic	Uncertain benefits
	Financial Constraints
	Economic Performance
	Financial Risk
Governmental	Lack of governmental support
	Lack of specific legislation and regulations and policies
Environmental	Market Factors
	Difficulty in sustaining the benefits of improvement
	Environmental and Market Policy
	Environmental performance
Social and Human Resource	Lack of training and knowledge by manpower
	Green Awareness
	Employees commitment and enforcement.
	Environmental and public peer pressure
Technological and Informational	Lack of Resources
	Infrastructure and technology
	Complexity of Programs and Designs to be implemented
	Form and complexity of information
	Operational Performance

Fig. 3. Barriers' Macro and Micro Categories

to improving environmental performance. Nevertheless, this effect can only be hypothesized since this study relies on a literature review, and it has yet to be possible to directly associate specific practices to the barrier with the mitigating effect. Thus, further empirical studies are needed to unveil and confirm this hypothetical effect.

Bundle	Lean Manufacturing Practice (LMP)
Supplier	JIT
Production Planning and Control	VSM
	PDCA
	Ishikawa Diagram
	5 Why's
	Spaghetti Chart
	DMAIC
	Pull/Kanban
	TPM
	SMED
	Lean Product Flow/One piece flow
	Flow Layout
Process Technology	Cellular manufacturing
	Poka Yoke
	Kaizen
	5S
Human Resource	Multifunctional workers
	Standardized work

Fig. 4. Lean Manufacturing Practices and Bundles

4 Conclusion and Future Development

Through the literature review, this study was able to answer research question RQ1 comprehensively and partially answer research question RQ2. Specifically, the output related to RQ1 identified many barriers that manufacturing companies face in improving their environmental performance, divided into six macro categories. As for RQ2, the literature returned several Lean practices that can impact environmental performance. These practices may have a mitigating factor on the barriers identified in RQ1. On the other hand, the literature review did not identify which Lean practices may mitigate each of the barriers identified above. Further studies are needed to answer question RQ2 fully. Specifically, after categorizing the barriers faced by manufacturing firms and lean practices documented in the existing literature, an analysis needs to be conducted to establish their interrelationship. Each general macro category and the corresponding underlying barriers collected from the initial research question can be linked to a specific impact factor related to the second research question. This impact factor represents a particular Lean practice that can enable manufacturing companies to overcome the identified barriers. The correlation can be derived from the analysis of multiple case studies that seek to investigate, starting from the set of barriers identified in this study, which Lean practices were able to mitigate these barriers. By critically analyzing the work conducted in this work, it is possible to determine some contributions both on the academic and company side. This research explores how lean practices can drive improvements in environmental performance, representing a compelling academic endeavour marked by its interdisciplinary nature and potential to bridge theory and practice. It fosters an understanding by integrating lean management and environmental sustainability, challenging traditional disciplinary boundaries, and promoting the assimilation of diverse theories and methodologies. Furthermore, the research's emphasis on cross-industry applicability highlights its relevance beyond specific sectors, inspiring industries to embrace a harmonious synthesis of efficiency and ecological responsibility collectively. Moving forward, this research offers numerous advantages to companies. Aligning operational efficiency with environmental responsibility assists organizations in navigating the intricate interplay between lean principles and ecological considerations. Furthermore, this research significantly contributes to sustainability dialogues and resource management. It empowers businesses to take the lead in operational excellence and environmental stewardship, reshaping industry norms and developing sustainable regulatory frameworks.

References

1. Chiarini, A.: Sustainable manufacturing-greening processes using specific Lean Production tools: an empirical observation from European motorcycle component manufacturers. J. Clean. Prod. **85**, 226–233 (2014)
2. Afum, E., Sun, Z., Agyabeng-Mensah, Y., Baah, C.: Lean production systems, social sustainability performance and green competitiveness: the mediating roles of green technology adoption and green product innovation. J. Eng. Des. Technol. **21**(1), 206–227 (2021). https://doi.org/10.1108/JEDT-02-2021-0099
3. Caldera, H.T.S., Desha, C., Dawes, L.: Exploring the role of lean thinking in sustainable business practice: a systematic literature review. J. Clean. Prod. **167**, 1546–1565 (2017)
4. Jain, M.S., Sudarsan, J.S., Parija, P.P.: Managing construction and demolition waste using lean tools to achieve environmental sustainability: an Indian perspective. Environ. Sci. Pollut. Res. **30**(19), 57188–57200 (2023). https://doi.org/10.1007/s11356-023-26445-z
5. Nagadi, K.: Implementation of green, lean and six sigma operations for sustainable manufacturing. a review. Int. J. Prod. Manag. Eng. **10**(2), 159–171 (2022). https://doi.org/10.4995/ijpme.2022.16958
6. Khan, M.A., Ali, M.K., Sajid, M.: Lean implementation framework: a case of performance improvement of casting process. IEEE Access **10**, 81281–81295 (2022). https://doi.org/10.1109/ACCESS.2022.3194064
7. Díaz-Reza, J., García-Alcaraz, J., Figueroa, L., Puig, R., Muro, J.: Relationship between lean manufacturing tools and their sustainable economic benefits. Int. J. Adv. Manuf. Technol. **123**, 1–16 (2022). https://doi.org/10.1007/s00170-022-10208-0

8. Dieste, M., Panizzolo, R., Garza-Reyes, J.A., Anosike, A.: The relationship between lean and environmental performance: practices and measures. J. Clean. Prod. **224**, 120–131 (2019)
9. Fercoq, A., Lamouri, S., Carbone, V.: Lean/Green integration focused on waste reduction techniques. J. Clean. Prod. **137**, 567–578 (2016)
10. Cherrafi, A., Elfezazi, S., Chiarini, A., Mokhlis, A., Benhida, K.: The integration of lean manufacturing, Six Sigma and sustainability: a literature review and future research directions for developing a specific model. J. Clean. Prod. **139**, 828–846 (2016)
11. Inman, R.A., Green, K.W.: Lean and green combine to impact environmental and operational performance. Int. J. Prod. Res. **56**(14), 4802–4818 (2018). https://doi.org/10.1080/00207543.2018.1447705
12. Chen, P.-K., Fortuny-Santos, J., Lujan, I., López, P.: Sustainable manufacturing: exploring antecedents and influence of total productive maintenance and lean manufacturing. Adv. Mech. Eng. **11**, 168781401988973 (2019). https://doi.org/10.1177/1687814019889736
13. Iranmanesh, M., Zailani, S., Hyun, S., Ali, M.H.: Impact of lean manufacturing practices on firms' sustainable performance: lean culture as a moderator. Sustainability **11**, 1–20 (2019). https://doi.org/10.3390/su11041112
14. Habidin, N.F., Hibadullah, S., Fuzi, N., Ithnin, M., Latip, N.A.M.: Lean manufacturing practices, ISO 14001, and environmental performance in Malaysian automotive suppliers. Int. J. Manag. Sci. Eng. Manag. **13**, 1–9 (2017). https://doi.org/10.1080/17509653.2017.1288587
15. Negrão, L., Filho, M., Marodin, G.: Lean practices and their effect on performance: a literature review. Prod. Plan. Control **28**, 1–24 (2016)
16. Pinto Junior, M.J.A., Mendes, J.V.: Operational practices of lean manufacturing: potentiating environmental improvements. J. Ind. Eng. Manag. (JIEM) **10**(4), 550–580 (2017). https://doi.org/10.3926/jiem.2268
17. Dieste, M., Panizzolo, R., Garza-Reyes, J.A.: Evaluating the impact of lean practices on environmental performance: evidences from five manufacturing companies. Prod. Plan. Control **31**, 739–756 (2020). https://doi.org/10.1080/09537287.2019.1681535
18. Garza-Reyes, J.A., Kumar, V., Chaikittisilp, S., Tan, K.H.: The effect of lean methods and tools on the environmental performance of manufacturing organisations. Int. J. Prod. Econ. **200**, 170–180 (2018)
19. Muñoz-Villamizar, A., Santos, J., Grau, P., Viles, E.: Toolkit for simultaneously improving production and environmental efficiencies. Cent. Eur. J. Oper. Res. **29**, 1219–1230 (2021). https://doi.org/10.1007/s10100-019-00664-7
20. Minh, N.D., Nguyen, N.D., Cuong, P.K.: Applying lean tools and principles to reduce cost of waste management: an empirical research in Vietnam. Manag. Prod. Eng. Rev. **10**(1), 37–49 (2019). https://doi.org/10.24425/mper.2019.128242.
21. Jamil, N., Gholami, H., Saman, M.Z.M., Streimikiene, D., Sharif, S., Zakuan, N.: DMAIC-based approach to sustainable value stream mapping: towards a sustainable manufacturing system. Econ. Res.-Ekonomska Istrazivanja **33**(1), 331–360 (2020)
22. Ishak, A., et al.: Cleaner production implementation in an E-Waste recovery plant by using the Value Stream Mapping. J. Adv. Manuf. Technol. **12**, 55–68 (2018)
23. Parveen, C.M., Kumar, A.R.P., Rao, T.V.V.L.N.: Integration of lean and green supply chain - Impact on manufacturing firms in improving environmental efficiencies. In: Proceedings of the International Conference on Green Technology and

Environmental Conservation, GTEC-2011, pp. 143–147 (2011). https://doi.org/10.1109/GTEC.2011.6167659.
24. Miller, G., Pawloski, J., Standridge, C.: A case study of lean, sustainable manufacturing. J. Ind. Eng. Manag. **3**(1), 11–32 (2010). https://doi.org/10.3926/jiem.2010.v3n1.p11-32
25. Fuenzalida, C., Fischer, B., Arroyo, P., Salvatierra Garrido, J.L.: Evaluating environmental impacts of construction operation before and after the implementation of lean tools (2016)
26. Sîrbu, D., Băian, C.: Lean manufacturing benefits in a pharmaceutical production plant. Appl. Mech. Mater. **657**, 991–995 (2014). https://doi.org/10.4028/www.scientific.net/AMM.657.991
27. Yusup, M., Mahmood, W., Salleh, M.R., Azrul, M.: Review the influence of Lean tools and its performance against the index of manufacturing sustainability. Int. J. Agile Syst. Manag. **8**, 116–131 (2015). https://doi.org/10.1504/IJASM.2015.070605
28. Choudhary, S., Nayak, R., Dora, M., Mishra, N., Ghadge, A.: An integrated lean and green approach for improving sustainability performance: a case study of a packaging manufacturing SME in the U.K. Prod. Plan. Control **30**(5–6), 353–368 (2019). https://doi.org/10.1080/09537287.2018.1501811
29. Hübel, C., Schaltegger, S.: Barriers to a sustainability transformation of meat production practices - an industry actor perspective. Sustain. Prod. Consum. **29**, 128–140 (2022)
30. Pathak, S., Karwasra, K., Sharma, V., Sharma, V.: Analysis of barriers to green manufacturing using hybrid approach: an investigatory case study on Indian automotive industry. Process Integrat. Optim. Sustainabil. **5**, 545–560 (2021). https://doi.org/10.1007/s41660-021-00160-z
31. Kannan, D., Shankar, K.M., Gholipour, P.: Paving the way for a green transition through mitigation of green manufacturing challenges: a systematic literature review. J. Clean. Prod. **368**, 132578 (2022). https://doi.org/10.1016/j.jclepro.2022.132578
32. Escoto, X., Gebrehewot, D., Morris, K.C.: Refocusing the barriers to sustainability for small and medium-sized manufacturers. J. Clean. Prod. **338**, 130589 (2022)
33. Tanco, M., Kalemkerian, F., Santos, J.: Main challenges involved in the adoption of sustainable manufacturing in Uruguayan small and medium sized companies. J. Clean. Prod. **293**, 126139 (2021). https://doi.org/10.1016/j.jclepro.2021.126139
34. Ball, P., Lunt, P.: Enablers for improving environmental performance of manufacturing operations. IEEE Trans. Eng. Manag. **66**(4), 663–676 (2019). https://doi.org/10.1109/TEM.2018.2871613
35. Guo, H.: Analysing the barriers to green apparel manufacturing implementation. J. Fash. Mark. Manag. **27**(3), 531–560 (2023)
36. Singh, P., et al.: Analyse the critical success factor of green manufacturing for achieving sustainability in automotive sector, pp. 79–94 (2022)
37. Samad, S., et al.: Green supply chain management practices and impact on firm performance: the moderating effect of collaborative capability. Technol. Soc. **67**, 101766 (2021)
38. Behl, A., Singh, R., Pereira, V., Laker, B.: Analysis of Industry 4.0 and circular economy enablers: a step towards resilient sustainable operations management. Technol. Forecast. Soc. Change **189**, 122363 (2023)
39. Prasad, S., Rao, A.N., Lanka, K.: Analysing the barriers for implementation of lean-led sustainable manufacturing and potential of blockchain technology to overcome

these barriers: a conceptual framework. Int. J. Math. Eng. Manag. Sci. **7**(6), 791–819 (2022). https://doi.org/10.33889/IJMEMS.2022.7.6.051
40. Seth, D., Rehman, M.A.A.: Critical success factors-based strategy to facilitate green manufacturing for responsible business: an application experience in Indian context. Bus. Strategy Environ. **31**(7), 2786–2806 (2022). https://doi.org/10.1002/bse.3047
41. Shukla, G.P., Swarnakar, V., Singh, S.J.: Assessment of drivers and barriers of green manufacturing practices in Indian manufacturing companies. J. Inst. Engineers India Ser. C **104**(1), 45–54 (2023). https://doi.org/10.1007/s40032-022-00902-z
42. Piyathanavong, V., Garza-Reyes, J.A., Kumar, V., Maldonado-Guzmán, G., Mangla, S.K.: The adoption of operational environmental sustainability approaches in the Thai manufacturing sector. J. Clean. Prod. **220**, 507–528 (2019). https://doi.org/10.1016/j.jclepro.2019.02.093
43. Shokri, A., Antony, J., Garza-Reyes, J.A.: A new way of environmentally sustainable manufacturing with assessing transformation through the green deployment of Lean Six Sigma projects. J. Clean. Prod. **351**, 131510 (2022)
44. Garza-Reyes, J.A., Yu, M., Kumar, V., Upadhyay, A.: Total quality environmental management: adoption status in the Chinese manufacturing sector. TQM J. **30**, 2–19 (2017). https://doi.org/10.1108/TQM-05-2017-0052
45. Pande, B., Adil, G.K.: Assessment of the current state of sustainability in a manufacturing firm. Int. J. Prod. Perfor. Manag. **71**(4), 1254–1276 (2022). https://doi.org/10.1108/IJPPM-04-2020-0151
46. Hariyani, D., Mishra, S., Sharma, M.K., Hariyani, P.: Organizational barriers to the sustainable manufacturing system: a literature review. Environ. Challenges **9**, 100606 (2022). https://doi.org/10.1016/j.envc.2022.100606
47. Ball, P., MacBryde, J.: Developing a framework for adopting environmental manufacturing practices: learning from breweries. Prod. Plan. Control **33**(8), 758–773 (2022). https://doi.org/10.1080/09537287.2020.1834637
48. Malek, J., Desai, T.N.: Prioritization of sustainable manufacturing barriers using Best Worst Method. J. Clean. Prod. **226**, 589–600 (2019)
49. Gunasekara, H., Gamage, J., Punchihewa, H.: Remanufacture for sustainability: barriers and solutions to promote automotive remanufacturing. Procedia Manuf. **43**, 606–613 (2020)
50. Bhanot, N., Rao, P.V., Deshmukh, S.G.: Enablers and barriers of sustainable manufacturing: results from a survey of researchers and industry professionals. Procedia CIRP **29**, 562–567 (2015)
51. Goyal, A., Agrawal, R., Sharma, A.K.: Green quality circle: achieving sustainable manufacturing with low investment. Res. Conservat. Recycl. Adv. **15**, 200103 (2022)
52. Prakash, C., Barua, M.K., Pandya, K.V.: Barriers analysis for reverse logistics implementation in indian electronics industry using fuzzy analytic hierarchy process. Procedia. Soc. Behav. Sci. **189**, 91–102 (2015). https://doi.org/10.1016/j.sbspro.2015.03.203
53. Mittal, V.K., Sangwan, K.S.: Prioritizing drivers for green manufacturing: environmental, social and economic perspectives. Procedia CIRP **15**, 135–140 (2014). https://doi.org/10.1016/j.procir.2014.06.038
54. Abreu, M.F., Alves, A.C., Moreira, F.: Lean-Green models for eco-efficient and sustainable production. Energy **137**, 846–853 (2017). https://doi.org/10.1016/j.energy.2017.04.016

55. Thanki, S., Govindan, K., Thakkar, J.: An investigation on lean-green implementation practices in Indian SMEs using analytical hierarchy process (AHP) approach. J. Clean. Prod. **135**, 284–298 (2016). https://doi.org/10.1016/j.jclepro.2016.06.105
56. Mittal, V.K., Sindhwani, R., Kapur, P.K.: Two-way assessment of barriers to Lean-Green Manufacturing System: insights from India. Int. J. Syst. Assur. Eng. Manag. **7**(4), 400–407 (2016). https://doi.org/10.1007/s13198-016-0461-z
57. Mittal, V.K., Sangwan, K.S.: Development of a model of barriers to environmentally conscious manufacturing implementation. Int. J. Prod. Res. **52**(2), 584–594 (2014). https://doi.org/10.1080/00207543.2013.838649
58. Ghazilla, R.A.R., Sakundarini, N., Abdul-Rashid, S.H., Ayub, N.S., Olugu, E.U., Musa, S.N.: Drivers and barriers analysis for green manufacturing practices in Malaysian SMEs: a preliminary findings. Procedia Cirp **26**, 658–663 (2015)
59. Pojasek, R.: Framing your lean-to-green effort. Environ. Qual. Manag. **18**, 85–93 (2008). https://doi.org/10.1002/tqem.20198
60. Alves, A., Moreira, F., Abreu, M., Colombo, C.: Sustainability, lean and eco-efficiency symbioses, pp. 91–112 (2016)
61. Sundram, V.P.K., Bahrin, A.S., Othman, A.A., Munir, Z.A.: Green supply chain management practices in Malaysia manufacturing industry. Int. J. Supply Chain Manag. **6**(2), 89–95 (2017)
62. Eltayeb, T.K., Zailani, S., Filho, W.L.: Green business among certified companies in Malaysia towards environmental sustainability: benchmarking on the drivers, initiatives and outcomes. Int. J. Environ. Technol. Manag. **12**(1), 95–125 (2010). https://doi.org/10.1504/IJETM.2010.029983
63. Parmar, P.S., Desai, T.N.: Evaluating sustainable lean six sigma enablers using fuzzy DEMATEL: a case of an Indian manufacturing organization. J. Clean. Prod. **265**, 121802 (2020). https://doi.org/10.1016/j.jclepro.2020.121802
64. Bai, C., Satir, A., Sarkis, J.: Investing in lean manufacturing practices: an environmental and operational perspective. Int. J. Prod. Res. **57**(4), 1037–1051 (2019). https://doi.org/10.1080/00207543.2018.1498986
65. Ferrazzi, M., Portioli-Staudacher, A.: Using the lean approach for improving eco-efficiency performance: a case study for plastic reduction. In: Alfnes, E., Romsdal, A., Strandhagen, J.O., von Cieminski, G., Romero, D. (eds) Advances in Production Management Systems. Production Management Systems for Responsible Manufacturing, Service, and Logistics Futures. APMS 2023. IFIP Advances in Information and Communication Technology, vol. 689. Springer, Heidelberg (2023). https://doi.org/10.1007/978-3-031-43662-8_18
66. Ferrazzi, M., Portioli-Staudacher, A.: Applying the value stream map to streamline energy consumption: analysis of an Italian company. In: Alfnes, E., Romsdal, A., Strandhagen, J.O., von Cieminski, G., Romero, D. (eds) Advances in Production Management Systems. Production Management Systems for Responsible Manufacturing, Service, and Logistics Futures. APMS 2023. IFIP Advances in Information and Communication Technology, vol. 689. Springer, Heidelberg (2023). https://doi.org/10.1007/978-3-031-43662-8_10
67. Ferrazzi, M., Frecassetti, S., Staudacher, A.P.: Influence of the lean approach on corporate environmental Sustainability: a case study (2023)
68. Costa, F., Frecassetti, S., Rossini, M., Portioli-Staudacher, A.: Industry 4.0 digital technologies enhancing sustainability: applications and barriers from the agricultural industry in an emerging economy. J. Clean. Prod. **408**, 137208 (2023). ISSN 0959-6526

69. Graham, S., Cadden, T., Treacy, R.: Examining the influence of employee engagement in supporting the implementation of green supply chain management practices: a green human resource management perspective. Bus. Strat. Environ. **32**, 4750–4766 (2023)
70. Amoah, P., Eweje, G.: Barriers to environmental sustainability practices of multinational mining companies in Ghana: an institutional complexity perspective. Corp. Gov. **22**(2), 364–384 (2022)
71. Kirschke, S., Newig, J.: Addressing complexity in environmental management and governance. Sustainability **9**, 983 (2017)
72. McGrath, P., McCarthy, L., Marshall, D., Rehme, J.: Tools and technologies of transparency in sustainable global supply chains. Calif. Manag. Rev. **64**(1), 67–89 (2021)
73. Abreu, M.F., Alves, A.C., Moreira, F.: Lean-Green models for eco-efficient and sustainable production. Energy **137**, 846–853 (2017)

Investigating the Relationship Among Lean Manufacturing Practices to Improved Eco-Efficiency Performance: A Fuzzy DEMATEL Analysis

Matteo Ferrazzi(✉), Fu Ye, Stefano Frecassetti, and Alberto Portioli-Staudacher

Politecnico di Milano, Department of Management, Economics and Industrial Engineering, Via Lambruschini 4, b, Milano, Italy
matteo.ferrazzi@polimi.it

Abstract. The urgency to address environmental challenges has grown, Lean management has expanded its scope to incorporate environmental sustainability performance. However, there is a lack of studies on how specific lean management practices interacts with each other as a final objective of improving the environmental performances of a manufacturing firm. The objective of this study is to investigate the cause-effect relationships among Lean manufacturing practices for solid waste reduction. A set of Lean practices is extract from today's literature. Subsequently, a set of managers with more than five years of experience in implementing Lean practices give their opinion on the influence of the selected practices. In particular, the study will focus on the Apparel industry. Through the use of the fuzzy DEMATEL methodology, the cause-effect relationships of the Lean practices involved in this study are analyzed. The analysis of the DEMATEL approach responses showed that the Lean practices studied in this article can be divided in 5 different areas. In order to explain how the cause-effect relationships between various lean manufacturing practices, for the reduction of solid waste, manifest themselves; it was necessary to analyze how these new areas of practices interact with each other. In conclusion, the result of this research was able to analyze the role of lean manufacturing practices in reducing solid waste, and in particular what cause-effect relationships exist between the various practice.

Keywords: Lean manufacturing · Lean practices · DEMATEL · environmental sustainability

1 Introduction

In recent decades, the sustainability of the environment has become a vital and urgent global problem. Given the growing awareness of human-induced climate change, resource depletion, and ecological deterioration, it is becoming important to embrace sustainable practices [1]. The manufacturing sector is crucial in determining how the environment develops. Resource exploitation, energy use, waste production, and emissions

Published by Springer Nature Switzerland AG 2024
T. van Kollenburg et al. (Eds.): ELEC 2023, IFIP AICT 681, pp. 138–154, 2024.
https://doi.org/10.1007/978-3-031-63265-5_11

from manufacturing processes all contribute to environmental deterioration and climate change. There are many reasons for the manufacturing industry's ongoing transition to more environmentally friendly business practices [2, 3].

The urgency to address environmental challenges has grown, Lean management has expanded its scope to incorporate environmental sustainability performance. This integration acknowledges the need for integrating operational excellence with environmental responsibility [4]. According to numerous studies, the two philosophies have many things in common, and environmental performance enhancements can be seen as a "good spillover" of the Lean production philosophy [5]. Lean manufacturing has been shown to have indirect environmental benefits in many cases, but this synergistic effect is enhanced and brought to a higher level in businesses where Lean manufacturing and environmental sustainability are strategically aligned in the operation strategy [6, 7]. Another line of research emphasizes developing soft skills to create the ideal organizational culture within a company. This is crucial because "Lean Management is able to encourage employee involvement, and this commitment is important to ensure that green practices lead to an outstanding environmental performance" [7].

In recent years, research fields have examined the micro level perspective in an effort to understand the direct effects that each Lean technique and practice has on environmental sustainability performance [8, 9]. However, there is a lack of studies on how specific lean management practices interacts with each other as a final objective of improving the environmental performances of a manufacturing firm. Lean manufacturing is a comprehensive philosophy that promotes a culture of continuous improvement, waste reduction, and customer value generation rather than a collection of isolated techniques [10]. Unlocking the full potential of lean methods when applied to environmental performance requires a thorough understanding of how they interact. Organizations can find opportunities to improve operational and environmental outcomes by examining the dependencies and synergistic effects of various lean practices. The objective of this study is to investigate the cause-effect relationship of Lean manufacturing practices for solid waste reduction. A set of Lean practices will initially be selected from today's literature. Subsequently, a set of managers with more than five years of experience in implementing Lean practices will be asked to give their opinion on the influence of the selected practices in the literature. To limit one of the contextual factors, the experts were selected on the basis of a specific manufacturing sector. In particular, the study will focus on the Apparel industry. Finally, through the use of the DEMATEL methodology, the cause-effect relationships of the Lean practices involved in this study will be made explicit and analyzed. In conclusion, new bundles will be defined to explain the role of Lean manufacturing practices for better eco-efficiency performance.

2 Literature Review

The first step conducted was select a set of Lean manufacturing practices from the literature. The selected practices have already been studied in the literature to have a positive impact on eco-efficiency performance. In fact, the purpose of this review was to: (1) Identify well-known frameworks for Lean management practices and their bundles, (2) Classify the individual Lean Management practices in terms of their impact on eco-efficiencies performances, (3) Identify the research question.

2.1 Lean Practices and the Impact on Eco-Efficiency

The principles of lean management have gained prominence as a means to streamline operations, reduce waste, and enhance overall efficiency [11]. The convergence of these two critical paradigms–lean management and environmental sustainability–presents an opportunity for organizations to drive positive impacts on both their operational effectiveness and their contributions to a greener world. The pursuit of eco-efficiency, which involves minimizing resource consumption, waste generation, and emissions while maximizing value creation, aligns seamlessly with the foundational tenets of lean management.

Through the analysis of today's literature, we can see how various Lean manufacturing practices impact on different eco-efficiency performances. Lean manufacturing practices for production planning and control are frequently linked to scheduling techniques and fundamental concepts like just-in-time (JIT), with the aim of coordinating production with market demand. Lean planning and control, when compared to conventional manufacturing, greatly reduces scheduling waste, including the use of raw materials. Effective schedules lead to reductions in inventory, work-in-progress, resource use optimization, and fulfilment of client orders [12]; as a result, techniques like production levelling are positively correlated with reduced energy use, air pollutants, and solid waste [8, 12]. Moreover, the literature shows that organizational and continuous improvement cultures, together with employee engagement, are essential to improving environmental sustainability in manufacturing [9, 13, 14]. The Continuous Improvement (CI) or Kaizen approach is widely used in team-based work around the world [15, 16]. Furthermore, it is discovered that Lean manufacturing supports employee participation, which has been established as a critical moderator influencing the relationship between green practices and environmental performance [7, 17, 18]. The Lean Continuous Improvement culture interacts with Lean practices related to process and equipment, as well as supplier relationship to improve their effects on manufacturing organizations' long term sustainable performance. [19].

Based on literature review, it can be seen that the majority of studies show a positive effect of in manufacturing practices on eco-efficiency performance. In addition, the Lean manufacturing practices investigated are not only limited to 'hard' practices. A fundamental role is also played by practices involving Lean culture, which are identified as 'soft' practices.

2.2 Research Objective

The Literature review has demonstrated a growing interest in exploring the interaction of Lean management principles and environmental sustainability. Various studies have delved into the impact of Lean practices on environmental measures, with a particular emphasis on how these practices contribute to reducing waste, energy consumption, and emissions [13, 20–22]. A noticeable trend in existing research is the study of Lean practices in isolation, focusing on their individual effects on environmental performance. In some cases, scholars have analyzed the influence of Lean tools and principles combined in defined Lean bundles (such as the ones proposed by Shah and Ward or by Panizzolo), providing valuable insights into their collective impact [19, 23, 24]. While these efforts have enriched the understanding of Lean's potential environmental benefits, a critical gap in the literature remains. The intricate interplay and interdependence among various Lean practices have often been overlooked. This gap is significant because Lean management is inherently an interconnected system of practices [10, 16]. Therefore, this study seeks to address this research gap by exploring the relationships and cause-effect interactions between different Lean practices within the context of solid waste reduction. Specifically, the research question of this paper is: "How the cause-effect relationship arise among Lean manufacturing practices used for reducing solid waste in manufacturing firms?".

Solid waste reduction was chosen as the focal metric for several compelling reasons. First and foremost, the majority of academic literature acknowledges the unequivocally positive effect of Lean production on solid waste reduction [13]. This metric is a widely tracked indicator in both academic research and industrial practice [8]. Additionally, solid waste reduction possesses a distinct advantage over other environmental metrics, such as water usage, in terms of visibility, tangibility and tracking [8, 25]. It provides a clear and quantifiable measure of environmental improvement, making it easier for both researchers and practitioners to assess and comprehend the impact of Lean practices.

3 Methodology

The research methodology can be divided into two distinct but interconnected phases. In the initial phase, we conducted an exhaustive literature review. From this review, a list of 34 Lean practices emerged. These practices were not chosen solely for their contribution to solid waste reduction; instead, given that many research papers discuss Lean practices on their broader environmental impact, they were selected based on their recurring mentions in the literature and their perceived relevance to overall eco-efficiency.

Following the initial selection, Lean practices were further refined and organized. They were categorized into two fundamental groups: soft and hard practices, following guidance from [16, 26–29]. Subsequently, hard practices were sub-categorized into Process Technology and Production Planning & Control bundles, while soft practices were divided into Managerial-based and Employee-based, guided by [1] and [29]' frameworks respectively. The outcome of this reduction and compression phase resulted in a refined set of 22 Lean practices as shown in table 1. These practices are used for the analytical framework and research.

Table 1. Final sample of 22 Lean manufacturing practices

Lean Bundles	Code	Lean Manufacturing practices
Production Planning & Control	PC1	Pull production/takt time
	PC2	Total Productive Maintenance (TPM)
	PC3	Set-Up reduction (SMED)

(continued)

Table 1. (*continued*)

Lean Bundles	Code	Lean Manufacturing practices
	PC4	Statistical process control (SPC)
	PC5	Smoothed (levelled) production Heijunka
	PC6	Root cause analysis for problem solving
Process Technology	PT1	Cellular manufacturing
	PT2	Autonomation (jidoka)
	PT3	One-piece-flow (continuous flow)
	PT4	Value Stream Map (VSM)
	PT5	Total Quality Management (TQM)
	PT6	5S
	PT7	Layout size and shape
	PT8	Visual management
Managerial based	SM1	JIT delivery by suppliers
	SM1	Workforce training and awareness
	SM1	Management commitment and support
	SM1	Customer involvement
Employee based	SE1	Standardized work
	SE1	Employee engagement
	SE1	Continuous Improvement (kaizen)
	SE1	Kaizen events

3.1 Fuzzy DEMATEL Approach

The second phase of the methodology explain the application of the DEMATEL on the 22 Lean practice selected before. DEMATEL stands out in its approach, relying on directed graphs known as digraphs, which provide an advanced means of categorizing factors into distinct cause and effect groups. This method surpasses undirected graphs in terms of informative representation, allowing for a more profound understanding of how factors influence one another.

The DEMATEL process unfolds as follows, primarily following the guidance of [30]. Consider a system composed of a set of elements, denoted as $S = \{s1, s2,\ldots, sn\}$. For modeling, specific pairwise relationships are established, denoted by the mathematical relation R. To ensure the smooth application of the DEMATEL method, essential definitions are introduced:

Definition 1: The scale used for pairwise comparisons consists of five levels, with scores of 0, 1, 2, 3, and 4 signifying "No influence," "Low influence," "Medium influence," "High influence," and "Very high influence," respectively.

Table 2. Lean experts selected

Expert n	Job position	Experience in Lean	Geographic area of influence
1	Lean consultant and Manager	24	India, Bangladesh, Vietnam
2	Lean consultant and Manager	23	Sri Lanka
3	Lean consultant and Manager	20	Sri Lanka, India, Pakistan, Jordan
4	Supply Chain Manager	13	Switzerland
5	Lean Practitioner and Continuous Improvement Projects Leader	12	Bangladesh, Sri Lanka
6	Deputy Manager Industrial Engineering/Lean	6	Pakistan
7	Lean manufacturing Team Leader/Executive	5	Turkey

Definition 2: The initial direct-relation matrix Z is an n x n matrix generated through pairwise comparisons that assess both the degree of influence and the direction between criteria. Each element z_{ij} represents the extent to which criterion i impacts criterion j.

$$Z = \left[z_{ij}\right]_{nxn} \tag{1}$$

Definition 3: The normalized direct-relation matrix X, represented as $X = [x_{ij}]_{nxn}$, with values satisfying $0 \leq x_{ij} \leq 1$, is obtained using specific mathematical formulas. Importantly, all elements on the principal diagonal are set to zero.

$$X = s \cdot Z \tag{2}$$

$$s = \frac{1}{\max\limits_{1<i<n} \sum_{j=1}^{n} z_{ij}}, i, j = 1, 2, \ldots n \tag{3}$$

Definition 4: The total-relation matrix T is computed using a formula (3), where I signifies the identity matrix.

$$T = X(I - X)^\wedge(-1) \tag{4}$$

Definition 5: Within the total-relation matrix T, the sums of rows and columns are designated as D and R, respectively. These sums are calculated using formulas (4)–(6), with D representing the sum of rows, and R representing the sum of columns.

$$T = t_{ij}, i, j = 1, 2, \ldots, n. \quad (5)$$

$$D = \sum_{j=1}^{n} t_{ij} \quad (6)$$

$$R = \sum_{j=1}^{n} t_{ij} \quad (7)$$

Definition 6: A causal diagram is created by plotting the dataset ($D + R$, D–R). The horizontal axis is constructed by adding D to R, while the vertical axis is formed by subtracting D from R.

In practical decision-making scenarios, inherent imprecision often prevails due to uncertainties in goals, constraints, and potential actions [30, 31]. Decision outcomes in such fuzzy or imprecise environments rely heavily on subjective judgments, characterized by vagueness and imprecision [30]. To address these challenges, fuzzy set theory, offers a mathematical framework for managing vagueness in decision-making. Unlike binary logic, which uses crisp sets with values of either 0 or 1, fuzzy logic employs numerical values in the range of 0 to 1, representing degrees of partial truth.

Within the domain of fuzzy logic, fundamental definitions are essential:

Definition 7: A fuzzy set $\tilde{A}$, denoted as $\tilde{A}$, is a subset of a universe of discourse X, represented as ordered pairs. It is characterized by a membership function $\mu_{\tilde{A}}(x)$ that maps elements from X to values in the range [0, 1], signifying the degree of truth that x belongs to the fuzzy set $\tilde{A}$.

$$\tilde{A} = \{(x, \mu_{\tilde{A}}(x))\}, \ x \in X \quad (8)$$

Definition 8: A fuzzy set Ã of the universe of discourse X is convex if.

$$\mu_{\tilde{A}}(\lambda x_1 + (1 - \lambda)x_2) \geq \min(\mu_{\tilde{A}}(x_1), \mu_{\tilde{A}}(x_2)) \forall x \in [x_1, x_2], \text{ where } \lambda \in [0, 1] \quad (9)$$

Definition 9: A fuzzy set $\tilde{A}$ is considered normal if

$$\max \mu_{\tilde{A}}(x) = 1 \quad (10)$$

Definition 10: A fuzzy number $\tilde{N}$ is a subset within the universe of discourse X that is both convex and normal.

Definition 11: The α-cut of the fuzzy set $\tilde{A}$ in the universe of discourse X is defined as

$$\tilde{A}_\alpha = \{x \in X | \mu_{\tilde{A}}(x) \geq \alpha\} \quad (11)$$

Definition 12: A triangular fuzzy number $\tilde{N}$ is defined by a triplet (l, m, r) and the membership function $\mu_{\tilde{N}}(x)$ is defined as

$$\mu_{\tilde{N}}(x) = \begin{cases} 0, & x < l, \\ (x - l)/(m - l), & l \leq x \leq m, \\ (r - x)/(r - m) & m \leq x \leq r, \\ 0, & x > r, \end{cases} \tag{12}$$

where l, m, and r are real numbers and $l \leq m \leq r$.

4 Results

In the previous chapter, we discussed the development and methodology of our analytical framework based on the DEMATEL method. This section focuses on its practical application, detailing the steps taken for data collection and analysis.

Step 1: Defining research objectives and strategy. In this phase, we precisely defined research objectives. Our main aim is to comprehensively analyze the relationships between various Lean practices and their impact on solid waste reduction in manufacturing firms. We used a survey-based research strategy for its broad reach and efficiency.

Step 2: Setting evaluation factors and fuzzy linguistic scale. Here we focused on developing the survey instrument used for data collection. To ensure ease of use and alignment with the DEMATEL method's matrix format, we chose Microsoft Excel for this purpose. We placed a strong emphasis on framing precise questions, directing respondents to structure their assessments using the query: "How much does Practice X impact Practice Y in the reduction of solid waste?" This approach ensured clarity and precision in their responses, aligning with our research goals.

As perceptions of Lean practices can vary, according to [10], aligning definitions was deemed crucial, we offered comprehensive definitions of each Lean practice to standardize the respondents' knowledge levels. These definitions were derived from the extensive literature review and the reductionism phase of our research.

Step 3: Obtaining and combining opinions of experts. Recognizing the context-dependent nature of Lean practices [10, 32] it was necessary to ensure the consistency and facilitate meaningful comparisons of the collected data. Thus, we focused our study only on the Textile and Apparel, this sector is in relatively early stages of Lean management adoption [33–36]. Moreover the selection of Lean experts were based on specific criteria. These criteria included possessing substantial experience in the sector mentioned before, having a minimum of five years of hands-on experience in Lean management [37]. We assemble a panel of 7 experts as shown in table [2]. Such numbers are aligned with the recommendation of [38] who suggested to gather between 5 and 15 respondents for such method.

Step 4: Executing the analytical procedure and analyzing structural models. In this critical phase of the study, the analytical procedure unfolded as follows for each of the initial direct-relation matrices. Initially, the normalized direct-relation matrix was derived by applying formula (1) and (2). Subsequently, the total-relation matrix was established using formula (3).

Table 3. Prominence and net effect

Code	D	R	D + R	D-R	Cause/Effect
PC1	3,396	4,274	7,670	-0,878	effect
PC2	3,343	3,698	7,041	-0,355	effect
PC3	3,273	3,893	7,165	-0,620	effect
PC4	2,918	3,372	6,290	-0,454	effect
PC5	3,527	4,186	7,713	-0,658	effect
PC6	4,019	3,852	7,871	0,167	cause
PT1	3,504	3,417	6,920	0,087	cause
PT2	3,348	3,575	6,923	-0,227	effect
PT3	3,990	4,154	8,144	-0,163	effect
PT4	3,496	3,571	7,067	-0,074	effect
PT5	3,911	4,436	8,347	-0,525	effect
PT6	3,569	3,553	7,122	0,016	cause
PT7	2,787	2,635	5,422	0,152	cause
PT8	3,719	3,241	6,960	0,478	cause
SM1	3,113	3,646	6,759	-0,533	effect
SM2	4,153	3,307	7,460	0,846	cause
SM3	4,698	3,717	8,415	0,981	cause
SM4	3,247	3,107	6,354	0,139	cause
SE1	4,109	3,952	8,061	0,157	cause
SE2	4,253	3,667	7,920	0,585	cause
SE3	4,467	4,208	8,674	0,259	cause
SE4	4,612	3,989	8,601	0,622	cause

To visualize the intricate web of causal relationships among Lean practices for solid waste reduction, a causal diagram (Fig. 1) was constructed by mapping the dataset of (D + R, D–R) (Table 3). The creation of this diagram was particularly insightful as it offered a visual representation of the factors' relative importance (prominence) and their roles as either causes or effects in the Lean ecosystem. To further enhance the clarity of these relationships and to extract the more meaningful insights, a systematic approach was taken. The dataset (D + R, D–R) was divided into four distinct quadrants based on the mean value of (D + R). To pinpoint influential relations with precision, two distinct thresholds were introduced for the creation of the Influential Relation Map. The first threshold was calculated by taking the mean value and adding 1.5 times the standard deviation of the values within matrix T. This threshold effectively identified relations that were significant in the context of the study. Furthermore, to isolate relations of even higher significance, a second threshold was established. This threshold was set equal to the mean value plus 2 times the standard deviation of matrix T.

Fig. 1. Causal Diagram

For instance, in the Textile and Apparel sector, the application of these thresholds revealed the existence of 36 influential relations, representing the top 7% of the entire matrix concerning the lower-bound threshold. Additionally among these 36 relations, it unveiled 13 exceedingly significant relations, comprising the top 3% of the matrix for the upper-bound threshold. These influential relations formed the core of the subsequent analysis, shedding light on the critical interactions between Lean practices and their impact on solid waste reduction within the specific sector.

5 Discussions

Looking at the disposition of the lean practices in the prominence relation matrix and the impact relationship matrix we can distinguish 5 clusters of practices of interest (Fig. 2). The assessment criteria for the creation of clusters are described below.

Group 1: practices that have a high "Relationship" value and a high "Prominence" value. This group includes practices that have an effect on other practices but are not impacted by any other.

Group 2: practices that still have the same "Prominence" value as group 1. They are at the same time impacted and impact other practices in turn.

Group 3: practices with a low level of "Prominence" but a high level of " Relation". They are independent practices, they are not impacted by any other practice and any practice has no impact on them.

Group 4: practices with a low level of "Relation". These are practices that are only impacted by weak relationships (yellow arrows in the graph) but do not impact any other practices.

Group 5: practices with a low level of "Relation" but a higher level of "Prominence" compared to the practices in group 4. In this group are practices that are strongly influenced (red arrows in the graph) by other practices in groups 1 and 2, but which in turn do not impact any other practices.

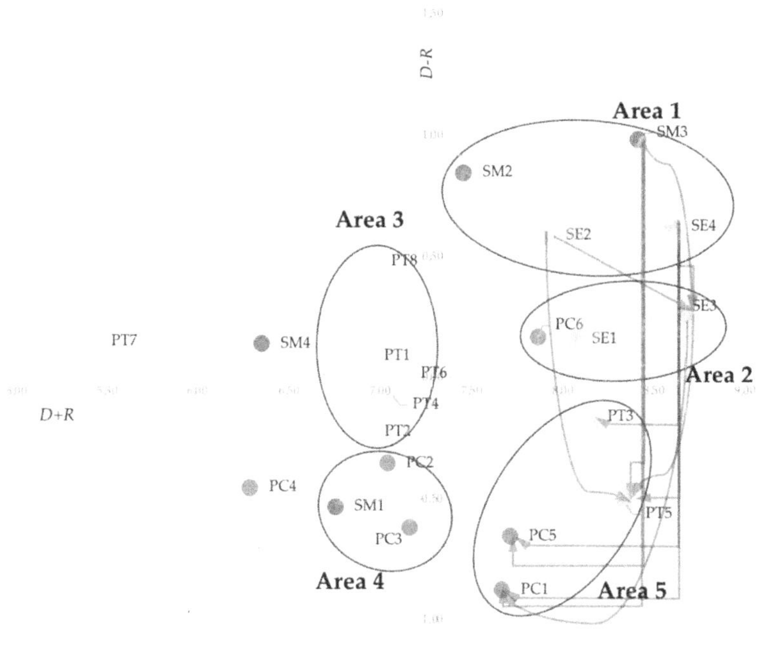

Fig. 2. Causal diagram with new areas

Area 1: SM3 Management commitment and support, SM2 Workforce training and awareness, SE4 Kaizen events, SE2 Employee engagement.

These practices not only exhibit the highest relation values but also boast relatively high prominence values. This dual distinction implies that they wield significant influence and play central roles in initiating Lean implementation for achieving solid waste reduction within the Apparel manufacturing sector. We can see that 11 out 13 of the strong cause effect relation arrows depart from this group, in particular from SM3, SE4 and SE2. All of this communicate that this group serve as the primary causal attributes that profoundly influence other Lean practices. Within this context, management commitment and support (SM3) emerge as critical components. They are vital not only in addressing employee resistance to change but also in sustaining this commitment throughout the Lean journey. Over the course of a protracted Lean improvement journey, this approach can become suboptimal, impacting employee morale and potentially jeopardizing project success [36]. Thus, the consistent and unwavering commitment of top management is indispensable, particularly in providing ongoing monitoring and effective decision-making support. Given the industry's heavy reliance on manual labor [36], effective employee training (SM2) becomes paramount. Ensuring that every employee comprehends the theoretical and practical aspects of Lean tools and the environmental impact of processes is crucial as they become catalysts for Continuous Improvement and Total Quality Management (TQM). More importantly is Employee engagement (SE2), where fostering a conducive working environment and involving the workforce in suggestion systems is key for a sustainable continuous improvement and an effective Total Quality management. Workers should feel motivated to contribute to the firm's progress without fear of repercussions for their suggestions and this is possible only when employee feel a strong sense of ownership for their processes and towards the firm. Kaizen events (SE4) play an important role in bringing people together, enhancing their engagement, by working toward a common goal and showcasing tangible results achievable within limited timeframes. Such practice results the strong causal attribute of many hard practices in Area 5 and in lower level of those in Area 4. This suggest how kaizen events can be a good initiator of many other Lean practices just as demonstrated by [8].

Area 2: SE3 Continuous Improvement (kaizen), PC6 Root cause analysis for problem solving, SE1 Standardized work.

These practices function as the linchpin for a complex web of interactions, connecting the fundamental Lean practices in Area 1 to the broader goals of solid waste reduction in Area 5. They serve as both the starting point for numerous second-order cause-effect relationships and the destination for second-order arrows originating from Area 1. All the practices in Area 1 strongly contribute to the effective seeding of a Continuous improvement culture within the company, suggesting that the Kaizen mindset is the result of strongly motivated, trained people who are empowered and supported by the managers. Continuous improvement has the highest prominence value in the model, highlighting thus how important is for Apparel companies to pursue a philosophy of never-ending innovation for waste reduction. This cultural transformation forms a virtuous cycle with Kaizen events (SE4) as the application of kaizen events leads to a stronger Continuous improvement which in turn create more opportunities for kaizen events to take place. Root Cause Analysis for Problem Solving (PC6) stands out as another vital element within this cluster. It underscores the importance of delving deep into issues to identify their underlying causes. While it plays a critical role in enhancing Total Quality Management (TQM) practices, it also benefits from the foundation laid by the support of management. Standardized Work (SE1) reveals its influence by impacting Total Quality Management (TQM) practices and shaping the kaizen mindset. However, it's important to acknowledge that Standardized Work is also influenced by the practices in Area 1, specifically SM3 and SE4. This symbiotic relationship underscores the critical role of these practices in setting the stage for the successful implementation of Standardized Work. This, in turn, becomes an essential component for ensuring consistent quality, thereby reducing scrap and rework, key factors in the journey toward solid waste reduction.

Area 3: PT8 Visual management, PT1 Cellular manufacturing, PT6 5S, PT4 Value Stream Map (VSM), PT2 Autonomation (jidoka).

In stark contrast to the high-profile practices in Area 1 and the mediatory role of those in Area 2, these Lean practices possess low prominence and, notably, close to zero relation values, with the exception of Visual Management, which maintains a relatively higher relation value. These practices collectively form a cluster characterized by their relative independence, suggesting that they are distinct tools that can be applied individually or in combination to reduce solid waste. This independence is further substantiated by the impact relationship map, which demonstrates that these practices neither significantly influence other Lean practices nor are greatly affected by them. Visual Management (PT8) stands out as an exception, as it exhibits a relatively higher relation value compared to the other practices in this cluster. While it may not directly impact other Lean practices to a substantial degree, Visual Management plays a pivotal role in providing transparency and real-time insights into operational processes.

Area 4: PC2 Total Productive Maintenance (TPM), SM1 JIT delivery by suppliers, PC3 Set-Up reduction (SMED).

These practices exhibit low prominence and low relation values, their direct impact on solid waste reduction is relatively limited in this industry. However, it's important to note that their successful implementation relies on the support and collaboration of practices within Area 1 and 2, particularly SM3, SE4 and SE3. Total Productive Maintenance (TPM) (PC2) emphasizes the importance of maintaining and optimizing equipment to prevent breakdowns and defects. JIT Delivery by Suppliers (SM1) focuses on the just-in-time delivery of supplies to reduce inventory and waste. Set-Up Reduction (SMED) (PC3) aims to minimize the time and resources required for equipment changeovers.

Area 5: PT3 One-piece-flow (continuous flow), PT5 Total Quality Management (TQM), PC5 Smoothed (levelled) production Heijunka, PC1 Pull production/takt time.

This area stands out with high prominence values but exhibits low relations with other practices, indicating that improving this area directly is challenging. Firms need to first focus on enhancing causal practices, primarily from Area 1 and, to a lesser extent, Area 2. Notably, these practices are technically demanding, being associated with production planning and process technology bundles. Total Quality Management (TQM) plays a central role in solid waste reduction among the hard practices as it holds the highest prominence among them. This is because stringent control over quality in the Apparel industry inherently leads to fewer defects and variations, thereby reducing solid waste and bolstering environmental benefits [34]. However, to effectively implement TQM, several critical causal attributes must be in place making it the practice with most prerequisites as it is affected by the most number of strong causal relationship, including commitment and support from management (SM3), Kaizen events (SE4), Employee engagement (SE2) and a culture of continuous improvement (SE3). To successfully implement JIT-related practices, there is a notable dependency on practices from Area 1, particularly Management Commitment and Support (SM3), Kaizen Events (SE4),

Employee engagement (SE2) and a significant contribution from Continuous Improvement (SE3). Additionally, Pull Production (PC1) is influenced by One-Piece Flow (PT3) highlighting the intricate dance of Lean practices required to achieve JIT production. The effectiveness of these practices to reduce solid waste aligns seamlessly with the observations made by [39], emphasizing the dynamic shift in demand patterns, especially with the rise of fast fashion trends. In response, companies must embrace flexibility to swiftly meet customer needs using Lean strategies such as JIT production. This entails producing only what is needed, in the right quantity, and precisely when required. By doing so, the accumulation of large product lots that often lead to overproduction and sub-optimal products is effectively avoided. The relatively low relation values are consistent with the assertions of [36], which underscore the necessity of complementing JIT production with other Lean tools. Notably, the engagement and motivation of individuals are pivotal in enabling the effective implementation of pull production system.

The final group of Lean practices in our analysis demonstrates notably low prominence values, suggesting that they may not significantly contribute to the goal of solid waste reduction within the Apparel industry. These practices are SM4: Customer Involvement, PT7: Layout Size and Shape, and PC4: Statistical Process Control (SPC).

6 Conclusion

This paper, is a first step to understand the cause-effect relationships of certain Lean manufacturing practices for the reduction of solid waste, and consequently for better eco-efficiency performance. The study is focused on analyzing the context of manufacturing companies in the Apparel sector, through the Fuzzy DEMATEL approach.

In particular, the analysis of the DEMATEL approach responses showed that the Lean practices studied in this article can be divided into 5 different areas. This kind of result was extremely useful in answering the research question. Indeed, in order to explain how the cause-effect relationships between various lean manufacturing practices, for the reduction of solid waste, manifest themselves; it was necessary to analyze how these new areas of practices interact with each other. The cause-effect relationships of each new area and analyzed in detail in Sect. 5. To summaries the most significant outcomes, we can say that the areas of Lean practices are divided into: "initiators", "mediators" and "impacted factors". The practices in area 1, are initiators. It is important to note that all practices in area one are soft lean practices (Management commitment and support, Workforce training and awareness, Kaizen events, Employee engagement). Practices that mediate between area 1 and area 4 and 5 are included in area 2. These practices are strongly influenced by the "initiator" practices, but at the same time have a strong influence on other practices. Finally, practices that are considered to be "impacted factors" are found in area 4 and 5. Area 5 contains practices that are most influenced by area 1 and 2. While the practices in area 4 are also influenced but more weakly than the practices in area 5. This type of study has shown how lean manufacturing practices are very interconnected with each other to have better eco-efficiency performance. In particular, we have seen how soft practices have an initiating role with respect to the other practices. This does not mean that soft practices have a greater impact on the reduction of solid waste, but that in order to implement practices such as those in area

5 (PT3 One-piece-flow (continuous flow), PT5 Total Quality Management (TQM), PC5 Smoothed (levelled) production, PC1 Pull production/takt time), it is first necessary to go to work on more cultural aspects of Lean. This kind of result is in line with other studies dealing with the impact of lean practices on the performance of manufacturing companies.

In conclusion, the result of this research was able to analyze the role of lean manufacturing practices in reducing solid waste, and in particular what cause-effect relationships exist between the various practices. This article partially fills the gap in the literature exposed in Sect. 2, and at the same time brings a better understanding of how lean practices can be used for environmental sustainability purposes. On the practitioner side, this study could be useful for companies that decide to implement lean manufacturing practices for performance and eco-efficiency issues. In fact, it could be a guideline for understanding what relationships exist between various lean practices. Further research can be conducted on this topic. First of all, it might be interesting to go and analyze other manufacturing sectors with the same approach. This could provide cross-sectoral feedback on the role of various Lean practices for eco-efficiency performance issues.

References

1. Bai, C., Satir, A., Sarkis, J.: Investing in lean manufacturing practices: an environmental and operational perspective. Int. J. Prod. Res. **57**(4), 1037–1051 (2019). https://doi.org/10.1080/00207543.2018.1498986
2. Garza-Reyes, J.A.: Green lean and the need for Six Sigma. International Journal of Lean Six Sigma **6**, 226–248 (2015). https://doi.org/10.1108/ijlss-04-2014-0010
3. Kleindorfer, P.R., Singhal, K., Wassenhove, L.N.: Sustainable Operations Management. Prod. Oper. Manag. **14**, 482–492 (2005). https://doi.org/10.1111/j.1937-5956.2005.tb00235.x
4. S., G.P., Resta Barbara, B.A., Dotti.: Lean Manufacturing and Sustainability: An Integrated View, in Advances in Production Management Systems. Initiatives for a Sustainable World, O. and M. R. J. and G. R. F. and S. M. T. and von C. G. and K. D. Nääs Irenilza and Vendrametto, Ed., Cham: Springer International Publishing, pp. 659–666 (2016)
5. King, A., Lenox, M.J.: Lean and green an empirical examination of the relationship between lean production and environmental performance. Prod. Oper. Manag. **10**, 244–256 (2001). https://doi.org/10.1111/j.1937-5956.2001.tb00373.x
6. Longoni., Cagliano, R.: Cross-functional executive involvement and worker involvement in lean manufacturing and sustainability alignment, International Journal of Operations & Production Management, **35**, 1332–1358, (2015) https://doi.org/10.1108/ijopm-02-2015-0113
7. Chen, P.-K., Lujan-Blanco, I., Fortuny-Santos, J., Ruiz-de-Arbulo-López, P.: Lean Manufacturing and Environmental Sustainability: The Effects of Employee Involvement, Stakeholder Pressure and ISO 14001. Sustainability **12**, 7258 (2020). https://doi.org/10.3390/su12187258
8. Dieste, M., Panizzolo, R., Garza-Reyes, J.A.: Evaluating the impact of lean practices on environmental performance: evidences from five manufacturing companies. Production Planning and Control **31**(9), 739–756 (2019). https://doi.org/10.1080/09537287.2019.1681535
9. Chiarini,: Sustainable manufacturing-greening processes using specific Lean Production tools: An empirical observation from European motorcycle component manufacturers, J Clean Prod, **85**, 226–233, (2014) https://doi.org/10.1016/j.jclepro.2014.07.080
10. Shah, R., Ward, P.T.: Defining and developing measures of lean production. J. Oper. Manag. **25**, 785–805 (2007). https://doi.org/10.1016/j.jom.2007.01.019

11. Frecassetti, S., Kassem, B., Kundu, K., Ferrazzi, M., Portioli-Staudacher, A.: Introducing Lean practices through simulation: A case study in an Italian SME. Qual. Manag. J. **30**(2), 90–104 (2023). https://doi.org/10.1080/10686967.2023.2171326
12. Panizzolo, R.: Applying the lessons learned from 27 lean manufacturers.: The relevance of relationships management. Int. J. Prod. Econ. **55**(3), 223–240 (1998). https://doi.org/10.1016/S0925-5273(98)00066-8
13. Dieste, M., Panizzolo, R., Garza-Reyes, J.A., Anosike, A.: The relationship between lean and environmental performance: Practices and measures. J. Clean. Prod. **224**, 120–131 (2019). https://doi.org/10.1016/j.jclepro.2019.03.243
14. Sobral, M.C., de Sousa Jabbour, A.B.L., Chiappetta Jabbour, C.J.: Green Benefits From Adopting Lean Manufacturing: A Case Study From the Automotive Sector, Environmental Quality Management, **22**(3), 65–72, (2013) https://doi.org/10.1002/TQEM.21336
15. Dr. Goyal, A., Dr. Agrawal, R., Kumar Sharma, A.: Green Quality Circle: Achieving Sustainable Manufacturing with Low Investment, Resources, Conservation & Recycling Advances, p. 200103, (2022) https://doi.org/10.1016/j.rcradv.2022.200103
16. Costa, F., Lispi, L., Staudacher, A.P., Rossini, M., Kundu, K., Cifone, F.D.: How to foster Sustainable Continuous Improvement: A cause-effect relations map of Lean soft practices. Operations Research Perspectives **6**, 100091 (2019). https://doi.org/10.1016/j.orp.2018.100091
17. Siegel, R., Antony, J., Garza-Reyes, J.A., Cherrafi, A., Lameijer, B.: Integrated green lean approach and sustainability for SMEs: From literature review to a conceptual framework, Journal of Cleaner Production, **240**. Elsevier Ltd (2019). https://doi.org/10.1016/j.jclepro.2019.118205
18. Pampanelli, B., Found, P., Bernardes, A.M.: A Lean & Green Model for a production cell. J. Clean. Prod. **85**, 19–30 (2014). https://doi.org/10.1016/j.jclepro.2013.06.014
19. Iranmanesh, M., Zailani, S., Hyun, S., Ali, M., Kim, K.: Impact of Lean Manufacturing Practices on Firms' Sustainable Performance: Lean Culture as a Moderator. Sustainability **11**, 1112 (2019). https://doi.org/10.3390/su11041112
20. Ferrazzi, M., Portioli-Staudacher, A.: Using the Lean Approach for Improving Eco-Efficiency Performance: A Case Study for Plastic Reduction, pp. 242–252. (2023) https://doi.org/10.1007/978-3-031-43662-8_18
21. Ferrazzi, M., Portioli-Staudacher, A.: Applying the Value Stream Map to Streamline Energy Consumption: Analysis of an Italian Company, pp. 125–136. (2023) https://doi.org/10.1007/978-3-031-43662-8_10
22. Ferrazzi, M., Frecassetti, S., Staudacher, A.P.: Influence of the Lean Approach on Corporate Environmental Sustainability: A Case Study, in IFIP Advances in Information and Communication Technology, Springer Science and Business Media Deutschland GmbH, pp. 285–294. (2023) https://doi.org/10.1007/978-3-031-25741-4_24
23. Sartal, A. I. Martinez-Senra, and V. Cruz-Machado, "Are all lean principles equally eco-friendly? A panel data study," *J Clean Prod*, vol. 177, pp. 362–370, Mar. 2018, https://doi.org/10.1016/j.jclepro.2017.12.190
24. García-Alcaraz, J.L, Morales García, A.S., Díaz-Reza, J.R., Jiménez Macías, E., Javierre Lardies, C., Blanco Fernández, J.: Effect of lean manufacturing tools on sustainability: the case of Mexican maquiladoras, Environmental Science and Pollution Research, **29**(26), 39622–39637 (2022) https://doi.org/10.1007/s11356-022-18978-6
25. Rothenberg, S., Pil, F.K., Maxwell, J.: LEAN, GREEN, AND THE QUEST FOR SUPERIOR ENVIRONMENTAL PERFORMANCE. Prod. Oper. Manag. **10**, 228–243 (2009). https://doi.org/10.1111/j.1937-5956.2001.tb00372.x

26. R. Che Mamat, B. Md Deros, M. N. Ab Rahman, M. Khalil Omar, and S. Abdullah, "SOFT LEAN PRACTICES FOR SUCCESSFUL LEAN PRODUCTION SYSTEM IMPLEMENTATION IN MALAYSIA AUTOMOTIVE SMES: A PROPOSED FRAMEWORK," *J Teknol*, vol. 77, Jun. 2015, https://doi.org/10.11113/jt.v77.6910
27. Bortolotti, T., Boscari, S., Danese, P.: Successful lean implementation: Organizational culture and soft lean practices. Int. J. Prod. Econ. **160**, 182–201 (2015). https://doi.org/10.1016/j.ijpe.2014.10.013
28. Gaiardelli, P., Resta, B., Dotti, S.: Exploring the role of human factors in lean management. International Journal of Lean Six Sigma **10**, 339–366 (2019). https://doi.org/10.1108/ijlss-08-2017-0094
29. Hernandez-Matias, J. C, Ocampo, J.R, Hidalgo, A., Vizan, A.: Lean manufacturing and operational performance. Interrelationships between human-related lean practices, Journal of Manufacturing Technology Management. (2019) https://doi.org/10.1108/jmtm-04-2019-0140
30. Wu, W.W., Lee, Y.T.: Developing global managers' competencies using the fuzzy DEMATEL method. Expert Syst. Appl. **32**(2), 499–507 (2007). https://doi.org/10.1016/j.eswa.2005.12.005
31. S. L. Si, X. Y. You, H. C. Liu, and P. Zhang, "DEMATEL Technique: A Systematic Review of the State-of-the-Art Literature on Methodologies and Applications," *Mathematical Problems in Engineering*, vol. 2018. Hindawi Limited, 2018. https://doi.org/10.1155/2018/3696457
32. Zaki Yusup, M., Hasrulnizzam Wan Mahmood, W., Rizal Salleh, M., Shahimy Mohd Yusof, A.: Review the influence of lean tools and its performance against the index of manufacturing sustainability, Int. J. Agile Systems and Management, **8**(2), 116–131 (2015)
33. Costa, L.B.M., Godinho Filho, M., Fredendall, L.D., Gómez Paredes, F.J.: Lean, six sigma and lean six sigma in the food industry: A systematic literature review, Trends in Food Science and Technology, **82**. Elsevier Ltd, pp. 122–133 (2018) https://doi.org/10.1016/j.tifs.2018.10.002
34. Raj, D., Ma, Y.J., Gam, H.J., Banning, J.: Implementation of lean production and environmental sustainability in the Indian apparel manufacturing industry: a way to reach the triple bottom line. International Journal of Fashion Design, Technology and Education **10**(3), 254–264 (2017). https://doi.org/10.1080/17543266.2017.1280091
35. Dora, M., van Goubergen, D., Kumar, M., Molnar, A., Gellynck, X.: Application of lean practices in small and medium-sized food enterprises. British Food Journal **116**(1), 125–141 (2014). https://doi.org/10.1108/BFJ-05-2012-0107
36. Jana, P., Tiwari, M.: Lean management in apparel manufacturing, in Lean Tools in Apparel Manufacturing: A Volume in The Textile Institute Book Series, Elsevier, pp. 1–16. (2021) https://doi.org/10.1016/B978-0-12-819426-3.00014-X
37. Laureani., Antony, J.: Standards for Lean Six Sigma certification, International Journal of Productivity and Performance Management, **61**(1), 110–120 (2011) https://doi.org/10.1108/17410401211188560
38. Chen, C.A: Using DEMATEL Method for Medical Tourism Development in Taiwan. (2012)
39. Maia, L.C, Alves, A.C., Leão, C.P.: Sustainable Work Environment with Lean Production in Textile and Clothing Industry. International Journal of Industrial Engineering and Management (IJIEM), **4**(3), 183–190 (2013) Available: www.iim.ftn.uns.ac.rs/ijiem_journal.php

The Contribution of SMED to the Sustainability of Organizations

J. C. Sá[1,2(✉)], R. C. M. Sales-Contini[1,3], Francisco J. G. Silva[1,4], José Dinis-Carvalho[5], P. Costa[1], and M. T. Pereira[1,2]

[1] School of Engineering of Porto (ISEP), Polytechnic of Porto, Rua Dr António Bernardino de Almeida 431, 4249-015 Porto, Portugal
cvs@isep.ipp.pt

[2] Associate Laboratory for Energy, Transports and Aerospace (LAETA-INEGI), Rua Dr. Roberto Frias 400, 4200-465 Porto, Portugal

[3] College of Technology São José dos Campos, Professor Jessen Vidal, Centro Paula Souza, São José dos Campos, SP, Brazil

[4] Institute of Science and Innovation in Mechanical and Industrial Engineering (INEGI), Rua Dr Roberto Frias 400, 4200-465 Porto, Portugal

[5] Production and Systems Department, University of Minho, Campus de Azurém, 4804-533 Guimarães, Portugal

Abstract. In the last decade, a trend towards a reduction in the setup time of machines has been observed in industries. The case study presented here was developed in a company dedicated to manufacturing tools and moulds for the automotive, energy, electronics, and aerospace industries. In this company, there are some machines with a high setup time. Having as an objective the reduction of the setup time, it was decided to implement the Single Minute Exchange of Die (SMED) in a cutting saw. To evaluate the impact of the implementation of SMED in terms of sustainability, the impacts in the three pillars of sustainability were evaluated: economic, social, and environmental. The SMED implementation allowed a reduction of the machine setup time by about 43%. Regarding environmental sustainability, it was possible to verify an increase in energy consumption, as well as an increase in lubrication oils, which led to an increase of about 2 048,90 € in the productive cost of the machine. However, despite these cost increases, the workers' productivity rate was also increase, reducing the environmental impact by piece produced. The obtained results make us conclude that these machine lean tools have impacted both positively and negatively those three indicators of sustainability, all due to the decrease in setup time.

Keywords: SMED · Lean philosophy · Sustainability · Lean Tools

1 Introduction

Lean philosophy is a type of management focused on eliminating waste, which is classified into seven types: waiting, transportation, overprocessing, overproduction, defects, inventory, and motion [1]. According to Ohno [2] waste that exists along the production flow is a loss creator and as such must be removed. Recognizing their location is

Published by Springer Nature Switzerland AG 2024
T. van Kollenburg et al. (Eds.): ELEC 2023, IFIP AICT 681, pp. 155–168, 2024.
https://doi.org/10.1007/978-3-031-63265-5_12

crucial to identifying them, and this should be done on the shop floor as this is where they occur [3]. Lean philosophy was a new way of managing companies, and became evident that has provided expressive differences in productivity, quality, and product development, explaining by that way the success of Japanese industry at the time [4] and became recognised as a major competitive advantage [5]. Several authors such as Lander and Liker [6], James-Moore and Gibbons [7], and McDonald et al. [8] define the most important areas of Lean philosophy to be flexibility; waste elimination; optimization; involvement with people and process control. In addition, several authors have also created tools/techniques to help companies implement the Lean philosophy, the main one being the creator of Value Stream Mapping (VSM), which focuses on detecting the waste formed along the production lines [9]. Other lean tools support is Daily Kaizen, Gemba Walk, Obeya Room, A3 Report, Waste Identification Diagram (WID), Visual Management, Yokoten, 5S, Standard Work, One Point Lesson (OPL), Total Productive Maintenance (TPM), Single Minute Exchange of Dies (SMED), among other [10].

Shingo [11] developed SMED over 19 years, passing through three large companies where he implemented this tool: Mazda, Mitsubishi and Toyota Motors Company. SMED starts from a preliminary stage where internal and external setups are not differentiated and three conceptual stages: i) first stage: where internal and external setups are separated, ii) conversion of internal setup into external setup and, finally, iii) rationalization of all aspects of the setup operation. SMED also allows for promoting safety in the workplace, simplifying setups, reducing skilled operators by standardizing and simplifying activities (promoting operator flexibility, compensating for the absence or lack of operators) and also promoting teamwork, finding solutions to reduce work effort and reducing machine downtime [12–14]. This will enable the development of a more sustainable production environment. This proposal is in line with the United Nations Sustainable Development Goals (Agenda 2030) [15], which relate to decent work and economic growth (Goal 8), building resilient infrastructure, promoting sustainable industrialisation and fostering innovation (Goal 9), and ensuring the reduction of costs in manufacturing processes, thereby enabling a more sustainable production environment (Goal 12).

In practical terms, SMED has allowed a reduction in setup time in a packaging production sector from 5–6 h to 2.5 h [16]; in the operation of a mechanical press for a lift company, a gain of 1,628. 1,628 per year was achieved [17]; on an electron beam machine used in the automotive industry, the setup time was reduced by around 50% [18]; in a company producing cold technical profiles used in the construction industry, a reduction of around 10.8% in the OEE - Overall Equipment Effectiveness - level was observed [19]; and in the cutting and packaging section of a cork processing plant, a reduction in setup time of around 24% was achieved, i.e. 9% more than expected [20].

Applying the SMED, this paper presents a study performed in a company manufacturing high-precision moulds and tools for the automotive, electronics, energy, oil and gas and aeronautics industries. The methodology was implemented in the raw material cutting sector, namely in a semi-automatic sawing equipment, to identify and implement process improvements that can impact the company's sustainability. In order to relate the implementation of SMED to the increase in the company's sustainability, the various impacts on the three pillars of sustainability were studied, and these impacts were calculated before and after the implementation of the SMED methodology.

2 Methodology

2.1 Case Study

The case study was carried out in a company manufacturing moulds and tools, both in steel, aluminium and, more recently, plastic.

The SMED was implemented to carry out the study of the impacts on the sustainability of the company in raw materials' cutting operations. The object of study is the operational processes of a semi-automatic saw (FMB brand, model MAJOR). This saw is not fully automatic, as it requires the operator to adjust to the cutting conditions, such as: automatically adjusting the workpiece to its cutting length, adjusting the cutting angle and setting the cutting speed pointed out for that material. However, the act of cutting itself is fully automatic, with only the start button having to be clicked.

When used at a zero inclination (0°), this saw allows to cut re-bonded rods up to 260 mm in diameter and rectangular sections up to 260 mm thick and 370 mm width. It also has a total operating power of 1.94 kW (Fig. 1).

Fig. 1. Semi-automatic saw (FMB, model MAJOR) used for cutting raw materials.

2.2 SMED: Methodology of Implementation

This tool included the following phases, all represented in the three stages of SMED:

(1) Problem identification, making a video recording to check which actions cause the increase in setup time; (2) Improvement planning, making the action plan based on the waste and improvement opportunities identified in the video; (3) Action plan, to develop the necessary works to improve the setup time; (4) Monitoring, and questioning the workers, at the end of the application of the methodology, if they agree with the

application of the methodology, and if they agree with their work conditions; (5) Evaluation of the results, commenting on the results obtained and also planning the actions to be carried out in the future.

The SMED usually consisted of three stages: (1) separate the setup time into internal setup and external setup, using a checklist to identify them; (2) check the operating conditions, and (3) improve the transport of raw materials. After the first stage, the work was mainly focused on the second stage, the transformation of internal setup into external setup, thus trying to decrease, or if possible, remove the setup time while the saw is stopped. This would require not only preparation of the operating conditions but also an attempt to standardize the operators' functions. Finally, in the third stage, not only some setup times that can already be done externally were reduced, in order to have a lower percentage of time used in setup, but also some implementations were suggested for the future that would allow this tool to be further boosted. The main actions performed are described below.

Stage 1 - Separation of Internal Tasks and External Tasks

The first task to be done was a checklist with the setup times of the machine, using a video of a setup. The video allowed to observe 16 h lost in setups per day, i.e., 8 h of work per day per worker. To decrease the time waste in internal setup, it was necessary to identify all the setup times present in the operation of these workers. To do this, we used the 2 h video for each shift, thus being able to observe 25% of each worker's working day. After that, the operating conditions were checked, i.e., whether the workers have the necessary conditions to perform their tasks, analyzing if the workers had all necessary tools and the corresponding work position.

Stage 2 - Transformation of Internal Tasks into External Tasks

In this stage, internal tasks were transformed into external tasks. The company has a perfect factory management tool that allows to advance with the preparation of operating conditions: the centralized software iCFaR integrated into the ERP PRIMAVERA, speeding up the access to all information and also helping in strategic, tactical and operational decision-making, coupled with the accuracy of financial information.

With this technology, it was possible to obtain all data regarding the parts produced: the date of delivery to the customer; the expected date for the manufacturing start; the type of raw material; and the dimensions of the raw material necessary for the production of the part; operating range of the part's manufacture (machines through which it passed until it is complete); need for subcontracting, the location and the surface treatments or heat treatments to which the part was subjected.

However, it was first necessary to understand which actions lead to the highest rate of internal setup in relation to external setup and to understand whether it was possible to transform these internal setups into external setups, or, if not, to substantially reduce the setup time associated with this action. To make this possible, the percentages of internal setup and external setup times were calculated for each action causing setup time. Next, it was necessary to understand which of these tasks can be converted from internal into external tasks. To do this, it was necessary to identify which tasks could not be performed while the machine was running.

Stage 3 - Improvement

In the last stage of the SMED implementation, tools' standardization was applied, thus trying to reduce the setup time associated with their demand. To organize the stock, shelves were purchased that allowed the separation of all standardized tools, categorizing them by type and measure. Finally, measures were suggested to further reduce the overall setup time.

To verify the efficiency of the SMED implementation, the following three sustainability criteria were evaluated: Economic, Environmental and Social. In the Economic category, the criteria of Production capacity (H), costs and profits derived from setup (€) were evaluated, in the Environmental category, Energy consumption (kWh) and Oil consumption (L) were accessed and, finally, in the social category, the Labor associated with the transport of loads (J).

3 Results and Discussion

After the application of the three SMED stages, a new 2 h video recording was made, but this time only on the second shift, the one with higher percentage of internal setup compared to external setup.

3.1 Results of SMED Implementation to Setup Times

After checking the existing tools in the production area, properly training the employees and implementing SMED, it was found that the time taken to carry out the tasks had reached the expected time. Table 1 shows the setup times for the second shift. SMED reduced the internal setup time by approximately 50%, so these figures would be expected to be achieved in this case study.

Figure 2 shows the percentage difference between the elapsed time with setup and out-of-setup time, and Fig. 3 shows the percentage of in-setup versus out-of-setup, before and after the implementation of the SMED. In both Figures, the increase in the time spent out of setup and with external setup is observed after the SMED implementation.

Table 1. Setup times after SMED implementation (hh:mm:ss).

Setup Tasks	Running time	Setup Total Time	Internal Setup	External Setup
Identify which raw material to use for the next manufacturing order	00:02:10	00:02:10	00:02:10	00:00:00
Locate and place in the machine the raw material needed for the next OF	00:03:20	00:05:30	00:03:20	00:00:00
Start the cutting process	00:03:30	00:00:10	00:00:10	00:00:00
Find a specific standardised	00:06:10	00:00:30	00:00:00	00:00:30
Find a specific standardised	00:07:40	00:00:30	00:00:00	00:00:30
Find a specific standardised	00:14:25	00:03:20	00:00:00	00:03:20
Identify which raw material to use for the next manufacturing order	00:15:10	00:00:40	00:00:00	00:00:40
Locate and place on the pallet the raw material needed for the next OF	00:18:45	00:03:35	00:00:00	00:03:35
Put the raw material that was left on the pallet into the machine	00:19:15	00:00:30	00:00:30	00:00:00
Start the cutting process	00:19:25	00:00:10	00:00:10	00:00:00
Receive material from a supplier	00:45:40	00:08:30	00:00:00	00:08:30
Identify the material with the manufacturing order number and place it on the pallet	00:52:10	00:06:30	00:00:20	00:06:10

(*continued*)

Table 1. (*continued*)

Setup Tasks	Running time	Setup Total Time	Internal Setup	External Setup
Identify which raw material to use for the next manufacturing order	01:12:20	00:00:20	00:00:20	00:00:00
Locate and place in the machine the raw material needed for the next OF	01:14:40	00:02:20	00:02:20	00:00:00
Start the cutting process	01:14:50	00:00:10	00:00:10	00:00:00
Creation of a transport guide that allows parts to be sent to suppliers	01:21:30	00:02:00	00:00:00	00:02:00
Find a specific standardised	01:24:40	00:01:30	00:00:00	00:01:30
Identify which raw material to use for the next manufacturing order	01:30:10	00:00:30	00:00:00	00:00:30
Locate and place on the pallet the raw material needed for the next OF	01:35:05	00:04:55	00:00:00	00:04:55
Put the raw material that was left on the pallet into the machine	01:30:20	00:00:20	00:00:20	00:00:00
Start the cutting process	01:32:25	00:00:10	00:00:00	00:00:10
Receiving material from a supplier	01:48:30	00:04:40	00:00:00	00:04:40
Find a specific standardised	01:55:10	00:02:25	00:00:00	00:02:25
Worker's snack	02:10:00	00:00:10	00:00:00	00:00:10
Total setup times	02:10:00	00:51:35	00:09:30	00:25:15
	Running time	**Setup Total Time**	**Internal Setup**	**External Setup**

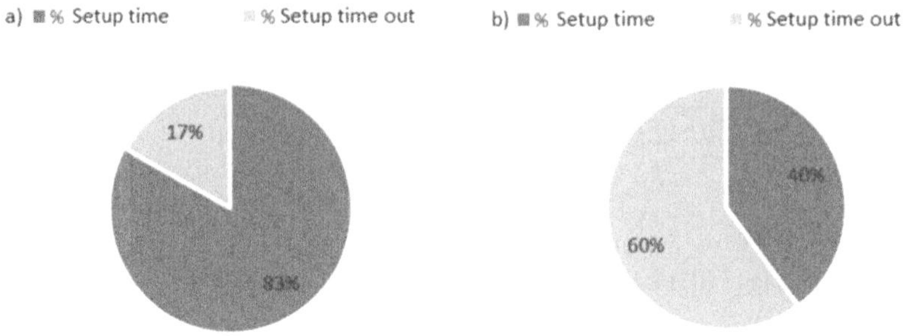

Fig. 2. Percentage of setup time vs. out-of-setup time: a) before and b) after SMED implementation.

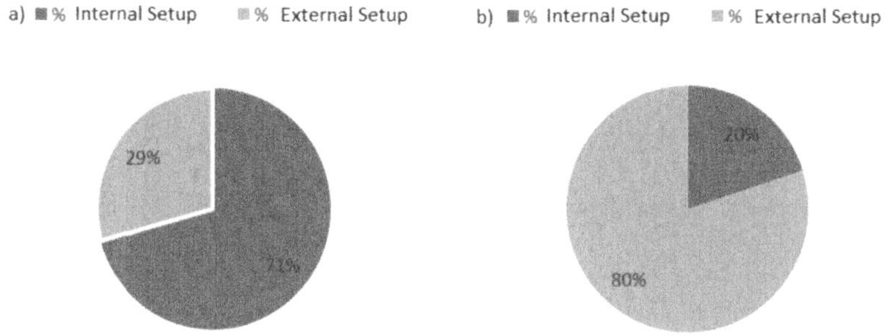

Fig. 3. Percentage of internal setup time vs external setup: a) before SMED and b) after SMED.

3.2 Analyzing the Three Sustainability Criteria

Following the results of the application of this tool to setup times, it was necessary to define the indicators to be analyzed and quantify their impact, as defined in Sect. 2.2.

3.2.1 Increased Machine Production Capacity

Due to the application of the SMED, the total daily setup time was reduced by 43%, thus allowing the operator to anticipate some tasks while the machine was cutting. With this, the operator can prepare a new part to be cut in the cutting machine during the cutting operation. Thus, the wasted time after the machine stops will decrease considerably, resulting in a productivity increase of the machine. This fact is supported by the results of the previous subchapter, where there was a reduction of internal setup of about 51%.

In order to transform this information into numbers, the production records of the cutting machine were analyzed before the implementation of the methodology and after. However, it was difficult to obtain a comparison through the unit number of pieces cut, as there are pieces that take much longer to cut than others, due to the high hardness of the raw material or its higher dimensions. Therefore, it was decided to compare the results according to the daily production hours. To help analyze the production hours of the machine operators, the iCFaR tool was used, which allows a search by operator code, where the production time of the machine in question on the designated day is indicated. Three random days were then chosen before the methodology was implemented and the data represented in Table 2 was obtained.

Table 2. Productive flow regarding three random days before SMED.

	Total Time (h)	Production Time (h)	Machine Downtime (h)	Number of cut pieces
Day 1	16	07:56:00	08:04:00	374.00
Day 2	16	08:50:00	07:10:00	312.00
Day 3	16	07:24:00	08:36:00	248.00
Average	16	08:03:20	07:56:40	311.33

Next, three random days after the implementation of the three SMED stages were analyzed (Table 3).

Table 3. Productive flow regarding three random days after SMED.

	Total Time (h)	Production Time (h)	Machine Downtime (h)	Number of cut pieces
Day 1	16	14:24:00	01:36:00	528.00
Day 2	16	12:52:00	02:08:00	384.00
Day 3	16	14:16:00	01:44:00	382.00
Average	16	14:10:40	01:49:20	431.33

It was found that there was an increase of about 38% in the hourly rate used to cut the parts, also translating into an increase in the unit quantity of parts cut. However, as previously mentioned, this increase cannot be considered for comparison, because as proven by the previous results, in Table 2 a day was visualized with 374 parts cut, but with a productive hourly rate of 49.58%, while in Table 3 a day was visualized with 382 parts produced at an hourly production rate of 89.17%. This is because the parts that needed to be cut were either harder or larger than on the previous day. Translating these values into invoicing, it was estimated that the company charges an average rate of 45 €/h to the customer, so it is possible to calculate the increase in revenue due to the increase in production capacity. Thus, the company's turnover influenced by the operator's hourly rate increased by about 176%, a very relevant rate for its future, since, according to Fig. 4, it increases, on average, from 65 659 € to 135 636 € (about 206%), using the number of working days of the year 2022 (254 days) and the average wage (6,50 €/h) for each operator considered.

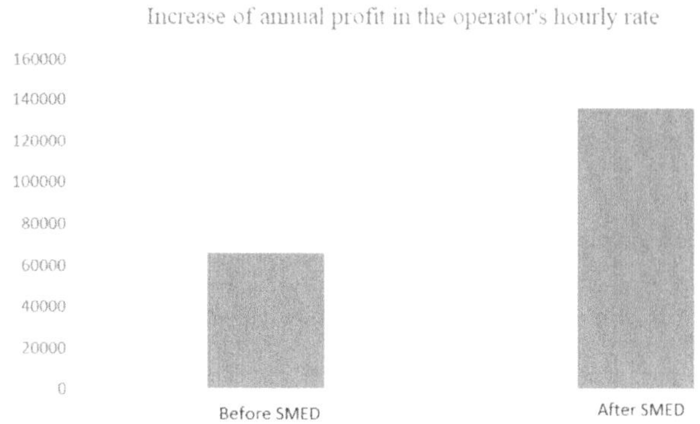

Fig. 4. Comparison of the annual profit (€) on the operator's hourly rate, pre- and post-SMED.

3.2.2 Energy Consumption

Energy consumption is the factor that most influences the environmental sustainability pillar of the company under study. In order to be able to calculate the amount of energy consumed in the workstation in question, three possible stages were considered for the cutting machine, these being: production stage, standby stage and off stage. The production stage is active when the machine is running. Sufficient power is supplied to the machine ensuring the required cutting speed for the machine. This mode is mostly active during working hours, except for downtime, breakdowns, or setups. The waiting stage is activated when it is necessary to stop the cutting machine for some reason, such as a lack of raw material to cut or even a lack of manufacturing orders, when it is necessary to make an internal setup, or when it is necessary to have some kind of maintenance, either on the machine or on the electrical system of the company. Off-stage only exists at the end of the two shifts, i.e., between 00:30 h and 07:00 h, as it does not pay to leave the power on when nothing was produced.

Thus, the total energy consumed in this workstation is given by the calculation of the total energy, $Total\ Energy = Ep + Ee + Ed$, where "Ep" is the energy associated with production, "Ee" is associated with waiting and "Ed" is associated with the energy spent with the machine switched off, which in this case is zero. It is also known that the energy output associated with the machine in production is 4.4 times greater than the energy spent in the standby stage. Considering the same number of working days considered previously (254 days) and the daily time as 16 h - two shifts - it is possible to define the number of annual working hours of the machine for each stage before and after the application of the SMED, using the average times of the previous subchapter.

Knowing that the electrical power required for the machine in the waiting state, i.e., without performing the cutting process, using only the energy for lubrication, is 0.44 kW, it was finally possible to calculate the energy consumed per year before and after the application of the SMED methodology. The values are: before the SMED application: 5 016,78 kWh and after the SMED application: 7 343,13 kWh, in other words, an increase by 46.37%.

3.2.3 Oil Utilization

Most of the machines in a factory are subject to the lubrication process. In this process, cooling/lubricant fluids are used, which allow the metal to be machined without suffering surface damage. In the machine considered in this case study, this is no exception. The cutting saw needs to be lubricated to fulfil its function. For this purpose, the machine is already integrated with a self-lubrication system, the intensity of which can be adjusted by the operator. To find out the average oil consumption of this machine, before and after the implementation of the SMED, a stopwatch was needed in which the operator could deposit from time to time 20 L of oil - which is the volume of the machine's storage tank, designated for its section. Measurements of the oil deposited allowed to conclude that oil consumption has also increased. This is due to the minimization of the internal setup (higher productivity, less time wasted). The oil cost per litre is 6.20 €, which is mixed with water at a rate of 60% oil and 40% water. Thus, there was a 130% increase in daily oil consumption, resulting in an annual expenditure of 3 680,46 €, compared to 2 049,78 € before SMED. Because the oil consumption increased, it seems that environmental sustainability was deteriorated. However, more oil consumed corresponds to a even better productivity, decreasing the volume of oil consumed per part produced, improving by that way the environmental sustainability.

3.2.4 Annual Working Costs

This indicator aims to analyze the impact of the section costs related to the change in the setup time of the section. This cost can be divided into two points: Operating cost, which includes the work cost of the operators, as well as all the costs associated with the operation of the machine, and energy cost, which includes the increase in energy consumption. In the operating cost, the cost of operators' salaries was considered, as well as the increase in oil costs. As for the operators' salary, it does not depend on the setup time, as it did not change. Thus, there was a daily cost of 104 €, making up for an annual cost of approximately 26 416 €. As for the cost of the oil that allows the machine to operate, it has already been calculated in the previous subchapter, which is 3 680,46 €, increasing by 1 630,68 €. Thus, an annual operating cost of approximately 30 096,50 € was obtained approximately, compared to the previous 28 465,82 €.

Considering the energy cost of 0.179778 €/kWh (average value charged in 2022) by the most energy operators in Portugal, which must be multiplied by the energy consumed by the machine annually, there was thus an increase of 418,22 € per year in the energy consumed by the machine, which is not very significant, since the increase in invoicing due to the increase in productivity, prevailed over this increase in energy cost.

3.2.5 Work Associated with Cargo Transport

The calculation of the energy spent by the operators before SMED implementation shows, for the situation before the implementation, the average weights of the loads transported daily, the average number of journeys, both to the entrance and to the place where the raw material is stored, and the total distance calculated by the sum of the multiplications between the distances by the number of times they were travelled is represented by $Work\ (J) = Load\ Mass\ (kg) * g\ (m/s^2) * Total\ distance\ (m)$.

Finally, the daily energy expended by the operators in the form of labor to take the raw materials was studied. After the SMED implementation, it was foreseen that the number of times the operators would have to go to the place where they store the raw materials would increase, because due to the decrease in the setup time, the operators were able to increase the productive time, thus needing to fetch many more times raw materials to be able to fulfil this increase of production. In addition, a decrease in the load mass to be moved was still expected, due to the implementation of the use of the forklift to move the pallets and the use of handles. This shows how the social sustainability has been improved through this work. The results obtained after the implementation of the methodology were compared with the previous results in Fig. 5.

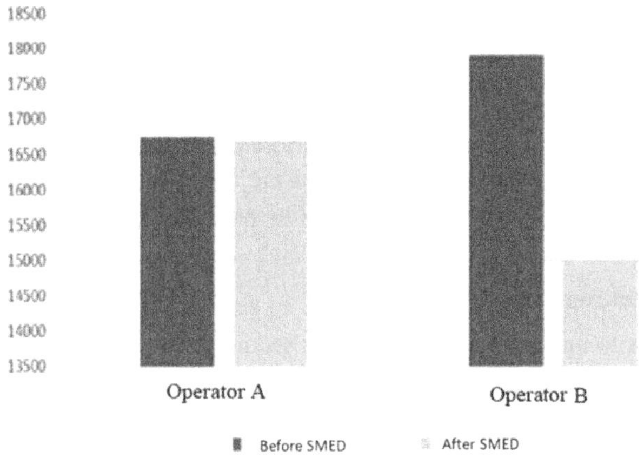

Fig. 5. Comparison of operator work (J) before and after SMED implementation.

4 Conclusion

The main objective of this work was to implement a SMED in a company, starting by analyzing the historical setup time of the saw and dividing it into internal and external setups. As the initial internal setup percentage was 71%, the main objective was to reduce it to 21%, i.e., a reduction of 50% in the total setup time.

Once the target was defined, a recording was made to understand the initial state of the setup. After analyzing the footage, the setup times of the operators during these 2 h of recording were mapped to identify which tasks were internal and which were external to setup. The tasks were then externalized and standardized into an operational mode. Finally, possible improvements for this workstation were identified to optimize the setup.

Through the implementation of SMED, it was concluded that in 4 months, the approximate reduction of the general setup time was 43%, while the reduction of the internal setup was 51%, thus exceeding the initial goals. Although these results are attractive, both financially and in terms of productivity, this system also has its weaknesses. According to the environmental sustainability analysis, we can see that energy consumption has increased, as well as the use of oils for lubrication, which, already considering the economic sustainability, causes an increase in the productive cost of the machine of about 2 048,90 €. However, considering the new production rates, the consumptions per part are lower, contributing to increase the overall sustainability. Indeed, despite the increases in energy and oil consumptions, in the end, it pays off financially, because an increase in the productivity rate of the workers has been achieved, which has resulted in an annual increase in turnover of around 69 977 €, and therefore an estimated increase in profit for this job from 62 707 € to 130 635,41 € (around 208%).

Thus, it can be stated that, taking into account the focus of this work – a raw material cutting machine (saw), SMED can help in reducing the wasted times in setups, increasing the productivity, which also positively impacts on the environmental and social sustainability of the process. In this case, economical and environmental sustainability were dealt jointly, and social sustainability was worked separately, but regarding the same focus.

References

1. Pereira, A.M., Silva, M.R., Domingues, M.A., Sá, J.C.: Lean six sigma approach to improve the production process in the mould industry: a case study. Qual. Innov. Prosper. **23**(3), 103–121 (2019)
2. Ohno, T.: Toyota Production System: Beyond Large-Scale Production, 1st edn. Productivity Press, New York (1988)
3. Imai, M. Kaizen, G.: A commonsense approach to a continuous improvement strategy. Libr. J. **122**, (1997)
4. Pacheco, D. A. de J. Teoria das Restrições, Lean Manufacturing e Seis Sigma: limites e possibilidades de integração. Production **24**(4), 940–956 (2014)
5. Pakdil, F., Leonard, K.M.: Implementing and sustaining lean processes: the dilemma of societal culture effects. Int. J. Prod. Res. **55**(3), 700–717 (2017)
6. Lander, E., Liker, J.K.: The Toyota production system and art: making highly customized and creative products the Toyota way. Int. J. Prod. Res. **45**(16), 3681–3698 (2007)
7. James-Moore, S.M., Gibbons, A.: Is lean manufacturing universally relevant? An investigative methodology. Int. J. Oper. Prod. Manag. **17**(9), 899–911 (1997)
8. McDonald, T., van Aken, E.M., Rentes, A.F.: Utilising simulation to enhance value stream mapping: a manufacturing case application. Int. J. Logist Res. Appl. **5**(2), 212–232 (2002)
9. Rother, M., Shook, J.: Learning to See: Value Stream Mapping to Add Value and Eliminate Muda. Lean Enterprise Institute (LEI), Cambridge Center, Cambridge (2003)
10. Ferreira, C., Sá, J.C., Ferreira, L.P., Lopes, M.P., Pereira, T., Silva, F.J.G.: iLeanDMAIC - A methodology for implementing the lean tools. Procedia Manuf. **41**, 1095–1102 (2019)
11. Shingo, S.: A Revolution in Manufacturing: The SMED System. Productivity Press, New York (1985)
12. Handfield, R.B., Pannesi, R.T.: Antecedents of lead-time competitiveness in make-to-order manufacturing firms. Int. J. Prod. Res. **32**(12), 5611–6513 (2007)
13. Monteiro, C., Ferreira, L.P., Fernandes, N.O., Sá, J.C., Ribeiro, M.T., Silva, F.J.G.: Improving the machining process of the metalworking industry using the lean tool SMED. Procedia Manuf. **41**, 555–562 (2019)
14. Sousa, E., Silva, F.J.G., Ferreira, L.P., Pereira, M.T., Gouveia, R., Silva, R.P.: Applying SMED methodology in cork stoppers production. Procedia Manuf. **17**, 611–622 (2018)

15. ONU. Transforming our world: the 2030 Agenda for Sustainable Development, 2015/2018 (2015)
16. Ulutas, B.: An application of SMED methodology. World Acad. Sci. Eng. Technol. **79**, 1–4 (2011)
17. Joshi, R., Naik, G.R.: Application of SMED methodology-a case study in small scale industry. Int. J. Sci. Res. Publ. **2**(8), 1–4 (2012)
18. Martins, M., Godina, R., Pimentel, C., Silva, F.J.G., Matias, J.C.O.: A practical study of the application of SMED to electron-beam machining in automotive industry. Procedia Manuf. **17**, 647–654 (2018)
19. Vieira, T., et al.: Optimization of the cold profiling process through SMED. Procedia Manuf. **38**, 892–899 (2019). (Faim 2019)
20. Silva, A., Sá, J.C., Santos, G., Silva, F.J.G., Ferreira, L.P., Pereira, M.T.: A comparison of the application of the SMED methodology in two different cutting lines. Qual. Innov. Prosper. **25**(1), 124–149 (2021)

Social Lean Production

Hoshin Kanri for Social Enterprises - Co-visualizing Values-Based Strategic Plans

Alinda Kokkinou[1,2](✉) and Charlotte Köbus[1]

[1] AVANS University of Applied Sciences, Hogeschoollaan 1, Breda, The Netherlands
kokkinou.a@buas.nl

[2] Breda University of Applied Sciences, Mgr. Hopmanstraat 1, Breda, The Netherlands

Abstract. Social enterprises are a hybrid type of organization that prioritize social and/or ecological values while needing to remain financially sustainable. Social enterprises face several challenges due to this hybrid business model, including aligning internal stakeholders in trading off between social/ecological values and financial value, and communicating these to external stakeholders. Using a single case-study approach, the present study demonstrates how Hoshin Kanri can be modified to fit the needs of social enterprises. The Hoshin Kanri diamond, a diamond shaped X-matrix, is developed by enriching the X-matrix to include terminal and instrumental values to ensure a better fit with the values-driven nature of social enterprises. The empirical data showed that this approach enabled the case company to prioritize according to its values and concurrently reflect on whether its activities were contributing to its social mission or merely necessary to ensure financial sustainability, contributing to both internal communication and communication with external stakeholders. The organization perceived this modified Hoshin Kanri approach as beneficial to help them articulate, prioritize and communicate objectives and activities that contributed to their growth in a way that felt congruent with their values.

Keywords: Continuous improvement · Lean · Social Enterprise · X-Matrix · Non-Profit · Policy Deployment

1 Introduction

Social enterprises (SEs) are values-driven organizations that seek to create or sustain social and/or ecological value through a financially self-sufficient business model [1–3]. SEs play an important role in providing products and services that meet communities' social needs [1] and have therefore been recognized for their contribution towards social issues [4]. SEs contribute to issues such as well-being (e.g. social integration), community creation (e.g. encouraging people to care for the environment and/or each-other) and environmental sustainability (e.g. preservation of the environment) [5–7]. SEs form an important part of the social economy, which also includes non-profits, cooperatives, and hybrid businesses [1]. SEs are positioned on a continuum spanning from non-profit

Published by Springer Nature Switzerland AG 2024
T. van Kollenburg et al. (Eds.): ELEC 2023, IFIP AICT 681, pp. 171–186, 2024.
https://doi.org/10.1007/978-3-031-63265-5_13

organizations to purely commercial for-profit organizations [8, 9]. While non-profit organizations rely on donations and/or subsidies to finance their operations, SEs rely for a substantial part on commercial activities [8] and therefore face the challenge of trading-off between social/ecological values and financial value without engaging in mission drift [2].

SEs encounter several challenges compared to purely for-profit organizations. First, SEs are perceived as less efficient and productive than their for-profit counterparts [1, 10]. SEs also are hindered by stakeholders' lack of awareness of their business model [4]. Typical managerial tools developed for profit organizations have limited application for SEs [10, 11] as they prioritize financial goals and underestimate the importance of the outputs related to their social and/or ecological values. These issues can be attributed to SEs' outputs being difficult to quantify and therefore rendering more conventional measures of productivity and efficiency inappropriate to capture their true contribution [1]. SE's are also perceived as less competitive than commercial businesses [12, 13] and their business model as more expensive [14]. Furthermore, the pursuit of efficiency has a negative connotation for SEs [5] as they worry that pursuing financial value will put them at risk of "mission drift" [25]. In the context of SEs, mission drift can happen when an organization prioritizes financial value over its social or environmental values [25, 36], for example when the continuity of the organization is threatened [15]. SEs are therefore more challenged by their hybrid business model both on the input side and output side.

Lean management was proposed as vehicle for SEs to translate their values and strategy to an actionable set of performance measures that could be used to guide operational decision-making, communicate with stakeholders and concurrently monitor financial and social objectives [10]. Hoshin Kanri is a Lean tool particularly appropriate for strengthening the link between strategy and annual planning cycle [16]. However, documented cases have exclusively investigated deployment of Hoshin Kanri by for-profit organizations, albeit in the context of Corporate Social Responsibility (CSR) as an alternative to the Balanced Scorecard (BSC) [17]. Moreover, despite the prevalence of Hoshin Kanri and policy deployment, relatively little research has been conducted on how these tools can be deployed by smaller organizations [18].

Previous research has shown that adoption of Lean by SEs is possible, but in modified form [11]. Like most management tools, Hoshin Kanri "as is" is not appropriate for SEs as it lacks the explicit focus on core values and ideals which provide meaning and engage workers. The main purpose of this study is to develop and modify Hoshin Kanri, and specifically the X-matrix, in such a way that it fits the values-driven character of SEs. The main research question is: *how can Hoshin Kanri's x-matrix be modified to fit the values-driven characteristic of SEs?* The answer to this question contributes to the further development of "social lean production" [11]. After a brief recap of the literature, the methodology section describes the action research used to develop Hoshin Kanri for SEs in cooperation with a case company. The findings section details the outcomes of the action research. Implications for theory and practice are discussed in the last section.

2 Existing Body of Knowledge and Contribution

This section introduces how continuous improvement (CI) and lean contribute to organizational performance, what Hoshin Kanri entails, and what distinguishes social enterprises from purely for-profit organizations. The conclusion of this section captures the main intended contribution of how the X-matrix can be adapted to advance the match with the values-driven character of social enterprises.

2.1 Continuous Improvement and Lean

Organizations deploy CI to achieve "*sustained improvements regarding effectiveness and efficiency*" which include quality, speed, flexibility, cost, and sustainability outcomes [15]. CI is defined as "*a culture of sustained improvement targeting the elimination of waste in all systems and processes of an organisation*" [19] and is an umbrella term that includes tools and models such as the European Foundation for Quality Management (EFQM) model and 5S, and more comprehensive methodologies such as the Toyota Production System (TPS), Six Sigma and Total Quality Management (TQM) [15, 19, 20]. The most well-known CI methodology is Lean management, also referred to as Lean Production, Lean Philosophy, or simply as Lean. The origins of Lean can be traced back to Henry Ford who over a century ago planted the seeds of mass production [12] and the subsequent development of TPS by Taiichi Ohno. His work was imported back to the West by Womack *et al.*'s [13] popular book "the Machine that Changed the World." CI and in particular Lean have been shown to improve long term organizational performance from a triple bottom line perspective [21, 22].

Lean's fundamental principle is the identification and removal of wasteful activities, defined from the customer's perspective as not adding value, and commonly referred to by the Japanese term *muda* [23]. Lean has evolved from being perceived as a set of tools including line balancing, 5S method, Single Minute Exchange of Dies (SMED), Value Stream Mapping (VSM) and visual management [24, 25] to a complex and more philosophical business system referred to as Lean production or Lean thinking [23, 26, 27]. From this perspective, Lean is considered more of a business philosophy, with the corresponding impact on aspects the organizational architecture which include developing strategies and corresponding metrics and targets, aligning operations with strategy through plans and actions, and monitoring the results using the defined metrics and targets [28].

Lean strategies can be placed on a continuum between cost-reduction and people-centered strategies [11]. A related perspective is that of hard and soft practices of lean [29] where hard practices are defined as the technical and analytical tools used to improve processes, and soft practices as those related to management, people and their relations. Hard practices include SMED, JIT, Kanban and statistical process control (SPC), while soft practices include training employees, small group problem solving, and customer involvement. While both hard and soft practices are necessary for a successful lean implementation, their relative importance may be industry specific [29]. For example, in the context of Work Integration Social Enterprises (WISE), hard practices do not seem to be appropriate for vulnerable workers [11].

Starting with the automotive industry [30], CI and Lean have been implemented in both manufacturing and service industries [31, 32], including aerospace [33], construction [34] and hospitality [35]. Lean has also been studied in the context of SMEs [36–38], healthcare [39] and education [40, 41], contexts that show some commonalities with SEs. SEs tend to be similar to SMEs in size, legal structure and entrepreneurship [1]. Like SMEs, governance at SEs is relatively centralized as ownership tends to be closely linked to management [18]. Decision-making tends to be informal. Combined with an operational focus, these characteristics lead to a lack of focus on strategic planning and development. SEs also resemble organizations in the education and healthcare industry, as their missions supersede financial goals and play an important role in public policy [42].

2.2 Hoshin Kanri and the X-Matrix

A key feature of Lean and TQM is the alignment between strategic objectives, tactical plans and activities of middle management, and the work done by operations employees [42] through a coherent and structured framework promoting employee involvement [16]. While several names are used to refer to this process, including policy deployment, management by policy, policy control and policy management, its essence is best captured by its Japanese name: Hoshin Kanri where hoshin means "compass", "policy", or " aim" and kanri refers to "management" and "control of the company's focus" [43]. Jolayemi [43] distinguishes between a Western type Hoshin Kanri which includes a strategic component, and the original Japanese type Hoshin Kanri which only focuses on policy deployment.

Hoshin Kanri is defined as "*a methodology for strategic planning that communicates the strategic vision of an organization throughout the organization*" [44]. This is executed through a four-phase cycle summarized by the acronym FAIR [16, 42]. During a "focus" (F) phase, management is stimulated to distillate the organizational strategy into a few strategic priorities, also known as "vital few objectives" [43]. In the subsequent "alignment" (A) phase, Hoshin policies are developed to connect available resources to the strategic priorities in a participatory manner. During the "integrate" (I) phase, the Hoshin policies are integrated in operational activities, usually using implementation plans. The final "review" or "responsiveness" (R) phase consists of the assessment of the Hoshin policies and their results, and the formulation of corrective actions, typically for the subsequent cycle. Even though Hoshin Kanri focuses on the mechanistic aspects of policy deployment and is distinct from strategy formulation which remains the responsibility of leadership, the Western type deployment of Hoshin Kanri still requires organizations to have solid mission, value, and vision statements prior to formulating long- and medium-term plans and goals and developing annual plans [43].

The main objectives of Hoshin Kanri are to reinforce the link between strategy and annual planning cycle [16], recognize the most important change opportunities for organizations and identify the best actions to take to achieve these changes [45]. Hoshin Kanri replaced management by objectives in Japan the 1960s, as it was perceived to be more flexible, an advantage given the prevailing economic conditions [45]. Hoshin Kanri is also frequently compared to the Balanced Scorecard (BSC), another strategic planning and management tool used to align strategy with day-to-day operations. Compared to the top-down nature of management by objectives and the BSC approach, Hoshin Kanri incorporates more employee empowerment and involvement and gives a greater role to consensus building through organization-wide communication [44]. Instead of management-imposed targets and measures, Hoshin Kanri encourages employees to set targets and objectives [43], seek consensus [16] and use employee self-assessment to monitor performance [45]. This is enabled by a unique feature of Hoshin Kanri nicknamed "catchball."

Catchball was named after a children's game where a ball is thrown from one person to another [17] and is defined as "the relative up, down, and horizontal discussions and joint analysis necessary for effective determination of objectives, strategies, targets and means" [43]. Catchball is thus characterized by a two-way dialogue occurring top-down and bottom-up. This communication at all levels of the organization contributes to the organization buy-in necessary to achieve results and solve problems [17, 44].

Another important element of Hoshin Kanri and the implementation of the FAIR cycle is the X-matrix. The X-matrix provides a structured framework linking strategic objectives, goals, tactics, KPIs and actors [42]. The X-matrix is a square matrix, where the four sides depict in clockwise direction: strategic objectives, tactical improvement initiatives, KPIs, and long-term goals. A separate section links actors (e.g., teams) to the tactical improvement initiatives. The intersection of the columns and rows is used to specify the strength of the relationship between the two elements [17]. This makes the X-matrix a very strong visual tool for management to structure and support Hoshin Kanri. Hoshin Kanri has been successfully implemented by large for-profit organizations including AT&T, Bridgestone, Exxon, Hewlett-Packard, Nissan, Rover, Texas Instruments, Tyco, and Xerox [16, 17, 43]. More recently, Hoshin Kanri has been deployed by organizations pursuing a CSR strategy as an alternative for the Balanced Scorecard (BSC) [17].

Implementations of Hoshin Kanri frequently center around the use of the X-matrix, and thus take organizational objectives and goals as starting points. Comprehensive Hoshin Kanri implementations require organizations to have well formulated mission, value, and vision statements as inputs for their long term goals [43]. Yet, in a review of the literature, Jolayemi [43] found that only 30% of the reviewed articles included value statements. Value statements "*describe what an organization holds dear and cares about*" [43] and are particularly relevant for the strategic direction of SEs. The current square visualization of the X-matrix omits value statements, even though these are meant to be an integral part of Hoshin Kanri, reducing its actionability for SEs who are characterized by their values-driven nature.

2.3 Social Enterprises and Values

SEs are defined as "*values-driven 'hybrid' businesses that operate in the ill-defined space between the for-profit and non-profit worlds*" [3]. To give some nuance to this definition, for-profit companies are value-driven which entails that they generate and extract financial value for shareholders by delivering value (used here as a descriptor of qualities with worth) to their customers. Social enterprises are often value *and* values-driven. The singular and the plural version of the word often refer to different meanings. Those in the field of psychology and sociology most often use values in its plural form as a set of human values which are considered as abstract beliefs about what is of value in life in general [46–48]. Human values are different from goals, as they can never be achieved, but are always worth pursuing. Human values are often captured by one word like: equality, sustainability, etc.

Rokeach [48] further distinguishes *terminal values*, which are desired end-states like 'freedom' and *instrumental values* which are desired ways of being like 'honest' (abstract beliefs close to virtues) [49]. In a value system values of an individual or a group are prioritized. SEs actively try to promote prioritized human values while paying attention to not hindering other human values (avoid effects that are considered harmful to society/ecology) that are less central to their mission, which makes them more values-driven and values-sensitive than for-profit organizations [50].

Hence, SEs try to balance the pursuit of a social or environmental mission related to a community benefit funded through trade activities [1]. Whether legally required to or not, SEs typically reinvest the majority of their profit in their mission. From their perspective, if not directly reinvested in their mission, profit could be considered a form of waste [51].

2.4 Lean, Hoshin Kanri and the X-Matrix for Social (Values-Driven) Enterprises

The application of CI methodologies by SEs has received limited attention [10, 11], with a few exception. In the context of WISE, Signoretti and Sacchetti [11] examined human-centric lean practices such as standardization, job rotation, teamwork, and employee empowerment. Training was seen as necessary to support these practices. They found that it was possible for WISE to realize the people-centered approach through lean practices, but that these practices have to be modified to fit the needs of the WISE organization and vulnerable employees. Applying the lean practices without adjustments to the particular context of WISE jeopardized efficiency and the WISE organization's social mission. Similarly, Zanchi et al. [52] examined the impact of lean practices on neurodiverse people (e.g. manifesting autism, Attention Deficit Hyperactivity Disorder (ADHD), and/or dyslexia traits) and found that Lean practices could potentially support neurodiverse people.

The limited empirical evidence thus shows that SEs could benefit from CI methodologies if they are adapted to the specific SE context [10, 11]. From this perspective, policy deployment, Hoshin Kanri and the X-matrix are promising tools for organizations pursuing alignment between their vision, mission, values, and long and short term goals [43]. In practice, the X-matrix only ensures alignment between strategic objectives, goals, tactics, Key Performance Indicators (KPIs) and actors [42]. Enriching the X-matrix in such a way that it fit with their values-driven nature might help SEs to articulate and communicate goals and plans that can help them to sustain - or even grow - their company, in a way that feels congruent with their values [3].

3 Methodology

Action research was adopted as the methodological framework for this study. Three steps for data collection and analysis were adopted as described by Pieroni et al. [53] based on their interpretation of Mathiassen's [54] framework for engaged scholarship. These steps included: (1) diagnosing the problem, (2) planning and executing the action, and (3) evaluating the action. The data collection and analysis conducted for each step are described below, after the description of the case company and illustrated in Fig. 1.

3.1 Case Presentation

The action research was conducted in partnership with a WISE organization operating in the Netherlands. What was meant to be a one-off charity event led to the inception of the case company in 2015. The case company started with a sewing workshop where vulnerable people were given the opportunity to find their way back to social and professional fulfillment in a way and at a pace that fit them. To meet the diverse interests of the beneficiaries a bicycle workplace was added. The case company is also in the process of developing a garden, restaurant, and t-shirt printing.

The Management Team (MT) of the case company consists of the founder and the chief operating officer who together act on strategic, tactical and operational levels. They oversee the daily operations of the various workshops (textile and bicycle), the development of the new workshops (garden, restaurant, and t-shirt printing), recruitment and coaching of employees and volunteers, procurement, and accounting. The MT also is responsible for setting the strategy and communicating with external stakeholders. This includes negotiating with subsidy providers, governmental organizations such as unemployment agencies and the municipality, but also reporting to their board.

Interviews with the management team were conducted on four separate occasions as shown in Fig. 1.

3.2 Action Research

Action research is a particular form of engaged scholarship, defined as "*a participatory form of research for studying complex real world problems based on the different perspectives and understandings of key stakeholders*" [54]. Action research is more specifically focused on the intervention that will deal with a specific problem, and through which the research will contribute to academic knowledge. For this study, the approach of external action research was adopted, as the researchers remained independent of the professional context, yet worked alongside the professional practitioners to develop and execute the intervention [55].

While action research encompasses a vast array of activities and methods, it typically consists of planning, acting, observing, and reflecting stages [55]. For the purpose of this study, we adopted Pieroni et al. [53] three step approach which fit better with the study purpose and as illustrated in Fig. 1. Their first step, diagnosing, consisted of identifying the organizational problem and scientific problem [54]. The organizational problem was identified through a first telephone interview with the founder and refined through a second interview with the two-person management team. In between the two interviews, a literature review was conducted to connect the organizational problem to existing theory and identify the gap. Literature on CI and SEs was examined to frame the problem experienced by the case company. The initial phone interview was documented through extensive notes, and a follow up e-mail summarizing the key points of the interview. The group interview was recorded and transcribed, freeing up the researchers to make observations and take notes.

The planning and taking action step consisted of identifying based on the organizational problem and additional literature review a potential solution and developing it. Subsequently, a workshop was conducted during which the researchers and MT members of the case company experimented with a potential solution. The workshop was recorded and transcribed. The output of the workshop was also documented through photographs.

The evaluation steps consisted of a group interview with the case company MT immediately after the workshop and e-mail correspondence several weeks after the workshop to document results and reflections.

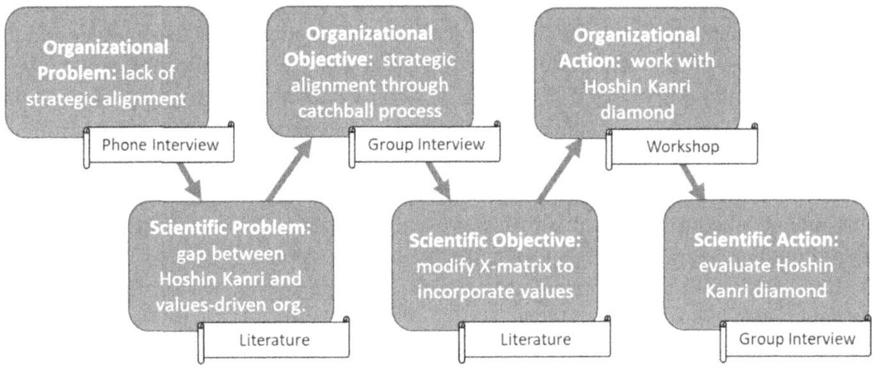

Fig. 1. Illustration of the action research design.

4 Findings

4.1 Diagnosing the Problem: Lack of Strategic Alignment

The case organization's vision is to be a place where people develop a sense of self and a sense of belonging with the eventual purpose to find a sustainable place in society and/or the labor market. Through their work in the workshops, vulnerable people are coached to develop themselves and their work skills. The case organization also emphasizes ecological aspects, by focusing on recycling and upcycling in their production processes.

At the time of the initial phone call and first interview, the case organization was encountering several challenges. First, the case organization grew from 1 to 9 employees, and from one to two workshops (textile and bicycle). This significantly increased overhead costs, requiring the organization to carefully monitor its revenue streams. In addition to the 9 employees, the case organization worked with pools of volunteers and the vulnerable employees who were also its beneficiaries. As the size of the organization increased, so did the coordination challenges. At the time of the interview, the MT was contending with the decision whether to add an organizational layer and appoint an operational manager or find a way to maintain the flat organization structure. Maintaining a flat organization structure fitted with the organization's values of inclusivity and equality. However, the MT was finding it difficult to combine the strategic, tactical, and operational tasks and was feeling the need to delegate some tactical and operational tasks, in particular the day-to-day problem solving across both locations.

Another issue that was emerging was how to keep the diverse workforce engaged and their decisions aligned with the organization's vision. The MT perceived that they were underpaying their employees and relying on their intrinsic motivation to serve vulnerable people. Recruiting new employees was therefore challenging, especially in the tight labor market. Once employees were hired, they also needed to embrace the organization's vision and social mission. The case organization's MT was experiencing the challenge of ensuring that mission drift did not occur.

Finally, as the case organization was growing and working with an increasing number of stakeholders, the pressure to document and quantify their performance and output was increasing. This was in strife with the MT's natural inclination to let stakeholders see and feel for themselves how happy people were working in the workshops. As the founder described a recent encounter with a stakeholder "*I thought, surely you can see these people, delve deeper, instead of just wanting to hear some numbers.*" [translated from Dutch]. However, the MT also felt the necessity to do so, and was participating in a programme to define, quantify, and measure impact.

During the second interview, the possibilities offered by Lean were discussed with the MT. Specifically, the researchers discussed the potential for strategic alignment and performance measurement in combination with the respect for people pillar of Lean. Lean was seen as a way to increase employee's (team) problem solving skills and empowerment in a way that aligned structure with the MT's desire for an inclusive and egalitarian organizational culture. Hoshin Kanri and in particular the catchball process were presented as promising avenues to ensure strategic alignment, ensure that employees felt ownership over the case organization's vision, increasing employee empowerment and reducing the need to add an organizational layer. The organizational objective for the action research was therefore to achieve strategic alignment through the catchball process.

4.2 Developing and Enacting the Modified Hoshin Kanri

A framework for Hoshin Kanri incorporating terminal and instrumental values was developed by reviewing previously documented applications of Hoshin Kanri by for profit-organizations (see Sect. 2.2). From the researchers' perspective, Hoshin Kanri and its tools were considered appropriate as they addressed several issues of importance of SEs. First, the catchball process inherent to Hoshin Kanri was perceived as beneficial to the process of strategic alignment that the case company considered necessary to avoid mission drift. Second, the use of the X-matrix and its powerful visualization was seen as helpful for management to prioritize between strategic, tactical, and operational issues. Third, the inclusion of terminal and instrumental values to the X-matrix was seen as a way to help the MT identify ways to document and quantify their performance in a way that fit their values.

Fig. 2. Hoshin Kanri diamond as filled in during the workshop

A two-hour interactive workshop was designed to take advantage of the strong visual appeal of the X-matrix. The goals of the workshop were threefold: (1) provide the case company's MT with a tangible outcome that they could continue working with, (2) familiarize them with the process of translating values to concrete actions, and, in reverse, prioritizing actions that fit with their values, and (3) familiarize them with the catchball process. The X-matrix incorporating terminal and instrumental values was transformed from a square to a diamond shape (see Fig. 2), leading to the "Hoshin Kanri diamond". The workshop consisted of a short explanation of this new diamond-shaped X-matrix and the concepts of terminal and instrumental values, guiding the case company's MT in filling in the Hoshin Kanri diamond, and a reflection on the process and whether the goals were achieved.

The Hoshin Kanri diamond was drawn and hung on the wall (see Fig. 2). The case company's MT members were asked to write out their organization's values, long term objectives, and activities on post-its and subsequently stick them on the Hoshin Kanri diamond, with the most important ones closest to the center. Yellow post-its were used for the current situation and pink post-its for the desired situation if it deviated from the current situation. The researchers guided them through questions in defining values, distinguishing between terminal and instrumental values, and in ranking them. Occasionally the conversation deviated to important issues the case company was facing that were only tangentially related or out of scope for the workshop. These included for example issues of legislation, and relations with external stakeholders and were still important to better understand the context in which the case company's MT members were operating.

During the workshop extensive discussions took place going back-and-forth from relatively abstract terminal values to more concrete actions. This back-and-forth process was very important in helping the case company's MT members crystallize their values and link them to activities. Example questions that were asked by the researchers were: "if this value is so important to you, how does it translate to goals and activities?" and conversely, "why is this activity is important, how does it link to your values?" For example, discussion was needed to crystallize the difference between terminal values such as "a world where people feel connected to each other" and "equality" and the instrumental values needed to achieve terminal values "learning with and from each other" and "patience."

Through this discussion, the case company's MT members were able to articulate what was in their opinion a more coherent set of terminal and instrumental values but more importantly, also reconcile it with the necessity to ensure funding for the organization. Concretely, when moving from values to actions, social values were prominently featured in the discussion. Terminal and instrumental values revolved primarily around the social mission of the organization. Sustainability (from an environmental perspective) was also identified as a terminal value yet subordinate to the social terminal values of connection and equality. However, when discussing short term goals (defined as one-year goals), financial sustainability featured more prominently as necessary to ensure the continuity of the organization. A concrete benefit of using the diamond-shaped X-matrix was thus that the case company's MT members could clarify for themselves, but also articulate to external stakeholders, the relationship between their social and environmental values and short-term financial objectives. The ability to distinguish between their values-driven nature as expressed by the terminal and instrumental values, and the need to pursue short term financial objectives made them less warry of mission drift.

4.3 Evaluating the Modified Hoshin Kanri

During a short interview at the end of the two-hour workshop, and in subsequent communication, the diamond shaped Hoshin Kanri was evaluated. First, the case company's MT recognized the usefulness of Hoshin Kanri, and the X-matrix, in prioritizing activities that helped them pursue their social mission. They also perceived it as a useful exercise to verbalize their espoused values. The hands-on nature of the workshop also resulted in tangible and useful output for them.

Conversely, the case company's MT also appreciated the opportunity this exercise gave them to reflect on why they undertook certain activities even if they did not explicitly link to what they believed to be their social mission. By distinguishing between terminal and instrumental values, and long-term and short-term goals, they were better able to verbalize the difference between their social mission, and the activities needed to ensure financial sustainability. The diamond-shaped X-matrix was in that way a powerful visual tool that contributed to this message.

While originally the diamond-shaped X-matrix was developed to help the case company's MT in aligning their internal employees with their vision for the company, they also identified communication with external stakeholders as a potential benefit. Specifically, the case company's MT mentioned the need to help their board understand the peculiarities of social enterprises. The diamond-shaped X-matrix and the verbalization of values vs. goals was seen as an important tool in this communication. Similarly, the X-matrix's explicit link between values, goals, activities and KPIs was seen as useful in defining appropriate KPIs for the organization to communication with external stakeholders.

5 Discussion and Implications for Theory

The present study demonstrated how Hoshin Kanri and the X-matrix were adapted to incorporate terminal and instrumental values, meeting the need of SEs for a tool that is congruent with their values. The study reports on a case study where the diamond-shaped X-matrix, a new approach to visualizing a strategy that is more explicitly linked to values, was applied. Like most management tools, Hoshin Kanri "*as is*" lacked an explicit focus on core values and ideals, yet these are aspects that provide meaning and engage employees of values-driven organizations.

The study thereby contributes to the limited body of research on "lean social production" [11, 52], examining how CI methodologies and tools can be adapted to meet the particular needs of SEs stemming from the hybrid business model [10, 11]. SEs encounter several challenges that can be aided by the proposed modifications to Hoshin Kanri and the X-matrix. The modifications presented in this paper concerned primarily the "focus" (F) phase of the FAIR cycle [43] and its visualization through the X-matrix. Through a diamond-shaped X-matrix, terminal and instrumental values were added to the existing process of distillation of the organizational strategy into strategic priorities and corresponding actions. This new approach enabled the distinction of activities directly linked to the organization's values, and those that were merely necessary for its financial sustainability. This was a particularly important outcome as mission drift is an important concern for SEs [2, 56, 57]. The diamond-shaped X-matrix gave the SE a powerful and visual way to explain how it prioritized its activities given its values and strategic objectives, making it possible to distinguish between social and financial aspects in a coherent way. This was relevant for communication with internal stakeholders and external stakeholders.

Employees of SEs need to navigate complex decision-making, trading-off between social and financial objectives. To avoid risks related to mission drift, alignment is needed between strategic, tactical, and day-to-day operational decisions [58]. As SEs grow, this need becomes more pronounced, and communication between different layers of the organization becomes more necessary. The catchball process and X-matrix are useful Hoshin Kanri tools that can support these communication processes.

SEs need to communicate their values but also report on their performance to external stakeholders. A challenge for SEs is that their hybrid business model and unique organization culture is not always familiar to (potential) customers, governmental organizations and/or board members [6, 58]. Anchoring their communication in common business tools such as Hoshin Kanri does contribute to SEs tailoring their communication to the previous knowledge of their external stakeholders. Furthermore, by helping SEs define meaningful to them key performance indicators and linking them to their goals and activities, the Hoshin Kanri diamond contributes to the need for SEs to document and quantify their performance and output [1, 10].

For practitioners, the present study demonstrates the use of a particular CI tool that can meet the need of values-driven organizations to incorporate values in their policy deployment processes. This approach is not limited to SEs. Any organization looking beyond merely financial goals can benefit from this approach to (1) crystallize its values, (2) ensure that goals are consistent with values, (3) critically reflect on projects and select appropriate projects to prioritize, (4) communicate internally and (5) communicate to external stakeholders.

6 Conclusion, Limitations and Further Research

The present study contributes to the concept of "social lean production" an avenue for lean to contribute to a more inclusive society. This topic merits further attention from researchers. Nevertheless, the present is only based on a single case study of a WISE organization in the Dutch context and of one CI tool. Further development of the Hoshin Kanri diamond would benefit from application in different settings. Furthermore, the evaluation of this approach is based on perceptions of value of the intervention right after the session and does not provide any insight into effects of the intervention in the long run.

The inclusion of terminal and instrumental values in the co-visualisation of a values-driven strategy was reported to be beneficial to help the organization at hand to articulate, prioritize and communicate objectives and activities that contributed to their growth in a way that felt congruent with their values. While the reported experience of the session and the expected effects are important, other forms of research could give insight into the actual effects. Finally, as the evaluation was done in part face to face, it is probable that the evaluation of the MT was pleasing the researchers and that the experienced downsides were held back. Future research might employ alternative data collection methods to reduce the effect of interviewee bias.

Acknowledgements. We would like to acknowledge funding received from the Dutch Taskforce for Applied Research (SIA). This publication is part of the project *Lean for Social Enterprises* (project number KIEM.K23.01.147) funded by the Taskforce for Applied Research (SIA) and the Dutch Research Council (NWO).

References

1. Abbott, M., Barraket, J., Castellas, E.I.-P., Hiruy, K., Suchowerska, R., Ward-Christie, L.: Evaluating the labour productivity of social enterprises in comparison to SMEs in Australia. SEJ. **15**, 179–194 (2019). https://doi.org/10.1108/SEJ-09-2018-0064
2. Battilana, J.: Cracking the organizational challenge of pursuing joint social and financial goals: social enterprise as a laboratory to understand hybrid organizing. M@n@gement **21**, 1278–1305 (2018)
3. Vickers, I., Lyon, F.: Beyond green niches? Growth strategies of environmentally-motivated social enterprises. Int. Small Bus. J. **32**, 449–470 (2014). https://doi.org/10.1177/0266242612457700
4. European Commission: The Social Business Initiative of the European Commission (2015)
5. Verloop, W., Hillen, M.: Social Enterprise Unraveled: Best Practices from the Netherlands. Warden Press, Amsterdam (2014)
6. Davies, I.A., Haugh, H., Chambers, L.: Barriers to social enterprise growth. J. Small Bus. Manage. **57**, 1616–1636 (2019). https://doi.org/10.1111/jsbm.12429
7. Defourny, J., Nyssens, M.: Social enterprise in Europe: recent trends and developments. Soc. Enterp. J. **4**, 202–228 (2008). https://doi.org/10.1108/17508610810922703
8. Battilana, J., Lee, M., Walker, J., Dorsey, C.: In search of the hybrid ideal. Stanf. Soc. Innov. Rev. **10**(3), 50–55 (2012)
9. Dees, G.: The Social Enterprises Spectrum: Philanthropy to Commerce. Harvard Business Review, Cambridge (1996)
10. Kokkinou, A., van Kollenburg, T.: Lean for social enterprises: doing the right things. In: McDermott, O., Rosa, A., Sá, J.C., Toner, A. (eds.) ELEC 2022. IFIP Advances in Information and Communication Technology, vol. 668, pp. 261–272. Springer, Cham (2023). https://doi.org/10.1007/978-3-031-25741-4_22
11. Signoretti, A., Sacchetti, S.: Lean HRM practices in work integration social enterprises: moving towards social lean production. Evidence from Italian case studies*. Ann. Public Coop. Econ. **91**, 545–563 (2020). https://doi.org/10.1111/apce.12283
12. Kay, A., Roy, M.J., Donaldson, C.: Re-imagining social enterprise. SEJ **12**, 217–234 (2016). https://doi.org/10.1108/SEJ-05-2016-0018
13. Ryan, P.W., Lyne, I.: Social enterprise and the measurement of social value: methodological issues with the calculation and application of the social return on investment. Educ. Knowl. Econ. **2**, 223–237 (2008). https://doi.org/10.1080/17496890802426253
14. Bandyopadhyay, C., Ray, S.: Social enterprise marketing: review of literature and future research agenda. MIP **38**, 121–135 (2019). https://doi.org/10.1108/MIP-02-2019-0079
15. van Kollenburg, T., Kokkinou, A.: What Comes After the Transformation?: Characteristics of Continuous Improvement Organizations. In: Powell, D.J., Alfnes, E., Holmemo, M.D.Q., Reke, E. (eds.) Learning in the Digital Era, vol. 610, pp. 259–268. Springer International Publishing, Cham (2021). https://doi.org/10.1007/978-3-030-92934-3_26
16. Tennant, C., Roberts, P.: Hoshin Kanri: implementing the catchball process. Long Range Plan. **34**, 287–308 (2001). https://doi.org/10.1016/S0024-6301(01)00039-5
17. Chiarini, A.: Corporate social responsibility strategies using the TQM: Hoshin Kanri as an alternative system to the balanced scorecard. TQM J. **28**, 360–376 (2016). https://doi.org/10.1108/TQM-03-2014-0035
18. Löfving, M., Melander, A., Elgh, F., Andersson, D.: Implementing Hoshin Kanri in small manufacturing companies. JMTM **32**, 304–322 (2021). https://doi.org/10.1108/JMTM-08-2020-0313
19. Bhuiyan, N., Baghel, A.: An overview of continuous improvement: from the past to the present. Manag. Decis. **43**, 761–771 (2005). https://doi.org/10.1108/00251740510597761

20. Rijnders, S., Boer, H.: A typology of continuous improvement implementation processes. Knowl. Process Manag. **11**, 283–296 (2004). https://doi.org/10.1002/kpm.208
21. Negrão, L.L.L., Godinho Filho, M., Marodin, G.: Lean practices and their effect on performance: a literature review. Prod. Plan. Control 1–24 (2016). https://doi.org/10.1080/09537287.2016.1231853
22. Camacho-Miñano, M.-M., Moyano-Fuentes, J., Sacristán-Díaz, M.: What can we learn from the evolution of research on lean management assessment? Int. J. Prod. Res. **51**, 1098–1116 (2013). https://doi.org/10.1080/00207543.2012.677550
23. Hines, P., Holweg, M., Rich, N.: Learning to evolve: a review of contemporary lean thinking. Int. J. Oper. Prod. Manag. **24**, 994–1011 (2004). https://doi.org/10.1108/01443570410558049
24. Drohomeretski, E., Gouvea da Costa, S.E., Pinheiro de Lima, E., Garbuio, P.A. da R.: Lean, Six Sigma and Lean Six Sigma: an analysis based on operations strategy. Int. J. Prod. Res. **52**, 804–824 (2014). https://doi.org/10.1080/00207543.2013.842015
25. Koning, H.D., Does, R.J.M.M., Bisgaard, S.: Lean Six Sigma in financial services. IJSSCA **4**, 1 (2008). https://doi.org/10.1504/IJSSCA.2008.018417
26. Åhlström, P., et al.: Is lean a theory? Viewpoints and outlook. IJOPM **41**, 1852–1878 (2021). https://doi.org/10.1108/IJOPM-06-2021-0408
27. Shah, R., Ward, P.T.: Defining and developing measures of lean production. J. Oper. Manag. **25**, 785–805 (2007). https://doi.org/10.1016/j.jom.2007.01.019
28. Bhasin, S.: Performance of organisations treating lean as an ideology. Bus. Process. Manag. J. **17**, 986–1011 (2011). https://doi.org/10.1108/14637151111182729
29. Bortolotti, T., Boscari, S., Danese, P.: Successful lean implementation: Organizational culture and soft lean practices. Int. J. Prod. Econ. **160**, 182–201 (2015). https://doi.org/10.1016/j.ijpe.2014.10.013
30. Womack, J.P., Jones, D.T., Roos, D.: The Machine that Changed the World. Simon and Schuster, New York (2007)
31. Kokkinou, A., van Kollenburg, T., Touw, P.: The road to operational excellence is scenic: tales of continuous improvement journeys. In: Presented at the 2022 EurOMA Conference, Berlin (2022)
32. Li, J., Papadopoulos, C.T., Zhang, L.: Continuous improvement in manufacturing and service systems. Int. J. Prod. Res. **54**, 6281–6284 (2016). https://doi.org/10.1080/00207543.2016.1228235
33. Chakravorty, S.S., Hales, D.N.: Sustainability of process improvements: an application of the experiential learning model (ELM). Int. J. Prod. Res. **55**, 4931–4947 (2017). https://doi.org/10.1080/00207543.2016.1277278
34. Zimina, D., Pasquire, C.L.: Applying lean thinking in commercial management. J. Financ. Manag. Prop. Constr. **16**, 64–72 (2011). https://doi.org/10.1108/13664381111116098
35. Farrington, T., Antony, J., O'Gorman, K.D.: Continuous improvement methodologies and practices in hospitality and tourism. IJCHM **30**, 581–600 (2018). https://doi.org/10.1108/IJCHM-03-2017-0141
36. Knol, W.H., Slomp, J., Schouteten, R.L.J., Lauche, K.: Implementing lean practices in manufacturing SMEs: testing 'critical success factors' using necessary condition analysis. Int. J. Prod. Res. **56**, 3955–3973 (2018). https://doi.org/10.1080/00207543.2017.1419583
37. Achanga, P., Shehab, E., Roy, R., Nelder, G.: Critical success factors for lean implementation within SMEs. J. Manuf. Tech. Manag. **17**, 460–471 (2006). https://doi.org/10.1108/17410380610662889
38. Dora, M., Kumar, M., Van Goubergen, D., Molnar, A., Gellynck, X.: Operational performance and critical success factors of lean manufacturing in European food processing SMEs. Trends Food Sci. Technol. **31**, 156–164 (2013). https://doi.org/10.1016/j.tifs.2013.03.002

39. Henrique, D.B., Filho, M.G., Marodin, G., de Sousa Jabbour, A.B.L., Chiappetta Jabbour, C.J.: A framework to assess sustaining continuous improvement in lean healthcare. Int. J. Prod. Res. **59**, 2885–2904 (2021). https://doi.org/10.1080/00207543.2020.1743892
40. Kokkinou, A., van Kollenburg, T.: Top down or bottom up: perspectives on critical success factors of lean in institutes of higher education. In: Powell, D.J., Alfnes, E., Holmemo, M.D.Q., Reke, E. (eds.) Learning in the Digital Era, vol. 610, pp. 32–41. Springer International Publishing, Cham (2021). https://doi.org/10.1007/978-3-030-92934-3_4
41. Kokkinou, A., van Kollenburg, T.: Critical success factors of lean in higher education: an international perspective. IJLSS (2022). https://doi.org/10.1108/IJLSS-04-2022-0076
42. Barnabè, F., Giorgino, M.C.: Practicing lean strategy: Hoshin Kanri and X-Matrix in a healthcare-centered simulation. TQM **29**, 590–609 (2017). https://doi.org/10.1108/TQM-07-2016-0057
43. Jolayemi, J.K.: Hoshin Kanri and Hoshin process: a review and literature survey. Total Qual. Manag. Bus. Excell. **19**, 295–320 (2008). https://doi.org/10.1080/14783360701601868
44. Wilson, R., Cudney, E.A., Marley, R.J.: Current status of Hoshin Kanri. TQM (2023). https://doi.org/10.1108/TQM-07-2022-0216
45. Roberts, P., Tennant, C.: Application of the Hoshin Kanri methodology at a higher education establishment in the UK. TQM Mag. **15**, 82–87 (2003). https://doi.org/10.1108/09544780310461080
46. Maio, G.R.: Mental representations of social values. In: Advances in Experimental Social Psychology, pp. 1–43. Elsevier (2010). https://doi.org/10.1016/S0065-2601(10)42001-8
47. Schwartz, S.H.: Universals in the content and structure of values: theoretical advances and empirical tests in 20 countries. In: Advances in Experimental Social Psychology, pp. 1–65. Elsevier (1992)
48. Rokeach, M.: The Nature of Human Values. Free Press, New York City (1973)
49. Tuulik, K., Õunapuu, T., Kuimet, K., Titov, E.: Rokeach's instrumental and terminal values as descriptors of modern organisation values. Int. J. Organ. Leadersh. **5**, 151–161 (2016)
50. McCabe, L.A.: Human values of entrepreneurship: an empirical analysis of the human values of social and traditional entrepreneurs. Regent University (2012)
51. De Zwart, J.: Is There such a thing as a lean philosophy? In: McDermott, O., Rosa, A., Sá, J.C., Toner, A. (eds.) Lean, Green and Sustainability, vol. 668, pp. 3–13. Springer International Publishing, Cham (2023). https://doi.org/10.1007/978-3-031-25741-4_1
52. Zanchi, M., Gaiardelli, P., Pezzotta, G.: The role of lean management practices in the valorisation of neurodiverse people in production. In: McDermott, O., Rosa, A., Sá, J.C., Toner, A. (eds.) Lean, Green and Sustainability, vol. 668, pp. 14–22. Springer International Publishing, Cham (2023). https://doi.org/10.1007/978-3-031-25741-4_2
53. Pieroni, M.P.P., McAloone, T.C., Pigosso, D.C.A.: Developing a process model for circular economy business model innovation within manufacturing companies. J. Clean. Prod. **299**, 126785 (2021). https://doi.org/10.1016/j.jclepro.2021.126785
54. Mathiassen, L.: Designing engaged scholarship: from real-world problems to research publications. Engaged Manag. ReView **1** (2017). https://doi.org/10.28953/2375-8643.1000
55. Gray, D.E.: Doing Research in the Real World. Sage, Los Angeles (2014)
56. Cornforth, C.: Understanding and combating mission drift in social enterprises. Soc. Enterp. J. **10**, 3–20 (2014). https://doi.org/10.1108/SEJ-09-2013-0036
57. Young, D.R.: The state of theory and research on social enterprises. In: Gidron, B., Hasenfeld, Y. (eds.) Social Enterprises, pp. 19–46. Palgrave Macmillan, London (2012). https://doi.org/10.1057/9781137035301_2
58. Spear, R., Cornforth, C., Aiken, M.: The governance challenges of social enterprises: evidence from a UK empirical study. Ann. Public Coop. Econ. **80**, 247–273 (2009). https://doi.org/10.1111/j.1467-8292.2009.00386.x

Education

Integration of a Robot Solution in a Manufacturing Environment: A Serious Gaming Approach

Meike Froklage(✉) and Mitchell van Roij(✉)

HAN University of Applied Sciences, Arnhem, The Netherlands
{meike.froklage,mitchell.vanroij}@han.nl

Abstract. This paper presents a serious game for the implementation of a robot in high variety/low volume (HVLV) production environments. Students and practitioners are able to experience and reflect on the complexity of integrating a robot solution in HVLV production processes. By simulating a production environment, players experience how to assemble an increasing variety of products, transport parts and products, visualize information flows and perform quality checks. During the game, the players are challenged to determine which process step needs to be automated. They experience the challenges of integrating a robot and determine how to overcome these challenges. Aspects regarding the reconsideration of process design, standardization, product design and information provision are analysed with the aim of reducing waste as much as possible. Results from a small sample of robotics experts and students show that the I-Robot game is fun and insightful. In addition, the pre-defined learning outcomes seem to be well reflected in the game. This 90-min serious game can be used in a wide range of courses and training programs, is low-tech and allows the players to focus completely on the integration within the process and systems and not solely on the technical possibilities of the robot itself.

Keywords: Serious gaming · lean robotics · robot integration

1 Introduction

Currently, many manufacturing companies face a shortage of technical employees. The number of open vacancies is growing and will most likely not decrease in the near future [1]. One solution to overcome this problem is to implement robot solutions [2]. Robot solutions can support employees with their tasks and thus increase production [3]. However, implementing a robot solution also provides new challenges regarding the flexibility of production processes. High Variety – Low Volume (HVLV) environments have an everchanging customer demand and are therefore reliant on flexible production processes. When implementing a robot solution in such an environment, it could result in unwanted downtime, defects and ultimately aversion to the robot solution. A main barrier for the successful implementation of a robot solution is a shortcoming in the

Published by Springer Nature Switzerland AG 2024
T. van Kollenburg et al. (Eds.): ELEC 2023, IFIP AICT 681, pp. 189–200, 2024.
https://doi.org/10.1007/978-3-031-63265-5_14

standardisation regarding the coordination between process steps, in the connectivity between information systems and in the process quality [4]. We state that a successful implemented robot solution requires an integrated process: the concept of integral robotization. Integral robotization focuses on the connectivity and coordination with other processes and systems to embed the robot solution in the complete organisation. However, both the necessity and the complexity of a well-structured connectivity and coordination with other production processes and systems with the robot solution is often difficult to grasp.

A way to help (future) operations managers understand the challenges and frustrations of implementing robot solutions in production processes is through serious gaming. Serious games are designed to change behaviours and impart knowledge and are widely used in training situations [5]. They can replicate real context in a simplified manner and could be used for experiential learning. Experiential learning uses experience, reflection and application to stimulate learning processes [6] and could therefore help to create an overall understanding of digitization and technologies which will change employees' acceptance [7]. This paper presents an experiential learning exercise in the form of a serious game to give students and practitioners insight into the complexity of implementing robot solutions in an HVLV production environment. The following research question is posed: "To what extent does the I-Robot game generate insight into challenges related to integral robotization?".

Various serious games about robot implementation have been developed by other scholars, such as Matsas et al. [8] and Matsas and Vosniakos [9] who developed serious games with the aim of experiencing human-robot interaction and collaboration, and Vassigh et al. [10] who developed a game that supports learning experiences with a robot solution. However, a serious game that aims to clarify the importance of integral robotization is lacking. This study uses Malik and Bilberg's [11] iterative approach to robotization implementation as a guideline for the I-Robot game and complements it with insights from Bouchard's [12] approach. We draw insights from these approaches, as both focus on aspects on integrated robot implementation.

This paper is structured as follows. Firstly, the study provides a theoretical background in relation to the factors that influence the integration of a robotic solution in the production process. An overview is given of these factors and their influence on the design has been described. Secondly, the design of the game is explained. The game dynamics are explained, learning goals are defined and the connection with the influencing factors is described. Lastly, this game has been tested with a group of students to verify the game.

2 Game Description

The "I-Robot" game was developed to give students and practitioners an understanding of how to implement an integral robot solution and the different factors that influence this implementation. I-Robot is a low-tech game which allows the participants to focus on the integration of the robot solution within the process.

2.1 Background and Aim

Participants in the I-Robot game are challenged to successfully implement a robot solution in a fictional organisation by redesigning internal processes. The game simulates a production process where participants assemble products in a HVLV production environment (see Fig. 1). The product is made in four process steps. Between each step, an intermediate stock of two is present (visualised in Fig. 1 with a triangle). During the game, the customer places an order every 15 s. The participants need to deliver a correctly assembled product to the customer before a new order is placed. In the fourth process step, variation is added to the product. After three minutes, the play round ends and the Key Performance Indicators (KPIs) are registered.

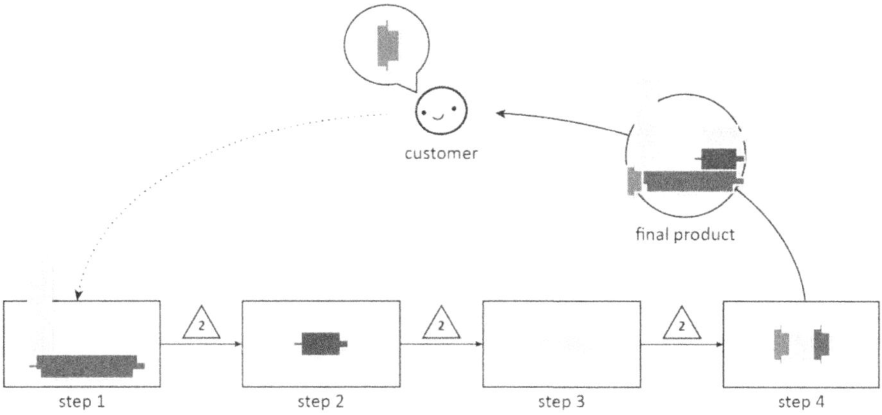

Fig. 1. Visualisation simulation production process first round

Over four play rounds, the participants learn to integrate a robot solution in a HVLV environment. In the game, the robot will be simulated by blindfolding a participant. When performing a task, people subconsciously take in a lot of information and convert it into action. By blindfolding a participant, information obtained through vision is removed. This results in an understanding of the information that is needed for the robot to be able to function well. In several rounds, the participants get the opportunity to redesign their process, integrate the robot and test it.

2.2 Game Dynamics

The game is played in four rounds. While the first round is played to get an understanding of the process and the second, third and fourth round are played to implement the robot and redesign the process to successfully integrate the robot. A successful robot integration can have multiple approaches. This study analyses and combines two approaches that elaborate on implementing a robot solution (see Fig. 2). Malik and Bilburg [11] propose an iterative approach: after each phase, the solution is evaluated and optimised. During this process, robot specifications, process connectivity and organisational factors are explored and determined. In contrast, Bouchard [12] only optimises the robot solution once it is implemented in the production process. Furthermore, his approach heavily focuses on the implementation of the robot solution in the process. Bouchard proposes a Value Stream Map (VSM) to analyse the current state of the process and design a future state of the robot solution. The VSM helps to identify process steps, activities, material flows, information flows and other process elements that are involved with a process or transformation [13]. The "I-Robot" game draws on Malik & Bilburg's iterative approach, whilst also including Bouchard's current and future state process visualisation to analyse and optimise the process.

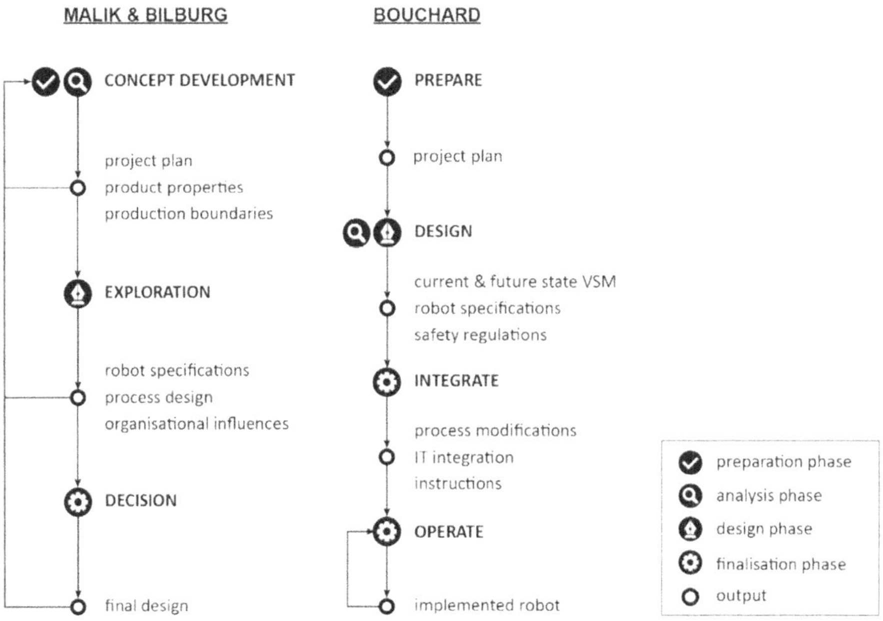

Fig. 2. Overview of Malik and Bilburg's [11] and Bouchard's [12] approach

When comparing Bouchard's approach with that of Malik and Bilburg, the steps taken can be categorised into four phases: the preparation, analysis, design and finalisation phase. These four phases are also included in the approach the participants use during the game (see Fig. 3). During these phases, the participants identify factors that have an influence on the redesign of the robot solution. As a result, the participants learn the approach to implement a robot solution and the importance the influencing factors have on this implementation.

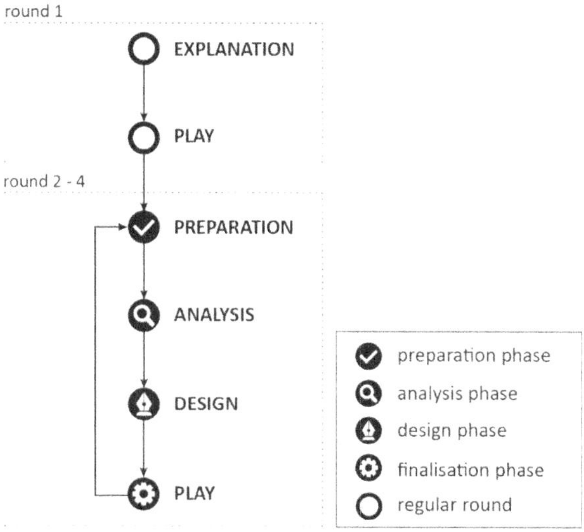

Fig. 3. Approach during the game

Preparation Phase. During the preparation phase, the project plan is made. A project plan helps to manage an efficient implementation process [14]. In the game, this is simulated by creating a plan once a new project starts (the scenario changes). The participants assign new roles, decide their scope and determine new KPIs. Furthermore, in line with Hussain, et al. [15], we pose that involving employees in this phase is essential for the success of the robot implementation. Explaining the necessity to change and helping employees to understand why a robot solution is needed, what implications and possibilities it brings for them and the organizations, may help to create greater employee involvement [16]. Also, getting this employee involvement helps define the scope of the robotizing task. Employees often have a good idea of the actions they perform within a task and can therefore provide necessary information for the robotization project. Involving employees early in the robotization project also helps to counteract resistance to change, promotes participation during the project, enhances trust and can help define roles and responsibilities [15, 17]. Therefore, all decisions are made collaboratively.

Analysis Phase. Once the project plan is made, the current state of the process is analysed. During the game, the process is analysed using a VSM. By mapping out the process steps, value-adding and non-value adding activities are identified. This information can be used during the design phase to determine where a robot solution should be implemented. Once a process step has been selected, the activities within this step are further elaborated upon. This is done by a task analysis or a breakdown of the current situation [14]. By doing so, possible bottlenecks that could hinder the robotization are further identified. In addition to the activities, the information that is needed to perform the actions is also identified. This information potentially needs to be converted into data for the robot solution to work.

Design Phase. The knowledge gained during the analysis phase, is used during this phase to design the future state of the robot solution. The future state should include the task allocation of the operator and robot. According to Johnson et al. [18], it is important that the tasks of the operator and robot are well aligned with each other. Robots and humans each have their benefits and disadvantages which need to be included in the implementation. Additionally, another important factor is the supply and disposal of the materials [19]. This includes the feeding policy and the storage of the products. Finally, the future information flow should be defined. When implementing a robot solution in a process, it collaborates with both humans and machines. Enhancing such cooperation between humans and other machines requires effective information exchange [20]. Therefore, information mapping is paramount.

To identify the consequences on the overall process of the robot solution, a future state VSM can be used. In addition to process-related factors, other factors such as the layout of the robotic cell to improve efficiency [21] and safety regulations are also identified and determined during the design phase. Because the game is focused on providing an understanding of process-related factors when implementing a robot solution, these factors are not included in the game.

Finalisation Phase. Once the robot solution is designed, it is finalised: the solution is tested, information systems are connected, the layout is modified and the robot solution is implemented in the production process. In the game, the finalisation phase is simulated by playing a new round with the participants' proposed changes.

2.3 Storyline

During the game, the participants encounter various scenarios in the gaming rounds to which they must respond. By experiencing these scenarios, the participants become aware of the challenges when implementing a robot.

Round 1: The first round is played to get the participants acquainted with the production process and their tasks. Once they are comfortable with the production process, the second round begins.

Round 2: In the second round, the participants are notified by the management team that a robot needs to be implemented in the production process. The participants determine the bottleneck of the process and where the robot needs to be placed to solve this bottleneck. Once the process step is identified, the participants will first get the opportunity to brainstorm themselves to come up with ideas to redesign the process to fit the robot.

Round 3: During the third round, the participants are informed about different tools they can use to integrate the robot within their process. Firstly, the actions in the robotised process step are identified. Next, the information the robot misses to perform those actions properly is identified. The participants are coached in different ways to embed information within the process itself so the robot is able to perform their tasks. This can be done through standardisation or with the use of moulds to provide information to the 'robot' about the placement of the components when assembling. During this scenario, the participants are focused on the process step of the 'robot' and the steps before and after.

Round 4: In the last round, the variety of the product increases and the participants need to use production order cards which describe the HVLV products. Whereas the third round was focused on the process step of the robot, during this round, the participants will need to analyse and redesign the complete process to integrate the 'robot'. This not only includes the activities that need to be performed, but also how the information is embedded in the process.

3 Method

3.1 Sample and Background

To gain understanding on the effectiveness and learning experience of the I-Robot game, we invited both domain experts in the field of robotics (robot integrators, teachers and researchers) and students to play the game. We played two sessions, in which one session was played with only domain experts (5 participants) and the other with only students (7 participants). The total number of participants was therefore 12. The length of each session, including the explanations and debriefings, was around 3 h. The actual length of gameplay ranged between 60 and 80 min. All sessions had the same experienced facilitator and an observer. Both groups played the same scenarios.

3.2 Data Collection and Analysis

We used a multi-method approach for data collection. This approach consists of a post-game debriefing session in the form of a focus group. Focus groups are useful in generating a rich understanding of participants understandings and believes and thus providing us insight in their learning processes [22]. The post-game debrief consists of an open question in which participants were asked to list a maximum of three main insights gained by playing the game. The answers on the open questions are collected and categorized in relation to the expected learning outcomes.

Additionally, participants were asked to fill out a post-game questionnaire, in which they are asked about their experience based on the learning objectives defined by us. The questionnaire used consists of a 7-point Likert scale, in which the participants are asked, by means of a number of statements, to what extent they "Strongly Disagree" (1), or "Strongly Agree" (7). In this way, we gained insight into the extent to which the game contributed to the learning objectives related to the concept and challenges of integral robotization. The response rate to the questionnaire was 100%. The data did not show any missing values, so all the data was included for analysis.

4 Results

This section describes the results that emerged from the post-game debriefing session and the linkage to the predetermined learning outcomes. It also presents the results of the questionnaire that both the domain experts and students completed after the game.

Table 1. Citation examples of learning experiences and classification codes

ID	Citation content	Codes
1:1	There are many possibilities to standardise supply	Match supply and output & standardisation
1:6	Awareness of information processing and senses (human-robot)	Job classification between human and robot
1:7	Awareness of what humans can do and what robots can do	Job classification between human and robot
1:8	Necessity of precision of parts placement	Match supply and output& standardisation
1:10	How to organise the preparation (supply) of robot processes	Match supply and output
1:13	The increased interdependence of the process and the robot after the robot deployment	Increased process interdependency
1:15	Even more insight into testing, evaluating and improving the robot solution	Continuous improvement
1:17	Production can be flexible with a robot solution, but requires change in the process	Flexible production possibilities

The answers from the open questions, in which participants were asked to write down the three most memorable learning experiences, were systematically analysed, coded and linked to the learning objectives defined by the researchers. Table 1 provides a summary of some of the outcomes and the researchers' classification. It is striking that the participants remembered the aspects of the (standardised) coordination of the supply and removal of products to the robot solution the most. In addition, the participants indicate that the game makes it very clear how much information we as humans process, what information a robot needs and how this affects the division of tasks between humans and robots. Interestingly, the participants also indicated that the game illustrates well the need for experimentation and evaluation of processes and the robot solution. This was an unforeseen learning outcome of the game.

Table 2 gives an overview of the participants' general thoughts about the game. Although both the students and domain experts described the game as entertaining, it is striking that the domain experts generally found the game more entertaining than the students. Also, the standard deviation of the domain experts is generally lower, which may indicate that they generally agree more with each other than the students. Based on this sample, both the students and the domain experts conclude that the various challenges of integral robotization are nicely simulated in the game.

Table 2. General student and robotic expert reactions to the game

Question	Students		Experts		Overall	
	Mean	SD	Mean	SD	Mean	SD
This game is fun to play	5.86	0.35	6.80	0.45	6.25	0.60
The aim of the game is clear	6.14	0.83	6.40	0.55	6.25	0.72
The rules of the game are clear	5.86	0.83	6.40	0.55	6.08	0.76
The game is challenging	5.00	0.93	6.60	0.55	5.67	1.11
I would recommend the game to others	5.57	0.73	6.80	0.45	6.08	0.86
I have gained insight into the complexity of integral robotization	6.14	0.83	6.20	0.84	6.17	0.80

Note: Responses on a 7-point scale from 1 (strongly disagree) to 7 (strongly agree). N = 12

Table 3 shows a more detailed picture of the defined learning objectives and how the participants recognize them in the game. These learning objectives are derived from the approach of Malik and Bilburg [11] and Bouchard [12] and the factors that need to be identified during these approaches. What is striking about the results is that in general the domain experts score higher than the students, but that the students have a lower standard deviation. In addition, both the students and domain experts indicate that the game well illustrates the importance of the supply and removal of products for robot solutions (6.43 for students) and (6.80 for the domain experts). They also indicate that the game well illustrates the need for standardization for robot solutions (6.57 for students) and (6.60 for domain experts). Despite the many positive responses to the different learning objectives, the students and domain experts also agree on learning objectives that are less emphatically simulated by the game, namely gaining insight into the differences between local and global information and the relationship with robotization projects. Students score this learning objective at 4.43 and the domain experts at 4.80.

Table 3. Learning objective scores of students and domain experts

Question	Students		Experts		Overall	
	Mean	SD	Mean	SD	Mean	SD
This game illustrates the importance of coordinating supply and removal for robot solutions	6.43	0.49	6.80	0.45	6.58	0.60
This game illustrates the importance of standardisation for the robot solution	6.57	0.49	6.60	0.55	6.58	0.49
This game challenges me to determine a good scope for the process to be robotised	5.14	1.25	4.80	1.64	5.00	1.35
I have gained insight into the importance of information for the robot solution	6.14	0.64	5.60	0.89	5.92	0.76
I can perform a task analysis 5.on a process step to be robotised	5.33	1.11	5.40	1.34	5.36	1.15
I have gained insight into rearranging tasks for the robot solution	5.71	0.70	5.60	0.55	5.67	0.62
I have gained insight into the division of tasks between humans and robots	6.14	0.64	6.00	0.71	6.08	0.64
I have gained insight into the difference between local and global information	4.43	1.40	4.80	1.64	4.58	1.44
I have gained insight into how a process mapping method can contribute to determining the process step to be robotised	5.43	0.90	4.80	1.92	5.17	1.34
I have gained insight into how you can effectively deploy a robot solution in a high variety low volume production environment	5.86	0.83	5.40	0.55	5.67	0.75

Note: Responses on a 7-point scale from 1 (strongly disagree) to 7 (strongly agree). N = 12

5 Discussion

This study posed the following research question: "To what extent does the I-Robot game generates insight into challenges related to integral robotization?" and based on the preliminary results, we can assume that the I-Robot game helps participants to identify various challenges in relation to integral robotization. One of the key challenges for implementing robot solution is the alignment of the supply and disposal of material [19]. Both the domain experts and students in our sample indicate that this challenge is well simulated in the game. Additionally, another important challenge is the human-robot task allocation [18]: which tasks need to be performed by a human and which by a robot? According to the answers to the open questions and the questionnaire, this challenge and it's associated learning outcomes are well simulated in the game. Despite the small sample, this outcome indicates that this game properly simulates the challenges of coordinating the supply and removal of products and human-robot task allocation. Lastly, the participants indicate that the game effectively emulates the handling of information derived from human sources and its subsequent translation into robotic solutions. This is in line with Zhang et al. [20]. However, the participants contend that the comprehensive integration of this information processing is inadequately represented in the game.

In the future, the game should be developed more to include the importance of information flows and processing. Additionally, future research should focus on testing the game more thoroughly to determine if all the predetermined challenges of integral robotization are tackled accordingly. To achieve this, more data needs to be generated in larger samples to strengthen our findings in relation to the game. Notwithstanding the aforementioned concerns, it is our contention that the I-Robot game possesses the potential to serve as a valuable introductory tool for individuals, including students and practitioners, seeking to gain knowledge and experience in the field of integral robotization.

References

1. SEO Economisch Onderzoek. Arbeidsmarktkrapte technici: Ontwikkelingen, verklaringen en handelingsperspectieven (2022)
2. Gan, Z.L., Musa, S.N., Yap, H.J.: A review of the high-mix, low-volume manufacturing industry. Appl. Sci. **13**(3), 1687 (2023)
3. Lakshmi, V., Bahli, B.: Understanding the robotization landscape transformation: A centering resonance analysis. J. Innov. Knowl. **5**(1), 59–67 (2020)
4. Sordan, J.E., Oprime, P.C., Pimenta, M.L., Lombardi, F., Chiabert, P.: Symbiotic relationship between robotics and Lean Manufacturing: a case study involving line balancing. TQM J. **34**(5), 1076–1095 (2022)
5. Gouveia, D., Lopes, D., De Carvalho, C.V.: Serious gaming for experiential learning. In: 2011 Frontiers in Education Conference (FIE), Rapid City, South Dakota, USA (2011)
6. Kolb, D.A.: Experiential Learning: Experience as the Source of Learning and Development. Prentice-Hall, Upper Saddle River (1984)
7. Arents, J., Greitans, M.: Smart industrial robot control trends, challenges and opportunities within manufacturing. Appl. Sci. **12**(2), 937 (2022)

8. Matsas, E., Batras, D., Vosniakos, G.C.: Beware of the robot: a highly interactive and immersive virtual reality training application in robotic manufacturing systems. In: 19th Advances in Production Management Systems (APMS), Rhodes, Greece (2013)
9. Matsas, E., Vosniakos, G.C.: Designing an interactive serious game to investigate acceptability of human-robot collaboration in manufacturing. In: IEEE Virtual Reality 2015 Doctoral Consortium, Arles-Provence, France (2015)
10. Vassigh, S., Peterson, E., Bogosian, B., Tubella, J.: The robotics academy: an immersive learning game for training industrial roboticists. In: Building Technology Educator's Society (2021)
11. Malik, A.A., Bilberg, A.: Framework to implement collaborative robots in manual assembly: a lean automation approach. In: 28th DAAAM International Symposium on Intelligent Manufacturing & Automation, Zadar, Croatia (2017)
12. Bouchard, S.: Lean Robotics: A Guide to Making Robots Work in Your Factory (2017)
13. Stadnicka, D., Litwin, P.: Value stream mapping and system dynamics integration for manufacturing line modelling and analysis. Int. J. Prod. Econ. **208**, 400–411 (2019)
14. Zhang, J., Fang, X.: Challenges and key technologies in robotic cell layout design and optimization. Proc. Inst. Mech. Eng. Part C: J. Mech. Eng. Sci. **231**(15), 2912–2924 (2017)
15. Hussain, S.T., Lei, S., Akram, T., Haider, M.J., Hussain, S.H., Ali, M.: Kurt Lewin's change model: a critical review of the role of leadership and employee involvement in organizational change. J. Innov. Knowl. **3**(3), 123–127 (2018)
16. Pierce, J.L., Gardner, D.G., Dunham, R.B.: Management organizational change and development. Manag. Organ. Behav.: Integr. Perspect. **18**, 627–657 (2002)
17. Morgan, D.E., Zeffane, R.: Employee involvement, organizational change and trust in management. Int. J. Hum. Resour. Manag. **14**(1), 55–75 (2003)
18. Johsnon, M., Bradshaw, J.M., Feltovich, P.J., Jonker, C.M., van Riemsdijk, M.B., Sierhuis, M.: Coactive design: designing support for interdependence in joint activity. J. Hum.-Robot Interact. **3**(1), 43–69 (2014)
19. Pocachard, J., Klement, N., Jouve, C., Quenehen, A.: Methodology to select the best part presentation in cobotics. Procedia Manuf. **51**, 125–132 (2020)
20. Zhang, J., Luo, H., Xu, J.: Towards fully BIM-enabled building automation and robotics: a perspective of lifecycle information flow. Comput. Ind. **135**, 103570 (2022)
21. Han, B.T., Cook, J.S.: An efficient heuristic for robot acquisition and cell formation. Ann. Oper. Res. **77**, 229–252 (1998)
22. Morgan, D.L., Krueger, R.A., King, J.A.: The Focus Group Guidebook. Sage, Newcastle upon Tyne (1998)

Using Games and Simulations to Facilitate Generative Conflict

Bruno Pešec[1,2(✉)] and Andrew Kidd[2]

[1] Ashridge Executive Education: Berkhamsted, Hertfordshire, UK
[2] Playing Lean, Oslo, Norway
bruno@playinglean.com

Abstract. Lean educators and practitioners often find themselves in conflict with existing structures, ways of work, and habits. We can differentiate destructive and generative conflict. The former usually leads to waste. The latter, on the other hand, has the potential to further the individuals' capability development, enhance their social skills, and contribute to mature discourse.

Games and simulations provide a safe environment to surface and explore conflict, thus defusing escalation of violent tensions before they begin. Creating a simulacrum of reality through situations perceived as "outside" allows the participants to engage in generative conflict without tensions rising and escalating to violent behaviours. In this paper, the authors explore the connection between play and social success, as well as several examples of using a board game to facilitate generative conflict.

Keywords: Educational Games · Game-Based Learning · Social Success · Conflict · Lean Startup

1 Introduction

Workplace conflict affects 90% of US workers [1], with only 6% of work conflicts stemming from personality/culture differences or fighting over resources. The top three sources of workplace conflict were reported as a lack of communication/miscommunication (33%), conflicting priorities (23%), and a lack of understanding about the urgency/time-sensitive nature of a task (13%). And more than 1 in 3 (36%) of the respondents said that loss in productivity is the most significant consequence of conflict, citing a range of distractions which left them with only 46% of their working week available for the primary duties of their job.

Similarly, in a recent annual report of their Q12 employee engagement survey, Gallup reported that the majority of the world's employees are "quiet quitting" [2]. They report that 23% of the global workforce is engaged, defining this as highly involved in and enthusiastic about their work and workplace (Gallup 2023, 94). However, 18% reported as loud quitting (actively disengaged) and

Published by Springer Nature Switzerland AG 2024
T. van Kollenburg et al. (Eds.): ELEC 2023, IFIP AICT 681, pp. 201–208, 2024.
https://doi.org/10.1007/978-3-031-63265-5_15

59% as quiet quitting (not engaged), causing Gallup to estimate the cost of low engagement in the global workplace at US$8.8 trillion, which accounts for 9% of global GDP.

This phenomenon coincides with the increase in team working, especially in knowledge work, where teams work collaboratively, communicate frequently, and mutually depend on one another for success. This increases the potential for task and relationship conflict [3, 70].

Lean games and simulations can be used for more than introducing various lean concepts. [4] They create a safe environment to surface and resolve conflict, tensions as well as other issues. This paper presents three cases where a specific board game has created situations the authors classify as conflict. We discuss the importance of generative conflict for non-routine tasks as well as interplay of play and social success.

2 Theoretical Background

2.1 Generative and Destructive Conflict

Increased potential for task and relationship conflict, in turn, can amplify the impact of cognitive biases such as naïve realism and fundamental attribution error [3, 64–65], which can undermine personal or team credibility [5] or authority [6, 275].

Edmondson speaks directly to this as most people intuitively recognise that each of us engages in a tacit "calculus" in which we assess the risk associated with a given interpersonal behaviour quickly and effortlessly as we face a micro-decision point. She also links this risk-aversion to the idea of "learning anxiety" [7, 325], which Schein identified as a challenge to be overcome during the first stage of Lewin's "Three-Step Model of Change" [8].

But are all conflicts destructive? Jehn [9] argues that it depends on the task type performed. Through interviews and observations, Jehn found that conflict was destructive for routine, standardised tasks. However, disagreements were generative for novel tasks, promoting open discussion of task issues such as critical evaluation of problems and decision options. Participants reported that task-related conflicts decreased thoughtless agreement and complacency.

2.2 Play and Social Success

What is play? How does it benefit us and why would we do it?

Play is a roomy subject, broad in human experience, rich and various over time and place, and accommodating pursuits as diverse as peekaboo and party banter, sandlot baseball and contract bridge, scuba diving and Scrabble [10]. Whilst this description may resonate with us, it only reveals a little beyond an experience in time and space that can be characterised by a few examples. Eberle suggests that there are six basic elements to the process of play. Play is an ancient, voluntary, 'emergent' process driven by pleasure that yet strengthens our muscles, instructs our social skills, tempers and deepens our positive emotions, and enables a state of balance that leaves us poised to play some more. And it's in this definition that we see play adequately conceptualised, enabling us to understand our motivation for play, as well as its value. A paradox of pleasure, growth and connection, play, it seems, is a vehicle for learning.

Clinical psychologist Jordan Peterson draws parallels between developmental psychology (Jean Piaget) and the subfield of affective neuroscience (Jaak Panksepp) in the process of social skill acquisition [11, 14–17]. Peterson suggests that participation in the process of play develops the players of that game as they learn the skills needed to negotiate the goals and rules governing cooperation and competition. A point further explored by a study into play as a springboard for adult social competence in human and non-human primates [12].

A 2013 study looked at social skills as predictors of communication, performance and quality of collaboration in project-based learning [13]. The researchers found that effective collaborative learning depended on the social skill configuration. Here, homogeneous and/or high-level social skill configurations tend to be more favourable than heterogeneous and/or low-level social skill configurations, especially for social skills that focus on communal goals (as cooperation/compromising and prosocial behaviour/openness). The authors went on to recommend that groups would benefit from social skill development before they engaged in collaborative work.

2.3 Playing Lean

Playing Lean is a turn-based board game for teaching the Lean Startup, a methodology for developing business, products, and services. The game is designed for 4 to 16 players, divided in up to four teams. Each team manages a fictional startup in shared industry. The first team to reach 100 000 customers, so called early majority [14], wins. The game is played in turns divided into planning and execution phase. During the former, players discuss their product development, experimentation, and sales strategies. They also have to assign employees to accomplish specific tasks before their planning times runs out. If they don't, that means their business hasn't got anything done in that turn. See [4,15,16] for in-depth coverage of gamification behind Playing Lean and how it teaches the Lean Startup methodology.

For this article, we want to focus on how Playing Lean introduces conflict and tension within and between teams. Since there is a limited set of actions a team can do every turn (develop product features, attempt a sale, conduct an experiment, bid at an auction), the players must negotiate how they want to direct their employees. That often leads to disagreement between team members, especially when players have different professional backgrounds. At the same time, there is a limited number of customers in the market. The game divides customers into tiers (innovators, early adopters, late majority) and uses the network effect in sales (teams cannot sell to late majority if there are no early adopter customers, and early adopters won't buy unless there are some innovators who already tried the product). This makes it important to move quickly and secure early customers, otherwise the slow-moving team risks ending locked out of certain customers. All of these factors risk causing conflict as they stir competitiveness between the teams, their strategies, and tactical choices.

3 Case

A large international company headquartered in Europe has been on a transformational journey for several years. They've been investing in developing lean and agile capabilities on all levels of the organisation. As part of their upskilling programme, they've also invested in game- and simulation-based workshops.

In this case we will focus on a specific workshop that was attended by managers in product-oriented roles. Sample included ten participants, of which one was a senior manager, seven were line managers, and two were support function managers.

The workshop consisted of (a) brief theoretical introduction to the lean startup methodology, followed by (b) four hours of gameplay, followed by (c) facilitated reflection. In the last part participants were asked to identify cases (i) where what they experienced in game conflicts with what they experience in their daily work, and (ii) how can they leverage that insight to create positive change, no matter how "small." Data, i.e. the discussion that transpired during facilitated reflection, was collected in the form of written notes and transcripts.

The data was analysed live, by discussing what patterns have emerged in the responses to questions posed during the facilitated reflection. This discussion was then captured in a single report, which was then discussed once more. Equal attention has been given to actions and their consequences as well as lived experience of thereof.

4 Discussion

We have collated participants' responses into three areas relevant to the lean startup methodology: build-measure-learn loop, pivoting, and experimentation. We discuss what role conflict played in each case below. The quotes are from various participants.

4.1 Build-Measure-Learn Loop

In Playing Lean, the only way to have a guaranteed sale is by first understanding what the customers wants (expressed in specific product features), developing said features, and then selling to that customer. It is possible to over-deliver (i.e., have more features than they asked for), but not under-deliver. Conducting learning experiments is the only way to learn what the customer wants.

> *"In the game we learn from the experiments, and get insight into what our customers wanted, and put that insight into building features and understanding whether we're able to sell to certain parts of the market.*

In the business analyst team, we do a lot of measurement in terms of understanding what the best approach or best solution to problems would be through insight and data. In the current project, we run into problems because we've come into the project when already a lot of the decisions have been made, but we are still able to do the likes of value based scoping to understand in terms of our backlog of work what is the best benefit.

Once we get into it in a more agile way, with an iterative approach, we obviously have measurement, learning and building as we go along, and we can understand as we're building iteratively how successful that is, and pivot if we need to and continue that cycle."

In this case the workshop participants connected their in-game experience to an on-going conflict they experience within the organisation when it comes to level of autonomy and flexibility when it comes to product development. At the moment they are addressing this conflict by relying on their social skills as well as sub-processes like analysing smaller parts of the product to determine areas which haven't been decided on and where they can still create some value.

4.2 Pivoting

Pivoting, "changing strategy while retaining one's original vision" [17, 10], is in essence conflict between pathways or chosen options. During the game it is relatively easy to pivot: employees can be assigned to any activity, features can be removed and added, and previous customers cannot be lost. This allows the participants to experience the benefits of changing course whilst maintaining their initial objective—to win their first 100 000 customers. Since in-game pivot is almost always based on the customers' needs, it usually results in better in-game performance as well.

"We often build very big products over a long period of time. It's difficult sometimes to pursue our product and proposition teams to build smaller products and learn from something, and then take those learnings on board to alter whatever we're building. There have been cases where they'd be forced to build smaller products by the fact that we haven't been able to launch everything in time.

A huge amount of pressure needs to be applied to the ... team to go down that route. And we gain a huge amount of benefit from launching smaller increments, and learning from them and then pivoting slightly to eventually build a much more tailored product to what the customers actually want, opposed to what we think the customer wants or what consultants are telling us the customers want.

We do pivot, and we do that based on fixed timelines and deliverability or non-deliverability and being forced to change. The thing I've learned today is the definition of where you're going is a business model level in this framework, and actually in terms of your product-market fit. And you learn that as you develop the product.

What we're experiencing in our day to day is we've decided what our market fit should be, what our product design should be and we just keep pushing till we can deliver that initial concept, rather than learn the design from learning and building."

Having experienced first-hand the value of adjusting course based on market-data, the participants are better resourced to engage in generative conflict in their organisation.

4.3 Experimentation

Business experimentation is a process of rapidly testing business-related assumptions to speed up the product and business development process. During the game, players can assign their employees to conduct various business experiments like customer interviews, landing page tests, prototyping, and so on. Whenever they run an experiment successfully, they learn what the customer is willing to pay for.

"Our culture is not to experiment, we have an organisation in which we are cascaded the ideas, and we're asked to deliver the ideas. Customer needs and deciding what product strategy is right, is almost like a pyramid where at the very tip of that pyramid there may be some small type of experimentation done by the product teams, and at the base where people are doing the work there's little experimentation.

By then the work is already defined. We might play with different looks on an app, might play with different nooks and feel of the journey, but the direction in which it is going is preordained. Even when we do some experimentation it's discarded because it doesn't fit the goals and the strategic direction that's already been decided.

There is a lack of understanding the value experimentation would actually give to the programs. Senior buy-ins, senior understanding, senior inclusion and participation in experimentation, in design sprints, that would drive the value through the delivery program is probably missing."

In organisations, the conflict arises between the perception of reality, or inside-out thinking, and customers' reality, or outside-in thinking. Understanding what the customers want is often a better strategy than forcing them to purchase products that were developed without their needs being considered at all. Through play, participants identified opportunities where they could challenge the existing processes and procedures to become more customer-oriented, thus increasing the organisation's chance of success.

4.4 Implications for Practitioners

As we've seen, task-related conflict can be destructive. However, for non-standard tasks, it provides a dynamism that ensures ideas are debated and the opportunity for co-created solutions to win on their merit. Such a perspective suggests two kinds of work designs—execution-as-efficiency and execution-as-learning—which can be placed on a process-knowledge spectrum describing the uncertainty in the work [3, 229–234].

The spectrum model asserts that routine operations are sufficient to manage execution-as-efficiency for situations of low uncertainty. By contrast, for situations of high uncertainty work requires innovative operations to manage execution-as-learning. This is especially useful for high-risk endeavours, such as launching a new product or investigating a new market, where mistakes will be made, and tensions will run high. There is no question that lean practice *is* execution-as-learning, which Edmondson describes as "getting the work done while simultaneously working on how to do it better." [3]

Play creates a safe space for learning to take place. Players explore work-related, psychological, and interpersonal risk-taking to create new insights and, more importantly, deepen social bonds with colleagues through shared experience. And structured games can bridge classroom knowledge with specific skills [18], compounding the effectiveness of the learning experience.

5 Conclusion

In this paper we explored the difference between generative and destructive conflict, relationship between play and social success, and how a board game for teaching Lean Startup, a methodology for developing business, products, and services. We investigated how games and simulations can create safe environment for generative conflict, from which participants can learn and grow. Consequently, they can then take that insight into their own organisations to instigate generative conflict where it matters.

Using games and simulations might be a sound first step when learning outcomes include lessons and insight that might be in conflict with the participants' established norms, beliefs, and lived experience. By creating the safe space for them to learn and fail, the educator has in turn created space they themselves need to further challenge the learners. Hence, we would like to invite lean practitioners and researchers to continue exploring play and conflict as fertile ground for lean transformations and change efforts.

References

1. Workfront: The State of Enterprise Work (2015)
2. Gallup: State of the Global Workplace 2023 Report: The Voice of the World's Employees (2023). https://www.gallup.com/workplace/349484/state-of-the-global-workplace.aspx
3. Edmondson, A.C.: Teaming: How Organizations Learn, Innovate, and Compete in the Knowledge Economy. Jossey-Bass (2012)

4. Pešec, B.: Taking the playing lean experience online: the case of using a board game to teach lean startup remotely. In: Powell, D.J., Alfnes, E., Holmemo, M.D.Q., Reke, E. (eds.) Learning in the Digital Era, IFIP Advances in Information and Communication Technology, vol. 610, pp. 299–307. Springer, Heidelberg (2021). https://doi.org/10.1007/978-3-030-92934-3_30
5. Prekel, T.: The 3 Rs - Respect. recognition and relatedness - essentials in conflict resolution. SSRN Electron. J. (2012)
6. Hawkins, P., Smith, N.: Coaching, Mentoring and Organizational Consultancy: Supervision, Skills and Development, 2nd edn. Open University Press, Maidenhead (2013)
7. Schein, E.H.: Organizational Culture and Leadership, 5th edn. Wiley, Hoboken (2016)
8. Lewin, K.: Frontiers in group dynamics: concept, method and reality in social science; social equilibria and social change. Human Relat. **1**(1), 5–41 (1947)
9. Jehn, K.A.: A multimethod examination of the benefits and detriments of intragroup conflict. Adm. Sci. Q. **40**(2), 256 (1995)
10. Eberle, S.G.: The elements of play: toward a philosophy and a definition of play. Am. J. Play **6**(2), 214–233 (2014)
11. Peterson, J.B.: Beyond Order: 12 More Rules for Life. Allen Lane (2021)
12. Palagi, E.: Not just for fun! Social play as a springboard for adult social competence in human and non-human primates. Behav. Ecol. Sociobiol. **72**(6), 90 (2018)
13. Notari, M., Baumgartner, A., Herzog, W.: Social skills as predictors of communication, performance and quality of collaboration in project-based learning: Social skills in project-based learning. J. Comput. Assist. Learn. **30**(2), 132–147 (2014)
14. Moore, G.A.: Crossing the Chasm: Marketing and Selling Disruptive Products to Mainstream Customers, 3rd edn. HarperBusiness, an imprint of HarperCollins Publishers (2014)
15. Rasmussen, T., Øxseth, S.: Playing lean: gamification of the lean startup methodology. Master's thesis, Norwegian University of Life Sciences, Ås/Norwegian University of Life Sciences (2016)
16. Pešec, B.: Improving the impact of remote Playing Lean workshops through action inquiry and critical reflexivity. Int. J. Lean Six Sigma **14**, 1144–1167 (2022)
17. Eisenmann, T.R., Ries, E., Dillard, S.: Hypothesis-driven entrepreneurship: the Lean Startup. Harvard Business School Entrepreneurial Management Case (2011)
18. Holland, C., Ulrich, D.: Critical thinking cards: an innovative teaching strategy to bridge classroom knowledge with clinical decision making. Teach. Learn. Nurs. **11**(3), 108–112 (2016)

The Influence of Learning Styles on the Perception of Lean Implementation Effectiveness by Employees

Matteo Zanchi(✉), Beatrice Colombo, and Paolo Gaiardelli

Department of Management, Information and Production Engineering, University of Bergamo, Viale Marconi 5, Dalmine, BG, Italy
{matteo.zanchi,beatrice.colombo,paolo.gaiardelli}@unibg.it

Abstract. Despite the well-known effects and benefits that Lean Management (LM) methodologies potentially bring to manufacturing companies, many firms still struggle with enabling the full potential of LM practices, thus reaching the desired effects. Motivation represents a crucial factor in setting in motion the cycle of continuous improvement and achieving considerable results over the long term. Ensuring and maintaining the right motivation can be quite challenging. This is particularly true when dealing with LM programs, which typically demand several years to effectively transform people's mindset. Furthermore, the disparity in mindset between companies that have recently embraced lean thinking and those from which the so-called Toyota Way originated its founding principles adds to the complexity of this task. Based on a real case study conducted in an Italian manufacturing company, the aim of this paper is to understand how the implementation of a Lean program within a factory is actually perceived by blue and white-collar workers. Given the broad spectrum of personal preferences and inclinations that differentiate each individual, the analysis was built by establishing a correlation between learning styles of the participants and predisposition toward Lean methodologies, which has resulted in a wide variety of both positive and negative outcomes. Such results highlight the need for a different design of the training program to tailor it more effectively to the needs of each worker, thereby triggering a positive reaction that over time can maintain high motivation among the operators in the full embrace of Lean methodologies.

Keywords: Lean manufacturing · 5S · SMED · Kolb's Learning Style Inventory (LSI) · Dunn and Dunn Learning Style Model · Single case study

1 Introduction

The urge of modern companies to maximize productive efficiency, to carve out a niche in the highly competitive sector of manufacturing production, has led many organizations to attempt implementing Lean practices and methodologies based on the so-called "Toyota Production System" (TPS), within their processes [1]. However, the deployment of such

Published by Springer Nature Switzerland AG 2024
T. van Kollenburg et al. (Eds.): ELEC 2023, IFIP AICT 681, pp. 209–220, 2024.
https://doi.org/10.1007/978-3-031-63265-5_16

practices does not always lead to the expected results. This is mainly because a successful Lean program heavily relies on the ability to support the cultural change process over time, which is typically necessary when adopting such practices. It is well-known that any Lean optimization program requires several years before showing relevant and stable results that indicate the actual transformation of the company's culture [2]. In the field of research regarding Lean Management (LM), a well-established approach differentiates between hard and soft practices [3]. Hard practices refer to technical and analytical tools employed to enhance production systems, while soft practices encompass managerial concepts and principles, individuals and relationships. Soft practices play a vital role in attaining superior outcomes, although the successful execution of hard practices strongly indicates enhanced operational performance within the context of lean practices [3]. As noted by Rodriguez et al. [4], the efficacy of implementing hard practices is heightened when carried out concurrently and consistently with the implementation of soft practices.

In this respect, people involvement across all hierarchical levels results to be a highly crucial factor, exactly since the 'People' element constitutes one of the founding pillars to trigger the process of Kaizen, necessary to properly sustain the streamlining process of production activities over the long term [5]. Projecting the mentality of management and of shopfloor workers on such a forward-looking perspective requires, though, a strong and constant motivation among all the company components to keep the change process vivid.

Instilling the right level of interest into LM methodologies can be pursued through the adoption, in the first instance, of "ready-to-use" Lean techniques and practices. These tools are easy and rapid to implement, but at the same time very impactful, and concur toward the creation of a participative climate within the company [6]. Examples, in this sense, include tools like 5S and SMED, which offer highly visible results in a short period of time [7]. These tools contribute to creating a strong sense of commitment among teamwork members, driven by the curiosity sparked by remarkable outcomes and the desire to assess long-term benefits [8]. At the same time, the adoption of Lean practices is known to have non-negligible effects on working fields which should lead to the creation of a more stimulating workplace [9]. However, the perception of the working environment may differ from person to person and, thus, achieving high levels of motivation is possible only in the case where the working context results to be befitting in respect of workers' preferences.

From these premises, this paper aims to depict how the first-stage adoption of Lean strategies and tools may influence the perception of working personnel to external stimuli characteristic of the workplace, in light of individual predisposition. The research is built on a single case study of a company producing aluminum extrusion dies, where a Lean optimization program has been launched over the last few years and is currently developed upon the implementation of 5S and SMED practices. The implementation schedule has been paired up, in the initial stage, with a training program designed by the research team (made up of 3 experts on LM topics), and intended to both the company optimization team and shopfloor workers, to train personnel on general LM principles and on 5S and SMED methods and tools.

The results obtained from the research, based on data collected through a research protocol administered to the personnel, concern two particular aspects: i) the reaction to changing environmental/occupational stimuli and ii) the personal predisposition, intended in the concerned research as "learning styles", for which various theoretical models available in scientific literature were referred to.

Following this brief introduction, the paper is structured as follows: Sect. 2 provides the theoretical background on LM tools, with a specific focus on 5S and SMED practices, and different models of "learning style"; Sect. 3 illustrates the methodology used to carry out the research, while Sect. 4 presents the main results obtained along with the related discussion and considerations. Finally, Sect. 5 concludes the paper by highlighting the main relevance of the paper, discussing the limitations of the study and suggesting possible future research directions.

2 Theoretical Background

In accordance with the goal of the research, the theoretical background has been built upon a summary of existing learning style models.

2.1 Learning Style Models

With the advent of the Industry 5.0 concept, which puts the human factor under the spotlight of scientific research in the production engineering field [10], an increasing interest toward topics concerning training and learning aspects has emerged over the last years. However, dealing with people and studying human behavior is not as straightforward as studying physical phenomena. Indeed, each individual is unique, leading to high variability when studying human subjects in different contexts. In this regard, over the past decades, researchers have attempted to frame the way people behave in terms of learning, developing various models to depict people's attitudes toward learning styles, namely being:

- Dunn and Dunn Learning Style Model (LSM) [11]
- Gregorc's Style Delineator (GSD) [12]
- Honey and Mumford's Learning Styles Questionnaire (LSQ) [13]
- Jackson's Learning Styles Profiler (LSP) [14]
- Kolb's Learning Style Inventory (LSI) [15]
- Myers-Briggs Type Indicator (MBTI) [16]
- Neil Fleming's VARK Model [17]
- Vermunt's Inventory of Learning Styles (ILS) [18]

Among these, two models have gained a noticeable relevance, either for their applicability to industrial environments, rather than for their multi-perspective nature that allows for a holistic approach to the subject of learning: the Learning Style Model (LSM) proposed by Dunn [11] and the Learning Style Inventory (LSI) created by Kolb [15]. They are briefly described in the following.

Dunn and Dunn Learning Style Model (LSM). One of the advantages of this model is that it focuses on examining a person's learning preferences rather than fixing their flaws or criticalities. Indeed, LSM incorporates physiological, environmental, and social interaction aspects in addition to motivational factors. Consistently, the questionnaire, designed on the basis of the principles described by the authors, identifies preferences for 22 factors that are classified into five different categories:

1. Environmental - that is, an individual's preference for places where quiet prevails rather than noisy environments; or for spaces that are more or less bright, or characterized by high or low temperatures (*stimuli* respectively being sound, light, temperature, and seating).
2. Emotional - linked to an individual's preference for solo or group work, for the presence or absence of a recognized authority, or for the need to please others (*stimuli* respectively being motivation, responsibility/conformity, task persistence and structure).
3. Sociological - stimulus linked to the person's need for career advancement, to the possible empowerment of the individual, or to the need to have certain directives (*stimuli* respectively being alone/peer, authority and variety).
4. Physiological - factors that significantly influence the learning process, such as a greater inclination to learn at different times of the day (be it morning or evening), or the need to move to increase one's performance as much as to remain stationary (*stimuli* respectively being auditory, visual, kinesthetic, tactile, intake, morning/evening, late morning, afternoon and mobility).
5. Psychological - strand incorporating the information elaboration process, global versus analytical, impulsive versus reflective behavior (*stimuli* respectively being reflective/impulsive and analytic/global).

In our particular case, Dunn and Dunn's model was used to describe the influence of work-related stimuli on the employee's motivation to learn Lean logics and, consequently, on greater commitment to their implementation in the long term.

Kolb's Learning Style Inventory (LSI). The LSI is widely recognized as one of the most influential models on learning styles. Based on the idea that individuals often have distinct preferences for specific activities, it is structured around a questionnaire aimed at identifying these preferences and capturing individual variations in learning. It is important to note that learning styles are not fixed traits but rather concern preferences that may vary slightly depending on the context/situation. Indeed, learning entails the resolution of conflicts between opposing approaches to adapting to the world, making it inherently tense. There are four types of learning skills: from i) concrete experience (CE); ii) reflective observation (RO); iii) abstract conceptualization (AC), and iv) active experimentation (AE). These four capacities are placed on two independent axes, with concrete experience opposing abstract conceptualization on the first axis, and active experimentation opposing reflective observation on the second axis. Based on these dimensions, Kolb identified four types of learning styles:

1. Convergent - Individuals belonging to this group, characterized by their proficiency in abstract conceptualization and active experimentation, exhibit strong abilities in problem solving, decision making, and the practical application of ideas. They excel

in solving conventional intelligence tests, display emotional self-control, and tend to gravitate toward technical problem-solving rather than interpersonal matters.

2. Divergent - The focus lies on concrete experience and reflective observation within this group. Individuals in this category demonstrate ingenuity and possess a heightened awareness of the meanings and values associated with various aspects of life. They have the ability to perceive concrete situations from multiple perspectives, displaying a preference for observation over immediate action. They exhibit a genuine interest in people and tend to be more oriented toward emotions and feelings.
3. Assimilative - Preference is given to abstract conceptualization and reflective observation within this group. Individuals belonging to this category show a fondness for inductive reasoning, drawing conclusions from specific instances to form general principles. They possess a propensity for creating theoretical models and are more intrigued by abstract ideas and concepts rather than interpersonal dynamics. Their focus lies on the logical validity of ideas rather than their practical realizability.
4. Accommodative - The focus lies on concrete experience and active experimentation within this group. Individuals in this category thrive on engaging in hands-on activities, making plans, and seeking out new experiences. They excel at adapting to changing circumstances and tend to solve problems intuitively through trial and error. They possess a natural comfort with social interactions, although there may be instances where they exhibit impatience and assertiveness.

3 Methodology

As for the methodological aspect, this research was conducted in three distinct stages. First, a literature review was carried out to assess existing learning styles models. Google Scholar was the primary database used to gather papers or books on the topic. The identified learning styles models were then evaluated and validated by three Lean experts with both theoretical and practical knowledge. Specifically, Dunn and Dunn [11] and Kolb [15] models were found to be the most effective in achieving the research goal. The former was used to assess how and to what extent the various stimuli affect the learning style before and after the implementation of a lean program. The latter, instead, was adopted to evaluate the way in which the learning process of an individual takes place, identifying their cognitive profile.

At this point, a research protocol consisting of close-ended questions reflecting the aims of the two selected models was designed. The first part, based on the Dunn and Dunn's model, comprised 17 questions out of original 22, as some *stimuli* were grouped according to their category. For instance, auditory, visual, kinesthetic, and tactile *stimuli*, which are the channels through which our brain processes information from the five senses, were grouped into a single category identified as "Perceptual". Respondents were asked to express three evaluations relating to the *stimulus* considered on a five-level scale: the first concerning their preference for the stimulus (Preference), the second evaluating their perception of the stimulus prior to the implementation of the SMED and 5S project (Before), and the last evaluating the stimulus after the implementation of the lean project (After). Subsequently, a value from 1 to 5 was associated to the options composing each question. This allowed the researchers to compute the effectiveness of each *stimulus*, namely the Lean's ability to bring the reaction closer to or further away from the preference of a specific *stimulus*, as follows:

$$\text{Effectiveness} = |\text{Preference} - \text{Before}| - |\text{Preference} - \text{After}| \quad (1)$$

The second part, based on Kolb's model, utilized ten blocks of four statements each, to which respondents assigned a value between 1 and 4 based on their affinities. This enabled the identification of the cognitive profile of each participant. In detail, by summing up the points assigned to each phase of the four-stage cycle per block and plotting them on the Cartesian axes, a quadrilateral was identified. The triangle with the largest area represents the learning style of the respondent.

Third, a single case study was performed to address the aim of the research. Indeed, this methodology can make a significant contribution to knowledge and theory building when analyzing complex interactions between different variables under observation. Moreover, it helps avoid a superficial approach that is often associated with multi-case analyses [19, 20]. The company under investigation (henceforth, Alpha) is a leading manufacturer of extrusion dies located in Northern Italy, whose mission is focused on creating an independent and innovative firm with a strong potential for growth. In 2021, Alpha accounted for a turnover of around € 50 million. Its production serves various markets, including transportation, building, automotive, aerospace, and industrial at a global level. In 2021, Alpha started a lean project with the aim of implementing SMED and 5S techniques. The research team supported the company in the training and implementation process while simultaneously administering the aforementioned research protocol to both blue-collar (9) and white-collar (7) employees, for a total of 16 people, to achieve the research objective. Lastly, the collected data were analyzed to draw initial general conclusions on the investigated topic.

4 Results and Discussion

With regard to the considered sample, results show a prevalence of Accommodative and Assimilative learning-oriented people, both in respect of the total sample considered (37.5% and 31.25% respectively) and particularly among personnel working on the shopfloor (44.44% for both), referred to in Tables 1, 2, 3, 4, 5 and 6 as S (Shopfloor). On the other hand, Divergent and Convergent learning-oriented individuals are less represented in the sample (12.5% and 18.75% overall), with almost no presence of such individuals in the Shopfloor population (1 individual belonging to the Convergent family and 0 to the Divergent). However, such discrepancy is not observed within the optimization team (referred to as T - Team) that supervised the implementation of the Lean project. Here, while considering with due concern to the boundedness of the sample size, the distribution of individuals belonging to all the different learning-style families is fairly homogeneous.

Globally, the learning category that best responds to work-related stimuli following the implementation of the Lean tools is the Assimilative one (with a mean of 9.60 effectiveness score), followed by the Accommodative (6.50 points) and the Convergent (6.33) groups. Divergent individuals have, on the other hand, experienced the least benefits from the adoption of 5S and SMED logics (5.50).

Table 1. Effectiveness scores - Aggregate analysis

Learning Style	S				T		Mean
Accommodative	6	5	10	3	3	12	6.50
Divergent					8	3	5.50
Assimilative	14	6	10	8	10		9.60
Convergent	2				8	9	6.33

When stratifying the results between the two populations, S and T, it can be observed that the Assimilative individuals perceive the effectiveness of Lean in both roles (although there is only one employee in the T group with an Assimilative cognitive profile). The same partially applies for the Accommodative group, although there is some variability in terms of effectiveness (some values are equal to 3 and thus indicate a low overall effectiveness).

What distinguishes the two populations, however, is the perception of Lean among the Convergent individuals. In the case of the shopfloor operators (S), they do not perceive significant benefits in terms of stimuli as a result of the implementation of 5S and SMED tools with the associated training program. Conversely, the implementation team (T) experienced great effectiveness from the adoption of Lean practices in terms of work-related stimuli. It is not possible to provide a detailed analysis by role for the Divergent individuals because the total population coincides with that of the implementation team. This discrepancy between S and T populations, contextually for the Convergent learning style may derive from the diversity in job roles, more practical for the former and managerial for the latter. This could generally draw more attention from the optimization group toward the adoption of Lean logics in the long-term, rather than the shopfloor personnel.

To gain more insights into the possible causes of such a difference, and to provide a more comprehensive analysis, the results have also been analyzed contextually to the different dimensions of work-related stimuli, as described by the Dunn and Dunn model.

Table 2. Effectiveness scores - Emotional dimension

Learning Style	S				T		Mean
Accommodative	5	4	5	−2	−1	8	3.17
Divergent					2	1	1.50
Assimilative	5	4	5	2	5		4.20
Convergent	2				2	3	2.33

Emotional *stimuli* represent the class reporting the best results in terms of effectiveness between all the different work-related dimensions, with a high degree of homogeneity among the participants (also in relation to different roles). This evidence confirms, once again, the validity of Lean tools in creating a strong sense of responsibility among personnel at all hierarchical levels. Furthermore, the empowerment and involvement of the operators in designing their workplaces according to the 5S principles has significantly raised the motivation of the employees, crucial factors as underlined in scientific literature [21].

The learning-style category that witnessed the best results in terms of Emotional stimuli is the Assimilative (4.20), opposed to the Divergent that shows the worst outcomes in this sense (1.50).

Table 3. Effectiveness scores - Sociological dimension

Learning Style	S				T		Mean
Accommodative	2	2	3	−3	4	5	2.17
Divergent					2	1	1.50
Assimilative	−1	2	2	4	4		2.20
Convergent	0				3	3	2.00

Second stimuli class most positively affected by the adoption of SMED and 5S practices is the Sociological one, despite the effectiveness being strongly polarized between S (1.22) and T (3.14) samples. Lean, in fact, stimulates team working between employees belonging to different departments. This has proven to be beneficial in achieving higher operational performance over the long term [22]. In this case, the best respondents are the people with an Assimilative cognitive profile (2.20) closely followed by Accommodative ones (2.17). Divergent subjects are, on the other hand, the ones witnessing the fewest benefits (1.50). The high variability also found for Accommodative and Convergent within the S and T populations proves again the discrepancy of results depending on the role held.

Table 4. Effectiveness scores - Psychological dimension

Learning Style	S				T		Mean
Accommodative	0	2	0	5	1	2	1.67
Divergent					1	0	0.50
Assimilative	3	3	3	−1	2		2.00
Convergent	0				4	2	2.00

Stimuli belonging to the Psychological category show just a mild improvement (overall 1.69 points) in terms of effectiveness with regards to the sample's preferences, although being consistent between S and T populations. In this case, the most benefits have equally been experienced by Assimilative and Convergent (2.00), although for the latter there is an actual discrepancy between shopfloor personnel (0.00) and optimization team (3.00). This difference may be attributed to distinct approaches to work. Blue-collar workers tend to be more analytically and impulsively oriented, whereas the implementation crew leans toward a global and reflective approach, aligning better with the problem-solving skills typically associated with this group. On the other hand, the least advantages in terms of work-related stimuli have instead been witnessed by Divergent subjects (0.50).

Table 5. Effectiveness scores - Physiological dimension

Learning Style	S				T		Mean
Accommodative	1	−1	4	4	1	−3	1.00
Divergent					5	2	3.50
Assimilative	6	−1	0	2	2		1.80
Convergent	0				0	0	0.00

Physiological stimuli are perceived with the mildest effectiveness among the considered categories (1.38 points overall). Divergent subjects are those who perceive the change of physiological stimuli deriving from the implementation of the Lean program as the most effective (3.50) among all the learning-style categories. Such a positive result for Divergent subjects shows how the stimuli now meet the needs of such people (especially in terms of flexible working hours, which aligns to the creative needs of these individuals). On the other hand, Divergent employees believe the change in Physiological stimuli not being particularly evident (0.00).

The only notable results within this category concern the "perceptual" (encompassing auditory, visual, kinesthetic and tactile *stimuli*) and "mobility" elements. The adoption of a coding system significantly improved the identification process of necessary tools for set-up operations. Simultaneously, it reduced the time needed and the distances employees had to travel to locate the required equipment within the department.

Table 6. Effectiveness scores - Environmental dimension

Learning Style	S				T		Mean
Accommodative	−2	−2	−2	−1	−2	0	−1.50
Divergent					−2	−1	−1.50
Assimilative	1	−2	0	1	−3		−0.60
Convergent	0				−1	1	0.00

Finally, Environmental *stimuli* are the only ones that have shown a deterioration, for nearly all the learning-style categories considered, following the implementation of the Lean program (average of −0.94 effectiveness points). The results are confirmed from both S and T populations, denoting the bad effects that SMED and 5S have surprisingly exerted on employees' perception of the working environment. However, it is clear that the Lean methodology does not aim to influence factors such as light, temperature and sound, so the negative result may not be very significant. The only criticism pertains to the possibility that this outcome could be influenced by the seating element. However, it is important to note that individual preferences for certain working postures might explain this occurrence. Therefore, it should not significantly undermine the validity of the Lean project within the considered context.

5 Conclusions, Limitations, and Future Research

In this paper, a single case study was conducted to understand how and to what extent lean techniques can affect the perception of employees, who are characterized by different learning styles, to external stimuli characteristic of the workplace.

The results demonstrate that, on the whole, implementing LM methodologies in the case study brought work-related stimuli closer to the preferences of both shopfloor operators and the implementation team. However, the effectiveness of this alignment varied depending on the specific stimulus category under consideration. Specifically, the effectiveness was high for Emotional and Sociological stimuli, mild for Psychological and Physiological categories and, lastly, negative for Environmental stimuli. It is worth noting that the negative perception of Environmental stimuli may be attributed to the fact that Lean tools such as 5S and SMED do not directly address factors like sound, light, and temperature. Additionally, the negative perception mostly relies on the individual preferences, making it highly unpredictable.

Finally, the obtained outcomes can be crucial on a twofold perspective. Primarily for practitioners, as they offer guidance to managers on tailoring training programs to align with the prevalent learning-style orientation within a population and cater to the individual preferences of each person. This customization is aimed at not only enhancing the positive reception of Lean program implementations but also at mitigating potential negative perceptions that could erode long-term motivation in pursuing Kaizen principles. Secondly, to open up a new stream of research regarding teaching and learning, not related to typical academic training but rather the one that takes place in the workplace, which is useful in making business performance more effective in the long run. Such a topic, despite being widely addressed from a practical point of view, still exhibits very little material in the scientific literature.

Nevertheless, this work is not exempt from limitations typical of qualitative research. First, the generalizability of the results is undermined by the small sample of employees under analysis. This paves the way for future improvements of the current study. By widening the numbers involved, it would be possible to analyze and quantify the impacts of the investigated factors leveraging econometric techniques. Second, to consolidate the obtained results and insights, it is advisable to explore a broader range of companies across different sectors and countries, rather than relying solely on a single case study. Third, it is equally true that when dealing with human subjects, the classification by "learning style" only partially reflects their cognitive predisposition. Each individual possesses more complex dynamics and logics that require deeper considerations, in addition to those identified by the two models under examination.

References

1. Belekoukias, I., Garza-Reyes, J.A., Kumar, V.: The impact of lean methods and tools on the operational performance of manufacturing organisations. Int. J. Prod. Res. **52**(18), 5346–5366 (2014)
2. Mann, D.: The missing link: lean leadership. Front. Health Serv. Manag. **26**(1), 15–26 (2009)
3. Bortolotti, T., Boscari, S., Danese, P.: Successful lean implementation: organizational culture and soft lean practices. Int. J. Prod. Econ. **160**, 182–201 (2015)
4. Rodríguez, D., Buyens, D., Van Landeghem, H., Lasio, V.: Impact of lean production on perceived job autonomy and job satisfaction: an experimental study. Hum. Factors Ergon. Manuf. Serv. Ind. **26**(2), 159–176 (2016)
5. Liker, J.K., Convis, G.L.: Toyota Way to Lean Leadership: Achieving and Sustaining Excellence Through Leadership Development. McGraw-Hill Education, New York City (2012)
6. Zanchi, M., Gaiardelli, P., Powell, D.J.: The impact of different training approaches on learning lean: a comparative study on value stream mapping. In: Powell, D.J., Alfnes, E., Holmemo, M.D.Q., Reke, E. (eds.) ELEC 2021. IFIP Advances in Information and Communication Technology, vol. 610, pp. 109–117. Springer, Cham. https://doi.org/10.1007/978-3-030-92934-3_12
7. Dombrowski, U., MIelke, T.: Lean leadership–15 rules for a sustainable lean implementation. Procedia CIRP **17**, 565–570 (2014)
8. Gutierrez, J., Rojas, L., Saldivar, D., Rios, V., Aliaga, A.: Benefits of the 5's methodology in the manufacturing industry: a literature review 2017–2022. In: Proceedings of the LACCEI International Multi-Conference for Engineering, Education and Technology (2023)
9. Mascarenhas, R.F., Pimentel, C., Rosa, M.J.: The way lean starts–a different approach to introduce lean culture and changing process with people's involvement. Procedia Manuf. **38**, 948–956 (2019)
10. Nahavandi, S.: Industry 5.0—a human-centric solution. Sustainability **11**(16), 4371 (2019)
11. Dunn, R., Griggs, S.: The Dunn and Dunn learning style model and its theoretical cornerstone. In: Synthesis of the Dunn and Dunn Learning-Style Model Research Who, What, When, Where, and so What, pp. 1–6 (2003)
12. Gregorc, A.F.: Style as a symptom: a phenomenological perspective. Theory Pract. **23**(1), 51–55 (1984)
13. Honey, P., Mumford, A.: The Learning Styles Helper's Guide. Peter Honey Publications, Maidenhead (2000)
14. O'Connor, P.J., Jackson, C.J.: The factor structure and validity of the Learning Styles Profiler (LSP). Eur. J. Psychol. Assess. **24**(2), 117–123 (2008)
15. Kolb, D.A.: Experiential Learning: Experience as the Source of Learning and Development. FT Press/Prentice Hall, Englewood Cliffs (1984)
16. Myers, I.B., McCaulley, M.H., Quenk, N.L., Hammer, A.L.: MBTI Manual: A Guide to the Development and Use of the Myers-Briggs Type Indicator. Consulting Psychologists Press, Washington, DC (1998)
17. Fleming, N.D.: VARK Visual, Aural/Auditory, Read/Write, Kinesthetic. Bonwell Green Mountain Falls, Christchurch (2006)
18. Vermunt, J.D.: The regulation of constructive learning processes. Br. J. Educ. Psychol. **68**(2), 149–171 (1998)
19. Dyer, W.G., Jr., Wilkins, A.L.: Better stories, not better constructs, to generate better theory: a rejoinder to Eisenhardt. Acad. Manag. Rev. **16**(3), 613–619 (1991)
20. Yin, R.K.: Case Study Research: Design and Methods, vol. 5. Sage Publications, Thousand Oaks (2009)

21. Siegel, R., Antony, J., Govindan, K., Garza-Reyes, J. A., Lameijer, B., Samadhiya, A.: A framework for the systematic implementation of green-lean and sustainability in SMEs. Prod. Plan. Control **35**, 1–19 (2022)
22. Kurilova-Palisaitiene, J., Sundin, E., Poksinska, B.: Remanufacturing challenges and possible lean improvements. J. Clean. Prod. **172**, 3225–3236 (2018)

Current State of Practice in Developing Lean Six Sigma Training and Certification Programs -an Irish Perspective

Olivia McDermott[1](✉), Michelle Regan[2], Manjeet Kharub[3], Anna Trubetskaya[2], Michael Sony[4], and Jiju Antony[5]

[1] College of Science and Engineering, University of Galway, Galway, Ireland
Olivia.McDermott@universityofgalway.ie
[2] University of Limerick, Limerick, Ireland
[3] Department of Mechanical Engineering, CVR College of Engineering, Hyderabad, India
[4] Oxford Brookes Business School, Oxford Brookes University, Oxford, England
[5] Faculty of Business and Law, Newcastle Business School, Northumbria University, Newcastle Upon Tyne, England, UK

Abstract. The study aims to review how Lean Six Sigma training and certification programs are conducted in organisations to develop employee competence and advance the programs. The types of training and certification programmes, the approach to development, the critical factors for success and failure, and barriers to development were all investigated. A quantitative survey was conducted with Operational Excellence professionals from various Irish manufacturing industry sectors who had Lean Six Sigma programs. It was found external accreditations of LSS expertise were more prevalent than internal certifications in Irish organisations, and many organisations encouraged completing of continuous improvement projects with valid financial savings before individuals were certified. As well as this, a lack of management support, not setting aside time for the individuals to complete the training, and a lack of recognition and reward for completing training and projects were deemed critical failure factors. The findings from this study can be used to develop a best-practice Lean Six Sigma training and certification program that is open to all employees and is externally accredited. This paper is one of few studies that expose the current practice for designing a Lean Six Sigma training and certification programme in industry.

Keywords: Lean Six Sigma · Training Programme · Belt Certification · Continuous Improvement · Framework

1 Introduction

With the competitive nature of the industry globally to meet customer demands, there is an increased demand for process improvement initiatives to reduce cost and enhance innovation [1]. COVID-19 has also contributed to the growing demand and has increased

Published by Springer Nature Switzerland AG 2024
T. van Kollenburg et al. (Eds.): ELEC 2023, IFIP AICT 681, pp. 221–236, 2024.
https://doi.org/10.1007/978-3-031-63265-5_17

the need to identify waste in production processes with continuous improvement initiatives [2]. Continuous improvement is defined by the American Society of Quality (ASQ) as the improvement of products or services through incremental or transformational changes. However, the common denominator behind implementing these improvements is the employees or people interacting with the associated [3].

While Lean Six Sigma (LSS) training has been deployed extensively in the Manufacturing industry, including Medtech, Pharma and Automotive manufacturers, as well as in the services sector, there is limited research published to give insights into the lessons learned and best practices of the operational implementation and sustaining of a LSS training programme [4]. Several studies have investigated the importance of training, reward recognition and Leadership support for a LSS program, but few have delved into the tactical aspects of training and certification.

The main aim of the research project is to determine the best approach for developing a LSS training and certification programme in industry. The American Society of Quality (ASQ) has a well-recognised, reputable certification programme, which requires recertification every 3 years. However, many certification consultants exist who will offer a LSS certification for a minimal fee and minimum attendance at training and that do not require a project to be implemented in order [5, 6]. The International Standards Organisation (ISO) has published a standard for LSS competency assessment, but it has been widely criticised and companies have not embraced and leveraged it [5, 7–9]. A gap also exists in the research to determine the best pathway for companies within industry to develop continuous improvement training and build the capabilities of its employees. The lessons learned and best practices of companies implementing these training programmes will be investigated.

The main objectives of the researcher are as follows:

- *What is the current state of practice of LSS training and certification programs in the manufacturing industry?*
- *What are the critical success and failure factors for building a successful LSS training and certification framework?*

This research will investigate through a current state analysis of LSS application in the industry, using a quantitative benchmarking survey to assess the current best practice for LSS training and certification.

2 Literature Review

Lean (a reduction in waste) and Six Sigma (a reduction in variation) have been described as catalysts of change [10]. In any Operational Excellence program, it is important to have a solid foundation in using the right tools and methodologies for problem-solving [11, 12]. This requires using a structured approach, disciplined thinking and engagement by all employees in the programme [13, 14]. LSS training has been positively correlated with employee engagement [15].

LSS certification has historically been labelled a "belt", depending on the level achieved. The term "belt" was originally assigned to individuals who were project leaders trained in process problem solving, and companies often hire for roles in process improvement based on the level of belt attained [16]. However, despite problem-solving being a transferrable skill across roles and industries [17], one organisation's measure or definition of competency may not match another's.

Depending on the organisation, there may be basic white belt training and certification, but a yellow belt is generally the most basic training level, followed by a tiered level of training and progression to green and black belt levels [18]. The master black belt is the highest certificate to attain; at this level, an individual would often manage the lower levels and mentor, train and demonstrate the application of the Six Sigma methodology [19].

Research also showed that resource management is important for the effective implementation of LSS programs in organisations [20]. However, the 2 main drivers for the failure of LSS implementation can be a lack of culture change in implementing continuous improvement and a lack of training and education on these initiatives [21]. Practising the theory learned is another key success factor [22].

Many companies have internally developed training programmes to build the capabilities of their employees in LSS. However, the syllabus and content of these courses are not often publicly available. [23] carried out a review of LSS training programs and found that there was much variation in companies in the development of their internal pathways for belt certification. [24] suggested a standard should be built using the three elements of training, practical application and maintenance or recertification. Some certifications that are internally built into organisations require no application of the tools to demonstrate competence. In some organisations, successful completion of LSS certification has been linked to promotion [25].

To respond and adapt to the future needs of an organisation, it was suggested that frequent repetition of implementation of the tools would be required to achieve different levels of competence [24]. The ISO 18404:2015 standard sets out LSS competencies for the implementation of the tools. However, it is not been embraced by organisations and has been critiqued for trying to measure "Lean-ness" [9]. Some companies use a return on investment (ROI) approach to determine what projects to prioritise as part of prioritising training and selecting LSS projects. However, the risk of not achieving or being able to measure a ROI can impact the programme's credibility and other employees' willingness to take the training[26].

In any LSS deployment and training program, there have to be proper criteria for the selection and prioritisation of projects, as poorly selected and defined projects lead to delayed results and also a great deal of frustration [27]. Having an identified project before commencing training is recommended. Rogers [16] discussed a selection of appropriate personnel to become certified as a LSS belt practitioner and the importance of soft skills training as these individuals may be leading, coaching, mentoring and project managers at certain levels of an organisation.

Overall, despite theoretical-based training and certification programs, e.g. the ASQ or accreditation to a LSS standard, e.g. ISO 18404, the literature offers minimal guidance or case studies on the tactical best practices and recommendations on LSS training and certification implementation in organisations.

3 Methodology

A quantitative survey was utilised to answer the research questions. Surveys are inexpensive and fast methods of gathering data from a large number of people where meeting in person is not possible [28]. Surveys also gather information using a sample size that can elicit information about a larger population in an industry [29]. The objectives of the online survey were to gain a general sense of how LSS training and certification is carried out currently in the Irish industry, how accredited and rewarded, and the supporting contributing factors for developing a LSS training programme in the industry.

The survey questions were drafted based on the themes identified in the literature review, and the order of the questions was determined (See Table 1). A pilot of the survey was carried out to pre-test the process prior to distribution [30]. The pilot involved 5 continuous improvement professional participants working in the industry. The online survey (via MS Forms) allowed for the data to be obtained from the participants to be confidential. Once the participants agreed to take part in the study, the link for the online survey was then distributed online via 'LinkedIn Messenger' to a sample size of 150 individuals [31]. Flaws or risks associated with this type of data collection include ensuring the participants of the survey are representative of the population under investigation [29]. To ensure control here, the sample participants were selected. The sample consisted of employees from various industries, including Biotech, Pharmaceuticals, Medical devices, etc., as well as those in various roles and functions who have exposure to a LSS training programme. To ensure sufficient response rates, a deadline was given to the participants to complete the online survey, which has been shown to be effective in improving response rates [28]. Another risk associated with an online survey was the potential for participants to skip a question; this was controlled by ensuring each question must be answered in the Microsoft Form setting unless it was not required based on a previous answer (Siva et al. 2019). 110 valid survey responses were obtained, yielding a 30% response rate (surveys were disseminated to 330 people). All participants voluntarily agreed to be part of the study, any form of identifiable labelling was not made visible, and participant numbers were used as identifiers [32].

Table 1. Non Demographic Survey Questions

Questions	Literature Sources
Have you undertaken training through the LSS belt programmes? (i.e. Yellow, Green, Black Belts etc.) **Yes/No**	[18, 19, 33]
If Yes, what belt level have you been certified in? (Tick all that apply) **White Belt/Yellow Belt/Green Belt/Black Belt/Master Black Belt/None of the above**	[18, 19, 27, 33]
If certified to belt level, were the belts received? **Internal certifications/external certifications**	[18, 19, 27, 33]
What type of pathway (training source types) for LSS training exist in your organisation? Tick all that apply **Internal Belt Level Training & Certification/External Consultant Training & Certification/No Pathway/Other, Please Specify**	[7–9, 18]
In relation to the LSS training programme you attended /participated in, how were you certified to the relevant belt level? (Tick all that apply.) **Demonstration of theory or Learning (exam)/Demonstrated application of the learnings through a project/Maintenance of cert (recertification required periodically**	[5, 6, 8]
Are all employees required to participate in the Belt training programme in your organisation? **Yes/No**	[24, 33]
If Yes to the previous question, is there a minimum tenure expectation or job level required to participate in the training programme for LSS in your organisation?	[24]
Does senior Leadership support the LSS training programme**? Yes/No** **If yes, how is it supported?**	[13, 21, 34]
Is there a stipulation that the trainees attending LSS training in your organisation have a project to work on and a cost-benefit analysis/ROI in a plan? **Yes/No**	[14]
If Yes, how is this ROI or savings validated and tracked? Tick all that apply **Employee Feedback/Sharing of Learnings/Application and Implementation of Actions/Business Impact/Metrics Analysis/Cost Reduction/Other, Please explain**	[21, 35]
Is the LSS training programme in your company externally accredited (for example, by a university/accredited body)? **Yes/No**	[5, 18]
In your experience, what do you think are the critical success factors for developing a LSS training programme to develop LSS belts/skills in your organisation? Please tick all that apply **Strong LSS Culture/Pathway to progression in LSS developed (white to yellow to green)/Management Buy In /Recognition for completing the training (example: receiving a certification)/Tracking Performance of application of the learnings/Trainee Pre-Selection /Sponsor Required to sponsor project /project Identified prior to training/Other: Please specify**	[13, 24, 36]
In your experience, what do you think are the critical failure factors for developing a LSS training and certification programme in your organisation? **Lack of management support /lack of accreditation for the training/No standard pathway developed for continued learning/lack of time set aside for individuals to take this training/culture of seeing this as extra work/No return of investment required/Difficult to make changes in a highly regulated environment (included as part of application)/Lack of soft skill development (i.e. leadership/managing a team) /Other, Please Specify**	[14, 15, 22]
In your personal experience, what do you think is the biggest barrier to developing a LSS training programme and Belt Levels in industry?	[7, 9, 13]
Are the LSS training levels (i.e. belts) recognised by and rewarded by management in the organisation you work in? **Yes/No**	[14, 21, 37]

4 Results

4.1 Participant Demographics

Table 2 below identifies that 27% of the respondents who completed the survey worked in the Manufacturing industry by their sectors.

Table 2. Percentage of participants by their industry type

Industry	Percentage of Participants (%)
Pharmaceutical	20%
Med Devices	30%
Biotech	10%
Manufacturing (Electronics/Equipment)	20%
Food	10%
Other	10%

4.2 Training Levels

The level of experience in LSS training of the 120 participants who completed the survey was obtained. The participants were asked firstly, *"Have you received LSS training via a belt program? (i.e. Yellow, Green belts, etc.)"*. The results received indicate that 90% of the participants had been trained in some levels of LSS. This correlates with two studies by McDermott et al. [4, 38], where over 96% of Irish Pharmaceutical and MedTech companies were found to have a Lean, Six Sigma or LSS program.

4.3 Belt Certification Levels

The participants were then asked, *"What is the highest level of belts you are certified to?"* where they could select the highest levels of belts for which they had received certification. Of the responses obtained, 20% were certified at the highest belt level of the *"Master Black Belt"* level. Of those certified at a Master Black belt level, the majority had undertaken a specialised university Master in LSS, but none had completed, for example, the ASQ MBB certification or any other external MBB accreditation. 20% were certified to a *"Black belt"* level, 40% were certified at a *"green belt"* level, while the remaining 20% were certified at a basic *"yellow belt"* or *"white belt"* level. None of the participants had no belt certification, which, given that the researchers approached OpEx personnel and Manufacturing participants, was not a surprise (Fig. 1).

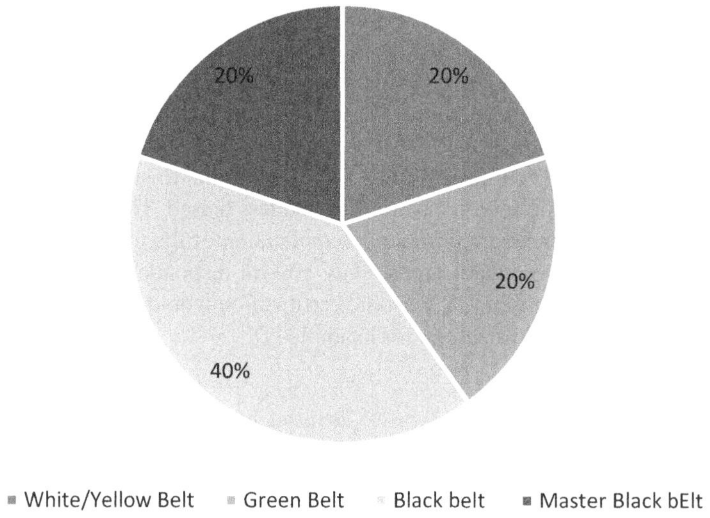

Fig. 1. Graph of the type of LSS Belts (X-axis) by the percentage of participants with certifications received (Y-axis). (Color figure online)

4.4 Internal versus External Accreditation

30% of the participants had certifications that were solely accredited outside of their company (for example, by attending a university or by exam from an external organisation e.g. ASQ). In comparison, another 50% had certifications from an external trainer working with their organisations (see Table 3). Only 11% of the respondents stated that they were certified by their own organisation's certification program (with no external trainer/consultancy/organisation involvement). The remaining respondents did not answer or selected not applicable. This result suggests that externally accredited certification were of higher importance for the participants and the organisations that they work in.

Table 3. Source of belt certification

Source of certification	%
External trainer (hired by the organisation)	50%
External qualification/accreditation (e.g. university/ASQ)	30%
In-house certification program	10%
Not applicable/other	10%

4.5 The Training and Certification Pathway Components

60% of the respondents selected *"Demonstrated application of learnings through a project"* in order to be certified in their organisations as opposed to just demonstrating theory or learning via an external exam (e.g. ASQ belt certification exams, which were selected by 30%). One large multinational, for example, did not have an internal certification process and required all their Black Belts and Green Belts to sit the ASQ certification exams as they deemed those more prestigious and less biased. These responses indicate that demonstrating competency through the application of the tools and project implementation is important to organisations. Only 10% of respondents stated that they had no certification pathway (Table 4). Periodic certification would be a requirement by the ASQ in their black belt certification, for example [18].

Table 4. Type of Certification pathway

Type of Certification Pathway	%
Demonstrate application of learning via a project	60%
Organisation supporting a Theory/learning exam (e.g. university/ASQ/other)	30%
None	10%

4.6 Requirements to Participate in the Training Program

The next question asked was, *"Are all employees required to participate in the LSS training programme?"* 90% of respondents indicated that not all employees were required to complete the internal training, but further analysis found that it was "*expected*" training to be undertaken in the respondents manufacturing areas. Only 10% stated it was required or mandated training. In relation to the question, *"Is there a minimum tenure expectation or minimum grade level required to be able to participate in the training programme?"* -99% responded no or that the question was not applicable. However, while it was not explicitly stated that there was a minimum tenure or grade required, it would be expected that certain job grades and roles would align with different belt levels - for example, production operators would not normally complete Black Belt training. Black Belt training is more expensive than other belt level training, particularly if carried out by an external supplier; thus, organisations are more selective about who they send on this training. If carried out by in-house trainers -trainer time and resources can be limited so that places are prioritised based on project urgency and class space constraints. Also, a Black Belt is expected to be able to understand and apply statistical and data analysis tools as well as facilitate projects, and this would not be in the remit of a lower-grade employee.

4.7 Leadership Support

Next, regarding the question on leadership support, 60% of the respondents indicated there was leadership support in the training by typing "*yes*" into the response field while 40% stated "*no*". There was a sub-question added for those who answered "yes" to the previous question in terms of how Leadership show support for LSS training. Answers here included leadership support being demonstrated by communications in relation to CI, and recognition of CI project successes as well as finance and budget being made available for external trainers to come on site or deliver training offsite.

4.8 Return on Investment Requirement

61.8% of respondents stated that a return on investment was required as a condition of undertaking LSS training (and potentially to receive subsequent certification). The respondents could select as many conditions as was applicable. Examples here included the demonstration that applying LSS tools and training would result in a saving for the company. This aligns with the responses to a previous question related to training programme contents, where 60% of the respondents selected "*Demonstrated application of the learnings through a project*" in order to be certified. In terms of how the return on investment is tracked, the respondents could tick all that applied. The return of investment through *"Business Impact/Metrics Analysis"* received the most responses, with 49 of the participants selecting this option, followed by *"Cost Reduction"*, where 45 of the participants selected this option (see Fig. 5). These results focus on data-driven results where an improved metric or financial saving would be seen. "*Application and Implementation*" (relating to implementation through a project), "*Learnings*" (relates to an improvement in the learner's ability) and "*Employee Feedback*" (relates to feedback from the learners of the training) all received a similar number of responses with greater than 30% of the 55 participants selecting these options. Finally, 35 of the participants selected "*Other*". Here, respondents were given the option to respond via an open text field and the inputs received were linked to various methods of tracking returns of investment. These included the number of CI opportunities implemented and measuring of improvement as seen in the metrics. All of these inputs aligned with the two biggest drivers, "*Business Impact/Metrics Analysis*" and "*Cost Reduction*", identified in this question.

4.9 Critical Success Factors and Critical Failure Factors for Developing a LSS Training Programme in Industry

Next, the critical factors in terms of 1) success, 2) failure, 3) barriers to the development of a LSS training programme, and 4) recognition and reward were analysed in the final section of the survey.

The top critical success factors that the participants felt were applicable could be selected (see Fig. 6) for developing a LSS training and certification program were 1) *"Management Buy-In"* (82 of the participants selected this option), 2) *"Strong LSS Culture"* (76 of the participants selected this option). The top drivers for success demonstrated a need for acceptance and support in the training courses from both management and the employees within a company during development and implementation. The categories "*Sponsor required to sponsor a project, tracking the performance of application of the learnings, Recognition for completing the training (example: receiving a certification), pathway to progression in LSS belts developed (white to yellow to green)* and *project identified prior to training*" were also considered significant (at least 40 of the participants selected each of these options) (Fig. 2).

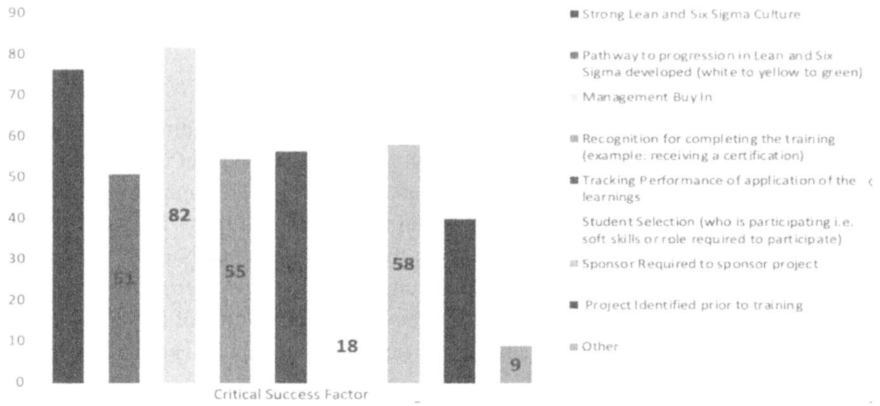

Fig. 2. The critical success factors in a LSS training programme (Color figure online)

The respondents also chose from a number of potential failure factors that they felt were applicable and selected all that applied. The top critical failure factor that received the most responses was a "*Lack of management support*", followed by a "*Lack of time set aside for individuals to take this training*" and "*Culture of seeing this as extra work*". The failure factor that received the least number of selections was "*no return of investment required*". Having a return on investment was more of a management priority and stipulation to ensure maximum return from training budget investment. In the open text field, some of the responses given included the following categories: a lack of engagement/culture in continuous improvement and behaviours associated with it, training and leadership support, the lack of potential problems to solve to be able to apply the learnings and finally closure/sustainability of the projects.

An open-text field response allowed respondents to write in their own words about barriers to developing training and certification. The majority of the responses (nearly half) were related to a lack of leadership support or management buy-in for a LSS programme. The remainder of the responses identified were in relation to a lack of resources applied to projects or allocated to the LSS training programme. Just 10% of the responses identified the culture in an organisation as the biggest barrier to a LSS programme (see Table 5).

The final question of the survey investigated the topic of recognition and reward for completing a LSS project or for getting certified in their organisations. 80% of respondents selected "*yes*" for this question and stated they felt recognised. This suggests

Table 5. The percentage of responses for the barriers identified for the development of a LSS training programme.

Barriers to the Development of a LSS Training Programme	Percentage of the total responses (%)
A lack of leadership support or management buy-in	48%
A lack of resources applied or allocated	25%
Culture of an Organisation	10%
Understanding LSS and the need for it	5%
Blank/Other	12%

that it is important to consider recognition and reward when developing a LSS training programme.

5 Discussion

Based on the findings above from the research investigation conducted, a number of trends have been identified. Establishing and maintaining management support was a common theme observed across multiple questions asked to determine how successful LSS training programmes are designed. Lack of management support was also seen as a critical failure factor and a barrier to the development of a LSS training programme in industry. As well as this, demonstration of the application of the learnings from the training on a company problem was deemed important, as was certification based on demonstration of project completion and tool application. Antony et al. (2021) in their study on Many studies on the importance of Connecting the certification of projects to a final saving or return on investment by demonstrating the business impact through metric analysis was also seen as of high importance. The majority of organisations that took part had externally accredited LSS programs. This correlates with the finding that the majority of participants had received certification from an externally accredited organisation or trainer, with only 10% of the participants having an internal certification program. This suggests that a certification that is externally accreditable is of high importance to organisations. Conversely, given the cost of external trainers and accreditations, it could suggest a lack of internally qualified LSS personnel to deliver training. The popularity of external accredited training also highlighted by Louzada et al. in their 2023 study of belt certifications in Brazil. They found that personnel seeking LSS certifications can use external courses to obtain competencies required by the market, whether for promotion within their current organisations or in the search for a new employment [39].

Finally, half of the participants identified a lack of leadership support or management buy-in within a LSS training programme in industry as the biggest barrier to the development of a programme.

A conceptual framework of findings for developing a LSS training programme for industry can be developed using the recommendations above and leveraging the lessons learned from this study. The research was conducted with professionals, where the majority had experience of completing LSS training and were certified. Of the certifications received by the participants involved in the study, external accreditations were more prevalent. According to previous studies, internally built certifications gave rise to variation within the requirements for certification, so this would validate why most of the belts the participants received in this study are externally accredited [23]. However, the validity of external accreditation or trainers has also been critiqued in terms of the quality of their training and the fees charged [6, 9]. Different content levels can be found in the LSS courses offered by certification consultants, institutions and trainers which can cause problems for both organizations and professionals seeking to compare, evaluate, and select a training and certification partner [23]. Over half of the participants stated that the LSS training programmes were externally accredited when asked as part of the survey. This shows that working professionals in the industry prioritise externally accredited training programmes, and therefore, this should be a key consideration for the development of a LSS training programme in any organisation.

A limitation of any training programs in some of the organisations was that certification could be received without showing an application of the learnings or tools included in the training through the implementation of an improvement project. This does not measure employee competencies and ensure that tools are understood [12, 40, 41]. However, 75% of the participants responded that implementation through a project was required in order to be certified for completion of the training.

The study found that the majority of LSS training programmes were not mandatory, as not all employees were required to take them. However, further analysis of comments in the survey did find a higher expectation that manufacturing-based employees are trained or understated training. As well as this, a certain grade level or tenure was also not a requirement to be able to take the training. Setting a requirement such as this one could be seen as a potential roadblock, and the lack thereof implies that there are no obstacles to training.

This study has implications for the development of a LSS training programme in industry to form a pathway to follow. Leadership and management support is of high importance from the beginning of the development of the programme to ensure its success. This will ensure support for both those who are developing the programme as well as the participants. A strong culture of LSS will also enable the development of such a programme. During the training, a participant should demonstrate the application of the learnings through a project that leads to improvements where a return on investment can be seen. This is preferably in a data-driven approach, such as a metric analysis or as a cost-benefit. Following completion of the training, one should be certified, recognised and rewarded. Recognising and rewarding Lean improvement projects has been shown to support a Lean culture [22]. Sharing the knowledge of Lean implementation through recognition can also, in turn, increase the implementation of improvement projects by sharing best practices [14]. Finally, externally accredited certifications for participants have been seen to be more favoured according to the survey responses received in the research investigation.

This research study can be used to build on the best practices for companies within the industry to utilise when developing their LSS training and certification programmes. The findings provide a pathway for industry to follow and key critical factors for development. The critical success factors and failure factors outlined here are of high importance for owners when considering or initiating LSS training programmes. The output can be built into the standard work process for the owners, trainers and attendees of the training programmes to follow to ensure the success of the programme. From this, the effectiveness of the current design can be determined, and the depth and detail of the content in the LSS training can be analysed further. This will allow companies to continue to upskill their employees on LSS and build the capabilities of their organisations.

6 Conclusions

The best approach for developing a LSS training and certification programme in organisations has been brought to light by the findings from the research investigation. This is one of the few studies to demonstrate what a good design and development of a LSS training and certification programme looks like. Contributing factors to building a LSS training framework involve developing a programme that is open to all employees to take, and that also can be externally accredited. Furthermore, in order to be certified according to the findings, one must show application of the learnings through a project that has data-driven improvements.

The critical success factors and critical failure factors for developing a LSS training programme have also been revealed. The critical success factors of management buy-in and support are of high importance, as well as developing a strong LSS culture. Similarly, to prevent failure of a LSS training programme, management support is crucial in ensuring time is set aside for the individuals to complete the programme, as well as the cultural element of not seeing it as extra work. The novelty of the findings identified in this research paper can be used to form a best practice document for companies within industry to follow when developing a LSS training programme. As well as this, academic researchers can use this study to learn how industry develops their LSS training programmes. The current work, along with future research, can ensure that companies continue to determine the pathway to be taken for the training programmes related to LSS.

A limitation of the study is that it was only Irish; however, the majority of the companies that participated were all part of globally based multinationals whose LSS programs were standardised globally as mandated at a corporate level. Thus, the results have a high level of generalisability in relation to current training and certification practices globally.

Further research can be carried out in terms of a case study to dig deeper into the depth of the content and syllabus of the programmes in order to determine the effectiveness of the LSS learning objectives. As well as this, further research can be conducted on the maturity of LSS training programmes and the ability to recertify periodically once a programme has been developed. This will determine the sustainability of the programme implemented. Overall, the findings revealed a novel approach that can be used to successfully develop a LSS training programme in industry. By training workforces on LSS and building the capabilities of organisations, companies can react to problems that arise and continuously improve their processes and procedures.

References

1. Pavlović, K., Božanić, V.: Lean and Six Sigma Concepts – Application in Pharmaceutical Industry. In: International Journal for Quality Research. pp. 259–268. IQC, University of Kragujevac (2011)
2. Byrne, B., McDermott, O., Noonan, J.: Applying lean six sigma methodology to a pharmaceutical manufacturing facility: a case study. Processes **9** (2021). https://doi.org/10.3390/pr9030550
3. ASQ: Continuous Improvement Model - Continual Improvement Tools | ASQ. https://asq.org/quality-resources/continuous-improvement. Accessed 15 Sept 2023
4. McDermott, O., Antony, J., Sony, M., Healy, T.: Critical failure factors for continuous improvement methodologies in the Irish MedTech industry. TQM J. **34**, 18–38 (2022). https://doi.org/10.1108/TQM-10-2021-0289
5. Antony, J., McDermott, O., Sony, M., Cudney, E.A., Snee, R.D., Hoerl, R.W.: A study into the pros and cons of ISO 18404: viewpoints from leading academics and practitioners. TQM J. **33**, 1845–1866 (2021)
6. Oudrhiri, R., et al.: The place of ISO 18404:2015 in organisational improvement. TQM J. (2022). https://doi.org/10.1108/TQM-08-2021-0243
7. Antony, J., et al.: A global study on applicability of ISO 18404: 2015 for SMEs: an exploratory qualitative study. TQM J. **35**, 1917–1934 (2022)
8. Antony, J., McDermott, O., Sony, M., Powell, D., Snee, R., Hoerl, R.W.: Global study into the pros and cons of ISO 18404: a convergent mixed method study and recommendations for further research. Int. J. Qual. Reliab. Manag. (2021). https://doi.org/10.1108/IJQRM-10-2021-0356
9. McDermott, O., Antony, J., Sony, M., Swarnakar, V.: The misplacement of ISO 18404:2015 in organizational improvement: a point-counterpoint article. TQM J. (2023). https://doi.org/10.1108/TQM-01-2023-0019
10. Pepper, M.P.J., Spedding, T.A.: The evolution of lean six sigma. Int. J. Qual. Reliab. Manag. **27**, 138–155 (2010). https://doi.org/10.1108/02656711011014276
11. Antony, J., McDermott, O., Sony, M., Fernandes, M.M., Ribeiro, R.V.C.: A study on the Ishikawa's original basic tools of quality control in South American companies: results from a pilot survey and directions for further research. TQM J. **33**, 1770–1786 (2021). https://doi.org/10.1108/TQM-01-2021-0004
12. McDermott, O., Antony, J., Sony, M., Fernandes, M.M., Koul, R., Doulatabadi, M.: The use and application of the 7 new quality control tools in the manufacturing sector: a global study. TQM J. **35**, 2621–2639 (2023)
13. Albliwi, S., Antony, J., Abdul Halim Lim, S., van der Wiele, T.: Critical failure factors of lean six sigma: a systematic literature review. Int. J. Qual. Reliab. Manag. **31**, 1012–1030 (2014). https://doi.org/10.1108/IJQRM-09-2013-0147
14. McDermott, O., Antony, J., Sony, M., Looby, E.: A critical evaluation and measurement of organisational readiness and adoption for continuous improvement within a medical device manufacturer. 1–11 (2022). https://doi.org/10.1080/17509653.2022.2073917
15. Sunder M.V., Prashar, A.: Empirical examination of critical failure factors of continuous improvement deployments: stage-wise results and a contingency theory perspective. Int. J. Prod. Res. **58**, 4894–4915 (2020). https://doi.org/10.1080/00207543.2020.1727044
16. Rogers, D.: The Future of Lean Sigma Thinking in a Changing Business Environment. Productivity Press, New York (2016). https://doi.org/10.4324/9781315300269
17. Raja Sreedharan, V., Raju, R.: A systematic literature review of lean six sigma in different industries. Int. J. Lean Six Sigma. **7**, 430–466 (2016). https://doi.org/10.1108/IJLSS-12-2015-0050

18. ASQ: Six Sigma Belts, Levels & Roles—ASQ. https://asq.org/quality-resources/six-sigma/belts-executives-champions. Accessed 15 Sept 2023
19. Antony, J., Snee, R.: Leading role – identifying the skills master black belts and black belts need to be effective leaders. Six Sigma Forum Mag. (2010)
20. Lizarelli, F., de Toledo, J., Alliprandini, D.: Relationship between continuous improvement and innovation performance: an empirical study in Brazilian manufacturing companies. Total Qual. Manag. Bus. Excell. **32**, 981–1004 (2021). https://doi.org/10.1080/14783363.2019.1653178
21. Antony, J., Gupta, S., Sunder M.V., Gijo, E.V.: Ten commandments of Lean Six Sigma: a practitioners' perspective. Int. J. Prod. Perform. Manag. **67**, 1033–1044 (2018). https://doi.org/10.1108/IJPPM-07-2017-0170
22. Barclay, R.C., Cudney, E.A., Shetty, S., Antony, J.: Determining critical success factors for lean implementation. 1–15 (2021). https://doi.org/10.1080/14783363.2021.1894919
23. Laureani, A., Antony, J.: Standards for lean six sigma certification. Int. J. Prod. Perform. Manag. **61**, 110–120 (2012). https://doi.org/10.1108/17410401211188560
24. Antony, J., Snee, R., Hoerl, R.: Lean Six Sigma: yesterday, today and tomorrow. Int. J. Qual. Reliab. Manag. **34**, 1073–1093 (2017). https://doi.org/10.1108/IJQRM-03-2016-0035
25. Hendricks, C.A., Kelbaugh, R.L.: Implementing six sigma at GE. J. Qual. Particip. **21**, 48 (1998)
26. Gülyaz, E., Venugopal, V., Veen, van der A., Gorp, V.: Decision support framework for estimating return on lean six Sigma projects (2013)
27. Antony, J., Banuelas, R.: Key ingredients for the effective implementation of Six Sigma program. Meas. Bus. Excell. **6**, 20–27 (2002). https://doi.org/10.1108/13683040210451679
28. Babbie, E.R.: The Practice of Social Research. Cengage Learning, Boston (2020)
29. Ball, H.L.: Conducting online surveys. J. Hum. Lact. **35**, 413–417 (2019). https://doi.org/10.1177/0890334419848734
30. Saunders, B., et al.: Saturation in qualitative research: exploring its conceptualization and operationalization. Qual. Quant. **52**, 1893–1907 (2018). https://doi.org/10.1007/s11135-017-0574-8
31. Power, A.: LinkedIn: Facebook for professionals? Br. J. Midwifery **23**, 196–198 (2015)
32. Fowler Jr., F.J., Cosenza, C.: Design and Evaluation of Survey Questions. In: The SAGE Handbook of Applied Social Research Methods, 2nd edn., pp. 375–412 (2009)
33. Escobar, C.A., Chakraborty, D., McGovern, M., Macias, D., Morales-Menendez, R.: Quality 4.0—green, black and master black belt curricula. Procedia Manuf. **53**, 748–759 (2021). https://doi.org/10.1016/j.promfg.2021.06.085
34. Aij, K.H., Teunissen, M.: Lean leadership attributes: a systematic review of the literature. J. Health Organ. Manag. **31**, 713–729 (2017). https://doi.org/10.1108/JHOM-12-2016-0245
35. O'Connor, C., McDermott, O.: Cost of Quality in Construction. In: McDermott, O., Rosa, A., Sá, J.C., and Toner, A. (eds.) Lean, Green and Sustainability, vol. 668, pp. 307–317. Springer International Publishing, Cham (2023). https://doi.org/10.1007/978-3-031-25741-4_26
36. Gonzalez-Aleu, F., Van Aken, E.M., Cross, J., Glover, W.J.: Continuous improvement project within Kaizen: critical success factors in hospitals. TQM J. **30**, 335–355 (2018). https://doi.org/10.1108/TQM-12-2017-0175
37. Antony, J., Rodgers, B., Gijo, E.V.: Can lean six sigma make UK public sector organisations more efficient and effective? Int. J. Product. Perform. Manag. **65**, 995–1002 (2016). https://doi.org/10.1108/IJPPM-03-2016-0069
38. McDermott, O., Antony, J., Sony, M., Daly, S.: Barriers and enablers for continuous improvement methodologies within the Irish pharmaceutical industry. Processes **10** (2022). https://doi.org/10.3390/pr10010073
39. de Santi Louzada, P., et al.: Critical analysis of lean six sigma black belt certification courses offered in Brazil. TQM J. **35**, 1980–2002 (2023). https://doi.org/10.1108/TQM-08-2022-0254

40. McDermott, O., Walsh, P., Halpin, L.: A lean six sigma training providers transition to a 100% online delivery model. In: Powell, D.J., Alfnes, E., Holmemo, M.D.Q., Reke, E. (eds.) ELEC 2021. IFIP Advances in Information and Communication Technology, vol. 610, pp. 144–154. Springer, Cham (2021). https://doi.org/10.1007/978-3-030-92934-3_15
41. McDermott, O.: The digitalisation and virtual delivery of lean six sigma teaching in an Irish university during COVID-19. In: Powell, D.J., Alfnes, E., Holmemo, M.D.Q., Reke, E. (eds.) Learning in the Digital Era. ELEC 2021. IFIP Advances in Information and Communication Technology, vol. 610, pp. 132–143. Springer, Cham. https://doi.org/10.1007/978-3-030-92934-3_14

Improving the Success Rate of Lean-Themed Internships

Stephanie Monfils(✉)

AVANS University of Applied Science, Breda, The Netherlands
sl.monfils@avans.nl

Abstract. In the context of lean education, industry-university collaborations are an important mechanism for promoting knowledge exchange and fueling innovation. An important element of these collaborations are internships, which allow students to practice the transition from university to work while concurrently introducing or reinforcing existing lean knowledge in the organization. To train students to become young, skilled professionals, a practical learning experience is essential. The chances of dropping out of an internship can be reduced by a good approach in the context of a successful industry-university collaboration. Four elements make an industry-university collaboration successful. Those elements are institutional-, relational-, output- and framework factors and contribute to students completing internships successfully.

The present study documents the working mechanisms that result in successful lean-themed internships. First, meaning is given to the concept of success from the concurrent perspective of student, institution, and company. Subsequently cases are compared to identify elements that make the industry-university collaboration successful. Using a multiple case approach, the case of Care Simplifiers, an industry-university collaboration between Amphia hospital and Avans University of Applied Sciences is compared to other industry-university collaborations.

Keywords: Teaching · Internship · Lean · Healthcare · Personal growth

1 Introduction

The popularity of curricular internships as a way to prepare students for the labor market has been increasing [1]. Given the important challenges that will need to be addressed in the future, internships enable students to bridge the transition between the classroom and the world in which they will be working [2]. Internships also are beneficial for the hosting organization as they gain access to skilled human resources such as researchers or students [3]. By having students look at opportunities for continuous improvement with new, refreshing insights and applying relevant knowledge of Lean Management, organizations benefit from reduced workload and increased productivity [4]. For the hosting organizations, internships are also a way to acquire new knowledge and technology and thereby create competitive advantage [5]. Therefore, for internship programmes to be successful, they need to address these various stakeholders needs. An important

Published by Springer Nature Switzerland AG 2024
T. van Kollenburg et al. (Eds.): ELEC 2023, IFIP AICT 681, pp. 237–244, 2024.
https://doi.org/10.1007/978-3-031-63265-5_18

requirement is therefore for students to not drop out prematurely during this period of their study.

Internships are challenging for students, and dropout is a serious concern. Good supervision during internships is crucial in reducing internship dropouts. A well-structured on-site internship approach can significantly minimize the chances of early dropouts [6]. For students, internships are an important condition for obtaining a degree and a crucial preparation for entering the labour market. In February 2021, the Dutch government decided to invest extra in education. The main purpose of this investment was to repair the delays caused by the Covid-19 pandemic among Bachelor students, among others. Universities of applied sciences have invested heavily in extra student support and the prevention of study delays, trying to prevent students from dropping out prematurely as much as possible [7]. However, according to Deunk and Korpershoek [6], the corona crisis has caused a lot of extra stress for many students, and this has affected their study success.

Universities of applied sciences used additional educational resources to provide support and guidance for internships. This mainly involved support in guiding, training and coaching students in finding an internship through internship coordinators and internship agencies [7]. However, to prepare students as skilled professionals, practical learning experiences are essential during an internship. This can be accomplished by a relational approach that promotes student well-being. This approach emphasizes connection and increased interaction between teachers, practice supervisors, and students, as well as among students themselves. This approach strengthens students' sense of belonging [6]. A similar approach is used in the Care Simplifiers project.

The present paper describes the working mechanisms of the Care Simplifiers project, comparing the programme to approaches used at similar settings such as Silicon Venturing Rotterdam and VAKbekwaam. The aim is to achieve common working mechanisms for a successful internship regardless of the setting and advice is given to both universities and industries on how to improve the success rate.

2 Methods

The present study used a multiple case study approach, comparing internships programs to identify the common mechanisms leading to successful outcomes. Each internship context consists of a unique mix of stakeholders, including the hosting organization, the educational institution, and the individual students. This makes internship programs complex phenomena, and suited to a qualitative approach such as the multiple case study approach [8]. Several data collection techniques were used, including participant observation, interviews, and review of company documents. The internship organizations were selected to represent differing approaches to internships programmes with differing outcomes [9].

3 Within Case Analysis

3.1 Care Simplifiers

Care Simplifiers is a partnership between Amphia hospital and Avans University of Applied Sciences [4]. During their internships, Avans students from Business Administration programs work to simplify the healthcare process, contributing to increased quality of care and reduced work pressure. The sustainable cooperation between Avans University of Applied Sciences and Amphia Hospital has resulted in four to five students from Avans University of Applied Sciences doing internships at the hospital every semester since 2019. They work on relevant issues and improve processes using the Lean method. This 20-week program has produced great results for the healthcare institution and its patients, while also providing personal and professional growth opportunities for the students [4].

According to Rybnicek and Konigsruber's [3], there are four distinct elements that contribute to a successful industry-university collaboration. These are institutional factors, relational factors, output factors, and framework factors. Institutional factors refer to the participating institutions and include resources and structure. For example, every semester an internship is offered by Amphia to four or five Avans students from Business Administration programs. Relationship factors refer to the linking between those partners and include communication, commitment, trust and culture. On a regular basis, mutual exchange of information takes place between Amphia and Avans about the students, the planning and activities. In case of bottlenecks or questions, both parties know where to find each other and quickly switch to a solution or answer. Output factors refer to the desired results of the collaboration and include objectives, knowledge and technology transfer. Avans students use the DMAIC method to shape their research. DMAIC is the acronym for Define, Measure, Analyze, Improve and Control [10]. This research method is a structured problem-solving method of Six Sigma and aims to improve and optimize business processes. It is customary for Business Administration students to implement their proposed improvements instead of completing their internship with an advisory report. Framework factors refer to environmental aspects and include geographical distance, contracts and intellectual property rights. For example, the geographical distance between Amphia hospital and Avans University of Applied Science is 500 m.

Therefore, when applying this model to the internship approach used at Care Simplifiers, it is evident that all factors are present in sufficient measure. Amphia and Avans are both highly involved in the Care Simplifiers concept. Good, personal relationships form the basis for making collaboration possible. In addition, both parties share the same goals that students need to achieve. Geographical distance from each other is also a relevant success factor for cooperation [4]. These ingredients contribute to the successful completion of internship assignments within Amphia and it ensures that students do not drop out early.

From the student's perspective, the internship is successful if they have been able to make a contribution that benefits the hospital and leads to actual improvement. Additionally, personal growth is also considered a marker of success. This includes the development of self-confidence, communication skills, and the ability to cooperate effectively with stakeholders. So the student mainly names relational and output factors [4]. Avans and Amphia prioritize output factors, and for Avans, a successful internship entails completing professional products. These products consist of an A3, a tool to structure the thinking behind the problem-solving, an accountability report, and a presentation that reflects on the process and the generic competences of the program [11]. For Amphia, an internship is considered successful if results are achieved in terms of simplifying healthcare by designing smarter healthcare processes. But also when they have excited students to possibly work in healthcare in the future [12].

3.2 Other Programmes

Reekers [13] shows an approach which is very similar to the concept of Care Simplifiers. Silicon Venturing Rotterdam is a partnership between Albert Schweitzer Hospital and the center of Expertise Business Innovation of Rotterdam University of Applied Sciences. Students from various fields of study work together interdisciplinary with professionals from the hospital. This ultimately leads to useful innovative ideas. Every year, the hospital is surprised by its own corporate blindness, causing them to overlook real problems and solutions provided by the students. This is similar to Amphia. By working with students and the questions they ask, healthcare professionals are made to think about their way of working. This makes the collaboration fun and enriching. However, there are some essential differences. For instance, the emphasis is on product improvement rather than process improvement, and the students carry out their assignments in groups rather than individually. Nevertheless, the ingredients that contribute to success can be categorized in Rybnicek and Konigsruber's [3] model. Institutional factors are present including the high involvement of both the university and industry. In addition relationship factors are well established because communication lines between lecturers, students, and the organization are short. Moreover, the output factors are in place. As with Care Simplifiers, teaching programs are organized around the assignments, and students have a clear goal in mind. Like Care simplifiers, lecturers have held introductory talks with students to gauge their motivations for participating. The students participated each week in a weekly closure, similar to the two weekly progress sessions in Amphia where findings are presented.

There are also similarities with the study conducted by Den Hertog and van Hell [14]. 'VAKbekwaam' is a partnership between Gelre Hospital, Saxion University of Applied Sciences and Ede University of Applied Sciences. 'VAKbekwaam' is an internship variant to meet the need for better equipped nurses. During their internship period in the hospital, there is intensive supervision by work-supervisors. They act as role models. The close collaboration between the student, hospital, and educational institutions ensured that the gap between school and internship was minimized. At the end of their Bachelor education, these students were better able to start work as novice healthcare professionals. In this case as well, periodic active knowledge exchange took place between the various stakeholders. These so called Action Learning meetings were held once every fortnight at the hospital. These meetings were teaching moments in which current nursing ward situations were addressed. Intervision skills were also discussed.

4 Different Settings

Effective mechanisms in contexts other than healthcare and also resulting in a successful internship can be found at the Academy of Social Studies at the Avans University of Applied Science [15]. Second year students from the social pedagogical assistance programme struggled with fear of failure and unrealistic demands during their practice placement. Additionally, they tended to perceive feedback from their practice supervisors as personal disapproval, which discouraged them and led to internship dropout. To address these issues, the Academy added role models to their approach. They organized workshops facilitated by experienced 4th-year students who already completed the same internship. These 4th-year students offered guidance and shared their own experiences. By making themselves vulnerable, and offering valuable insights, the 2nd-year students were better prepared for the upcoming practical internship.

Lovers et al. [16] endorse this. The main reason for dropout in this study was the student himself. The transition to practice was felt to be too big, making the student uncomfortable socially and psychologically. Again, it were personal factors that caused internship dropout. By implementing mentorship and a peer support model, a smoother transition into the professional setting will be facilitated. The sharing of experiences and the support offered by more experienced peers significantly contributed to the success and retention of interns. They recommend a peer support model as described by Willekens [15].

Van Schilt-Mol [17] and Ros et. al. [18] once again confirm the effectiveness of the bi-weekly progress sessions implemented at the Care Simplifiers concept [4]. She demonstrates that this approach is a proven concept for every context. While the feedback inherently possesses subjectivity, it is the accumulation of multiple subjective judgments that leads to a robust, reliable and comprehensive evaluation of the student. Feedback gathered from various participants in these sessions play a crucial role in guiding student progress in the right direction.

Furthermore, Ros et al. [16] state that it is motivating for students to work on issues from real practice. This is also a lesson learned at the concept Care Simplifiers. Developing complex internship assignments with the involvement of industry professionals not only serves as a source of motivation for students but also ignites enthusiasm among the employees who assist them [4]. In their research they focus on future skills, such as collaboration-, problem-solving- and communication skills and the complexity of an assignment. By working on complex issues from the professional practice, students develop their future skills effectively. In this case the professional practice were industries from healthcare, education and ICT. For the industry, it was not always clear what to expect from students. Interests and conditions were not always discussed in advance. Good communication between student, teacher and work field is the key to success. They also state that working with an established methodology is supportive to achieving better quality. As already mentioned before, output factors induce clarity and relationship factors induces honesty. They both are essential elements in order for the Industry University Collaboration to succeed [3]. They concluded for an internship to be successful, the assignment should be complex enough to engage students' problem-solving and design skills, while also being feasible within the given time period.

5 Conclusion

Based on the case-comparison, in relation to my own experiences with the Care Simplifiers concept, it can be concluded that the success of an internship goes beyond the specific context in which it takes place. The chances of an internship being terminated early has much more to do with factors that can be traced back to Rybnicek and Konigsruber's [3] model. Focusing on these factors ensures that students are sufficiently equipped and are able to successfully fulfill their internship. On the other hand, premature internships should not necessarily be perceived as unsuccessful. Vosmer and Sturing [19] advise addressing positive developments so that both university and industry can finish the internship trajectory with a positive feeling. Students have experienced personal development and growth during their internship. In addition, students have concluded during their internship that the target group or sector does not suit them. This can also be perceived as positive because then they can start looking at what does fit. So despite an internship being terminated early, it does not mean that an internship has not been valuable.

According to the Personal Development papers written by the Avans students, fear of failure and taking 'negative' feedback personally, also occurs at the Care Simplifiers Concept. The structured approach from Avans and Amphia ensures that the students grow and become more and more self-confident during their internship. When the students dare to ask for help and the practice supervisor provides support in challenging work situations, they enhance their skills.

What are common working mechanisms that result in successful internships? The following advice is of use to those universities and industries that have implemented an internship program and are interested in improving the success rate of their program.

5.1 Communication

Communication is essential. During an internship, students grow in their role as project leaders by taking responsibility and directing their research [4]. Nevertheless, it is important for both the practical supervisor and the teacher to maintain good contact with the student and with the students among themselves. For the student counselling to run smoothly, there must be an open relationship in which people trust each other, where mistakes can be made and problems can be discussed. If it is difficult for a student to connect with stakeholders for any reason, the internship assignment will be extra difficult.

Specific points to consider:

- Organize feedback meetings at the university or in-company so that students can exchange experiences with each other
- Organize progress meetings between student, lecturer and practice supervisor (and other stakeholders) at the university or in-company so that student progress can be monitored.
- Have completed assignments or written products submitted before the start of a progress-meeting and provide feedback on the work.
- Involve students as much as possible in work meetings.
- Make sure there is room for equal input.

5.2 Objectives

Clear goals must be set during the internship about the final results. What concrete results should the internship assignment yield? For example, in the case of Care Simplifiers, it is not the intention to give advice on how to improve. The students must implement the advice. Specific points to consider:

- Set criteria for the final results.
- Create a schedule with dates and activities that must be met

5.3 Resources

The quality of an internship stands or falls with resources. If there is not enough staff to guide the students properly during the internship, then this will affect the quality and students may delay on their internship-assignment or worse, they may drop out prematurely. Specific points to consider:

- Set criteria what knowledge and skills the supervisors should possess
- Make the number of students per supervisor manageable.

The above points of attention help to minimize dropouts during an internship.

References

1. Franco, M., Silva, R., Rodrigues, M.: Partnerships between higher education institutions and firms: the role of students' curricular internships. Ind. High. Educ. **33**(3), 172–185 (2019). https://doi.org/10.1177/0950422218819638
2. Coco, M.: Internships: a try before you buy arrangement. SAM Adv. Manag. J. **65**(2), 41 (2000)
3. Rybnicek, R., Königsgruber, R.: What makes industry–university collaboration succeed? A systematic review of the literature. J. Bus. Econ. **89**(2), 221–250 (2019). https://doi.org/10.1007/s11573-018-0916-6
4. Monfils, S., Kokkinou, A.: Care simplifiers': students contributing to optimal healthcare. In: McDermott, O., Rosa, A., Sá, J.C., Toner, A. (eds.) Lean, Green and Sustainability: 8th IFIP WG 5.7 European Lean Educator Conference, ELEC 2022, Galway, Ireland, November 22–24, 2022, Proceedings, pp. 54–60. Springer, Cham (2023). https://doi.org/10.1007/978-3-031-25741-4_6
5. Santoro, M.D., Gopalakrishnan, S.: The institutionalization of knowledge transfer activities within industry–university collaborative ventures. J. Eng. Tech. Manage. **17**(3–4), 299–319 (2000). https://doi.org/10.1016/S0923-4748(00)00027-8
6. Deunk, M., Korpershoek, H.: Studentenwelzijn in het hoger onderwijs: Een overzichtsstudie van veelbelovende aanpakken voor docenten (teams), opleidingen en instellingen. Rijksuniversiteit Groningen (RUG) (2021)
7. Ministerie van Onderwijs: Cultuur en Wetenschap, "Nationaal Programma Onderwijs: Derde voortgangsrapportage (2022). Accessed 07 July 2023. https://open.overheid.nl/documenten/ronl-1b15f3ad38c9a7230aca488d15ce66346e9defc4/pdf
8. Yin, R.K.: Validity and generalization in future case study evaluations. Evaluation **19**(3), 321–332 (2013). https://doi.org/10.1177/1356389013497081
9. Gray, D.E.: Doing Research in the Real World, 3rd edn. Sage, Los Angeles (2014)

10. Salentijn, W.: LEAN en Six Sigma voor het Hoger Onderwijs: handleiding voor het toepassen van LEAN en Six Sigma. Noordhoff Uitgevers B.V., Utrecht (2017)
11. Academie voor Algemeen en Financieel Management, "Afstudeerwijzer Bedrijfskunde 2021–2022 (2021)
12. Avans Hogeschool: Avans en Amphia werken samen aan verbeteren zorg. https://www.avans.nl/onderzoek/expertisecentra/brede-welvaart-en-nieuw-ondernemerschap/lectoraten/improving-business/nieuws/2023/03/avans-en-amphia-werken-samen-aan-verbeteren-zorg. Accessed 07 July 2023
13. Reekers, M.: De Minor+ Silicon Venturing Rotterdam: Rapportage van een observatie. Hogeschool Rotterdam, Kenniscentrum Business Innovation. https://www.hbo-kennisbank.nl/details/sharekit_hr:oai:surfsharekit.nl:2e254032-1f46-4b27-986e-767d00cd8275
14. Den Hertog, R., Van Hell, M.: VAKbekwaam. ONDERW. GEZONDHEIDSZ. **34**(3), 22–25 (2010). https://doi.org/10.1007/s12477-010-0033-0
15. Willekens, A.: Het ervaringsdeskundige rolmodel: vierdejaars studenten bereiden tweedejaars voor op stage. Sozio-SPH **104**, 14–19 (2012)
16. Lovers, A., De Weerd, D., Plaggenmakers, M., Morren, H.: Uitgevallen en Opgevallen, Wat zijn de redenen van uitval in het stagejaar MW&D 2012–2013 van de Gereformeerde Hogeschool? Hogeschool Viaa, Zwolle, the Netherlands
17. Van Schilt-Mol, T.: Meerwaarde van integratieve leeromgevingen bij het verkrijgen van professionele oor-delen binnen programmatisch toetsen. Onderzoek Van Onderwijs, vol. 50, no. 3 (2021). https://www.tijdschriftovo.nl/art/50-6781_Meerwaarde-van-integratieve-leeromgevingen-bij-het-verkrijgen-van-professionele-oordelen-binnen-programmatisch-toetsen
18. Ros, A., Heldens, H., Swennenhuis, P.: Leren van complexe vraagstukken uit de praktijk: hoe complex mag het zijn? Onderzoek Van Onderwijs, vol. 50, no. 3 (2021). https://www.tijdschriftovo.nl/art/50-6767_Leren-van-complexe-vraagstukken-uit-de-praktijk-hoe-complex-mag-het-zijn
19. Vosmer, M., Sturing, R.: Een kwalitatief onderzoek naar stagiaires en stages binnen Ambiq. Hogeschool Saxion, Enschede, the Netherlands

Serious Games as a Lean Construction Teaching Method - A Conceptual Framework

Michele Tereza Marques Carvalho(✉), Andréa de Freitas Avelar, Marcos Brenol Renk, and Márcio Fernando Oliveira

Department of Civil and Environment Engineering, Universidade de Brasília, Campus Darcy Ribeiro, Brasilia 70830-303, Brazil
micheletereza@gmail.com

Abstract. The Information Technology (IT) revolution has transformed worldviews, spurring active teaching methods. In higher and technical education, serious games in virtual reality (VR) yield significant results. For this reason, this paper aims to show a conceptual and analytical tool for the design of serious games in virtual reality aimed at teaching the fundamentals of Lean Construction to undergraduate students in civil engineering. The implementation of Lean tools in civil construction promotes a lower time of production, decreases waste, increases the performance of workers and, obviously, reduces costs, increases the profit of business and improves the market positioning of companies. Based on a systematic literature review, whose results indicate that serious games (i) stimulate the practice of content, (ii) improve the ability to understand Lean principles, (iii) increase motivation and engagement, (iv) promote the development of interpersonal skills, (v) 70% of the games developed for teaching Lean do not use ITs and (vi) few studies refer to the perception, preparation and/or guidance of professors on the use of games. A didactic proposal was structured which, anchored in the scientific foundations of learning theories and in VR technology, is capable of filling the existing gap between the frontier of "knowing" and "knowing how to do", providing the student a procedural knowledge and creating a collaborative, didactic and effective tool, connecting theory contents with professional practice. This work's significant contribution is a conceptual framework for teaching Lean Construction, enhancing teaching practices, and reversing deficiencies in the learning process through hybrid education.

Keywords: Lean construction · Serious games · Virtual reality

1 Introduction

Traditional learning, where the teacher is always narrating his knowledge to the students, is not out of date, it is in transformation [1]. The revolution brought by Information and Communication Technology (ICT) has changed the way people see the world and active methodologies, in which the student assist to build knowledge, appear to help consolidate concepts and motivate the process of learning [2]. The digital games industry

Published by Springer Nature Switzerland AG 2024
T. van Kollenburg et al. (Eds.): ELEC 2023, IFIP AICT 681, pp. 245–254, 2024.
https://doi.org/10.1007/978-3-031-63265-5_19

has grown dramatically in recent years and the influence of this computing environment on society has caused several paradigm shifts and in Game-Based Learning (GBL) assuming increasing importance [1]. In this sense, according to Mouaheb el al. [3], "serious games" that are based on constructivist psychocognitive theories guarantee, among several characteristics, improvement of skills, understanding of phenomena and motivation. This follows the research by Aliu and Aigbavboa [4] that present active learning as instructional methods that involve the student.

In the field of civil engineering, Construction has constantly been viewed as a unique discipline that combines arithmetic, technical skills, and critical thinking for invention. Thus, there is a salient need to constantly enhance construction education to develop graduates who will meet the dynamic and ever- changing needs of the construction industry [4]. And "serious games" can bring the student closer to reality, increasing learning.

With a view to improving for the future, Singh et al. [5] claim that the application of Lean principles can help the construction industry, but although the concept has gained acceptance, it is difficult to put the tools and way of thinking into practice. Lean Construction (LC) has a proven track record of accomplishment, but there are still implementation issues, including those related to culture, leadership, training and partial adoption [5].

In order to change mindsets and generate knowledge, especially for new professionals, this article presents a framework for the development of a serious game using virtual reality technology aimed at improving the efficiency of the teaching and learning process through this management methodology based on Lean principles.

2 Literature Review

2.1 Lean Construction

LC has brought great contributions to civil construction since its inception, innovating production methods and processes. According to Koskela [6], Lean project delivery pursues three goals. Firstly it transforms inputs to outputs and gets production realized more efficiently. Secondly, itensures the flow of materials, composed of transformation, inspection, moving and waiting, to eliminate waste (or non- value adding activities). Thirdly it creates value for the client through the fulfillment of his / her objectives. These goals are complementary and should be integrated into the implementation of Lean construction [7, 8]. Lean construction frameworks, often known as Lean construction models, provide guidelines for the application of lean construction strategies that enable proactive control of the performance of construction projects [9]. The use of a framework to implement lean construction helps to achieve significant project success, especially in terms of cost, time and quality performance [10].

The application of Lean principles to construction permeates the teaching of Lean philosophy in Civil Engineering courses, in this sense, the use of games as a way of teaching Lean principles and practices has proven to be an innovative and engaging approach. This is because it allows the student to experience theoretical concepts in practice and develop problem-solving skills [11].

The research of Deif [12] looked at how different game elements can influence lean learning behavior among students. Based on the author's results, we can infer that gamification aligned with the learning cycle, which starts with motivation and then cognitive exercise within a social setting, is an efficient mechanism for teaching lean thinking in higher education.

2.2 Games-Based Learning

Games-based learning (GBL) are structured ways of playing, designed with the purpose of facilitating learning, the acquisition of knowledge, skills, values, beliefs or habits. They can help the user to understand certain subjects or concepts, support him to learn or improve skills, involving his own actions [13].

The application of educational games with a gamification approach can be a way to make the learning process more interactive and dynamic, which can lead to greater retention of knowledge and engagement of participants [14].

Garris, Ahlers, and Driskell [15] developed a model to show how a game supports learning outcomes. A game needs to be designed so that players are encouraged to repeat the game process, and during this interaction cycle players are engaged to acquire the target knowledge and skills. This structure emphasizes three main phases, namely: (a) the instructional attributes and characteristics of the game are incorporated as inputs to the learning model; (b) the input resources must be able to make a reaction in players such as engagement or fun, changing the users' behavior in order to provoke, for example, the concentration in a certain task. In this phase, users receive immediate feedback based on their performances; (c) the learning outcome happens.

In this regard, learning games incorporate specific pedagogical approaches and are declared to offer the following performance indicators: rule and objective, sensorial kick, control, challenge and interactivity [16].

2.3 Learning Mechanics and Game Mechanics

Learning and game principles in well-designed educational games, that is, pedagogical intentions can be translated and implemented through game mechanics [17].

A Serious Game mechanic is the design decision that concretely realizes the transition from a practice to a game mechanic element with the sole purpose of learning. It is the elements/aspects of the game that link the pedagogical practices (represented through learning mechanics) to the student's actions within the game [17].

2.4 Virtual Reality

VR technology creates the possibility of representing abstract concepts in a tangible way while generating student engagement and motivation in the learning process [18, 19]. In addition, VR provides the user with a new context to think about their behaviors and responses to the generated environment [20], which allows a positive impact on learning outcomes in relation to the training of students' technical and behavioral skills [21].

Aqlan et. al. [11] found that the assessed group that used virtual reality performed slightly better on the test compared to the group that only used simulation during the game. In addition, it was reported by students who used virtual reality that a more immersive and interesting experience was possible compared to those who used only simulation.

A VR experience can be used to teach lean principles in a more realistic environment than board games or other Lean simulation games [22].

3 Methodology

This paper addresses the proposal of a conceptual and pedagogical tool for the design of serious games in VR, aiming at teaching the fundamentals of LC to undergraduate students in civil engineering, emphasizing the principle "eliminate or reduction of non-value-added activities" applied to the task of "resizing a construction site".

In order to achieve this goal, this research was carried out in 3 steps: literature review, selection of frameworks related to serious games, and selection of structural and functional requirements relevant to the proposed theme.

The first step of the research involved a literature review on the application of LC and gamification as a teaching strategy. Academic databases, books and relevant papers in the area were consulted, with the aim of understanding the concepts of LC and exploring previous studies on educational games and gamification in the teaching of construction and civil engineering. The search terms used were: gamification OR game OR "serious game" AND Lean OR "Lean Construction" AND teaching OR learning OR "e-learning" OR "engineering education" OR "learning systems" OR "education computing". The search period was limited to between the years 2002 to 2023. After reading, articles that did not address the topics of interest (gamification, Lean and teaching) were excluded, as well as those that had restricted access. Thus, the studies considered relevant were analyzed in order to identify gaps and challenges for teaching Lean and how gamification could contribute to overcome them.

Based on the literature review, the second step consisted of the analysis and selection of educational game frameworks in VR, in order to identify bases for the development of a specific game framework for teaching one of the principles of LC, "Reduction of activities that do not add value". From this, it was elaborated, in the third step, which consists of the conceptual structure of a game. In order to create an engaging, immersive and interactive educational experience that allows students to understand and apply the principles of LC in a practical way, the context of the game takes place in a construction site, where the player is challenged to organize and manage all the activities. Below are the requirements used to design the educational proposal (Fig. 1):

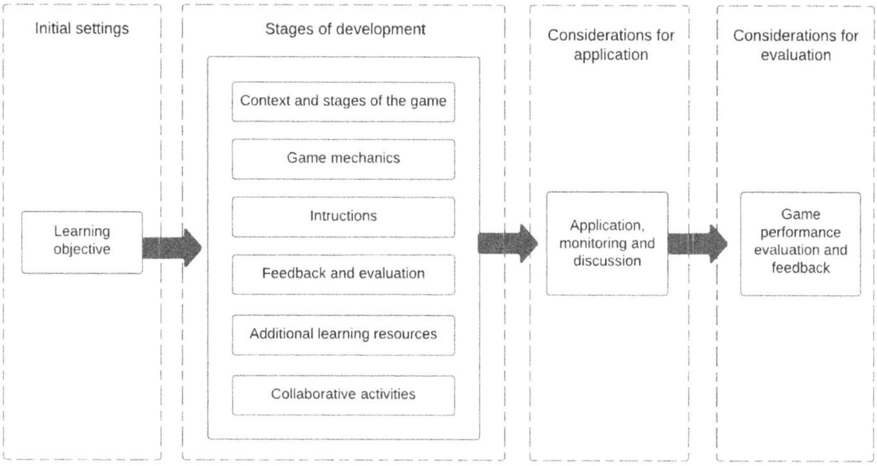

Fig. 1. Proposal's requirements (Source: Authors own)

In addition, using the results obtained from the literature review, the selection of frameworks and the adopted requirements, the proposed conceptual framework was developed, whose results and discussion are in the next section.

4 Results and Discussion

After an in-depth analysis of literature, it was observed that the number of board Lean games is significantly higher than the number of digital Lean games. About 70% of the examined studies are related to the development or application of face-to-face and/or board games, including the creation of realistic environments to simulate lean production. Table 1 shows a synthesis of the composition of the papers analyzed in the literature review, providing a summarized view of the different types of studies found, highlighting the predominance of board's games for teaching instead of gamification.

Table 1. Typologies of works for teaching Lean through gamification

Methodology	Lean		Lean Construction	
	Board games	Virtual games	Board games	Virtual games
Literature review	2	1	0	0
Game application/development	31	12	14	5
Evaluation of games/studies and others	5	4	4	0
Evaluation of game design	13		2	

As a result of this analysis, it is clear that only five papers address the application and/or development of virtual and digital games, which allows exploring the universe of gamification as a tool in learning LC. So, the development of frameworks to game structuring stands out as a significant contribution to academic advancement in this area. Offering guidelines and frameworks that facilitate the creation of effective educational games, providing a solid foundation for educational, intellectual and professional development. In this sense, Table 2 shows the papers that were used as a reference for the development of the educational tool that deals with the present research.

Table 2. Frameworks references

Papers	Authors
Real-Time Interaction and Cost Estimating within Immersive Virtual Environments	Balali et al., 2019
Empirical Bid or No Bid Decision Process in International Construction Projects: Structural Equation Modeling Framework	Guanghua et al., 2020
Framework for the implementation of lean construction strategies using the interpretive structural modelling (ISM) technique: A case of the Saudi construction industry	Sarhan et al., 2019
A conceptual framework for serious games	Yusoff et al, 2010
Simulation Game for Lean Leadership – Shopfloor Management combined with Accounting for Lean	Blöchla et al., 2017
Student-centred digital game–based learning: a conceptual framework and survey of the state of the art	Coleman, T; Money, A., 2020
Beyond playful learning – Serious games for the human-centric digital transformation of production and a design process model	Brauner, P., Ziefle, M., 2022

Most of the serious games's frameworks show the major components that create an effective model for learning through the use of serious games, including game attributes, learning activity, game mechanics, and game achievement. Every component inside this framework plays a role to ensure that learning would take place while playing the game. In accordance with these papers, We propose the framework as an appropriate basis for effective serious games design for designers and teaching practitioners.

The operation of the "LeanBuild" game - according to the educational tool framework shown in Fig. 2 - is carried out in five stages. Initially, we are collecting the player's input data, in order to register the performance and allow the analysis, per player, of the knowledge and results acquired.

The second stage deals with the presentation of the game's instructions, which aims to familiarize the player with the features, functions and with the context in which the educational activity takes place, thus promoting the ease of use and improving the players' performance. In the third stage, the task is presented to the student with the aim of developing critical and lean thinking skills, which, applied to a given construction site project, will lead, for example, to change the layout in order to reduce or eliminate activities that do not add value. Using the Unity platform will bring the game scenario to life and create an interactive virtual environment to play in VR.

VR technology is purposely inserted in this work because it provides the practice of a professional activity similar to the real world, generating engagement and motivation [18], increasing the effectiveness of learning [23].

In stage 4, the simulation takes place, moving the scenario according to the LC principle used. Activities appear in a single phase where players must reorganize the

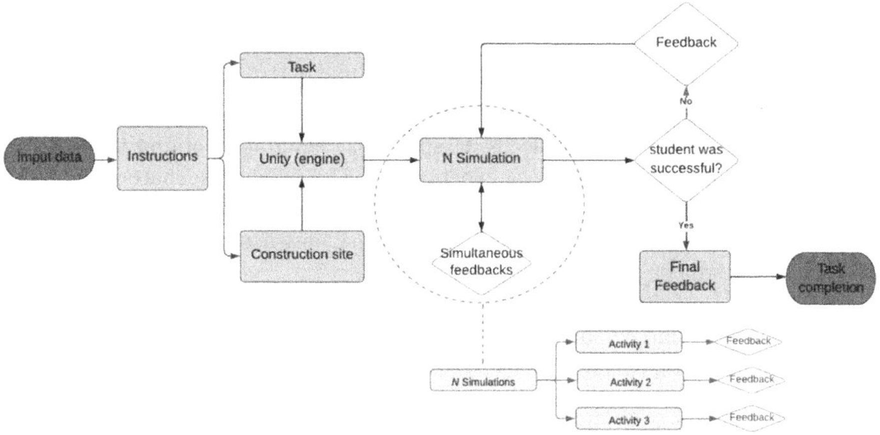

Fig. 2. Framework (Source: Authors own)

layout, redefine flows of materials, equipment and labor, in order to minimize travel time, maximize productivity and optimize the use of resources. For each move performed, feedback is offered validating the proposal to stimulate critical thinking. In the next stage, according to the final performance, scores and rewards are generated motivating and aligning the game mechanics to the learning process. According to the success or failure, the student can repeat the activity or finish the challenge. The possibility of repeating the task and reflecting on what was achieved facilitates the understanding of the content and provides greater student engagement [24, 25].

Therefore, GBL methods may be well-suited for formative assessment, e.g., to monitor students' learning and provide feedback based on students activities in the game, and help them identify weaknesses, strengths and areas that require further work [26]. For the same author, the game should contain features to practice skills such as decision making and problem solving amid uncertainty and change because project managers will face both success and failure in real-life projects.

In addition to the results presented, a suitable Game Development Framework (GDF) is chosen during the game design process, which can influence the effect of games themselves and also positively or negatively impact the learner. The findings indicate that games can be an effective learning medium and have a more beneficial impact than traditional classroom learning if they follow all the rules, suitable an appropriate context, and specific goals in the design of games [27].

5 Conclusion

The methodology adopted in this study allowed the development of a promising game framework for teaching Lean construction, in which the objectives - motivating students, providing practical experience, learning a certain content and developing managerial skills can be successfully achieved. It is possible to conclude that the traditional approach has difficulty in triggering changes in attitudes, and it is in this context that serious games play a fundamental role, by providing interdisciplinarity, practice and engagement in the engineering teaching scenario.

Another important factor to be observed is the ability that frameworks have to provide the flexibility to adapt to different contexts or areas of activity, as well as customization according to someone's specific needs. It is true that additional learning resources can be inserted into the game to enhance experience and knowledge, such as other simulations and real-world scenarios relevant to the civil engineer. This will help students to deepen their understanding of the principles of Lean Construction and connecting game information with theory taught in the classroom.

In this game specifically, the student will not only apply lean construction to help manage their work, but will also work on project practices through technical decisions that have an impact on operational, technical and financial aspects. This integrated approach allows a more effective connection between theory and professional practice, fulfilling the proposed objective of teaching students the application of the principle of reducing tasks that do not add value.

In addition, the pedagogical proposal developed, therefore, goes beyond the teaching of theoretical knowledge, stimulating the formation of professionals who are more complete and prepared to face the challenges of the construction industry.

A major limitation of this research was the difficulty of data due to the few works found in the specific area of activity. From the works analyzed in the literature review, it was identified that approximately 70% of the studies developed for teaching Lean through gamification do not use ITs.

t is suggested that future research explores other gamification methodologies, as well as the application of the framework in broader teaching environments and in different educational contexts. In addition, it is important to think of activities or phases that can be played in virtual teams or carried out in groups, fostering collaboration among students. Strategies such as the creation of challenges between teams or the segmentation, per player, of interdependent activities that require dialog boxes for the success of the stage or the game can be adopted, promoting the exchange of information, discussions about strategies and the application of the principles of the Lean Construction in a social context.

Acknowledgment. We thank FUB/UnB/DPG for supporting this research.

References

1. Aoki, R.L., Fiuza, P.J., Lemos, R.R.: Utilização de narrativas digitais em ambientes de aprendizagem baseada em jogos digitais: uma revisão sistemática da literatura. ETD - Educação Temática Digit. **20**(4), 1138–1160 (2018). https://doi.org/10.20396/etd.v20i4.8649913
2. Aulbur, W., CJ, A., Bigghe, R.: Skill development for Industry 4.0: BRICS skill development working group. Roland Berger GMBH (2016)
3. Mouaheb, H., Fahli, A., Moussetad, M., Eljamali, S.: The serious game: what educational benefits? Elsevier Ltd. (2012). https://doi.org/10.1016/j.sbspro.2012.06.465
4. Aliu, J., Aigbavboa, C.: Reviewing the trends of construction education research in the last decade: a bibliometric analysis. Int. J. Constr. Manag. **23**(9), 1571–1580 (2023). https://doi.org/10.1080/15623599.2021.1985777

5. Singh, A., Kumar, V., Mittal, A., Verma, P.: Identifying critical challenges to lean construction adoption. Construction Innovation, ahead-of-print No. ahead-of-print (2023). https://doi.org/10.1108/CI-09-2022-0229
6. Koskela, L.: Lean construction as a movement towards theory-based construction management (2011). http://Ljk.sdpublishing.org.uk
7. Koskela, L., Howell, G., Ballard, G., Tommelein, I.: The foundations of lean construction. In: Design and Construction: Building in Value, pp. 211–226 (2002)
8. Koskela, L.: Moving on – beyond lean thinking. Lean Constr. J. **1**(1), 24–37 (2004)
9. Kasiramkumar, T., Indhu, B.: An implementation framework for integrated lean construction system for Indian scenario. ARPN J. Eng. Appl. Sci. **11**, 9388–9394 (2016)
10. Al-Aomar, R.: A lean construction framework with Six Sigma rating. Int. J. Lean Six Sigma **3**(4), 299–314 (2012)
11. Aqlan, F., et al.: Integrating simulation games and virtual reality to teach manufacturing systems concepts. In: ASEE Annual Conference and Exposition, Conference Proceedings (2019). https://doi.org/10.18260/1-2-32991
12. Deif, A.: Insights on lean gamification for higher education. Int. J. Lean Six Sigma **8**(3), 359–376 (2017). https://doi.org/10.1108/IJLSS-04-2016-0017
13. Gredler, M.E.: Games and simulations and their relationships to learning. In: Jonassen, D. (ed.) Handbook of Research on Educational Communications and Technology, 2nd edn., pp. 571–581. Lawrence Erlbaum Associates Publishers, Mahwah (2004)
14. Stadnicka, D., Deif, A.: A gamification approach application to facilitate lean manufacturing knowledge acquisition. Manag. Prod. Eng. Rev. **10**(4), 108–122 (2019). https://doi.org/10.24425/mper.2019.131451
15. Garris, R., Ahlers, R., Driskell, J.E.: Games, motivation, and learning: a research and practice model. Simul. Gaming **33**(4), 441–467 (2002). https://doi.org/10.1177/1046878102238607
16. Djaouti, D., Alvarez, J., JesselL, J.P.: Can "Gaming 2.0" help design" Seriou s Games"? A comparative study. In: Proceedings of the 5th ACM SIGGRAPH Symposium on Video Games, pp. 11–18 (2010). https://doi.org/10.1145/1836135.1836137
17. Arnab, S., et al.: Mapping learning and game mechanics for serious games analysis. Br. J. Edu. Technol. **46**(2), 391–411 (2015). https://doi.org/10.1111/bjet.12113
18. Araiza-Alba, P., et al.: Immersive virtual reality as a tool to learn problem-solving skills. Comput. Educ. **164**, 104121 (2021). https://doi.org/10.1016/j.compedu.2020.104121
19. Persky, S.; MCBRIDE, C. Immersive virtual environment technology: A promising tool for future social and behavioral genomics research and practice. **Health Communication**, v. 24, n. 8, p. 677–682, 2009. https://doi.org/10.1080/10410230903263982. Acesso em: 28 mai. 2019
20. Smith, S., Ericson, E.: Using immersive game-based virtual reality to teach fire-safety skills to children. Virtual Reality **13**(2), 87–99 (2009). https://doi.org/10.1007/s10055-009-0113-6
21. Çakiroglu, U., Gokoglu, S.: Development of fire safety behavioral skills via virtual reality. Comput. Educ. **133**, 56–68 (2019). https://doi.org/10.1016/j.compedu.2019.01.014
22. Jacobsen, E., Strange, N., Teizer, J.: Lean construction in a serious game using a multiplayer virtual reality environment. In: Proceedings of 29th Annual Conference of the International Group for Lean Construction (IGLC), Lima, Peru, 14–16 July 2021, pp 55–64 (2021). https://doi.org/10.24928/2021/0160
23. Zhang, X., et al.: How virtual reality affects perceived learning effectiveness: a task–technology fit perspective. Behav. Inf. Technol. **36**(5), 548–556 (2017). https://doi.org/10.1080/0144929X.2016.1268647
24. Yusoff, A., et al.: A conceptual framework for serious games. In: 2009 Ninth IEEE International Conference on Advanced Learning Technologies, pp. 21–23. IEEE (2009). https://doi.org/10.1109/ICALT.2009.19

25. Avelar, A.: Serious games como artefatos digitais de aprendizagem: uma proposta para o ensino de engenharia civil. Dissertação de Mestrado em Estruturas e Construção Civil, Publicação E.DM-10A/21, Departamento de Engenharia Civil e Ambiental, Universidade de Brasília, Brasília, DF, 154 p. (2021)
26. Jaaska, E., Lehtinen, J., Kujala, J., Kauppila, O.: Game-based learning and students' motivation in project management education. Proj. Leadersh. Soc. **3**, 100055 (2022). https://doi.org/10.1016/j.plas.2022.100055
27. Ramlan, N.B., Abil, N.B.: The importance of game development framework (GDF): proposing an islamic game development framework with sustainability features. Int. J. Acad. Res. Bus. Soc. Sci. **10**(3), 633–644 (2020)
28. Balali, V., Zalavadia, A., Heydarian, A.: Real-time interaction and cost estimating within immersive virtual environments. J. Constr. Eng. Manag. **2**, 04019098 (2020). https://doi.org/10.1061/(ASCE)CO.1943-7862.0001752
29. Li, G., et al.: Empirical bid or no bid decision process in international construction projects: structural equation modeling framework. J. Constr. Eng. Manag. **146**, 04020050 (2020). https://doi.org/10.1061/(ASCE)CO.1943-7862.0001830
30. Sarhan, J.G., Xia, B., Fawzia, S., Karim, A., Olanipekun, A.O., Coffey, V.: Framework for the implementation of lean construction strategies using the interpretive structural modelling (ISM) technique: a case of the Saudi construction industry. Eng. Constr. Archit. Manag. **27**(1), 1–23 (2019). https://doi.org/10.1108/ECAM-03-2018-0136
31. Coleman, T.E., Money, A.G.: Student-centred digital game–based learning: a conceptual framework and survey of the state of the art. High. Educ. **79**, 415–457 (2020). https://doi.org/10.1007/s10734-019-00417-0
32. Brauner, P., Ziefle, M.: Beyond playful learning – serious games for the human-centric digital transformation of production and a design process model. Technol. Soc. **71**, 102140 (2022). https://doi.org/10.1016/j.techsoc.2022.102140

Applications of Lean

The Impact of SMED on Productivity and Safety

José C. Sá[1,2(✉)], Rita C. M. Sales-Contini[1,3], Francisco J. G. Silva[1,4], José Dinis-Carvalho[5], L. Cardoso[1], and Luis Fonseca[1,2]

[1] School of Engineering of Porto (ISEP), Polytechnic of Porto, Rua Dr António Bernardino de Almeida 431, 4249-015 Porto, Portugal
cvs@isep.ipp.pt

[2] Associate Laboratory for Energy, Transports and Aerospace (LAETA-INEGI), Rua Dr. Roberto Frias 400, 4200-465 Porto, Portugal

[3] College of Technology São José dos Campos, Professor Jessen Vidal, Centro Paula Souza, São José dos Campos SP, Brazil

[4] Institute of Science and Innovation in Mechanical and Industrial Engineering (INEGI), Rua Dr Roberto Frias 400, 4200-465 Porto, Portugal

[5] Production and Systems Department, University of Minho, Campus de Azurém, 4804 - 533 Guimarães, Portugal

Abstract. This article is the result of a case study that arose from the need for a plastic injection moulding company to adapt to an increase in the number of injection moulding machines and moulds. The acquisition of a company and the consequent transfer of its production to a manufacturing unit in Portugal increased the internal diversity of the existing machines and moulds, resulting in a constant need for tool changes, which posed a daily challenge to the operators, both at a technical and safety level. The very high set-up times of the new machines compared to the existing ones and the company's increasing concern about accidents/incidents occurring during this phase of the process led to the need for action to reduce them. SMED (Single Minute Exchange of Die) was initially applied to two different machine ranges. The application of SMED on both machine ranges allowed the identification of several wastes along the process, which were eliminated or reduced through the application of lean tools such as 5S, Visual Management and Standard Work. After completing SMED, it was possible to verify improvements of 46.10% and 44.19%, respectively, in the set-up time of the two machine ranges. The survey results of the employees involved in mould set-up, which analysed their perception of the impact of each measure, showed a positive impact of all the measures implemented. Overall, 100% of the employees agreed that lean practices positively impacted their perception of safety.

Keywords: Lean · Safety · Lean Tools · SMED · Lean Safety

1 Introduction

In a globalized economy, adaptation is the key to success to ensure their survival [1]. The last few years have put several industries to the test, and the automotive industry is one of the most affected, with very high levels of demand and where the basis of success

Published by Springer Nature Switzerland AG 2024
T. van Kollenburg et al. (Eds.): ELEC 2023, IFIP AICT 681, pp. 257–270, 2024.
https://doi.org/10.1007/978-3-031-63265-5_20

is flexibility and responsiveness [2]. In the face of these obstacles, companies need to reduce costs without compromising the quality of their products. Recent adaptations to new environmental requirements and standards are driving the industry towards rapid technological advancement while at the same time facing global geopolitical instability that has led to a shortage of raw materials and products. This scarcity further increases the need for companies to become more competitive as the cost of materials continues to rise, making it imperative to optimize resources to produce more effectively and efficiently.

In recent years, companies have been increasingly adhering to the lean philosophy, and its positive impact on their performance has been proven [3]. The Lean Philosophy is a concept first described in the book "The Machine That Changed the World", and its main objective is eliminating waste in the production process [4]. As the name suggests, lean means slim. The ideology is to do more with less to increase the product's value by consuming fewer resources.

To implement lean philosophy, several tools have been developed and implemented in organizations. These are the means to achieve a lean organization, where processes are optimized, and waste is eliminated [5, 6]. All activities performed that do not add value are considered waste. An activity that consumes excess resources will make the product or service more expensive and less attractive. It is indispensable for lean principles implementation to identify and eliminate existing waste [7] initially. Activities that do not generate value can account for up to 95% of an organization's time. Although all this time can be considered waste, it should be divided into two types: Pure Waste and Necessary Waste. The former can represent up to 65% of waste in organizations and involves all expendable activities such as non-productive meetings, de-locations, stoppages and breakdowns. The latter involves all activities essential for its creation, although they do not add value. Examples include setups and inspections of raw materials, which, even though necessary, should also be reduced [8]. According to the studies of Liker [9] and de Souza and Carpinetti [10], the most significant wastes were identified in seven categories, added later an eighth, which are: Overproduction, Waiting Time, Transport, Overprocessing, Inventory, Movements, Defects, and last and not least, non-utilization workers' knowledge.

Lean tools have as a fundamental principle the organization of the workplace to make it more efficient, clean and productive. A clean and organized workplace creates an environment that motivates the operator, leading to increased safety and product quality, generating less waste [11]. Employees must understand the benefits of applying lean tools in occupational health and safety (OHS) and that management is involved in motivating everyone [12].

Looking at the company's future, safety is seen as a critical point for its growth and can be continuously improved using lean tools [13]. The lean methodologies application must always consider the health and safety of those involved, as they are an integral part of the process. It can be considered that not taking care of employees is in itself a waste [14]. The use of lean tools can positively or negatively impact safety, although the impact is mostly positive [15]. If implementing Lean tools has a negative impact on employees, it cannot be considered the implementation of the Lean philosophy at all. It will instead be what is commonly called "fake lean" because adopting the lean philosophy presupposes involvement and respect for the workers and their activities! [16] Adopting the lean philosophy can never be considered valid if it only brings improvement in reducing and eliminating waste. To create a positive impact, it is necessary to involve everyone, particularly management, who should pay particular attention to the impacts of applying lean tools [17].

The goal of aligning lean with safety will always be to improve production performance and employee health [18]. Gnoni et al. [19] found that few studies have been conducted at the industrial level looking at safety in the application of lean tools. Hasle et al. [20] also reached the same conclusion, adding that the effects of lean tools on safety depended on the context in which they were applied. Most of the articles in which the subject is addressed were developed after 2016, although it is necessary to use terms such as lean tools and safety separately, and the term lean safety is still little used [21].

The attention given to safety after implementing lean tools has been increasingly targeted, and there are already several adaptations of the most used methodologies. Namely, SSM (Safety Stream Mapping), where Gonçalves et al. [22] combine VSM with WID (Waste Identification Diagram) [23], with a colour scheme they allow to obtain a macro view of the easy interpretation of the level of risks in the various locations/processes of a company. Also, Marques et al. [24] developed SEVSM (Safety Efficiency Value Stream Mapping), which combines VSM, OEE and SSM to observe process indicators and safety efficiency quickly. The ErgoSMED flowchart was developed by Marlene Brito and Gonçalves [25] to improve ergonomic conditions while applying SMED (Single Minute Exchange of Die) to reduce setup times.

SMED is a method developed by Shigeo Shingo in 1950 to reduce setup times [26]. Setup time is the interval between the manufacture of the last good part of a batch and the first good part of the next batch [27]. This time interval is critical for companies because it contains activities that do not add value to the product but are necessary for its production [28]. According to Shingo and Dillon [29], setup can be divided into two activity types, which can be internal or external. The first can be performed while the machine is stopped, such as assembling and disassembling tools, and the second can be performed while the machine is working, such as transporting materials and preparing tools.

The original application of the SMED methodology should be progressive and composed of 3 steps where several techniques are applied to optimize the setup [30]. Ferradás & Salonitis [31] proposed a SMED methodology applied in a supplier of the automotive industry with 33% improvements in setup time. This proposal consists of the following five steps: i) Classify activities, ii) Separate activities, iii) Convert internal activities into external ones, iv) Reduce internal activities and v) Reduce external activities.

Applying SMED in a plastic injection process generated gains of 36,79% in mould changeover time and reduced the number of failures due to the creation of procedures [32]. In a cork stopper encapsulation line, it was possible to reduce setup time by 43% with a monthly gain of 2 340€ [33]. Costa, Sousa, Bragança, and Alves [34] showed a gain between 53% and 67% in the setup times of mechanical presses in a metalworking company. Together with other lean tools, there were gains of up to 78% in distances travelled and 50% in WIP. The annual gains were 1 628,70€. Silva et al. [28] presented a study case of a floating floor-cutting line that benefited from the application of SMED, reducing the number of operators to perform the setup from three to two, using approximately the same time. Implementing SMED for mould changing in the plastic injection industry resulted in an 18% gain in mould changing and a 38% reduction in the number of activities [35]. In the studies of Rosa et al. [2] within a metal cable company for the automotive industry, it was possible to verify a 58.3% reduction in setup times after implementing SMED and other lean tools in just one week. Vieira et al. [36] observed that after implementing SMED in the production of metal profiles, it was possible to obtain an average improvement of 10.8% in OEE (Overall Equipment Effectiveness). Monteiro et al. [37] studied two milling machines (Vertical and Horizontal) in a metalworking company. Applying SMED in conjunction with other lean tools reduced setup times by 40% and 57%. In all analyzed studies, it was observed that when well implemented, SMED brings positive impacts to companies by reducing setup times, gains in time and increasing financial gains.

Therefore, this research aims to verify the impact of the SMED application on the reduction of setup times and the employees' safety perception of a "new plastic injection process". By using the SMED tool in combination with the lean tools 5S, visual management and standardization, it will be possible to analyze the improvement points in the setup phase and apply other lean methods, optimizing the entire mould assembly process.

2 Methodology

2.1 Case Study

The case study takes place within a plastics injection moulding company that has undergone a significant restructuring that has caused major changes in its equipment and processes. The previously existing injection process was developed from scratch for a large group of catalogue products. As a result, all machines and moulds were similar and were developed with the same principles, with a high level of standardisation between them. The transfer of the "new" injection moulding was done in a short time of one year, and the transferred machines and moulds, coming from different locations, were developed to different standards. The rapid growth of the injection moulding process made it difficult to adapt the existing operators and train the new ones that were hired.

For this effect, a set of improvements was implemented on the factory floor of a carpentry business in the various productive sections, evaluating workers' perception of this matter through 4 surveys of 9 questions. It was distributed to 12 employees working in the Finishing, Pre-Assembly, Assembly and Packaging sections, including Logistics and Quality since these were the sections where the project was already implemented.

After more than a year with the new process, stability had yet to be achieved, and it was noticeable that setup times were too high, leading to delays in planning. The time defined for the previously existing process was 1 h. In contrast, for the new process, 2 h was defined for a setup in which raw material is already ready for use, or 4 h in cases where it is necessary to dehumidify the material for that period in the portable greenhouses.

Due to limitations in the internal management system, it was not possible to analyse the setup times over time or the separation between the two processes. After consulting reliable records and interviews with operators, it was possible to conclude that the 2 h limit is exceeded most of the time. The process was initiated by the operator responsible for mould assembly, passing through the tuning phase until the start of production to the tuner's responsibility. Involving several movements, handling of high-temperature materials, chemical gases and moving moulds whose weight can exceed two tons, the setup phase became critical regarding operator health and safety. This situation was proven by the data collected in the company's Health and Safety department, where it can be observed that after the transfer, in the plastic injection process, 60% of the occupational accidents and 29% of the incidents happened in the setup phase. To analyse the safety factor during and after the implementation of the "new" process, the actions were recorded by video, and an employee survey was also conducted to understand to what extent the implemented actions, based on Lean tools, improved their safety perception. It is intended that employees feel that they work in a safer environment.

This research was focused only on the setups of the new project, where one of the main gaps is the need for more knowledge of the real-time spent on changing moulds.

The wastes throughout the setup were evaluated through the SMED, and several lean tools were used to reduce or eliminate them. Each mould's complexity impacts its setup time, and as a rule, the larger the mould, the longer it will take. Considering this differentiation, two ranges were created to evaluate and define the time needed for mould change. After analysing the specifications of existing moulds, the ranges were divided into those used on machines with a tonnage of less than and greater than or equal to 100 tons (Range $<$100t and range $\geq$100t). Relying on the company's experience with the existing injection moulding process, target times were set at 60 min for the lower tonnage range and 90 min for the higher tonnage range.

In this work, the following steps were carried out:

1. Identify the problem in the setups and record them on video.
2. Analysis of the videos with the application of SMED to identify waste and identification of activities with health and safety risks for employees.
3. Test improvement actions in the setup process using Lean tools.
4. Analyse the impact of the actions in reducing setup time and employee safety through a survey using the Likert Scale.

3 Results and Discussions

3.1 Analysis of Productivity Results

Through SMED, it was possible to understand where the biggest wastes of the injection mould setup process were. After understanding what these wastes were, several tools associated with lean were applied to optimize the process. Lean tools such as 5S were applied in the organization of tool trolleys and the arrangement of hoses, thermochillers and mould fittings. The use of Visual Management had the most significant impact on reducing setup time. By applying this lean tool to the colour of the hoses, the water dispensers, and the mould nozzles, operators reduced much of the time spent figuring out how to assemble the mould hoses. The setup preparation sheet also provides visual support in areas more difficult for operators to access. The adoption of standardization has also had a big impact on the process. Although some of the improvements have only been tested on a one-off basis to check their effect, one of the aims will be to roll them out to other machines and make them part of the process. Using blue hoses for water outlets, red for inlets, and nozzles on all moulds, the new parameter sheet on all moulds and the setup preparation sheet are the elements where standardization has been applied. In terms of time gains, it is possible to observe in Table 1 that there were significant gains in the two studied ranges of 46.10% and 44.19%. The value is quite approximate in both. Concerning the objective initially proposed for each range, it was possible to verify that it was achieved, with an improvement of almost 30% from what was proposed in the smaller tonnage machines.

Table 1. SMED final time analysis.

Range	Initial *Setup* Time (min)	Final *Setup* Time (min)	Registered improvement (%)	Goal Time (min)	% Goal
<100t	78.90	42.53	46.10%	60	70.88%
≥100t	155.05	86.53	44.19%	90	96.14%

After obtaining the results of the time savings in each setup, an analysis was carried out to estimate the annual savings for each machine, and on average, there are about 3 mould changes per week on the lower tonnage machines and 2.5 changes on the higher tonnage machines. Analysing Table 2, it is possible to gain 3.64 working days in the <100t range and 5.71 days in the ≥100t range. Multiplying these values by the number of existing machines, it had a value of 145 working days that could be used to produce parts, increasing the company's productivity effectively.

Table 2. Annual time savings after SMED application per machine

Range	*Setups* Molds by Week	Week Annual Work	*Setups* by Year	*Setup Time saved* (min)	Total time saved (h)	Saved days by year
<100t	3.0	48	144	36.37	87.29	3.64
≥100t	2.5	48	120	68.52	137.04	5.71

3.2 Safety Results Analysis

One of the aims of this research was to understand whether the implementation of SMED improved safety conditions. To verify these results, a way to measure them was discussed with the company management. In the long term, the results of internal audits and the number of safety accidents could provide more real measurements. In the short term, and to help decide which measures to implement definitively, a nine-question survey was developed and presented to obtain the operators' perception of the measures adopted. This survey aimed to verify the individual impact of the optimizations on activities previously identified as having safety risks. The identified risks of burns during purging due to hot material are already identified in the process, and safety equipment is already used to prevent them. No optimizations were made in this activity, nor was any question in the survey dedicated.

After approval by the company's management, the survey was anonymously distributed to the twelve employees qualified to perform the mould setup. The only employee data requested is the length of the contract with the company to analyze whether there are different perceptions between employees who joined before and after the new project. By analyzing the graph in Fig. 1, It can be seen that half of the employees joined the company in the last two years, and the rest were already familiar with the "old" injection moulding process of the factory. There were nine easy-to-answer questions for the employee, where a Likert scale was used for their evaluation. The scale values ranged from 1 to 5 with the following correspondences: 1-Totally disagree, 2-Disagree, 3-Neither agree nor disagree, 4-Agree, 5-Totally agree.

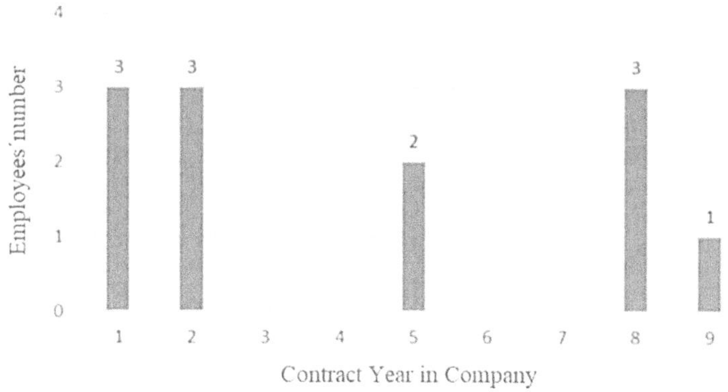

Fig. 1. Graph of the employee's contract years who perform setups.

The first question aims to verify whether operators feel that the introduction of the dispenser system has reduced the number of hoses and water on the floor, and therefore reduced the possibility of falling. Analyzing Fig. 2a, it is possible to see that 59% of the employees had a positive perception of the reduction of risks, while the rest did not feel any difference in risk.

The second question is still about the implementation of water dispensers. In this case, employees are asked if they feel that ergonomics are improved by using this system. The results are unanimous, where all employees report that there are benefits in terms of ergonomics, with half reporting that it improves completely (Fig. 2b).

At this point, employees were asked to give feedback on using the T-handle spanner. As shown in the graph in Fig. 3a, two-thirds of the employees feel that applying this measure reduces the effort required to loosen the KO compared to the conventional

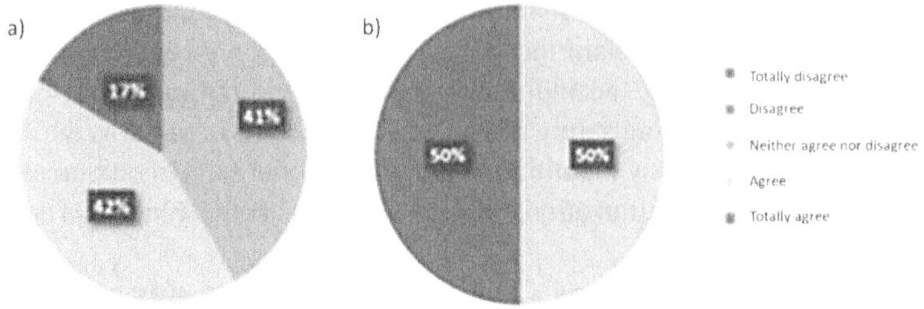

Fig. 2. a) Question 1 Results: The implementation of water dispensers inside the machine reduces the risk of falling hoses and water on the floor and b) Question 2 Results: The implementation of water dispensers inside the machine improves ergonomics by reducing movements to assemble the hoses.

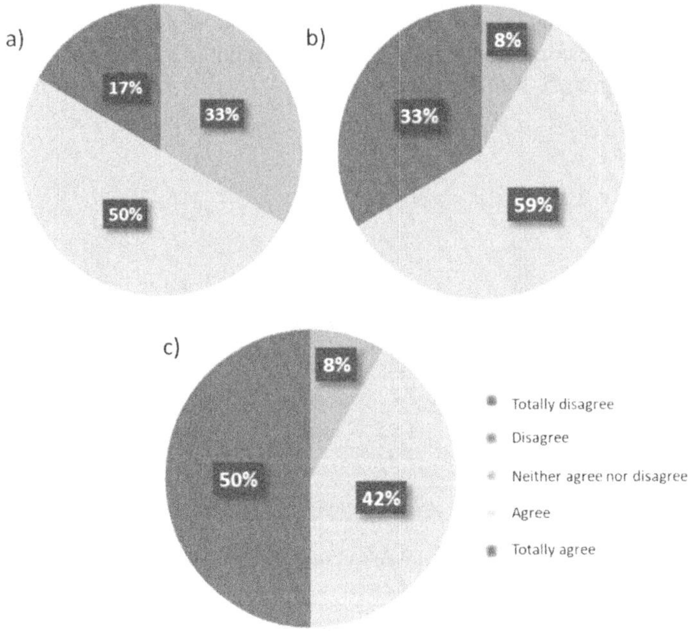

Fig. 3. a) Question 3 Results: Does the use of T-handle spanners reduce the effort required to loosen the KO?, b) Question 4 Results: The use of ratchet spanners improves ergonomics for tightening clamps in hard-to-reach areas, and c) Question 5 Results: The use of quick-release clamps improves ergonomics over conventional clamps.

sixth-row spanners normally used. The remaining employees felt the same with the application of this measure. One of the activities identified with the most complaints from operators was the tightening of clamps with hexagonal "L" spanners, especially in areas that are more difficult to access—according to the results shown in Fig. 3b, 92% of the employees agreed that the availability of the ratchets facilitated the task, with only one employee stating that the introduction of the ratchets had no impact. Question 5 aims to determine whether operators feel that the mould clamping conditions with the quick-clamping clamps are improved compared to the conventional ones. As mentioned during the work, these are quick and practical to place, while there are complaints regarding the difficulty in positioning the others and their falling during tightening. The results presented in Fig. 3c show that most employees consider this measure to be positive for their ergonomics, with half considering it to be a major improvement. At this point, the operators were asked if applying the colour-coding system on the hoses and moulds, with the support of the setup preparation sheet, improves ergonomics. The general result is positive with 75% of the employees feeling a positive impact of the measure and wanting it to be applied to the entire factory. They mentioned that this action reduces the need to look for the numbered markings on the moulds that are often difficult to see. 25% of the employees feel that applying this measure does not benefit their ergonomics when assembling the hoses (Fig. 4a). Question 7 aims to determine the operators' perception of the displacements by applying the various measures applied after SMED. Measures such as material pre-preparation and the organization of materials and tools aim to reduce these same trips. The survey's results (Fig. 4b) show that 58% of employees agree that these measures reduce the number of journeys. However, 34% feel that travelling has not been considerably reduced, and 8% (1 employee) disagree with the statement.

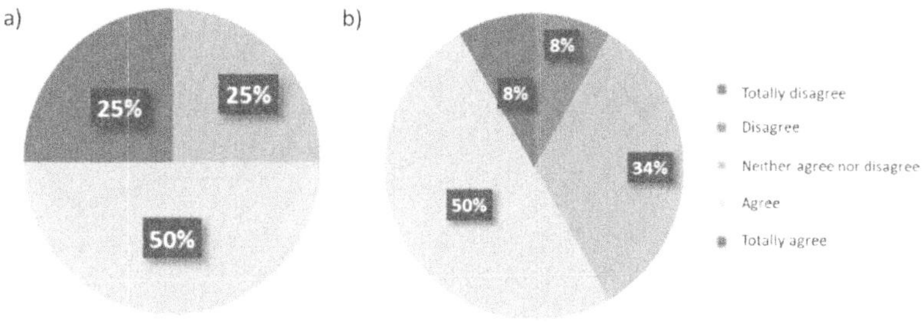

Fig. 4. a) Question 6 Results: The use of blue/red colour coding on hoses and moulds improves ergonomics when assembling hoses, and b) Question 7 Results: Reduced number of trips to find materials.

To verify the operators' opinions regarding the organization and cleanliness of the workplace. For this point, actions such as the organization of tool trolleys, reduction of hoses near machines and new locations for equipment were taken. According to the results in Fig. 5a, 42% of the operators feel that the measure had a positive impact, half of them think that there was no impact of the measures, and 8% disagree with the statement.

On the question with the worst results, the operators were asked why, and the majority agreed that the workplace would only be organized when everyone internalizes that they need to keep it organized and not just clean it sometimes. This point represents the 5th S of the 5S, where it is essential to maintain discipline and keep the workplace clean and organized and is perhaps the most difficult S to achieve. The last question asked aims to understand the opinion of the operators regarding lean tools and their safety

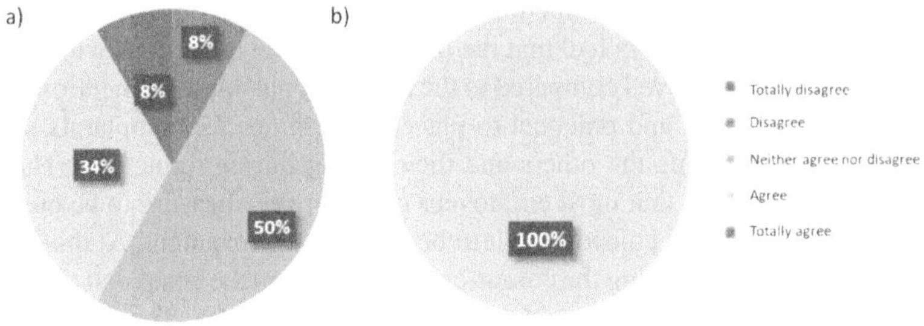

Fig. 5. Question 8 Results: The workplace is cleaner and more organized, and b) Question 9 Results: In general, do you feel that the new lean practices improve the Safety conditions at your workplace?

impact. Considering the results of the previous questions, positive results were already expected. All employees agreed that implementing lean tools will improve workplace safety (Fig. 5b).

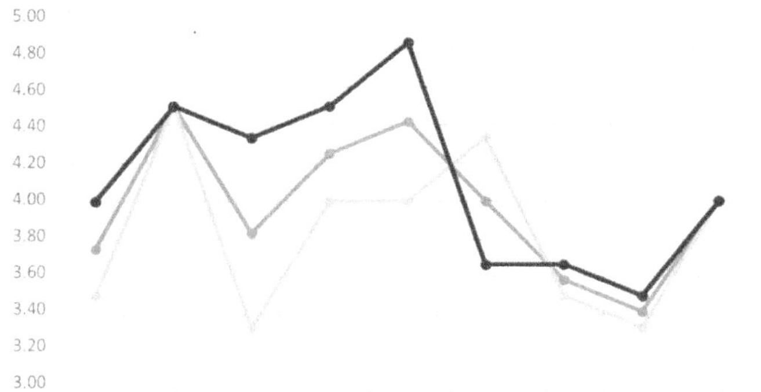

	1	2	3	4	5	6	7	8	9
Overall Average	3.75	4.50	3.83	4.25	4.42	4.00	3.58	3.42	4.00
Less than 2 years contract	3.50	4.50	3.33	4.00	4.00	4.33	3.50	3.33	4.00
More than 2 years contract	4.00	4.50	4.33	4.50	4.83	3.67	3.67	3.50	4.00

Fig. 6. Average survey results by question and contract year

After having all the results of the surveys, an analysis was carried out to determine the average of the values obtained on the Likert scale. The values of the employees who arrived before and after the new project were also separated to try to understand if their safety perception varies. These values can be seen in the graph and table in Fig. 6.

Generally, the questions with the most favourable results were 2, 5 and 4, with averages above 4. These results show that operators consider water dispensers to be an asset to their ergonomics, as well as quick-release clamps and the ratchet. These points coincide with those with a more significant reduction in setup time (hose assembly and clamp tightening). On the other hand, where there was not such a high average were questions 8, 7 and 1, with averages between 3.42 and 3.75, which, although the lowest, are still positive. Operators feel that the impact on the organization's cleanliness of the workplace and the number of journeys has only partially improved. The impact on the perception of the risk of falls with the use of dispensers is also not very high.

In questions 6, 5 and 3, there is a more significant discrepancy in opinion between those with more than two years of experience and those with less than two years of experience. In question 6, the greater value given to the code by employees with less than two years' contract is notorious, which could be because they need more experience. More experienced operators, with their greater knowledge, can identify where to connect the hoses more quickly and, therefore, do not compromise their ergonomics by looking for their position. In Question 5, operators with more experience attach more importance to the ergonomic impact of ergonomic clamps. This result may be related to the experience with these clamps in the "old" injection, where most machines use this system. The operators with less time in the company were trained with the standard clamps, so they don't feel the difference with the quick-clamping clamps. Also, in question 3, operators with more years in the company feel that using the "T" wrench brings more ergonomic benefits than newer operators. This difference can be explained by the history of operators with injuries and difficulties unscrewing the KO with another type of wrench.

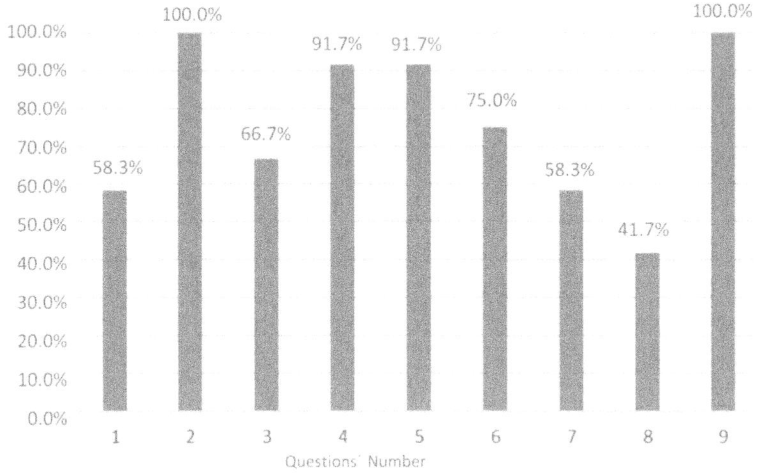

Fig. 7. Operators' percentage agreeing with studied measures.

The result of the agreement with the implemented measures can be consulted in the graph in Fig. 7, where it is possible to check the questions that were approved by the highest percentage of employees. For questions 2 and 9, there is 100% agreement, and the only question where less than half of the employees perceive improvements is the one relating to the tidiness and organization of the workplace, with 41.7%.

4 Conclusions

The main objective of this research was to apply SMED together with other lean tools to verify its impact on productivity and safety. In the first phase, by starting the recordings of the setups, it was possible to know the reality of the employees and their daily difficulties with the arrival of the new project. Many simple tasks that could be optimized naturally were not due to the size of the project and the short time in which everything was implemented. The workspace was disorganized, and all employees followed no standard.

With this SMED research, it was possible to demonstrate much wasted time and unnecessary movements that can be reduced or eliminated by applying lean tools while achieving safety improvements. Applying 5S, visual management, and standardization proved to be effective methods to reduce setup times for both machine ranges. For the <100t range of machines, there was a target of 60 min setup time, reduced from 78.90 min at the start of the work. At the end of applying all SMED steps, a final time of 42.53 min was recorded, which at the end of one year of work represents a gain of 3.64 days. In the ≥ 100t range, an initial setup time of 155.05 min was recorded, far from the target of 90 min. After applying SMED, the desired value was achieved with a final time of 86.53 min. At the end of one year, this difference represents a saving of 5.71 working days. The reductions in setup time in the two ranges were 46.10% and 44.19%, respectively.

The safety surveys answered by employees were intended to gain insight into the improvements from those who deal with the problems daily. The nine questions asked directly about the optimizations revealed that employees feel that their well-being and safety gain from the improvements in the process. All questions had a positive result, with the implementation of the water dispenser in the ergonomics of those who assemble the hoses (100%) and the last question where all employees agreed that lean practices positively impacted their safety perception. The surveys also showed that new employees value implementing tasks that improve ergonomics when they are more complex and require more experience. On the contrary, more experienced co-labourers feel that ergonomics improves more in simple tasks where they have only changed to a more suitable tool.

It is possible to verify that all the proposed objectives were successfully achieved, needing more than the final realization of the action plan for an effective improvement in the company. In short, in this research, it was possible to conclude that the application of SMED together with other lean tools not only allowed to save time that can now be used in activities with added value (production of parts) but also had a positive impact of the safety of the employees involved in the setup process.

Acknowledgements. The authors thank the Polytechnic Institute of Porto - Instituto Superior de Engenharia do Porto - IPP/ISEP for the infrastructure offered for the development of this project and Centro Paula Souza - College of Technology São José dos Campos, Professor Jessen Vidal, FATEC/SJC- Brazil for supporting the internationalization of the RJI project in partnership with IPP-ISEP- Porto Portugal.

References

1. Bevilacqua, M., Ciarapica, F.E., De Sanctis, I.: Lean practices implementation and their relationships with operational responsiveness and company performance: an Italian study. Int. J. Prod. Res. **55**(3), 769–794 (2017)
2. Rosa, C., Silva, F.J.G., Ferreira, L.P.: Improving the quality and productivity of steel wire-rope assembly lines for the automotive industry. Procedia Manuf. **11**(June), 1035–1042 (2017)
3. Jastia, N.V.K., Kodali, R.: Lean production: literature review and trends. Int. J. Prod. Res. **53**(3), 867–885 (2015)
4. Womack, J.P., Jones, D., Roos, D.: The machine that changed the world. Bus. Horiz. **35**(3), 81–82 (1992)
5. Choomlucksana, J., Ongsaranakorn, M., Suksabai, P.: Improving the productivity of sheet metal stamping subassembly area using the application of lean manufacturing principles. Procedia Manuf. **2**(February), 102–107 (2015)
6. Zhou, B.: Lean principles, practices, and impacts: a study on small and medium-sized enterprises (SMEs). Ann. Oper. Res. **241**(1–2), 457–474 (2016). https://doi.org/10.1007/s10479-012-1177-3
7. Belvedere, V., Cuttaia, F., Rossi, M., Stringhetti, L.: Mapping wastes in complex projects for lean product development. Int. J. Project Manage. **37**(3), 410–424 (2019)
8. Pinto, J.P. Pensamento Lean - ISBN: 978-989-752–032-7. Lidel - Edições Técnicas, lda (2014)
9. Liker, J.: The Toyota Way: Fourteen Management Principles From the World S Greatest Manufacturer, p. 330. McGraw-Hill, London (2004)
10. de Souza, R.V.B., Carpinetti, L.C.R.: A FMEA-based approach to prioritize waste reduction in lean implementation. Int. J. Qual. Reliab. Manag. **31**(4), 346–366 (2014)
11. Veres, C., Marian, L., Moica, S., Al-Akel, K.: Case study concerning 5S method impact in an automotive company. Procedia Manuf. **22**, 900–905 (2018)
12. Cordeiro, P., Sá, J.C., Pata, A., Gonçalves, M., Santos, G., Silva, F.J.G.: The impact of lean tools on safety—case study. Stud. Syst. Decis. Control **277**, 151–159 (2020). https://doi.org/10.1007/978-3-030-41486-3_17
13. Santos, G., Sá, J.C., Oliveira, J., Ramos, D., Ferreira, C.: Quality and safety continuous improvement through lean tools. In: Lean Manufacturing: Implementation, Opportunities and Challenges, pp. 165–188. Nova Science Publishers (2019)
14. Singh, C., Singh, D., Khamba, J.S.: Exploring an alignment of lean practices on the health and safety of workers in manufacturing industries. Mater. Today: Proc. **47**, 6696–6700 (2020)
15. Jilcha, K., Kitaw, D.: Lean influence on occupational safety and health in manufacturing industries (2016)
16. Liker, J.K.: Toyota Way: 14 Management Principles from the World's Greatest Manufacturer. McGraw-Hill Education, London (2021)
17. Hamja, A., Maalouf, M., Hasle, P.: The effect of lean on occupational health and safety and productivity in the garment industry – a literature review. Prod. Manuf. Res. **7**(1), 316–334 (2019)
18. Sakouhi, A., Nadeau, S.: Integration of occupational health and safety into lean manufacturing: Quebec aeronautics case study. Am. J. Ind. Bus. Manag. **06**(11), 1019–1031 (2016)
19. Gnoni, M.G., Andriulo, S., Maggio, G., Nardone, P.: "Lean occupational" safety: an application for a near-miss management system design. Saf. Sci. **53**, 96–104 (2013)
20. Hasle, P., Bojesen, A., Jensen, P.L., Bramming, P.: Lean and the working environment: a review of the literature. Int. J. Oper. Prod. Manag. **32**(7), 829–849 (2012)
21. Raquel, L., Alves, M.: Lean Safety - Estudo do impacto do Lean Seis Sigma na Segurança (2020)

22. Gonçalves, I., Sá, J.C., Santos, G., Gonçalves, M.: Safety stream mapping—a new tool applied to the textile company as a case study. Stud. Syst. Decis. Control **202**, 71–79 (2019). https://doi.org/10.1007/978-3-030-14730-3_8
23. Sá, J.C., Carvalho, D., Sousa, R.M.: Waste identification diagrams. CLME'2011 / IIICEM – 6º Congresso Luso-Moçambicano de Engenharia - 3º Congresso de Engenharia de Moçambique Maputo (2011)
24. Marques, J.P., Sá, J.C., Silva, F.J.G., Pereira, T., Ferreira, L.P., Santos, G.: Safety efficiency value stream mapping (SEVSM) - a new tool to support the implementation of Lean Safety. IOP Conf. Ser.: Mater. Sci. Eng. **1193**(1), 012124 (2021)
25. Brito, M., Vale, M., Leão, J., Ferreira, L.P., Silva, F.J.G., Gonçalves, M.A.: Lean and ergonomics decision support tool assessment in a plastic packaging company. Procedia Manuf. **51**, 613–619 (2020)
26. Wilson, L.: How to implement lean manufacturing. In: McGraw-Hill Professional Publishing (2009)
27. Ulutas, B.: An application of SMED methodology. World Acad. Sci. Eng. Technol. **79**(June), 100–103 (2011)
28. Silva, A., Sá, J.C., Santos, G., Silva, F.J.G., Ferreira, L.P., Pereira, M.T.: Implementation of SMED in a cutting line. Procedia Manuf. **51**, 1355–1362 (2020)
29. Shingo, S., Dillon, A.P.: Revolution in manufacturing: single-minute exchange of die system. 384 (1985)
30. Pellegrini, S., Shetty, D., Manzione, L.: Study and implementation of the single minute exchange of die (SMED) methodology in a setup reduction kaizen. In: 3rd 2012 International Conference on Industrial Engineering and Operations Management, vol. 3–6, pp. 2353–2363 (2012)
31. Ferradás, P.G., Salonitis, K.: Improving changeover time: a tailored SMED approach for welding cells. Procedia CIRP **7**, 598–603 (2013)
32. Ribeiro, P., Sá, J.C., Ferreira, L.P., Silva, F.J.G., Pereira, M.T., Santos, G.: The impact of the application of lean tools for improvement of process in a plastic company: a case study. Procedia Manuf. **38**, 765–775 (2019)
33. Sousa, E., Silva, F.J.G., Ferreira, L.P., Pereira, M.T., Gouveia, R., Silva, R.P.: Applying SMED methodology in cork stoppers production. Procedia Manuf. **17**, 611–622 (2018)
34. Costa, E.S.M.D., Sousa, R.M., Bragança, S., Alves, A.C.: An industrial application of the SMED methodology and other lean production tools. In: 4th International Conference on Integrity, Reliability and Failure, vol. 1(i), pp. 1–8 (2013)
35. Agung, D., Hasbullah, H.: Reducing the product changeover time using SMED & 5S methods in the injection molding industry. Sinergi **23**(3), 199 (2019)
36. Vieira, T., et al.: Optimization of the cold profiling process through SMED. Procedia Manuf. **38**(Faim 2019), 892–899 (2019)
37. Monteiro, C., Ferreira, L.P., Fernandes, N.O., Sá, J.C., Ribeiro, M.T., Silva, F.J.G.: Improving the machining process of the metalworking industry using the lean tool SMED. Procedia Manuf. **41**, 555–562 (2019)

A Systematic Literature Review on the Use of Lean Methodologies in Enterprise Sales Processes

Daniel O'Mahony and Olivia McDermott(✉)

College of Science and Engineering, University of Galway, Galway, Ireland
Olivia.McDermott@universityofgalway.ie

Abstract. The number of people involved in Sales and Sales support functions is significant. However, the profession experiences high levels of turnover, estimated at twice that of the labour force average. Staff turnover includes both voluntary and involuntary attrition. Problemistic Search Theory suggests that businesses look to re-organize their sales forces, rather than conduct root cause analysis, sales process improvement, or to develop its value proposition in the market. The aim of the study was to ascertain if Lean culture could benefit businesses and Sales teams by reducing the focus on individual rankings, encouraging a co-operative approach to sales, and focusing on the process. A systematic literature review was conducted related to the literature on Lean in Sales processes. The findings were that there is a scarcity of literature related to themes based on Lean principles in Sales. Where Lean was utilised value stream mapping, the relationship between inventory levels and sales, voice of customer, value propositions and Sales performance metrics were deployed. The study also found that the Lean Startup approach aligned with the Lean principal themes identified in the systematic literature review. This study is one of the first studies to look at Lean and its deployment and relevance with Sales processes.

Keywords: Lean · Sales · Revenue · Sales Targets

1 Introduction

One of the objectives of Lean management is to achieve better sales through better efficiency, better product design, and reduced costs. Even with better products and prices, increased Sales may not follow. The market communicates its requirements, back to the business, via the sales team. The sales team provides an important channel for the voice of the customer. Eliya Goldratt noted that as flow is achieved in the manufacturing plant that "the constraint moves into the market" [1].

The term "Lean" was first used to describe management practices in Japanese automotive manufacturers in the 1980's [2]. Since then, Lean management practices have been adopted in many industry sectors including construction, supply-chain, banking, insurance and healthcare [3, 4]. Nevertheless, Lean management is still mostly associated and embedded more within manufacturing. A 2023 survey of Lean projects in

Published by Springer Nature Switzerland AG 2024
T. van Kollenburg et al. (Eds.): ELEC 2023, IFIP AICT 681, pp. 271–286, 2024.
https://doi.org/10.1007/978-3-031-63265-5_21

Ireland for example found that 55% of Lean projects were conducted in manufacturing and engineering companies [5].

In the UK for example, the 2021 census estimates that over 1 million people work in Sales, Marketing, and Sales related occupations (not counting retail sales or customer service occupations) [6]. This compares to 268,000 people working in the Bioscience industries in the UK [7] and 182,000 working in the UK automotive manufacturing sector [8] . The U.S. Census counts over 5 million people with Sales related occupations, excluding retail and real estate sales workers [9].

The teachings of Dr. William Edwards Deming are considered to be one of the foundation of Lean management culture. Deming often commented on the role of Salespeople and Sales management in his writing. In his book "Out of the Crisis", Deming wrote about the inherent variation of Sales territories [10]. In "The New Economics", Deming wrote about the use of Sales commissions, Sales rankings, territories, cooperation in Sales teams, and intrinsic motivation [11].

Reports suggest that all is not well in the field of Sales and Sales management with current annual turnover of sales staff of 35% according to one study [12]. Other estimates put the attrition rate in the Sales profession to be twice that of the rest of the labour market average [13]. This rate of Sales attrition has a substantial negative impact on businesses. In the software industry, new Sales hires take on average over 5 months to become productive [14]. Constant changes in personnel mean more costs to hire and train replacement staff and represent a waste of human potential. There are opportunity costs to the business for Sales that are not initiated or closed. Included in the high rates of sales staff turnover is the concept of voluntary and involuntary attrition. Approximately two thirds of attrition is involuntary. In other words, sales staff are regularly terminated [14]. The main reason for voluntary and involuntary termination is failure to meet sales targets and quotas [15]. There is a widening gap between companies' expectations and sales and salespeople's ability to deliver.

A survey of over 2,900 sales representatives conducted in 2017 found that only 57% of respondents failed to reach their Sales targets [16] . In 2019, the LinkedIn survey of over 10,000 salespeople found that only 37% of representatives met their sales quota [17]. In other words, the majority of salespeople are seen as failures by their organizations. This acceptance of high turnover rates in Sales teams and the tolerance for "involuntary attrition" may be an example of problemistic search theory, where management reaches for changes within their immediate sphere of control, rather than analysing for the root cause of missed expectations [18, 19]. This study will investigate how Lean has been deployed in Sales processes and if Lean could improve Lean Sales processes.

Section 2 outlines the methodology utilised, Sect. 3 outlines the results, while Sects. 4 and 5 provide a discussion of the results and conclusion.

2 Methodology

A Systematic Literature Review (SLR) process was conducted for this paper. A systematic review provides a method to reduce bias by identifying, appraising, and collating data from a search of relevant studies [20]. The review followed the Tranfield methodology to plan the review, and to create inclusion and exclusion criteria [21]. A search of the full academic databases of SCOPUS and Web of Science was carried out using the search string "Lean" AND "Sales". The search was restricted to journal articles and conference papers and was not time limited. The journal search data was exported from Scopus and from the Web of Science and converted to a .XLS file. The exported files included details on year of publication, author, title, abstract, and publication. Relevant articles were managed utilising Zotero referencing software. Each relevant article was reviewed, and the key themes identified and recorded [20].

The following inclusion and exclusion criteria were used for the search (Table 1).

Table 1. Selection Criteria

Selection Criteria	
Inclusion	*Exclusion*
– Journal and conference proceedings articles yielded from search term "Lean" AND "Sales" – Peer reviewed Articles – Articles exploring the use of Lean management tools, directly impacting sales processes – Articles relating to enterprise level or business-to-business sales processes	– Articles with non-Lean management discussions e.g., sales of Lean as 'non-fat' products – Articles in the English language – Measure of relevance. Articles must discuss the application of Lean in the sales process itself. For example, a broad assertion of Lean management in manufacturing leading to better sales is not sufficient – Articles relating to retail or e-commerce sales – Grey literature (dissertations, newspaper articles, commercial articles)

The initial search for the string "Lean" AND "Sales" identified 1,336 journal articles, made up of 975 articles from Scopus and 361 from Web of Science. The search results of both databases were combined into a single spreadsheet. A search for duplicates was carried out and 111 duplicate articles were found and separated. Removing the duplicates left 1,225 articles for further consideration.

Articles were filtered for inclusion or exclusion based on Yes, No, and Maybe tags in Microsoft Excel after reading the abstracts. The exclusion of some articles was relatively obvious; for example, articles appeared in the search results based on a discussion of "Lean" turkey meat or "Lean" diets or beef meat product sales. Other articles discussed the topic of Lean management in hospitality, warehousing, or retail environments, and these were also excluded based on the enterprise sales criteria from Table 1.

Overall, 1,112 articles were relegated out of the search, based on the "No" tag in the selection spreadsheet. From the initial list of 1,225 individual articles, 113 articles remained that were tagged as Yes or Maybe, based on the initial examination using the inclusion and exclusion criteria. The remaining articles were individually examined in detail against the inclusion/exclusion criteria. Other articles that discussed the sales topic in terms of the use of Lean management in retail or e-commerce applications were excluded also. The detailed examination of articles, based on the inclusion/exclusion criteria removed another 88 articles from the list, leaving a final relevant list of 25 articles. The screening process was outlined in Fig. 1.

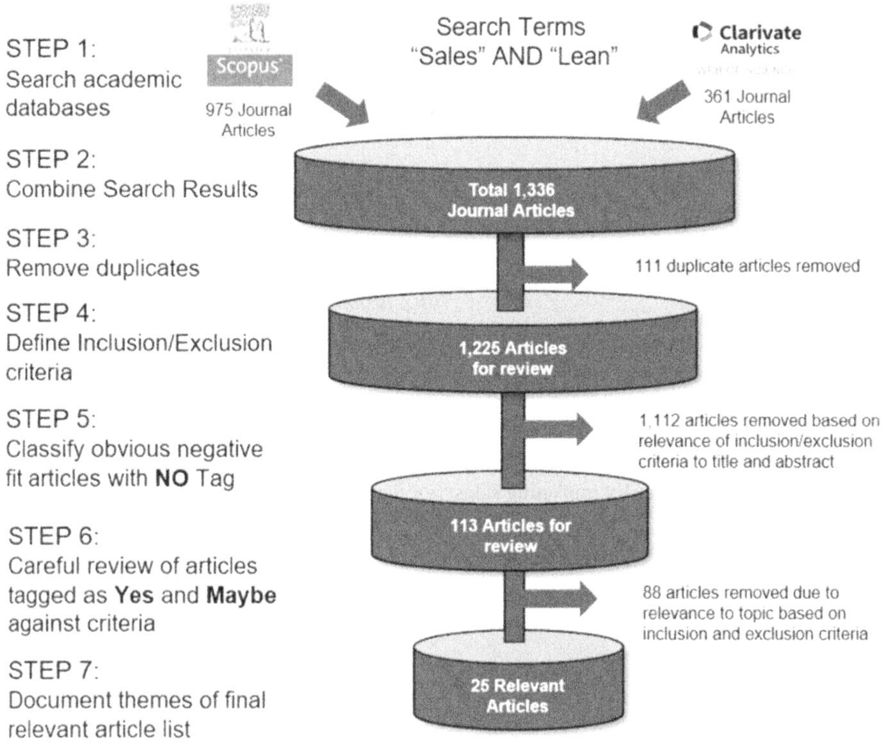

Fig. 1. Journal Articles selection funnel

3 Results

Of the final relevant articles for the "Lean" AND "Sales" search string, 68% (17) came from the Scopus database and 32% (8) came from the Web of Science database. No time limit was placed on the article search, but no relevant article was returned prior to 2001. The pace of publications was relatively low between 2001 and 2023. Between 2007 and 2010 six of the twenty-five identified articles were published. There was another publication spike between 2019 and 2022 with five articles published (Fig. 2).

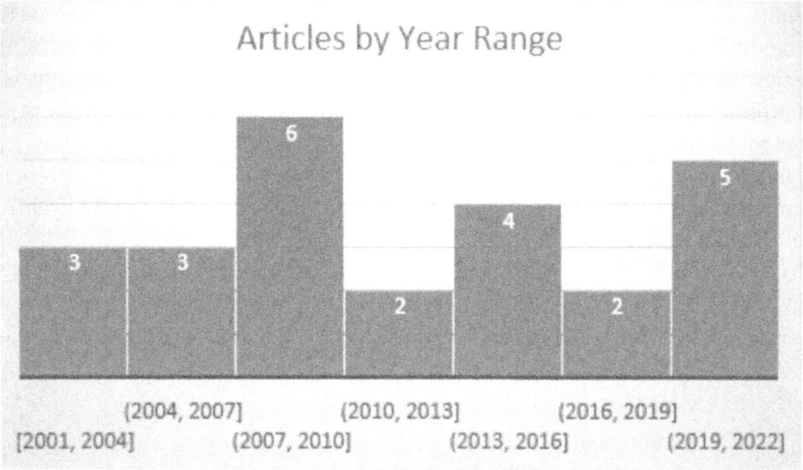

Fig. 2. Relevant articles by database source

Consideration was given to the publication source of the relevant articles. The 25 screened articles were spread consistently across a range of publications. The three most prolific publication titles with just two articles each on the topic of Lean and Sales were Production Planning & Control, Managing Automation and the Journal of Strategic Marketing, and Assembly (Fig. 3).

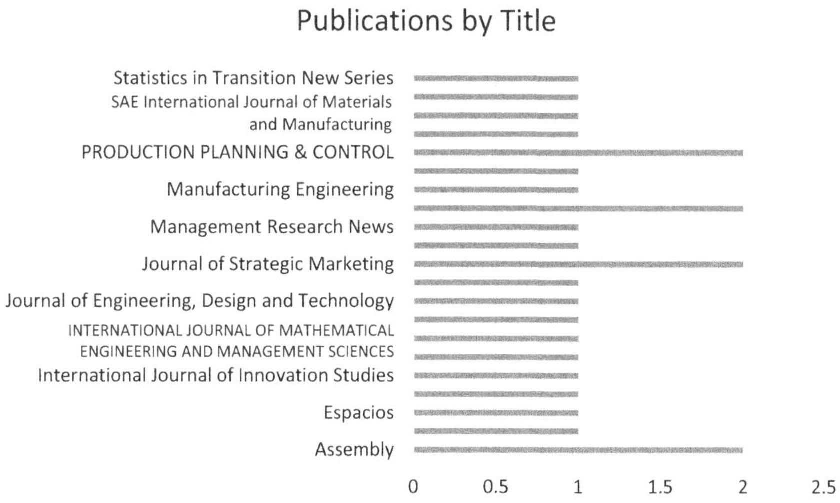

Fig. 3. Publication sources for relevant articles

Publications were also grouped by category. Eight categories of publications were identified: Design, Innovation, Lean, Marketing & Sales, Management, Manufacturing, Statistics, and Quality. Of these publication categories, the management category was the most prolific with 40% of articles coming from management themed journals. Another 28% of relevant articles came from journals in the manufacturing category. Only 12% of relevant articles came from journals associated with Sales and marketing. The remaining categories (Design, Innovation, Lean, Quality, and Statistics) were spread evenly with 4% of relevant articles each (Fig. 4).

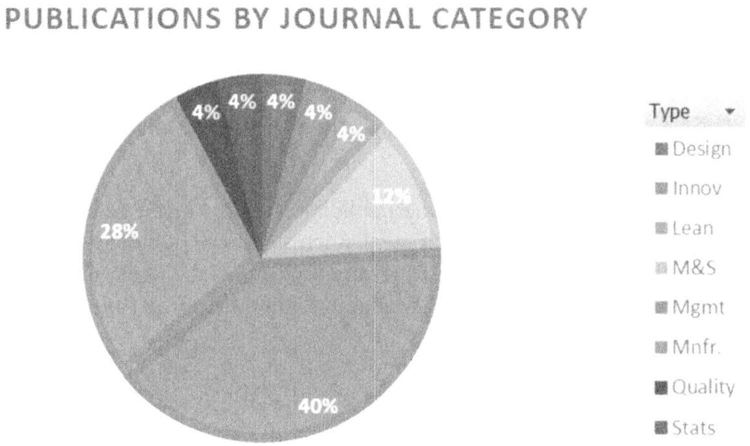

Fig. 4. Relevant articles by publication category

Each of the final 25 articles was examined for key themes. A primary theme was identified for each article, as well as secondary, and tertiary themes. The themes were tabulated in a spreadsheet (Table 2).

Table 2. Selected articles and their themes

#	Authors	Title	Yr	Source title	Primary Theme	Theme 2	Theme 3
22	De Mast J.; Kemper B.P.H.; Wiltjer A.; Does R.J.M.M	Quality quandaries: Deploying operational excellence at a financial service provider	2013	Quality Engineering	Value stream mapping in sales processes	General Lean in Sales and Admin	Selling time release
23	Barber C.S.; Tietje B.C	A research agenda for value stream mapping the sales process	2008	Journal of Personal Selling and Sales Management	Value stream mapping in sales processes	Sales process improvement	Value Proposition
24	Buzby C.M.; Gerstenfeld A.; Voss L.E.; Zeng A.Z	Using Lean principles to streamline the quotation process: A case study	2002	Industrial Management and Data Systems	Value stream mapping in sales processes	Takt time	Quotation process
27	Kunkera, Z; Tosanovic, N; Stefanic, N	Improving the Shipbuilding Sales Process by Selected Lean Management Tool	2022	MACHINES	Value stream mapping in sales processes	Customer Engagement	Sales process improvement
28	Wartati, D; Garza-Reyes, JA; Dieste, M; Nadeem, SP; Joshi, R; Gonzalez-Aleu, F	A Six-Sigma DMAIC Approach to Improve the Sales Process of a Technology Start-Up	2021	INTERNATIONAL JOURNAL OF MATHEMATICAL ENGINEERING AND MANAGEMENT SCIENCES	Value stream mapping in sales processes	Voice of customer	SPC in the sales process
29	Flinchbaugh J	Bring Lean to your sales team	2010	Assembly	Value stream mapping in sales processes	Sales process improvement	Cooperation
30	Moad J	Extending Lean into the enterprise	2008	Managing Automation	Sales process improvement	Value stream mapping in the sales process	Sales Training
31	Khan, SA; Kaviani, MA; Galli, BJ; Ishtiaq, P	Application of continuous improvement techniques to improve organization performance: A case study	2019	INTERNATIONAL JOURNAL OF LEAN SIX SIGMA	Sales process improvement	Value stream mapping in the sales process	General Lean in Sales and Admin

(*continued*)

Table 2. (*continued*)

#	Authors	Title	Yr	Source title	Primary Theme	Theme 2	Theme 3
32	Lyonnet, B; Toscano, R	Towards an adapted Lean system - a push-pull manufacturing strategy	2014	PRODUCTION PLANNING & CONTROL	Inventory levels and sales	Sales forecasting	New product introduction
33	Wallace, T	SALES AND OPERATIONS PLANNING: WHERE IS IT GOING?	2008	BUSINESS FORECASTING: PRACTICAL PROBLEMS AND SOLUTIONS	Inventory levels and sales	Sales forecasting	Sales & Ops Planning
34	Schonberger R.J	Producing in synch with sales: Manufacturers have two opposite ways of equipping factories to respond quickly to customer demand	2014	Assembly	Value Proposition	Sales marketing budgets	Quick response manufacturing
35	Zawada P.; Okrasa W.; Warchalowski J	Flow management system for maximising business revenue and profitability	2020	Statistics in Transition New Series	Inventory levels and sales	TOC and Sales	Systems thinking
35	Holweg, M; Pil, FK	Successful build-to-order strategies start with the customer	2001	MIT SLOAN MANAGEMENT REVIEW	Inventory levels and sales	Sales forecasting	Quick response manufacturing
37	Flórez Rendón A.L.; Cogollo Flórez J.M	Relationship between practices of improvement engineering and sales of micro, small and medium enterprises	2017	Espacios	Adoption of Lean and better sales	Inventory levels and sales	Innovation and sales
37	Lane N	Searching for strategy in sales	2009	Journal of Strategic Marketing	Sales process improvement	Customer Engagement	Sales Process Metrics
38	Gudem M.; Steinert M.; Welo T.; Leifer L	Redefining customer value in Lean product development design projects	2013	Journal of Engineering, Design and Technology	Value Proposition	Customer Engagement	Voice of customer

(*continued*)

Table 2. (*continued*)

#	Authors	Title	Yr	Source title	Primary Theme	Theme 2	Theme 3
41	Schonberger, RJ	Extending the pursuit of flow (Lean) management to encompass sales, general and administrative functions	2020	PRODUCTION PLANNING & CONTROL	Inventory levels and sales	TOC and Sales	Sales & General Admin
42	Nieto Cubero J.; Gbadegeshin S.A.; Consolación C	Commercialization of disruptive innovations: Literature review and proposal for a process framework	2021	International Journal of Innovation Studies	Customer Development	Sales Performance and Incentives	Voice of customer
45	El-Sayed M	Value Streaming Through Customer Participation in Product Realization	2016	SAE International Journal of Materials and Manufacturing	Voice of customer	Value proposition	Value stream mapping in product development
45	Piercy N.; Rich N	The implications of Lean operations for sales strategy: From sales-force to marketing-force	2009	Journal of Strategic Marketing	Selling to Lean companies	Sales Training	Systems thinking
46	Paul L.G	Shaping up for growth	2007	Managing Automation	General Lean in Sales and Admin	Systems thinking	
46	Jayamaha, NP; Wagner, JP; Grigg, NP; Campbell-Allen, NM; Harvie, W	Testing a theoretical model underlying the 'Toyota Way' - an empirical study involving a large global sample of Toyota facilities	2014	INTERNATIONAL JOURNAL OF PRODUCTION RESEARCH	General Lean in Sales and Admin	Inventory levels and sales	Sales Training
47	Holmes F.B	Is your office as Lean as your production line?	2007	Manufacturing Engineering	Systems thinking	Lean in Accounting	
48	Maddy K	Driving changes with Lean manufacturing	2007	SMT Surface Mount Technology Magazine	TOC and sales	Systems thinking	
51	Joetan E.; Kleiner B.H	Incentive practices in the US automobile industry	2004	Management Research News	Sales Performance and Incentives	Sales staff turnover	Customer Engagement

The primary theme is the main topic of discussion in the selected articles with the secondary and tertiary themes in each article offer supporting topics. The primary theme in one article may appear as a secondary or tertiary theme in another. The primary themes from the 25 final articles are considered in isolation in Fig. 5.

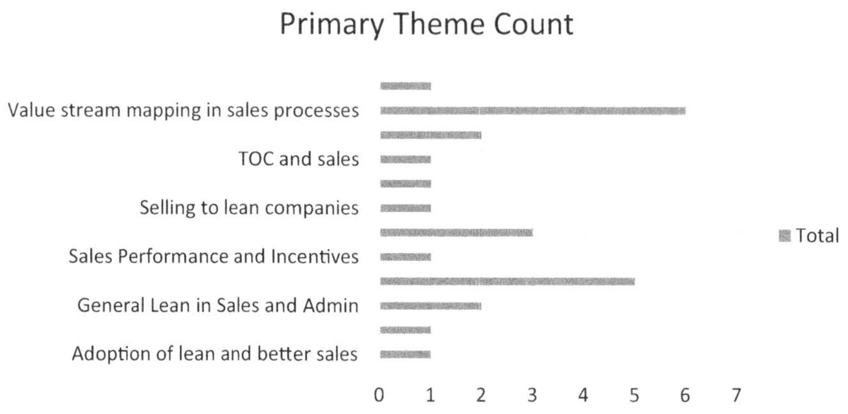

Fig. 5. Primary theme of relevant articles

The three most common primary themes in the final 25 articles appear, in order, as value stream mapping in the sales process (6), consideration of inventory levels and sales (5), and sales process improvement (3). The use of Lean management tools in Sales and General Administration (S&GA) processes and the development of value propositions occur in two articles each. All themes are considered together in Fig. 6.

When each theme is considered together as a primary, secondary, and tertiary theme then inventory levels and sales appear most frequently (7 articles). Value stream mapping in the Sales process is next most frequent, appearing 6 times. Across all theme levels the topics of Sales process improvement and systems thinking occur five times each. Across all theme levels, the voice of customer and value propositions occur four times in the final article list.

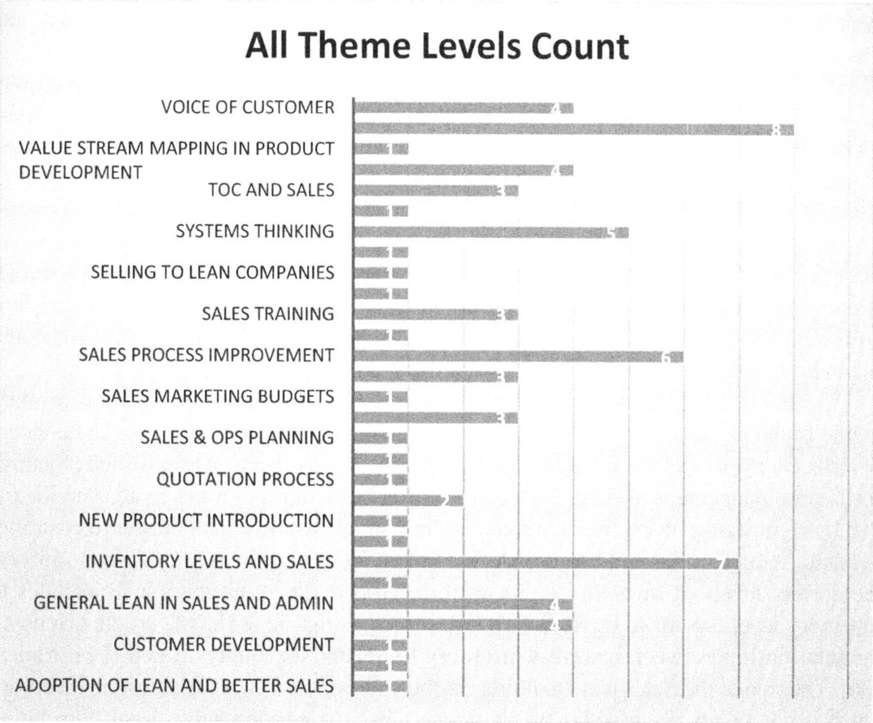

Fig. 6. Breakdown of relevant articles by primary, secondary, and tertiary themes

4 Discussion

The most common primary theme identified in the tabulated analysis is the use of Value Stream Mapping (VSM) deployment within Sales processes. The objective of VSM is to point to where a process may be streamlined and made to be more productive. One study outlined the application of VSM in the financial services sector. It found that 40% of a salesperson's time was taken up with non-customer facing time such as meetings, training, and travel [22]. The study postulated that €173,000 could be saved through more efficient meetings and knowledge exchange. Another study compared manufacturing wastes with Sales process wastes. Overproduction was compared to engagement with unqualified leads. Delays in getting customer information and approvals was identified as time waste. Excess inventory was compared with out-of-date or untargeted marketing materials etc. [23]. Based on four case studies the paper estimated that customer value add time in the sales process ranged from 14%–38%. The use of cycle time and Takt time measures in the quotation process is discussed in another article [24]. To gain better efficiency in the Sales process, Sales managers traditionally looked to either the application of technology or the resetting of the structure of the Sales organization [25, 26]. Barber and Tietje argue that the application of Lean methodologies and VSM could be used as a third method of sales process improvement [23].

A paper on value stream mapping in a European shipbuilding yard provided a very practical example of the gains offered by Lean methodologies applied to the Sales process [27]. The paper describes how the average Sales cycle time for the business, from inquiry to order, was 8 months. A Lean project calculated that the 75% of this time was spent on non-productive time. By creating a value stream map the study was able to identify where company representatives and empirically cost the sales process. As a result of changes initiated through the VSM study the shipbuilding company was able to reduce the time of the sales cycle by 60%. Another article discussed the use of value stream mapping in the sales process of a technology start-up [28]. By focusing on customer waiting time the company was able to reduce the overall sales process time and reduce customer complaints. The use of the value stream mapping tool was also discussed as a secondary or tertiary theme in other articles [29–31].

The theme of inventory levels and sales was the second most common primary theme found in the analysis and the most common across all theme levels. The concept of reduced inventory levels and just-in-time production has been an established objective for Lean management principles since the earliest discourses on the topic. The idea is that by right sizing inventories companies can free up cashflow, react faster to customer demand, reduce costs, and capture market-share. However, the role of Sales to inform the correct levels of inventory is not well developed. The contribution from Sales to inventory levels seems to be limited to Sales forecasting [32–35]. One article discussed the relationship between incorrect inventory levels and discounts offered to customers [36]. The role of the Sales team to represent the voice of customer to determine inventory levels is not widely discussed in the literature. One article found only a weak correlation between flexible manufacturing and better sales [37].

The third most common primary theme in the tabulated analysis was "Sales process improvement". This theme was also joint third across the combined themes ranking. One paper discusses transformation of the Sales process so that Sales and marketing efforts align, customer relationships are developed and the goals of the sales team align with the strategic objectives of the organization [38]. To achieve this transformation, the author suggests that greater cooperation is needed to manage the cross-functional buyer/seller relationship and that new performance measurements are required by the organization. Another article describes the difficulties of persuading a Sales team to adopt Lean methodologies. A case study was presented where Sales representatives were encouraged to record customer information so that regression analysis could be conducted on Sales opportunities, to determine their likelihood of success. Most Sales team members adopted the methodology but those that did not were let go [30]. Other articles describe the use of questionnaires in the Sales process as part of project selection and prioritization [27, 31].

Value proposition was the next most common primary theme and scored highly across all theme levels. One article highlighted the differences between the vendor's perception of value and that of the customer. [39]. Empirical measures of value, favoured by an engineering-based approach to value proposition, did not account for intangible benefits, customer psychology, and feelings. It can be difficult for designers to put themselves in the position of the customer. The roles of the salesperson to bridge this gap was not developed in detail. One application of Lean values in the Sales process is seen in the concept of Lean Startup [40]. The Lean Startup methodology uses the Osterwalder canvas to determine customer value proposition, via an iterative process, that involves getting out and meeting customers. The Lean Startup was referenced by some of the relevant articles [41, 42]. In the Lean startup method, only the founder can engage with customers and develop the value proposition. A salesperson communicating back to the business that the vendor's value proposition was inadequate risks involuntary attrition [43]. This limits the application of Lean start-up methods in small and medium businesses (SMEs) and larger enterprises. The Osterwalder canvas has however been used by larger companies, including IBM and Ericsson [44] . One relevant article described 33 practices to determine customer value [41]. The article did not contain one reference to the role of the salesperson to value determination. This approach would assume that value proposition is determined within the business and communicated in one direction by the sales team.

The theme of "Voice of Customer" scored relatively strongly across all theme levels. Only one article had voice of customer as its primary theme [45]. The paper discussed the voice of customer in the product realization process and customer value proposition. However, there is no mention of the role of the salesperson in the voice of customer discussion.

The theme of "systems thinking" appears five times at all theme levels in the tabulated results. Systems thinking may defined as positioning the sales function in the wider company and supply chain context. Not only does the salesperson have an external customer but there are also internal customers within their organization [46–48]. Customer data must be shared across the organization to achieve smooth transactions between the vendor and the customer. Systems thinking was highlighted in an article focused on selling to Lean companies. Manufacturers such as Nissan and Toyota work with their vendor's sales team to ensure that the salesperson has visibility of the impact of the vendors parts on the shopfloor process [49]. The sales team is expected to proactively seek out problems and to provide consistent after-sales services.

The theme of sales performance metrics and incentives was discussed as a secondary and tertiary themes in three articles. In one article, an argument is made to change Sales performance metrics in the unchartered territory of disruptive technology sales, when using Lean Startup methods [42]. Also, when selling to companies with a culture of Lean management, the performance metrics of the sales team should be appropriate [49, 50]. The risks associated with poor performance metrics were highlighted in two articles [38, 51].

5 Conclusion

Lean management has its origins in manufacturing but is now widely adopted across a range of business processes. The sales process is fundamental to business success. This study investigated the prevalence of Lean deployment in Sales processes and the themes pertaining to Lean application to Sales processes. A structured examination of the literature found twenty-five articles that focused on the application of Lean management in Sales processes. This study has implications for theory and practice. From a theoretical viewpoint it highlights how Lean can improve Sales processes and that there is a lack of literature on the topic. From a management implications point of view Sales management teams can benchmark Manufacturing Lean processes to enable improvement of Sales and Sales processes. A limitation of the study is the limited literature available related to Sales and Lean deployment. Future research could investigate more case study analysis of how Lean has been implemented in Sales processes.

References

1. Goldratt, E.: Beyond the Goal (2013)
2. Krafcik, J.: Triumph of the lean production system - proquest. Sloan Manag. Rev. **30**, 41–53 (1988)
3. McDermott, O., et al.: Lean six sigma in healthcare: a systematic literature review on motivations and benefits. Processes **10**, 1910 (2022). https://doi.org/10.3390/pr10101910
4. McDermott, O., et al.: Lean Six sigma in healthcare: a systematic literature review on challenges, organisational readiness and critical success factors. Processes **10**, 1945 (2022). https://doi.org/10.3390/pr10101945
5. Enterprise Ireland: Lean Consultants Directory - Enterprise Ireland (2023)
6. UK ONS: UK Office for National Statistics Industry and occupation, England and Wales - Office for National Statistics. https://www.ons.gov.uk/employmentandlabourmarket/peopleinwork/employmentandemployeetypes/bulletins/industryandoccupationenglandandwales/census2021. Accessed 08 Oct 2023
7. GOV.UK: Bioscience and health technology sector statistics 2020. https://www.gov.uk/government/statistics/bioscience-and-health-technology-sector-statistics-2020/bioscience-and-health-technology-sector-statistics-2020. Accessed 05 Oct 2023
8. SMMT UK: UK Automotive. SMMT (2023)
9. U.S. Census Bureau: Detailed Occupation by Sex Education Age Earnings: ACS 2019. https://www.census.gov/data/tables/2022/demo/acs-2019.html. Accessed 08 Oct 2023
10. Edwards Deming, W.: Out of the Crisis, pp. 345–346. MIT Center for Advanced Engineering Study. MIT Press, Cambridge (1982)
11. Edwards Deming, W.: The New Economics for Industry, Government, Education by Deming, W. Edwards: Very Good Soft cover, 1st ed. Boston Book World. MIT Press, Cambridge (1993)
12. Chaine, A.: Why Is Turnover So High In B2B Sales? https://www.linkedin.com/pulse/why-turnover-so-high-b2b-sales-anthony-chaine/. Accessed 30 Sept 2023
13. Richardson, R.: Measuring the impact of turnover on sales. J. Pers. Sell. Sales Manag. **19**, 53–66 (1999)
14. The Bridge Group: Sales Development Metrics & Compensation (2023)
15. Dooly Inc.: Sales Happiness Index (2022)
16. LinkedIn: Announcing LinkedIn's 3rd Annual State of Sales Report 2018 (2018)
17. LinkedIn: The LinkedIn State of Sales Report 2020 (2020)
18. Posen, H.E., Keil, T., Kim, S., Meissner, F.D.: Renewing research on problemistic search—a review and research agenda. Annals **12**, 208–251 (2018). https://doi.org/10.5465/annals.2016.0018
19. Audia, P., Greve, H.: Organizational learning from performance feedback: a behavioral perspective on multiple goals (2020). https://doi.org/10.1017/9781108344289
20. Uman, L.S.: Systematic reviews and meta-analyses. J. Can. Acad. Child Adolesc. Psychiat. **20**, 57–59 (2011)
21. Tranfield, D., Denyer, D., Smart, P.: Towards a methodology for developing evidence-informed management knowledge by means of systematic review. Br. J. Manag. **14**, 207–222 (2003). https://doi.org/10.1111/1467-8551.00375

22. De Mast, J., Kemper, B.P.H., Wiltjer, A., Does, R.J.M.M.: Quality quandaries: deploying operational excellence at a financial service provider. Qual. Eng. **25**, 298–306 (2013). https://doi.org/10.1080/08982112.2013.783599
23. Barber, C.S., Tietje, B.C.: A research agenda for value stream mapping the sales process. J. Pers. Sell. Sales Manag. **28**, 155–165 (2008). https://doi.org/10.2753/PSS0885-3134280204
24. Buzby, C.M., Gerstenfeld, A., Voss, L.E., Zeng, A.Z.: Using lean principles to streamline the quotation process: a case study. Ind. Manag. Data Syst. **102**, 513–520 (2002). https://doi.org/10.1108/02635570210450190
25. Hunter, G.K., Perreault, W.D.: Making sales technology effective. J. Mark. **71**, 16–34 (2007). https://doi.org/10.1509/jmkg.71.1.016
26. Zoltners, A.A., Sinha, P., Lorimer, S.E.: Sales force effectiveness: a framework for researchers and practitioners. J. Pers. Sell. Sales Manag. **28**, 115–131 (2008). https://doi.org/10.2753/PSS0885-3134280201
27. Kunkera, Z., Tošanović, N., Štefanić, N.: Improving the shipbuilding sales process by selected lean management tool. Machines **10**, 766 (2022). https://doi.org/10.3390/machines10090766
28. Wartati, D., Garza-Reyes, J.A., Dieste, M., Nadeem, S., Gonzalez Aleu, F.: A six-sigma DMAIC approach to improve the sales process of a technology start-up. Int. J. Math. Eng. Manag. Sci. **6**, 1487–1517 (2021). https://doi.org/10.33889/IJMEMS.2021.6.6.089
29. Flinchbaugh, J.: Bring lean to your sales team. Assembly. **53**, 56 (2010)
30. Moad, J.: Extending Lean into the Enterprise (2008). https://www.socialmediatoday.com/content/extending-lean-enterprise
31. Khan, S.A., Kaviani, M.A., Galli, B.J., Ishtiaq, P.: Application of continuous improvement techniques to improve organization performance: a case study. Int. J. Lean Six Sigma **10**, 542–565 (2019). https://doi.org/10.1108/IJLSS-05-2017-0048
32. Lyonnet, B., Toscano, R.: Towards an adapted lean system – a push-pull manufacturing strategy. Prod. Plan. Control **25**, 346–354 (2014). https://doi.org/10.1080/09537287.2012.702867
33. Wallace, T.: Sales and operations planning: where is it going? In: Gilliland, M., Tashman, L., and Sglavo, U. (eds.) Business Forecasting: Practical Problems and Solutions. John Wiley & Sons, Incorporated, Newark (2016)
34. Schonberger, R.J.: Producing in synch with sales : manufacturers have two opposite ways of equipping factories to respond quickly to customer demand. Assembly **57** (2014)
35. Zawada, P., Okrasa, W., Warchalowski, J.: Flow management system for maximising business revenue and profitability. Stat. Trans. New Ser. **21**, 193–206 (2020). https://doi.org/10.21307/STATTRANS-2020-062
36. Holweg, M., Pil, F.: Successful build-to-order strategies: start with the customer. Sloan Manag. Rev. **43** (2001)
37. Flórez Rendón, A.L., Cogollo Flórez, J.M.: Relationship between practices of improvement engineering and sales of micro, small and medium enterprises. Espacios **38** (2017)
38. Lane, N.: Searching for strategy in sales. J. Strateg. Mark. **17**, 191–197 (2009). https://doi.org/10.1080/09652540903064639
39. Gudem, M., Steinert, M., Welo, T., Leifer, L.: Redefining customer value in lean product development design projects. J. Eng. Des. Technol. **11**, 71–89 (2013). https://doi.org/10.1108/17260531311309143
40. Ries, E.: The Lean Startup: The Million Copy Bestseller Driving Entrepreneurs to Success. Penguin (2011)
41. Schonberger, R.J.: Extending the pursuit of flow (lean) management to encompass sales, general and administrative functions. Prod. Plan. Control **31**, 1098–1109 (2020). https://doi.org/10.1080/09537287.2019.1699971

42. Cubero, J.N., Gbadegeshin, S.A., Consolación, C.: Commercialization of disruptive innovations: literature review and proposal for a process framework. Int. J. Innov. Stud. **5**, 127–144 (2021). https://doi.org/10.1016/j.ijis.2021.07.001
43. Blank, S., Dorf, B.: The Startup Owner's Manual: The Step-By-Step Guide for Building a Great Company. John Wiley & Sons, Hoboken (2020)
44. Barquet, A.P.B., Cunha, V.P., Oliveira, M.G., Rozenfeld, H.: Business model elements for product-service system. In: Hesselbach, J., Herrmann, C. (eds.) Functional Thinking for Value Creation, pp. 332–337. Springer, Heidelberg (2011). https://doi.org/10.1007/978-3-642-19689-8_58
45. El-Sayed, M.: Value streaming through customer participation in product realization. SAE Int. J. Mater. Manuf. **9**, 552–557 (2016). https://doi.org/10.4271/2016-01-0344
46. Paul, L.G.: Shaping up for growth. Manag. Autom. **22**, 34–36 (2007)
47. Holmes, F.B.: Is your office as lean as your production line? Manuf. Eng. **139** (2007)
48. Maddy, K.: Driving changes with lean manufacturing. SMT Surf. Mount Technol. Maga. **21** (2007)
49. Piercy, N., Rich, N.: The implications of lean operations for sales strategy: from sales-force to marketing-force. J. Strateg. Mark. **17**, 237–255 (2009). https://doi.org/10.1080/096525409 03064738
50. Jayamaha, N.P., Wagner, J.P., Grigg, N.P., Campbell-Allen, N.M., Harvie, W.: Testing a theoretical model underlying the 'Toyota Way' – an empirical study involving a large global sample of Toyota facilities. Int. J. Prod. Res. **52**, 4332–4350 (2014). https://doi.org/10.1080/00207543.2014.883467
51. Joetan, E., Kleiner, B.H.: Incentive practices in the US automobile industry. Manag. Res. News. Res. News **27**, 49–56 (2004). https://doi.org/10.1108/01409170410784248

The First Chapter of a Regional Deployment of a Continuous Improvement Program in a Medical Device Company

C. Molnar and Olivia McDermott(✉)

College of Science and Engineering, University of Galway, Galway, Ireland
Olivia.McDermott@universityofgalway.ie

Abstract. This study aims to design a model and framework for LSS Deployment in a global multinational Medical Device company commencing with a regional implementation. The DMAIC problem solving training methodology was utilised to design and deploy a model for LSS deployment by designing Continuous Improvement Leadership and Problem solving training. A strategy for LSS deployment was agreed upon and implemented via a pilot. Several projects were completed, and Leadership was involved in training and coaching programs to prepare them for their roles in CI deployment. This study provides a detailed case study of how one organisation deployed and launched the first steps of a continuous improvement program through leadership involvement and training development across all functions of the organisation regionally.

Keywords: LSS · DMAIC · Leadership · Strategy · Training

1 Introduction

The medical technology sector provides innovative products to patients worldwide improving their quality of life. It is a highly regulated sector under continuous pressure from regulatory authorities to stay compliant and to reduce costs (to do more with less) whilst introducing new capabilities and generating growth opportunities (Brown et al., 2008). Process optimisation and gaining better product quality, efficiency, cost reduction, customer satisfaction, and bottom-line savings - are still being strived for. Driven by this need "many organisations are searching for a new formidable improvement strategy to address the gaps and complexities in today's market environment"(Iyede et al., 2018). Continuous improvement supports organisations to address these needs by doing things in the most efficient, effective, and productive way every day, everywhere, and by everyone (Gonzalez-Aleu et al., 2018). It does so by utilising Lean Six Sigma (LSS) with the objective of removing waste and reducing variation (George, 2002).

Within the medical device industry, this challenge is magnified by the need to comply with different global specific regulatory and associated medical device regulations and quality standards such as ISO 13485. The standard removes the emphasis from

Published by Springer Nature Switzerland AG 2024
T. van Kollenburg et al. (Eds.): ELEC 2023, IFIP AICT 681, pp. 287–305, 2024.
https://doi.org/10.1007/978-3-031-63265-5_22

continuous improvement and customer satisfaction and places it on meeting regulatory requirements, risk management, and maintaining effective and validated changes (McDermott *et al.*, 2022a, b; McGrane et al., 2022, Nicholas *et al.*, 2020). This focus on regulatory compliance results in difficulty and reluctance to make changes once a product is approved and validated due to the effort and risk involved (Brown et al, 2008). There is limited evidence in the literature of Lean or LSS application in medical device manufacturing, however, its application is on the increase. McDermot et al. (2022a, b) found that that over 95% of Irish Medtech companies have a CI program.

The medical device company where this case study has been conducted began its continuous improvement journey a few years ago. Initially, the need was highlighted in manufacturing at both a global and regional level. More recently, a global continuous improvement function was created to drive the implementation of CI cross-functionally within the transactional area of the business in collaboration with manufacturing. It was recognised that whilst continuous improvement excellence existed in pockets of the organisation it was less mature in other areas of the business. There was a need to provide LSS education across the transactional and manufacturing business which would lead to - through the implementation of LSS projects - increased customer satisfaction, improved product and service quality, and reduced cost. This paper is a case study on the first six months of the EMEA regional continuous improvement strategy implementation as aligned with the global continuous improvement strategy.

This research aims to implement LSS in a European-based medical device organisation as part of a global program deployment. The aims of the study are:

- to demonstrate the benefits of educating the workforce in LSS.
- to investigate the importance of leadership training as a critical success factor in LSS implementation and sustainability.
- to demonstrate that LSS brings results such as improved productivity, reduced leadtimes, and increased customer satisfaction.

Section 2 outlines the literature review, Sect. 3 the methodology, while Sects. 4, 3 and 6 outline the Results, Discussion and Conclusion, respectively.

2 Literature Review

It's evident that organisations have had varied success with LSS implementation (Antony et al., 2022). Their success depends on many factors which are financial performance, an organisation-wide LSS culture, organisation-wide innovation culture, continuous training, and retraining employees on LSS, linking LSS to the customer, project selection strategy, communication, recognition and compensation systems, social benefits, and green benefits (Sony et al., 2020). Workforce education and involvement in LSS projects are highlighted as a key Critical Success Factors (CSFs) by a succession of authors (Albliwi et al., 2014; Antony et al., 2018). The importance of investing heavily in educating the workforce in LSS as a key driver of its successful implementation (Swarnakar et al., 2021). Leadership buy-in is seen as the main enabler for LSS success in organisations according to (Laureani and Antony, 2017, 2019) but the study does not specifically address how this is supported through the education of leaders. Laureani and Antony

(2017) identified ten leadership characteristics that enable success in LSS deployment: being visible, good communications, inspirational, consistency, directed, leading by example, flexibility, embracing LSS as a philosophy, having clearly defined roles and responsibilities, and being able to construct a strategy. Leaders can only support a LSS strategy if they understand it and recognise the value it can bring to their organisation.

Creating leadership buy in for LSS can in part be achieved through LSS leadership education which supports the implementation of a continuous improvement culture in organisations. (Nelson and McDermott, 2023). Leadership therefore needs to fully understand the principles and practices of LSS (Albliwi et al., 2014).

When implemented properly, the benefits of LSS can be enormous, enabling organisations to do more with less: marketing, selling, manufacturing, and providing more of what customers want with fewer resources (Panayiotou and Stergiou, 2021). As the road to successful implementations is not very well defined, organisations discover that there is no magic formula with many potential failures along the way (Sony et al., 2019). (Brown et al., 2008) states that the implementation of continuous improvement strategies is not as widespread as expected in the sector.

Within the medical devices industry LSS is underdeveloped in the medical device industry due to its primary focus of meeting quality and regulatory requirements (Brown et al., 2008; Iyede et al., 2018; McDermott, Antony, Sony and Healy, 2022a, b) (Brown et al., 2008 and Iyede et al., 2018). Within the literature on LSS implementation in manufacturing rather than transactional environments (Antony et al., 2021) and at a project level (Nicholas, 2019). Much of the literature covers LSS implementation mostly in the manufacturing sector as the origins of LSS lie therein (Brown et al., 2008). There is a lack of literature on a systematic approach/strategy to support the development of successful partnerships with key leaders to commence continuous improvement in organisations. Instead, the literature focuses on the desired leadership styles (Laureani *et al.*, 2017). The impact of leadership buy in has been discussed by several authors (Nogueira et al., 2018 and Laureani *et al.*, 2019). Nogueira et al. (2018) stating that the empowering leadership style has a positive impact on the success of LSS implementation. This suggests that leader buy in can be best achieved by empowering them to introduce continuous improvement in their organisation through enabling support such as leadership training. This highlights the importance of partnering up with key leaders in the organisation and educating them to enable them to drive the implementation of LSS in their function. Tracking continuous improvement (CI) projects is key to successful LSS implementation. It provides a comprehensive view of the project or process being implemented, and its performance (Easton and Rosenzweig, 2012). According to the authors if something goes wrong in one phase of the project the whole project can go wrong therefore tracking the project will support its successful completion. by sharing the successes and failures of a well-developed and deployed problem-solving process. There are several software packages available to analyse LSS data such as JMP, Minitab and Power BI. These packages focus on data analysis utilising Six Sigma tools which can support effective decision making on Lean Six Sigma projects and draw conclusions from data sets and make decisions (Ozgur et al., 2015). However, they do not allow for the tracking of continuous improvement activities to support the scaling of continuous improvement in organisations. There is limited evidence of documented software solutions for LSS deployment except for those published by Coventry (2019) and Kutscher (2016). Coventry (2019) provides an overview of the continuous improvement software market identifying key players. Whilst Kutscher (2016) highlights KaiNexus as a software that allows employees at all levels to share ideas for saving money, generating revenue, and improving patient care.

3 Methodology

3.1 Introduction

The organisation in which this case study takes place is a multinational medical device manufacturer deploying an Operational Excellence program. DMAIC is a problem-solving methodology (de Mast and Lokkerbol, 2012) used to improve processes. In this paper, qualitative and quantitative methods were applied utilising DMAIC tools. They were complimented by a systematic review of journal articles to incorporate external lessons learned into each phase of the project thereby positively impacting on the results achieved whilst identifying literature gaps at the same time. The timeline for the project was over a 6-month period. During this time a strategic A3 template was utilised to provide visibility for the progress made prompting actions to keep the project on track and to support the confirmation of next steps towards project completion.

Table 1. Strategic A3 Template built on the DMAIC methodology

<table>
<tr><td colspan="5">Theme: Describe the Focus of the A3 Fiscal Year: 2021 Owner: Name Date: Day/Month/Year Target Condition: Month, Year</td></tr>
<tr><td>Define (Plan):
This year's Annual Goals / Objectives / Performance Targets</td><td colspan="4">Improve (Do)
Target Condition (Describe the desired condition and level of performance after implementing Actions / Sub-Projects)</td></tr>
<tr><td></td><td colspan="4" rowspan="3"></td></tr>
<tr><td>Reflection on Last Year's Activities relative to the Goals / Objectives / Performance Targets</td></tr>
<tr><td></td></tr>
<tr><td>Measure (Plan) (Current Condition: What is the current situation and level of performance ?)</td><td colspan="4">Implementation Plan</td></tr>
<tr><td rowspan="2"></td><td>Action Items / Sub-Projects ('child' A3)</td><td>Who</td><td>Whe</td><td>Status</td></tr>
<tr><td></td><td></td><td></td><td></td></tr>
<tr><td>Analysis (Plan) (Why does the current condition / situation and level of performance exist?):</td><td></td><td></td><td></td><td></td></tr>
<tr><td rowspan="3"></td><td colspan="4">Control (Study/Act)(Follow-up, recommendation, replication):</td></tr>
<tr><td colspan="2">Follow-up Plan</td><td colspan="2">Actual Results</td></tr>
<tr><td colspan="2"></td><td colspan="2"></td></tr>
<tr><td colspan="5">Additional Notes</td></tr>
</table>

An A3 is a structured problem-solving approach that provides a template for problem solving training (Matthews, 2018). The A3 integrated with DMAIC is a powerful tool that fosters learning, collaboration and guides the employees through projects until their completion (Bassuk and Washington, 2013). The Define, Measure and Analysis steps were aligned with the Planning Phase of Plan, Do, Check, Act (PDCA) (Sobek II and Smalley, 2008). The Improve step of DMAIC correlated with the Do Phase whilst the Control Phase contained the Check & Act Phases. Utilising PDCA will ensure continuous learning throughout every iteration of the continuous improvement implementation process.

3.2 DMAIC Pillars

As part of the project scoping 3 Pillars were identified as the key drivers of implementation. These were Educate, Partner and Publish recognised during a successful pilot program ran within one of the functions prior to the commencement of this project and based on literature reviewed. The Educate Pillar was set up with the objective of educating the workforce in continuous improvement tools and leadership skills as part of building out the CI Academy at the case study organisation. Its offerings will include both problem solving training (at various belt levels) and CI leadership courses. The Partner Pillar set out to enable strategic partners of the continuous improvement function to build a culture of operational excellence in their functional areas. Lastly, the Publish Pillar was established with the goal of making the CI wins visible to the entire organisation by publishing how the CI wins were achieved through the application of CI tools as well as the results/savings generated by the CI projects.

To compliment this overall strategy a CI execution strategy has also been developed to support our partners within their functions to grow into CI leaders leading to the sustainment of CI. This CI execution strategy was based on the three pillars of Standardise, Measure, and Improve. The objective of the Standardise Pillar was set to support the creation of standard work across the organisation. The Measure Pillar supports the creation of standard work performance tools such as visualisation boards and dashboards. The Improve Pillar supports standard work improvement by upskilling CI leaders and practitioners linking in with the Educate Pillar to provide the right courses as needed. In summary, the implementation methodology was built on the pillar structures as per Table 1.

Table 2. Continuous Improvement Pillars

Continuous Improvement Pillars	
CI Deployment Strategy	CI Execution Strategy
Educate	Standardise
Partner	Measure
Publish	Improve

The strategic A3 was completed as described in the DMAIC steps below.

3.3 Define (Plan)

To kick start the define stage, a global meeting was held to establish the global direction for introducing a Continuous Improvement culture and regional teams were created to commence the work. The global team agreed to initially focus on delivering a CI culture by training green belt candidates and their leaders to execute on pilot projects.

Following setting the global direction, the EMEA project team reflected on the current state of LSS in the three pillars (key activity streams) identified (Educate, Partner, and Publish) relative to the goals/objectives/performance targets (see Table 2) set within the region.

Within the Educate pillar, it was recognised that there was no belt training available apart from white belt and yellow belt training provided within one of the customer-facing functions. No green belt level training existed. With regards to CI leadership training there was no internal CI leadership training available.

In the Partner pillar, the team looked for evidence of CI partnerships between the functions. Whilst functions collaborated on projects these tended to be driven by the function's project needs and were typically not LSS projects. The results of LSS projects published were limited to vertical silos where CI education and work had already commenced. The team investigated the Current Condition of LSS in EMEA. This included confirming actual performance against last year's annual goals, objectives and performance targets and a reflection on same. The question the project team was looking to answer was "*How well did the region achieve the Target Condition?*". Once the Reflection activity was completed, the team looked to identify the Goals, Objectives, and Performance Targets of the project. In the Educate pillar the goal was identified as training one full cohort of green belt and leadership delegates (12 in each totalling 24). This included certification of delegates. In the Partner pillar, the goal was set to strategically select the delegates and the green belt projects in collaboration with functional leads. In the Publish pillar, it was agreed that the certifications would be published along with the outcome of, and lessons learned on the projects.

3.4 Measure (Plan)

In the measure phase, the review of Current Condition was undertaken. The question the team was looking to answer was "*What is the current situation and level of performance?* and "*How well did the region achieve the Target Condition?*" . In each of the pillars a metric was identified with its current performance recorded on a scorecard (see Table 3). Since no green belt and CI leadership training existed in the company prior to this project no current performance could be noted against these metrics.

Table 3. EMEA Scorecard Template – Current Performance

Metrics	Target	Actual
		Current (Aug 2020)
Educate		
Level 1 Leadership Training Metrics		%
Delegates trained	90%	0%
Completion rate (accreditation)	95%	0%
Completion rate (training)	95%	0%
Continuation rate	80%	0%
Conversion rate	50%	0%
Improvement Skills Metrics		
Delegates trained	90%	0%
Completion rate (accreditation)	95%	0%
Completion rate (training)	95%	0%
Completion rate (project)	100%	0%
Continuation rate	80%	0%
Conversion rate	100%	0%
Partner		
Delegates secured	100%	0%
Publish		
Project reports published on OneDrive	100%	0%

Along with the scorecard the team created a description of each of the metrics (see Table 4).

Following the review of the current condition and the setting of the metrics the team moved into the analyse phase of the project.

Table 4. Scorecard metrics descriptions

Educate pillar metrics
Leadership training metrics:
The leadership training metrics set were based on the overall goal of delivering the first EMEA Level 1 Leadership training and Coaching to 12 leaders.
Delegates trained metric:
90% of delegates trained (90% out of 12)
Completion rate metrics:
95% completion rate (accreditation) goal. 95% of candidates should receive their accreditation (no dropouts).
95% completion rate (training) goal. 95% of candidates should complete all their training and coaching sessions (12 modules and 6 coaching sessions).
Continuation rate metric:
80% continuation rate as measured by Leaders and matched Improvement Skills (green belt) delegates who identified their next improvement project to work on.
Conversion rate metric:
50% conversion rate (conversion = leaders nominate their direct reports to participate in either leadership or improvement skills 2021/22 courses).
Improvement Skills (green belt) training metrics:
The Improvement Skills training metrics were based on the overall goal of delivering the first EMEA Improvement Skills Training and Coaching to 12 EMEA delegates.
Delegates trained metric:
90% of delegates trained (90% out of 12)
Completion rate metrics:
95% completion rate (accreditation) goal. 95% of candidates should receive their accreditation (no dropouts).
95% completion rate (training) goal. 95% of candidates should complete all their training and coaching sessions (12 modules and 6 coaching sessions).
100% completion rate (project) goal as measured by successful green belt project submission.
Continuation rate metric:
80% continuation rate (same as defined above)
Conversion rate metric:
100% conversion rate (conversion = actual completion rate and is defined as Green Belt achieving successful process owner and countermeasure implementation for their project).
Partner pillar metrics
Onboarding metric:
100% of delegates onboarded (12 / 12)
Publish Pillar metrics
Project report metric:
100% of project reports published on OneDrive (12 / 12)

3.5 Analyse (Plan)

The purpose of the analyse phase is to formulate and formalise the system's requirements. This is accomplished by establishing what the system is to do, according to the requirements and expectations of the system's end users. The project team investigated why the current condition/situation and level of performance existed using the data from the Current Condition with the help of the 5 Whys tool and a Fishbone diagram. The analysis conducted resulted in the conclusion that broader buy-in was needed to implement continuous improvement by educating the workforce both at a Leadership and Problem solving training level. Without understanding the benefits of LSS and how it can be utilised it cannot be adapted by the company. Yet historically there has been no companywide LSS training available.

3.6 Improve (Do)

This phase deals with testing and standardising potential solutions. The team set the desired condition and level of performance after implementing actions/sub-projects. This included True North examples and a description of what the region will be like when the project is completed. It needed to include the new metrics that will enable the goals to be realised. An implementation plan was included to ensure timely completion of the actions/sub-projects identified with their owners and completion date set.

The project mantra of the company was set as CI for Everybody, Everywhere, Every day. The focus areas have been identified as follows: 1) establish a CI culture 2) coach and mentor local lean teams to deliver measurable and sustainable projects, 3) enable the Leadership team to engage and support their teams to deliver measurable and sustainable improvements/ROI.

The desired target condition was set as to deliver Level 1 CI Leadership and Problem solving training to 24 delegates (12 each) over a 6 month period. Training should lead to successful certification of all delegates via the company's training provider and successful completion of 12 CI projects leading to measurable business improvements. Performance against the metrics set as described earlier was to be measured in the control phase of the project. The implementation plan had 9 deliverables and was being monitored by the program manager in MS Project Plan.

3.7 Control (Study/Act)

The main objective of the control phase is to measure the new process characteristic and validate the improvement. Then implement a control plan and response plan to ensure the new process is strictly implemented. To achieve this objective, three focus areas have been established: follow-up, recommendation, and replication. A dashboard set up consisted of the below metrics (Table 5).

Table 5. Cohort 1 (C1) Dashboard Template

Metrics	Target	Actual
		C1 EMEA
Educate		
Level 1 Leadership Training Metrics		
No of Delegates	12	
Completion rate (accreditation)	95%	
Completion rate (training)	95%	
Continuation rate	80%	
Conversion rate	50%	
Improvement Skills Metrics		
No of Delegates	12	
Completion rate (accreditation)	95%	
Completion rate (training)	95%	
Completion rate (project)	100%	
Continuation rate	80%	
Conversion rate	100%	
Partner		
No of delegates onboarded		
Publish		
No of project reports published on OneDrive		

The team also decided when and how often it would communicate progress (up/down/across) the organisation. The team discussed how it will leverage the lessons learned and apply to other Functions/Departments/Regions. Feedback surveys were sent out to delegates after each training session followed by an analysis of responses in the Lean Management System (LMS) system to improve the training. Every training session was attended by the EMEA Continuous Improvement Director to observe the group and to support the conversations as needed. The lessons learned were fed into the next training cohort which kick started after the initial 6-month program.

Recommendations for improvements were gathered from candidates utilising the LMS system as well as a global meeting being held to discuss the combination of feedback received from all regions. These were utilised in the improvement being implemented for the next cohort. Lessons learned were fed into the next cohorts kick started in each of the regions to replicate the success of the first cohort and to prevent any of the issues that have surfaced in the first cohort.

4 Results

The aim of this study was to demonstrate the benefits of educating the workforce in LSS, to showcase the importance of leadership training and to demonstrate that LSS projects can lead to improvements in organisational performance. Table 6 below provides an overview of the CI training results achieved to date with the first EMEA cohort since its launch.

Table 6. Cohort 1 (C1) Dashboard Template

Metrics	**Target**	**Actual**	
		Cohort 1 (Current)	
Educate			
Level 1 Leadership Training Metrics	%	%	No
Delegates trained	90%	100%	12
Completion rate (accreditation)	95%	Due Sept	Due Sept
Completion rate (training)	95%	100%	12
Continuation rate	80%	Due Sept	Due Sept
Conversion rate	50%	Due July	Due July
Improvement Skills Metrics			
Delegates trained	90%	100%	12
Completion rate (accreditation)	95%	60%	7
Completion rate (training)	95%	100%	12
Completion rate (project)	100%	60%	7
Continuation rate	80%	Due Sept	Due Sept
Conversion rate	100%	Due July	Due July
Partner			
Delegates secured	100%	100%	12
Publish			
Project reports published on OneDrive	100%	60%	7

All 24 delegates put forward completed their training. Delegates were equally split between Leadership and Problem solving training (12 &12). Cohort delegates were made up of two functions representing centres of excellence of CI within the company. This allowed for the review of the results between all delegates and by function i.e., manufacturing and customer facing.

4.1 Benefits of Educating the Workforce in LSS

Each of the delegates reported on the cost savings of their project which is one of the key benefits of LSS training as a project needs to be delivered as part of the certification. With the Lean tools they learned how to reduce waste whereas with Six Sigma they focused on reducing variation – finding ways to make processes as consistent as possible. Eliminating waste and variance led to money savings on the projects which were then validated by finance either as hard saving, soft saving, or cost avoidance. Delegates were able to tangibly prove how LSS processes benefitted their project and thereby their function. For example, they were able to measure how much less product was thrown away because product quality improved, or how overtime was reduced, and products were made more efficiently. They were able to directly link the savings they made to the changes they introduced to the process utilizing LSS tools.

Another key result achieved was improved standardization by standardizing how problems are solved using the same tools and templates in the company. This aided the QMS as if all employees of an organization use the same process improvement method, then the company will be standardized across the board.

Standardisation can be further improved by using data analytics skills to evaluate data for trends and inconsistencies. Since the problem solving training course certified candidates up to green belt level, they learned to apply statistical tools such as statistical problem solving training, hypothesis testing, 2-Sample-t, regression, ANOVA etc. on their projects. The delegates reported feeling more comfortable with data and can apply it on future projects achieving greater improvements.

Another result was improved decision-making skills. Delegates learned to make decisions based on facts and figures rather than feelings. This helped them to get buy in for their projects and helped the project team as well as their business leaders to make decisions based on facts.

4.2 Importance of Leadership Training

On this project twelve leaders completed their continuous improvement leadership training from cohort 1. Every leader was assigned a leadership coach and (apart from attending twelve class-room based training sessions) they were scheduled to attend six one on one coaching sessions with their coach to support the introduction of CI in their function with the goal of sustaining CI long term. The focus of the CI leadership training has been on teaching the skills that make a great CI leader including self-awareness, how to lead a CI team, how to lead change, situational leadership and CI tools such as the X-matrix, improvement systems, leader standard work etc.

As part of the leadership training every leadership training delegate was assigned an problem solving training delegate from the problem solving training to sponsor. Their success as leader was therefore not only measured by whether they received certification for the leadership training but by whether the improvement coach delegate they have been sponsoring, successfully certified at a green belt level. The success of the problem solving training candidate was therefore seen as not only their success but reflective of their sponsor. Since seven problem solving training delegates have already been accredited this meant that 60% of the leaders successfully sponsored a problem solving training delegate through their training.

As a result of the training there has been an agreement between the leaders that there was a need for identifying the right projects and allocate resources to it at a functional level. They have commenced the introduction of a project intake process along with a periodic review of the projects approved until their successful completion. Overall, it was recognised that leadership in LSS is a huge and essential task.

4.3 LSS Project Results

Each problem solving training candidate trained selected a project to complete with their sponsor as part of their accreditation. Table 7 contains the table of projects completed by the certified delegates.

Table 7. C1 EMEA – Completed Projects List

Function	Project Title
Distribution Centre	Cost Reduction of non-conformaties
Customer Experience	Customer requests for information
Marketing	Trademark implementation
Contracts	Contract Performance
Engineering	Manufacturing Line Maintenance
Operations	Communications to the Manufacturing Group
Human Resources	Manufacturing Training Compliance

The first customer experience project set out to reduce the lead time of customer requests for additional product and company information from up to six weeks to 72 h. Additionally, it aimed to reduce the effort needed by employees to gather the response and introduce consistent answers to recurring questions. As a result of the project 16 h of employee time per requests were saved (based on an average of 750 requests per year). The second project ran at the Distribution Centre set out to reduce the scrap value of non-conformances by approximately 8%. After additional data analysis the focus of the project switched to a single product family (due to highest potential impact). As a result of the project a 51% reduction of scrap was achieved. This project will now lead to additional spin off projects leading to further improvements.

The first project at the manufacturing entity led by an engineering problem solving training delegate set out to reduce maintenance time on a particular product line by 50% (60 min down to 30 min). This goal was achieved. In fact, the project achieved 60 h extra availability to operations to manufacture product as the 30 min maintenance time remaining was moved to breaktimes. The new maintenance process now involves close collaboration of maintenance, calibration, and operations. Since the change was introduced there has been no downtime caused by scheduled maintenance. The second manufacturing entity-based project led by operations entitled "Communications to the Manufacturing Group" addressed the impact of lack of clear, timely and consistent communication to manufacturing team members which resulted in low engagement and morale. After introducing standard work through the various communication channels as well as a RACI, communication delivery to the group increased from 27% to 94%. The increased engagement resulted in increased productivity, reduced absence and increased involvement in problem solving training. It is anticipated that the improved retention will lead to reduced hiring and training costs as well as reduced scrapped associated with new hires and reduced level of backorders due to more stable workforce. It is evident from the above that LSS skills along with continuous problem solving training can kick start a company's continuous improvement journey.

5 Discussion

5.1 Invest in LSS Training and Resources

As a result of this project the first EMEA cohort of Leadership and Problem solving training delegates have completed their training. Additionally, the problem solving training delegates either achieved or are on track to achieve their green belt level accreditation in part through the completion of a green belt project. These achievements formed the first step in the successful adaptation of LSS into the company's regional continuous improvement strategy – (outlined visually in Fig. 1 below). To bridge the knowledge gap, external LSS experts were hired to collaborate on the development and delivery of the Leadership and Problem solving training Coach training.

Delegates were strategically selected from the manufacturing and customer facing areas of the business in an opportunity to demonstrate impact at a functional level. Aligning project selection to business problems is importance for an effective CI program (Antony et al., 2018) Additionally, the functions selected represent different parts of the value stream of the company's supply chain providing an opportunity for the exchange of cross-functional points of views and knowledge sharing (Snee and Hoerl, 2002).

It was recognised that there was a need for a Continuous Improvement (CI) Academy within the organisation providing different levels of leadership training as well as belt training. The Leadership and Problem solving training (green belt) training piloted were the first step in the development of the academy's offerings. In the longer term, leadership should also ensure that adequate staff is trained to drive LSS throughout the organization. Having dedicated CI personnel and trainers is an important organizational factor in any CI initiative ((McDermott, Antony, Sony and Looby, 2022a, b).

Feedback was sought from both Leadership and Problem solving training delegates on the training which highlighted the differences in readiness levels for CI within the organisation. Whilst much of the feedback was positive delegates were seeking more practical company ad industry specific examples of the tools. In some cases, company specific examples could be shared with the delegates but there were some where the need for standard work for CI tools was highlighted as a gap to be addressed. Course content was reviewed continuously based on feedback and the training itself was therefore going through a continuous improvement cycle.

During the development of the training, it has become evident that there was a much greater availability of manufacturing rather than transactional examples of LSS tool applications. This was confirmed in the literature review earlier in this paper by authors such as (Delgado *et al.*, 2010 and Nogueira et al., 2018).

Earlier in this paper, the importance of workforce education and involvement as well as leadership support were highlighted as key CSFs as written by a succession of authors, Swarnakar, Hilton, Panyiotou and Laureani (Swarnakar *et al.*, 2020; Hilton *et al.*, 2012 and Panayiotou, 2021; Laureani and Antony, 2018). This paper supports this theory. The gap identified in this paper is detail around how training targeted at leaders can support the growth of leadership support for CI in an organisation and what training should be provided for leaders to achieve this.

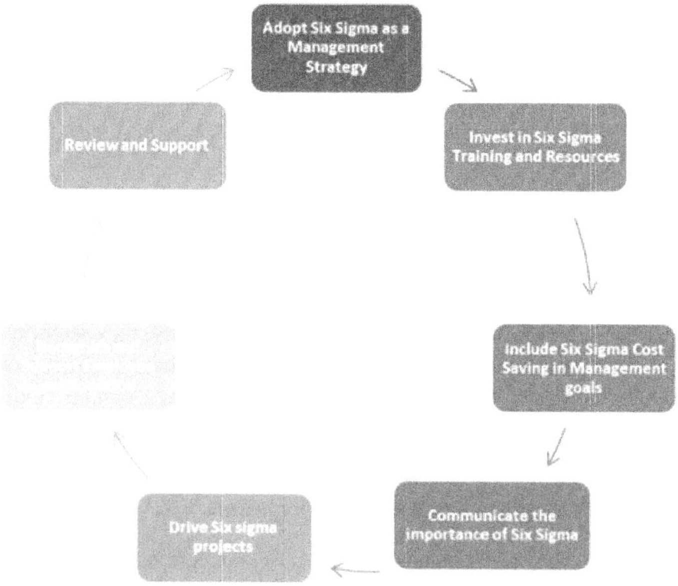

Fig. 1. Successful Adaptation of LSS

5.2 Include LSS Cost Saving in Management Goals

As part of the rollout of training the Continuous Improvement function partnered with Finance to support the development of standard work for the financial validation of savings generated by the projects. Whilst savings have been recorded today, they have not been systematically included in the overall cost calculations and savings as LSS projects at green belt level have previously not existed.

Having standard work and a software in place to record the financial savings will be of a great benefit as it will allow for the consistent view, categorisation and roll up of financial data associated with LSS projects. Thus, management and employees will start seeing LSS methodology as part of their responsibility and identify project opportunities leading to a LSS projects ideas database. The literature has highlighted that the tracking of LSS projects is key to its successful implementation (Coventry, 2019 and Kutscher, 2016).

5.3 Communicate the Importance of LSS

One of the key reasons for developing leadership training was to support top management in embracing and implementing LSS in their functions. Employees should have opportunities to share their concerns related to LSS adaption and leaders should provide clarity on everyone's role in the LSS adaption journey of the company. Communication Report outs have been organised for the green belts to report on the progress of their project as well as when the projects were completed to showcase their business impact. It has also become clear that there was a need for a formal process for presenting on the projects cross functionally.

5.4 Drive LSS Projects

It became clear that there was a need for LSS sponsors and champions within the functions partaking in the training to support the delegates through the DMAIC process of their project (Antony et al., 2018; Laureani and Antony, 2017). Leadership training delegates were completing their training in parallel with the problem solving training delegates and the leaders acted as LSS champions. Additionally, they support the project selection process and allocate resources for the project. There was intervention from leadership where there are bottlenecks in the progress of projects and periodical reviews were conducted.

5.5 Recognise and Support Employee Participation

Reward and recognition have been identified as a key success factor of LSS implementation (Antony et al., 2007; McDermott, Antony, Sony and Looby, 2022a, b). As part of the rollout of this project opportunities have been identified for participants to be rewarded and recognised for their efforts. All projects have been presented to leadership within the problem solving training delegates' function at the various DMAIC phases as well as being presented when they were completed both within their function and to cross functional senior leadership teams. A reward and recognition program has now been initiated as part of the implementation of the CI Academy with the goal of recognizing both leaders and problem solving training delegates partaking in the training.

5.6 Review and Support

The two functions partaking in the training both have their PMO in place which has proven to be a great enabler in supporting purpose, resource support, delegate selection (both leader and problem solving training) and project selection. Similar studies by Rosenfield Boeira and Rosenfield Boeira (2017) and Wegler (2019) have reported the importance of aligning LSS progress with a dedicated PMO to ensure LSS is integrated into the organization and to support tracking and tracing of projects and aid resourcing. Another important support factor identified was a healthy well established QMS system which meant that many processes were already well documented giving a good starting point for improvement projects. Many studies have demonstrated a correlation with having a well-defined QMS such as ISO 9001 as a precursor for implementing any CI program (Karthi et al., 2011; Sá et al., 2022). ISO 9001:2015 has a focus on continuous improvement and thus there is a synergy with combining CI programs to enhance the QMS effectiveness (Veena and Prabhushankar, 2019). However, a mature PMO and QMS were not present in all the pockets of the organization so as continuous improvement is rolled out across the rest of the organisation, additional support needed by these functions to deploy and integrate LSS. Having a strong project management process and well documented processes are foundational enablers of CI. Leadership should support these changes and ensure that the journey is in the right path and at right pace (Antony et al., 2018).

6 Conclusions

Lean Six Sigma is a journey; however, along the way, an organization will start to transform and move towards operational excellence. The approach and time taken to completely channel the organization's efforts towards LSS may vary depending on an organization's size, employee profile, organization culture, age of the company and so many other parameters. This project illustrated the benefits of rolling out LSS regionally by focusing on workforce education including Leadership training and the delivery of LSS projects with business impact. A limitation of this study is that it is a single case study based on one organization. However, as every Operational Excellence journey is different this study provides a valuable benchmark for other organizations.

This research has managerial implications for organizations considering a LSS journey to benchmark. From an academic point of view this case study adds to the state of the art literature in terms of educating on a LSS deployment journey. Future research will investigate a more longitudinal case study on the progress and results of the Operational Excellence company in a case study organization. Also investigating how Industry 4.0 will integrate with the LSS program to enhance it further and reduce non vale add waste is an opportunity for further study.

References

1. Albliwi, S., Antony, J., Abdul Halim Lim, S., van der Wiele, T.: Critical failure factors of lean six sigma: a systematic literature review. Int. J. Qual. Reliab. Manag. **31**(9), 1012–1030. Emerald Group Publishing Limited (2014).https://doi.org/10.1108/IJQRM-09-2013-0147
2. Antony, J., Downey-Ennis, K., Antony, F., Seow, C.: Can six sigma be the 'cure' for our 'ailing' NHS? Edited by Bowerman. J. Leadersh. Health Serv. **20**(4), 242–253. Emerald Group Publishing Limited (2007).https://doi.org/10.1108/17511870710829355
3. Antony, J., Gupta, S., Sunder, M.V., Gijo, E.V.: Ten commandments of Lean Six Sigma: a practitioners' perspective. Int. J. Product. Perform. Manag. **67**(6), 1033–1044. Emerald Publishing Limited (2018).https://doi.org/10.1108/IJPPM-07-2017-0170
4. Antony, J., Lancastle, J., McDermott, O., Bhat, S., Parida, R., Cudney, E.: An evaluation of lean and six sigma methodologies in the UK national health services. Int. J. Qual. Reliab. Manag. (2021)
5. Antony, J., et al.: An empirical study into the reasons for failure of sustaining operational excellence initiatives in organizations. TQM J. (2022). https://doi.org/10.1108/TQM-05-2022-0176
6. Bassuk, J.A., Washington, I.M.: The A3 problem solving training report: a 10-step scientific method to execute performance improvements in an academic research vivarium. PLoS One **8**(10), e76833. Public Library of Science San Francisco, USA (2013)
7. Brown, A., Eatock, J., Dixon, D., Meenan, B.J., Anderson, J.: Quality and continuous improvement in medical device manufacturing. TQM J. **20**(6), 541–555. Emerald Group Publishing Limited (2008).https://doi.org/10.1108/17542730810909329

8. Easton, G.S., Rosenzweig, E.D.: The role of experience in six sigma project success: an empirical analysis of improvement projects. J. Oper. Manag. **30**(7–8), 481–493 (2012). https://doi.org/10.1016/j.jom.2012.08.002
9. George, M.L.: Lean Six Sigma: Combining Six Sigma Quality with Lean Production Speed. McGraw-Hill, New York (2002)
10. Gonzalez-Aleu, F., Van Aken, E.M., Cross, J., Glover, W.J.: Continuous improvement project within Kaizen: critical success factors in hospitals. TQM J. 30(4), 335–355. Emerald Publishing Limited (2018).https://doi.org/10.1108/TQM-12-2017-0175
11. Iyede, R., Fallon, E.F., Donnellan, P.: An exploration of the extent of lean six sigma implementation in the West of Ireland. Int. J. Lean Six Sigma **9**(3), 444–462. Emerald Publishing Limited (2018).https://doi.org/10.1108/IJLSS-02-2017-0018
12. Karthi, S., Devadasan, S.R., Murugesh, R.: Lean six sigma through ISO 9001 standard-based quality management system: an investigation for research. Int. J. Product. Qual. Manag. **8**(2), 180–204. Inderscience Publishers (2011).https://doi.org/10.1504/IJPQM.2011.041845
13. Laureani, A., Antony, J.: Leadership characteristics for lean six sigma. Total Qual. Manag. Bus. Excell. **28**(3–4), 405–426. Routledge (2017). https://doi.org/10.1080/14783363.2015.1090291
14. Laureani, A., Antony, J.: Leadership and lean six sigma: a systematic literature review. Total Qual. Manag. Bus. Excell. **30**(1–2), 53–81. Routledge (2019).https://doi.org/10.1080/14783363.2017.1288565
15. Matthews, D.D.: The A3 Workbook: Unlock Your Problem-Solving Mind. CRC Press, Boca Raton (2018)
16. McDermott, O., Antony, J., Sony, M., Healy, T.: Critical failure factors for continuous improvement methodologies in the Irish MedTech industry. TQM J. (2022a)
17. McDermott, O., Antony, J., Sony, M., Looby, E.: A critical evaluation and measurement of organisational readiness and adoption for continuous improvement within a medical device manufacturer. Int. J. Manag. Sci. Eng. Manag. 1–11. Taylor & Francis (2022b). https://doi.org/10.1080/17509653.2022.2073917
18. McGrane, V., McDermott, O., Trubetskaya, A., Rosa, A., Sony, M.: The effect of medical device regulations on deploying a lean six sigma project. Processes **10**(11), 2303. MDPI (2022)
19. Nelson, S., McDermott, O.: Lean implementation in a painter/decorator micro enterprise: a case study. In: McDermott, O., Rosa, A., Sá, J.C., Toner, A. (eds.) Lean, Green and Sustainability. ELEC 2022. IFIP AICT, vol. 668, pp. 329–337. Springer, Cham (2023). https://doi.org/10.1007/978-3-031-25741-4_28
20. Nicholas, J.: Line Balancing Manual Assembly Processes using a Kaizen Blitz Approach in a Highly Regulated Industry, vol. 2, no. 1 (2019)
21. Nogueira, D.M.D.C., Sousa, P.S.A., Moreira, M.R.A.: The relationship between leadership style and the success of lean management implementation. Leadersh. Organ. Dev. J. **39**(6), 807–824. Emerald Publishing Limited (2018). https://doi.org/10.1108/LODJ-05-2018-0192
22. Ozgur, C., Kleckner, M., Li, Y.: Selection of statistical software for solving big data problems: a guide for businesses, students, and universities. SAGE Open **5**(2), 2158244015584379. SAGE Publications (2015). https://doi.org/10.1177/2158244015584379
23. Panayiotou, N., Stergiou, K.: Development of a retail supply chain process reference model incorporating Lean Six Sigma initiatives. Int. J. Lean Six Sigma (n.d.). https://doi.org/10.1108/IJLSS-04-2021-0079
24. Rosenfield Boeira, J.N. and Rosenfield Boeira, J.N. (2017), "First steps with lean", *Lean Game Development: Apply Lean Frameworks to the Process of Game Development*, Springer, pp. 9–21

25. Sá, J.C., et al.: A model of integration ISO 9001 with Lean six sigma and main benefits achieved. Total Qual. Manag. Bus. Excell. **33**(1–2), 218–242. Routledge (2022).https://doi.org/10.1080/14783363.2020.1829969
26. Snee, R., Hoerl, R.: Leading Six Sigma: A Step-by-Step Guide Based on Experience with GE and Other Six Sigma Companies, 1st edn. FT Press, Upper Saddle River, NJ (2002)
27. Sobek II, D.K., Smalley, A.: Understanding A3 Thinking: A Critical Component of Toyota's PDCA Management System, Productivity Press (2008)
28. Sony, M., Antony, J., Naik, S.: How do organizations implement an effective LSS initiative? A qualitative study. Benchmarking Int. J. **27**(5), 1657–1681. Emerald Publishing Limited (2020).https://doi.org/10.1108/BIJ-10-2019-0451
29. Sony, M., Naik, S., Therisa, K.: Why do organizations discontinue Lean Six Sigma initiatives? Int. J. Qual. Reliab. Manag. **36**(3), 420–436. Emerald Publishing Limited (2019)
30. Swarnakar, V., Bagherian, A., Singh, A.R.: Modeling critical success factors for sustainable LSS implementation in hospitals: an empirical study. Int. J. Qual. Reliab. Manag. **ahead-of-print**(ahead-of-print) (2021). https://doi.org/10.1108/IJQRM-04-2021-0099
31. Veena, T.R., Prabhushankar, G.V.: A literature review on lean, Six Sigma and ISO 9001:2015 in manufacturing industry to improve process performance. Int. J. Bus. Syst. Res. **13**(2), 162–180. Inderscience Publishers (2019). https://doi.org/10.1504/IJBSR.2019.098652
32. Wegler, S.: Lean Six Sigma Governance Modeling within the Project Management Office, The College of St. Scholastica (2019)

Implementing an Order Pull System into a Medical Device Company Using Define for Lean Six Sigma Methodology

Daniel O'Donoghue[1], Olivia McDermott[2(✉)], Anna Trubetskaya[1], Angelo Rosa[3], Manjeet Kharub[4], and Kathryn Cormican[2]

[1] Department of Engineering, University of Limerick, Limerick, Ireland
[2] College of Science and Engineering, University of Galway, Galway, Ireland
Olivia.McDermott@universityofgalway.ie
[3] Department of Mechanical Engineering, CVR College of Engineering, Hyderabad, India
[4] Department of Management Studies, Università LUM Jean Monnet, Bari, Italy

Abstract. This project aims to show how implementing continuous flow pull production with just-in-time Kanban processes in a Medical Device company can improve customer supply and thus mitigate device shortages in the Medtech supply chain. A case study in a medical device manufacturer utilised Define for Lean Six Sigma methodology for the design of a pull process and identification of waste in the process by using Value Stream Mapping and Kaizen events. A Pull model utilising Kanban and Hejunka was designed and implemented to produce products based only on customer demand signals. The device aged work orders in the process and waste reduced and overall service to the customer was improved while ensuring products were produced based on customer demand signals resulting in lead time and inventory reduction of over 60%, increased inventory turns, elimination of waste due to overproduction, holding inventory, and increased collaboration and communication between stakeholders. This is one of the few studies on implementing a Lean pull model in a medical device manufacturer and can be leveraged to improve supply chain accuracy and reliability. This study can demonstrate how supply chain shortages in devices that may affect patient treatments can be mitigated by embracing Lean methods.

Keyword: Leadership

1 Introduction

Quality management has always been fundamental to an organisation's success; it is needed to save money and remain competitive [1]. The ability to meet customer requirements is vital, and quality must be managed and include everyone within the organisation [2]. Many organisations are choosing Lean to aid quality management tools to assist with reducing cost, accelerating change, and protecting their reputation and see quality as crucial to attaining competitive advantage [3]. Driving the need for better quality and

Published by Springer Nature Switzerland AG 2024
T. van Kollenburg et al. (Eds.): ELEC 2023, IFIP AICT 681, pp. 306–326, 2024.
https://doi.org/10.1007/978-3-031-63265-5_23

operational excellence can help competition among organisations or stifle competitors, high customer expectations and ever-changing technology [4]. Lean and Six Sigma have been widely implemented in manufacturing because of their success rate in well-known organisations in increasing quality, speed, customer satisfaction and cost saving [5]. Where a design of a new process or product is required rather than simply improving an existing proves Design for Lean Six Sigma (DFLSS) has been demonstrated to ensure a process is "right first time" [6].

This research takes place in Company X, an EU member state-based Medical device manufacturer. The manufacturer is endeavouring to ensure a continuous supply of medical device sub-components to a sister plant in Asia where the components are assembled and thus ensure patients are not affected by adverse supply. There have been difficulties meeting customer demand due to shortages of the correct product in the EU-based manufacturing site, leading to last-minute order requests from their Asian plant. In addition, there is now a build-up of inventory in the production lines in the European manufacturing site due to variations in lead times within the manufacturing site from not fully understanding the customer demand. DFLSS will be utilised to identify a new process that will reduce waste, increase productivity, and have a continuous flow to meet customer demand. While there is much literature on Lean in manufacturing companies, there are scarce studies on Lean, Pull and Kanban implementation within the MedTech industry [7–9]. Some studies have attributed the lack of application of Lean in the medical device industry to the highly regulated nature of the industry which requires regulatory submissions to be made to different regulatory jurisdictional bodies when process changes are being made in order to maintain marketing authorisations [10]. However other studies have demonstrated high proliferation of Lean within the medical devices industry with up to 97% of the industry having Lean programs (McDermott, Antony, Sony and Healy, 2022; Trubetskaya *et al.*, 2022). However recent increased medical device legislation in Europe has meant increased stringency and controls in relation to device authorisation, coupled with a shortage of notified bodies to audit device manufacturers and backlogs in production and supply chain shortages caused by COVID-19 which has led to shortages of some medical devices in the global supply chain (McDermott, Antony, Sony and Healy, 2022; Melvin, 2022). Thus any opportunities to deploy Lean to improve the product supply chain and that does not impact the product (device) directly and eliminates regulatory product approval submissions are an opportunity for the medical device industry. Several studies have discussed the difficulties of Lean deployment in highly regulated industries such as the Medical Device or Pharma industry due to the delays in implementing changes if processes have to be revalidated [9, 10]. Indeed McGrane et al. (2022) discussed how a similarly scoped line installation project in a contract manufacturer versus a Medical Device manufacturer took about 4 months more to implement in a Medtech manufacturer.

This project aims to transform Company X's Supply Chain culture from a Lean push to pull by design a new press utilising DFLSS to deploying digital enabling Lean tools, processes and trained subject matter experts (SMEs) to enable smooth transition and adoption of Lean for one full value stream.

The research question (RQ) of this case study are to.

- Establish how a Pull program utilising DFLSS can be implemented to ensure right-first-time product release and maintenance of continuous supply to customers.

The structure of this paper is as follows. Following the introductory section, Sect. 2 provides a literature review, while Sect. 3 discusses the research design and methodology and provides the background of the study. Section 4 presents analyses of findings. Finally, Sect. 5 discusses the results, while Sect. 6 concludes with the practical lessons learned and future research opportunities.

2 Literature Review

Lean Six Sigma provides the methodology, approaches and tools needed for changing processes and is an efficient tool to prepare leaders to lead that change; while seeing improvements in people, quality, cost, and increased customer satisfaction, a systemic approach is required [13]. Lean is often referred to by many different names, such as "Lean Manufacturing", "Kaizen", and "Just-in-time", and the terms are substitutable in most cases [14]. Kaizen, or continuous improvement, is the management-driven environment that affects the organisation's cultural change to continuous improvement [15]. Lean and Kaizen are often mistakenly thought of as the same. Lean is finding and eliminating non-value-adding waste, while Kaizen seeks to find continuous incremental improvements in your process [16]. Value Stream Mapping can help you identify waste and use Kaizen events to facilitate these improvements. Leadership within the organisation must support a culture of continuous improvement and engage with its employees; this will allow Kaizen events to happen periodically and have targeted organisational changes[17].

Lean and responsive supply chains have transformed organisation's management of inventories [18]. Before the concept of Pull or Just in Time (JIT) was adopted in the Western world and prior to computers systems managing inventory, supply chains operated from manual Material Requirements Planning (MRP) combined with Master Scheduling, Rough-Cut Capacity Planning (RCCP), Capacity Requirements Planning (CRP) and Input/Output Control [19]. Just in Time (JIT) is an inventory-controlling tool used to manage levels of inventory. The fundamental principle of JIT is that the customer instigates the demand from the final operation, which triggers demand back through the supply chain, creating a "pull" system that issues the right parts at the right time with the right quantity [20]. Just-in-time production requires two components, Kanban and Heijunka (level production) [21].

Lean manufacturing aims to increase production by using fewer resources, removing wasteful activities and adding value to the final product (de Oliveira et al., 2019). The sustainability of Lean manufacturing relies on the engagement of the people in the organisation. Lean manufacturing has built its foundation on its people, and through this engagement, the success of future projects is dependent [22].

Lean investigates the mapping of end-to-end processes. Value Stream Mapping (VSM) is a Lean tool that allows analysis of a production process [23]. The VSM gives a graphical synopsis of the flow and information of production and its material while giving an insight into how they are connected and allows analysis of value-added steps, which in turn will allow improvements to be made along the value stream to find balance [24]. In addition, mapping out the current state from raw material to the customer allows you to see how it functions in real-time, identifies kaizens for the future state, and develops a deployment plan [25].

One of the key principles of Lean is a continuous flow, having continuous production without inventory build-up by facilitating the flow of material information and handling while improving productivity [20]. Pull production has received much applause because it is more attainable than continuous flow (Trubetskaya et al., 2022). The theory of Pull is to maintain levels of work in progress (WIP) at a continual level; a signal is sent from upstream processes once an order is initiated. One way to introduce pull is through supermarkets and Kanban, which allow products to be replaced promptly [19]. A supermarket is an inventory at the end of a pull system that stores items sorted by their part types in a first-in-first-out sequence. Whenever a part leaves the supermarket, a signal for reproduction is sent back to the production system [26]. Having a Kanban in place allows WIP to be regulated, smoother production flow, improved quality, and reduced cost [19]. The use of a supermarket will allow a quantity of material or product to be ready for use and will also help with scheduling production [20]. In addition, a JIT approach helps reduce non-value-added activities along the value stream [27]. Recent studies on Lean in Medtech companies have highlighted that Kanbans have advantages for establishing a level production flow [9].

Using tools such as Value Stream Mapping (VSM) incorrectly can have drawbacks instead of benefits; VSM is a hands-on approach and is dependent on the skill of the person carrying it out [28]. A cultural change is key in the deployment of Lean and affects the success of its introduction [29]. Lean research focuses on the implementation through phases but lacks a systematic approach and depends on people's common sense to use the correct set of tools and techniques [30]. Discussions of Lean implementation focus on deployment barriers, standards for implementation, and how to monitor after implementation but lack a framework to remove the barriers that affect implementation (de Oliveira et al., 2019). Changing leadership behaviour is more important as they influence quality management practices [31]. Lean can benefit the organisation, its people and, more importantly, its customers if implemented correctly. The introduction of Lean can eliminate waste and allow agile responses along the organisation's value stream [32]. Lean and six-sigma, combined with mutual techniques, give a more robust framework for implementation and sustaining into the future by having a bigger impact on customer satisfaction and problem-solving [23, 33].

Design for Lean Six Sigma (DFLSS) with it structured approach of Define, Measure, Analyse, Design and Verify (DMADV) has advantages for designing new processes rather than improving existing ones and has been effective particularly in new product design [34]. Studies have demonstrated the use of DFLSS for design of new housing [35], new processes [36] and new services [37].

3 Methodology

The case study approach is most suitable for an empirical study when work is scarce on the subject (Yin 2011), as there is in the case of literature related to Lean and Kanban implementation within the Medical Device manufacturing area [7, 39, 40]. Moreover, it further helps to understand the dynamics present within the presented context and setting to better understand the phenomenon under study (Yin 2016). In this instance, improving the continuous flow of products by implementing a pull system and maintaining customer supply in a medical device manufacturer is an understudied phenomenon; as such, a case approach was used. A single case study approach is applicable and useful if the phenomenon under investigation is unique, critical, and revelatory [42].

The organisation in the case study is based in an EU state, employs just under 500 support personnel, and has requested to remain anonymous. A push forecast process drives inaccurate inventory levels, and product mixes across product lines and results in high inventory and long cycle times. The company aid to design and implement a completely new process rather than "fix" the existing one. This project aims to transform the Company X Supply Chain culture from push to pull by deploying the DFLSS to design a new pull and kanban process, This new process will enable potentially more digital enabling Lean tools, processes and trained small and medium enterprise vendor (SMEs) to enable smooth transition and adoption for at least one full production value stream. A pilot program will allow introduction of new products onto the production line in a smoother, faster transition to pull manufacturing, and customers will receive what they want on time and in full following Lean principles [43]. As a new process will be designed for new product introduction the project will initially focus on one area – the metal inspection value stream of the device manufacturing site. to ensure cascading production and delivery instructions from downstream to upstream activities (pull) in which the upstream supplier produces nothing until the downstream customer signals a need (pull). The device components at the centre of this project are bought in from an external vendor, dimensionally and visually inspected, and go through a cleaning process before an interplant shipment, where they are assembled to make a device implant.

3.1 Lean Six Sigma Project Methodology Phases

The project will have five phases and will utilise the Lean Six sigma framework of Define, Measure, Analyse, Design and Validate (DMADV) and will utilise Lean tools and techniques. DMADV is a proven methodology for designing new processes correctly the first time due to its structured approach [44]. The project was aligned with the DMADV phases.

1. Define: This phase initiates the project by putting together a charter and defining the stakeholders via use of a Supplier, Input, Processes, Output, and Customer or SIPOC diagram.
2. Measure: This phase prepares the team for a successful implementation by creating a schedule, estimating correcting calculations for supermarket Kanbans, and beginning change management activities. This phase continues to execute the schedule and change management activities necessary to prepare stakeholders for the change. It also includes the physical and system implementation along with the initial tracking of metrics.
3. Analyse involved utilising data around supply and demand to establish what issues were in the existing processes in order to eliminate them in a newly design process.
4. Design resulted in a new proposed process and a "Future" Value steam Map.

5. Verify completed the improve and control aspects by closing the project but has measures to ensure the Pull System is sustained even after the project team disbands.

3.2 Define and Measure

Certain products within Company X are unsuitable for Pull based on their product lifecycle state or risk of recovery and therefore require a hybrid push-pull system [45]. To confirm whether a product fits the criteria for Pull, two criteria were used -the Surge Capacity capability and the stage of the product in its Life cycle. Surge capacity is the capability to expand beyond regular operations to accommodate a greater number of requests [46]. A lack of surge capacity leads to a higher risk of not recovering demand if the product inventory level falls. Company X's corporate goal is 85% forecast accuracy based on the estimated two months of prior customer demand. In terms of the Product Lifecycle Stage criteria, specifically, a new product can be volatile in demand levels as may be an end-of-life product and thus may not be suitable to realise the benefits of Pull. Product life stages can be broken into five stages, design, introduction, growth, maturity, and decline [47]. Each life cycle phase affects capacity and demand differently. For example, in the introduction, products are developed for a market, and demand is initially low; as it grows, demand increases, demand levels off during maturity, and during the decline, sales decrease [48].

After determining the few products that are not suitable for Pull, the final step is to prioritise the remaining products. This will allow the organisation to implement pull systems on critical products strategically. There are four decision factors below (Table 1) with instructions on determining eligibility for pull forecasting and kanban. Once the data has been gathered for each product or product family, the "Product Prioritisation" will help calculate the prioritisation rankings with appropriate weightings for inclusion in the pull system (Table 1).

Table 1. Decision factors and rating scale

Decision Factor	Suggested Weight	1 (Low)	2 (Med.)	3 (High)
Operational Capacity (Excess Capacity)	H	Excess Capacity: 5%	Excess Capacity: 15%	Excess Capacity: 30%
Raw Material Supply (Stability)	L			
Volume of Demand	M	1-15% of total volume	16-50% of total volume	50% or more of total volume
Stable Process Lead Time	M	10-20% variance	1-9% variance	0% variance

3.3 Analyse and Design

The aim of the project was to design a new process for pull from the start. Kaizen, Gemba, Value Steam Mapping and Non value add waste analysis were used to establish this.

A Gemba walk or going to the problem area and reviewing the process in real-time to gather the information was conducted to map the current state by walking the process end to end [26]. The next step completed a kaizen event to plan for the design of the technical elements of a Pull System. Kaizen is the Japanese term "change for good" and is an improvement method that is process oriented and should include people from all levels of the organisation [49]. An important aspect of this Kaizen Event will be to establish wastes in the process (Table 2) and create a VSM of the Current State as a precursor to the complete design of a new process. The data collected during the Gemba walk was applied to the map to create a completed current state map. This exercise identified areas in the value stream under study, such as the pre-cleaning area that would aid changing operations from a push to a customer-driven consumption-based replenishment system to improve the visibility of customer needs. Analysis of the current state (Fig. 1) identified inventory movement areas where in a new process design, Kanban, supermarkets, and pull signals could be established. From the Gemba walk, it was clear that overproduction was happening; components were issued without clear signals and sitting in a queue waiting to be worked on.

Analysis of the current state (Fig. 1) identified inventory movement areas where Kanban, supermarkets, and pull signals could be established. From the Gemba walk, it was clear that overproduction was happening; components were issued without clear signals and sitting in a queue waiting to be worked on.

Designing a new process.

The team started to design a future state "new" process (Fig. 2). A brainstorming session, was conducted to review the inputs, and output signals and identify supermarket locations (Fig. 2). For example, a supermarket Kanban would allow the team to hold a calculated inventory level and only build what was requested from the customer once a signal was received.

Initial physical implementation on the manufacturing floor was the next step. A brainstorming session after the Kaizen event identified the actions to implement Kanban's to stop overproduction and streamline the process. These actions included implementing Kanban cards, supermarket inventory levels, Kanban and visual systems, standard work and an overall audit process, a training plan and governance.

The team designed and created a digital Heijunka board (Fig. 3) which levels the release of production Kanban's for supply chain and operation team members. This aids production levelling and removes fluctuations in product flow [50]. Once a pull signal is received from the customer, the system will auto-generate a work order, which is sorted and placed into physical Kanban's and automated signals are sent throughout the system to start production.

During the Kaizen event, the team identified excess WIP sitting in production and not moving. Then, the team calculated the total Kanban quantity, which would communicate what part, quantity and location would be required to top up the material. These levels are important as they indicate when to start and stop production; when levels are low, orders are created to fill the Kanban and stop overproduction once the maximum level is reached [51]. Finally, the following equation was used, which dictates the supermarket size:

$$\text{Total Kanban quantity} = \text{Usage (per day) X Lead Time (days) X Safety Factor}$$

Table 2. Types of Waste Identified

Overproduction	Issue	New Design actions
Inventory	Excess inventory was being held in the warehouse and on production lines (particularly at the material supply stage) In general all areas were holding too much inventory	Kanban - a supermarket Kanban would allow the team to hold a calculated inventory level and only build what was requested from the customer once a signal was received Kanban's aid Visual management Install systematic/physical Pull signals Kanban cards
Transport	Moving inventory, components and finished goods	Kanban Visual Management Pull signals Hejunka
Motion	Looking for components	Kanban Cards/Visual Management Hejunka
Waiting	There were times where there was no orders to work on -not level loaded Stock outs of inventory	Pull process and signals -eliminate querying Hejunka
Under utilisation of employee skillset	Employees told to work on a "push" rather than a "pull" system	Standard work Kanban Cards 5S Hejunka
Over processing	Extra processing of inventory, orders handling	Standard work Pull system 5S Kanban signaling
Defects	Excess inventory leading to damage	Small work order sizes, less handling and Kanban signaling
Over production	Components were being issued despite no need to do so and subsequently were queued	Hejunka Pull signals Kanban

The safety factor is used to buffer usage and lead-time variability. A safety factor will incorporate reservations of processing time, supplier replenishment lead time, and demand variability[52]. Within the case study organisation, the typical safety factor is 1.5.

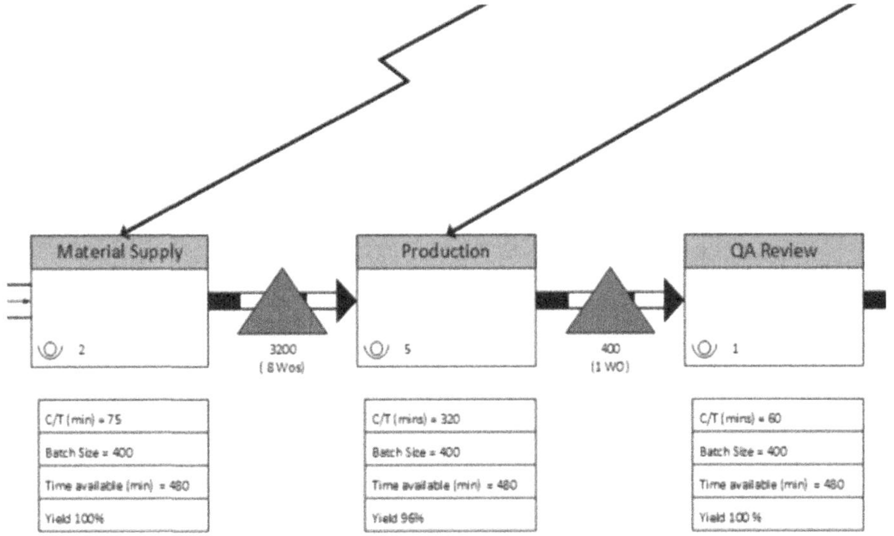

Fig. 1. Current state value stream map of the production process (Note: the process area of the VSM map where there is a key areas of focus is enlarged rather than demonstrate the entire map)

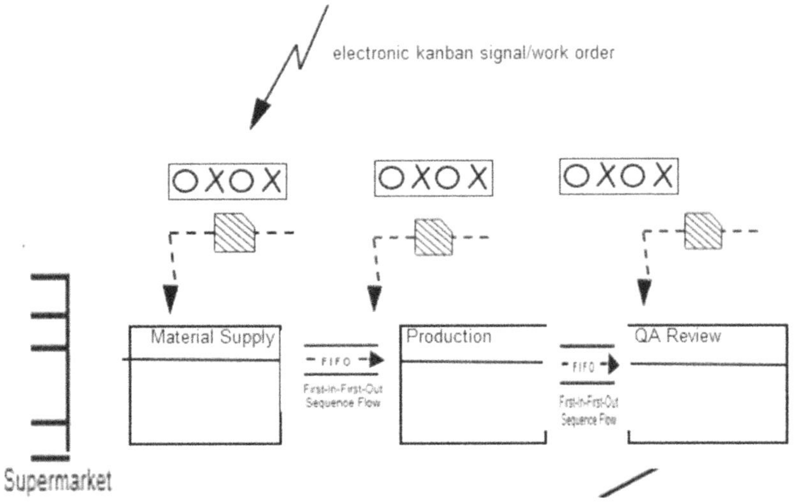

Fig. 2. New "Future" Value stream Map (only the area of interest is enlarged/represented here)

Next, the minimum and maximum Kanban bin size was calculated. The team opted to use a two-bin system where one card/bin is at the point of use (being consumed) and one card/bin is either in stock or re-stocked [21]. Once the first bin has been consumed, a trigger is sent to replenish, and material from the second bin can be used while the first is being re-stocked and is a repeating process [53]. Therefore, the Material Requirements

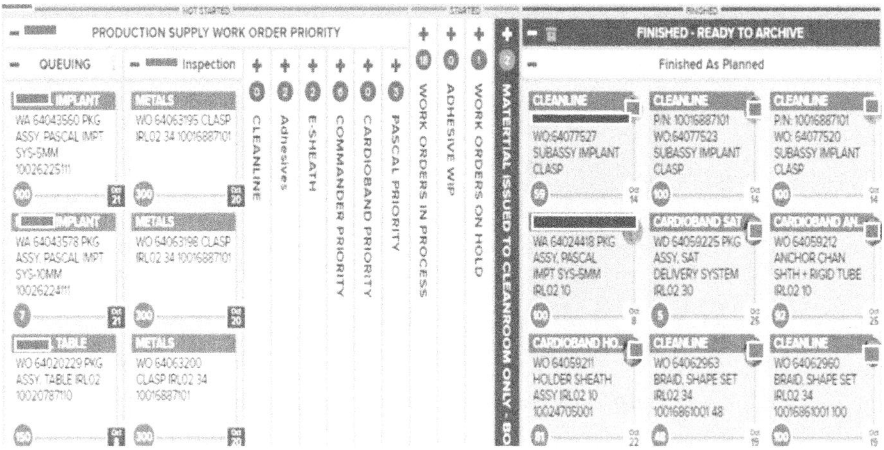

Fig. 3. Digital Hejunka Board

planning (MRP) system to needs to reflect the supermarket and WIP sizes and establish replenishment signals to create a signal to trigger work order creation (Table 3).

Table 3. Kanban bin size calculation

P/N	Descriptions	Lot size	Current Stock	In-transit	SNG weekly Demand	SG Daily go Rate (DGR)	Cycle-time	Safety Factor	2 Bin	KANBAN	ROUND to LOT Size
1234	BRAID,	100	248	0	238	48	3.0	1.5	2	428.4	500
3456	PADDLE, NARROW	300	579	0	474	95	3.0	1.5	2	853.2	900
5678	SUBASSY, CLASP	100	539	0	474	95	3.0	1.5	2	853.2	900
7891	CLASP, PLATE	300	522	0	474	95	3.0	1.5	2	853.2	900

After the Kaizen and initial implementation, a consistent governance process must be followed to ensure that the supermarket sizes and Kanban card quantities remain accurate to changing demand and other factors. In addition, to monitor the process and take a proactive approach to determine if the system is working, a dashboard is the tool used to monitor.

Next, the team set up physical locations and visual displays, enabling controls and allowing everyone to work in sync by clearly understanding what is required at that point in time. Figure 4 shows the storage of material prior to inspection. The material was stored in a cage with no clear indication of the required inventory levels nor was there a first in, first out (FIFO) operation in place. The raw material was kitted into smaller work order sizes when a work order was required.

The team brainstormed through various options on how to store pre-inspected material efficiently. The most important aspect of the physical storage was to ensure that inventory levels could easily identify abnormalities. Below, Fig. 5 shows an example of

Fig. 4. Material storage Pre-Pull implementation

the interim storage introduced for work orders before periodic pull signals were turned on. Work orders were kitted for the week based on the build plan and allowed all tiered levels in the process to visually see what was to be inspected each day through First in, first out (FIFO).

Fig. 5. Work order storage FIFO

The final steps were to train all personnel involved in the process in the new system, standard work and audit system established during the kaizen event. This was extremely important to align everyone involved who did not get to participate in the Kaizen or design the systems.

3.4 Verify

A digital kanban dashboard was created to ensure that the new system is working properly after implementation; Fig. 6 is a snapshot from the Kanban "health" report. This gives a visual real time image of the stock levels for all items on the Pull system. Ideally all items should be above 65% inventory or stock levels to ensure effective use and productivity of the production line.

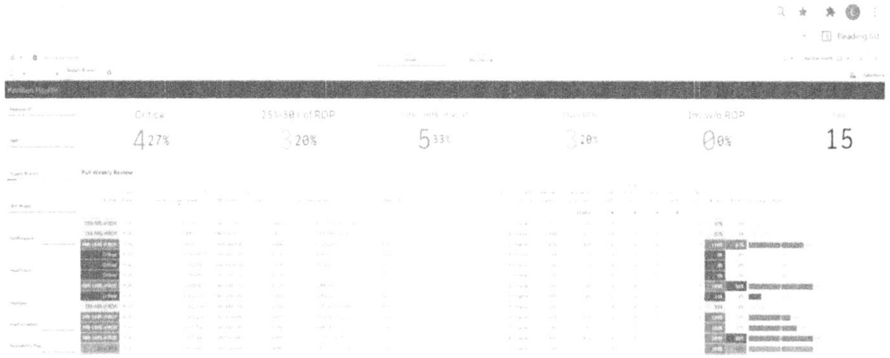

Fig. 6. Kanban Health Check (sized for example purposes only and to protect anonymity of case study organisation)

If any monitored metrics do not meet the site or operational standards, this will allow decisions to be made. For example, changes or decisions may be needed based on production and replenishment progress identify and take actions to mitigate for low-inventory items to avoid shortages and analyse Min/Max inventory values against actual demand so bin sizes can adjusted as demand changes over time. A check to ascertain if the minimum bin quantity by part number is below 50% triggers a systematic alert.

During the verify and monitoring phase, the team collected and brainstormed continuous improvement ideas for waste reduction and presence of wastes on the new design in terms of Transportation, Inventory, Motion, Waiting, Overproduction, Overprocessing and Defects (TIM WOODS). Any improvement ideas were reviewed by the team and a decision on whether suggestions were approved or not.

With the Pull System, some metrics must be tracked daily and weekly at the core team level to ensure the system performs as intended. The metrics to be measured are work-in-progress (WIP) inventory, lead time, and plan build versus actual build. These metrics will be incorporated into the Tier 1 and Tier 2 level plant metrics. Therefore, incorporating these meetings becomes an important part of the agenda and discussion. In addition to adding the metrics to the meetings, checking the Pull System levels and metrics was incorporated into the weekly management and project team Gemba walk. This allows all managers and supervisors to assess the system also.

4 Results

4.1 Qualitative Results

A set of short informal interviews was carried out with the Supply chain buyers, planners and schedulers to assess the effect of the new pull system. Some comments were extrapolated in Table 4.

Table 4. Planner feedback on the Pull system

"It was a quick implementation, It will be easy to use and easy to maintain. I can see this system working very well autonomously"
"The regional inventory in South America and North America almost immediately dropped by 5%. I expect more inventory right sixing as the demand signals reflect true customer demand"
"Previously the build plan for the following week was delayed until the end of the week and would delay the pick. Now the work orders are generated by Monday morning"
"I used to spend several hours a week manually reviewing and planning against the forecasts, now it automatic and transparent"

4.2 Quantitative Results

An essential metric for the Company X site is the schedule adherence to plan versus actual. The plan versus the actual schedule maintained accuracy during the implementation phase. For example, although the build plan was missed once, this was due to a component shortage from the supplier rather than an issue with the system.

While the monthly build plan percentages were good or performing well the team investigated gaps within the process to ensure the maturity of the process. When production started at company X's site and initially appeared in control before customer orders and production were ramped up -the backlog quickly went beyond eight days. As seen in Fig. 7, during the implementation phase of the new replenishment pull system, aged work orders were reduced from over 8 days to over 5 and then dropped to below three days once the automated system was introduced. This was due to work orders only being downloaded and processed when a signal came through from the customer (i.e. pull).

Yield is also a critical metric that the site measure. Moving to a pull system allowed the team to give live feedback to the supplier on issues that were received or found. For example, one-month post-implementation, some components were received in with defects. The reduction of WIP allowed for a faster reaction time on the line and allowed Company X to identify all supplier lots that had been affected. This allowed minimal impact on Company X's yield and prevented any defective product from leaving the site. Company X was thus also able to receive a credit note from the supplier for any incoming defects, which positively impacted company X's finances.

A full suite of supply chain metrics after the project is demonstrated in Table 5.

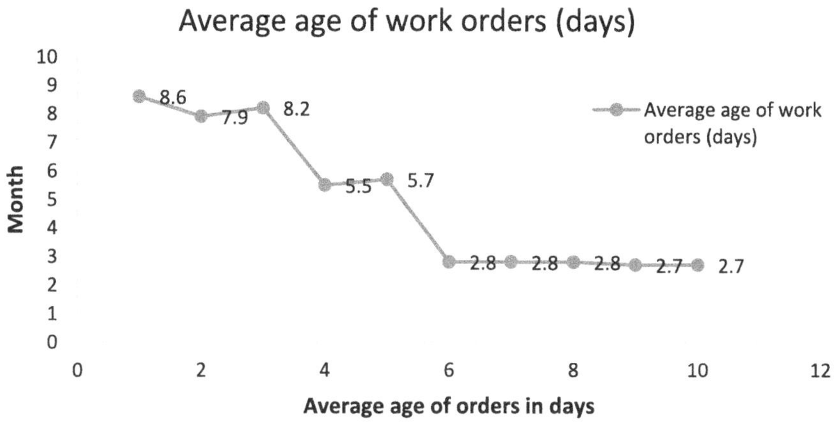

Fig. 7. Aged Work Orders before, during and after project (10 month period)

While many metrics were measured before the project some were new e.g. Number of suppliers onboarded to the pull/kanban system, the adherence to the 2 bin kanban system as well as the internal service level agreement of no more than 1 day for inventory to arrive from the supplier to the production floor once an order has been placed to ensure kanban replenishment. The researchers are prohibited from sharing exact cost and volume information to maintain the confidentiality and anonymity of the case study organisation.

Table 5. Supply chain metrics After project

Metric	*Improvement*
Production Planning/Schedule Adherence	*50%*
Capacity Planning Accuracy	*50%*
Work in Progress (WIP) Reduction	*20%*
Average Lead time reduction	*25%*
Number of Suppliers on board to pull/kanban system	*100%*
Finished goods productivity	*8%*
2 Bin system	*100%*
Internal Pull from Warehouse to Manufacturing Line	*50%*
Regional Inventory Levels	*50%*
Aged Work Orders	*62%*
Service Level Agreement adherence of 1 day (for delivery of components to floor)	*100%*

(*continued*)

Table 5. (*continued*)

Metric	*Improvement*
Raw material pull from vendor in euros	*33%*
Raw material pull from vendor in volume	*33%*
Raw material on hand in inventory planning	*100%*

Another benefit the team saw was the quality standards were not dropping. There were no quality nonconformance reports (NCRs) to address any deviations from company X's procedures due to the new pull implementation. The only NCR raised for the year was a discrepancy count unrelated to the project. The number of customer-related Field Corrective actions (FCAs) was maintained at zero, and no subsequent FCAs were raised due to the project (Table 6).

Table 6. Snapshot of Company X Quality scorecard post-project implementation

Quality Metrics	Goal	Past Quarter	Year to Date
Field corrective Actions (FCA)	<2	0	0
Non Conformance Reports (NCR's) closed	85% <45 days	1	1
Non Conformance Reports (NCR's) opened	n/a	1	1

5 Discussion

The research objective of this study was to demonstrate how the case study organisation implemented and piloted a pull program utilising Lean principles to ensure right-first-time product release and maintenance of continuous supply. The results from the project reveal that by implementing a pull system, significant savings in inventory and WIP can be achieved by removing waste from the process. These results align with the Lean literature in terms of the effect of a JIT Kanban system reducing WIP, inventory, and waste while continuously maintaining supply (Hopp and Spearman, 2004; Kumar and Panneerselvam, 2007).

The project was successful due to the focus on creating an automated system rather than a manual one. Utilising software to track the material flow in production systems, automatically generating and providing users with real-time value stream data and then allowing users to remotely supervise the performance of their production facility has been shown to be more efficient than manual tracking [55].

Much of the literature on Kanban implementation refers to the importance of training; leadership; commitment; teamwork; systematic quality management; communication; housekeeping; and visual management [56]. This study's results show that management support was important in resourcing the project, and teamwork was instrumental in developing an end-to-end pull system, JIT and Kanban system involving all stakeholders. The role of senior management played a critical role in the success of this project. The project team were enabled to design an entirely new process and thus enabled with the relevant IT support and financial budget to do this. The project had backing from the beginning, and the OMI audit's results echoed this support. Each area accessed under this project doubled its score in 2019, giving the team huge recognition. While completing the project, there was a 20% customer demand volume increase in Company X and by adapting the pull model ensured the company only produced what the customer demanded as new product lines transited to the pull system.

Housekeeping and utilising error proofing Poke Yoke helped optimise and design the system from the beginning and eliminated human errors. Visual management through the use of storage systems, digital Hejunka boards, key performance indicator scorecards and Kanban health checks helped aid in monitoring and managing the Kanban process. Digital Kanban's eliminated potential problems with physical Kanban cards being lost or lack of disciple in keeping them accurate [21, 56]. The digitisation of the Kanban was optimal for preventing non-value add wastes such as creating kanban cards manually [57, 58].

There were some difficulties to overcome in establishing systems to support JIT, ensuring that data was available and accurate and establishing accounting support for JIT and lack of JIT information which can be common in kanban implementation [59].

Sustainability is an important aspect of pull processes and Kanban's [56, 60]. The project team ensured that the implemented processes were sustainable using KPI scorecards, daily and weekly performance reviews, and Hejunka board tracking. In addition, a monthly compliance meeting was set up with the functional leaders to maintain positive results. Throughout this meeting, Kanban health will be reviewed, and any changes to inventory levels can be requested, by having these open discussions will eliminate old habits creeping into the process.

As mentioned previously, visual management enabled everyone to work in synchronisation by clearly understanding what was required at that point in time from a materials point of view. Visual controls such as the Kanban health dashboard contribute to the management of every process in a way that individuals alone cannot do by showing where the discrepancies occur. The system provided visibility of supermarket inventory levels to facilitate the decision-making on when to replenish an empty bin. This allowed communication and signalling between manufacturing and planning. Having a system set up of a pull system consisted of inputs and updates to information systems and the requisite work to configure those systems to support the implementation, maintenance, and facilitation of the pull activities.

Hassan *et al.* (2022) discuss the importance of management support and having a core project team for Kanban implementation. While there was a dedicated project team in this project in company X, they were limited in the total time they could give each week. However having autonomy to work on the Kaizen aided success [61]. The pull process Kaizen event meant time away from day-to-day roles, and this often-meant long days and frustrations as other business commitments had to be met. This did have a knock-on effect and caused a delay in rolling out the pull process to new production lines. The time required to assess the process, develop pull signals, and implement them does need dedicated resources to prevent other work from suffering due to a lack of focus.

6 Conclusion

The main aim of this project was to create a model utilising DFLSS in which new products could be implemented on a pull system. The study involved piloting and implementation of a pull model on a product line. As a result, the Pull system was fully implemented and reduced aged work orders from an average 8.2 days to 3.8 days over a 10 month period. This has given the organisation more flexibility to respond to changing demands and reduced inventory sitting in process.

Using Lean methodologies created a culture of engagement, focused the site on continuous improvement, and built people capabilities by training and educating people on Lean processes, tools, and systems. A cross-functional view allowed stakeholders from each area to have their opinions and concerns addressed. Taking this approach to all problems ensures a more robust system that will be sustained into the future. This study can provide a benchmark for other Medtech companies proposing to implement a pull model and can be leveraged by other organisations to leverage the learnings.

The limitations of this study are that as it was a single case study, it could be argued that the results are not generalisable. Also, the formula used to calculate inventory levels has proven to work within the organisation. However, further research is required to show if the hypothesis can be used in other businesses within company X to strengthen the conclusion. The potential benefits of this project are as a model to use when new products transfer to the European Union-based site. Future opportunities involve Company X working with their suppliers to ensure they do not encounter any supply chain bottlenecks, as there have been occasions where the suppliers have not had a shipment out on time, which has had an impact on production waiting on materials. In summary this study demonstrates how Lean and Kanban can be deployed in medical device manufacturing and ensure patient and customer continuity of supply thus avoiding potential exacerbation of patient health issues and supply chain shortages.

References

1. Hernandez-Matias, J.C., Ocampo, J.R., Hidalgo, A., Vizan, A.: Lean manufacturing and operational performance. J. Manuf. Technol. Manag. **31**, 217–235 (2020). https://doi.org/10.1108/JMTM-04-2019-0140
2. Evans, L.: Introduction to six sigma introduction to six sigma and process improvement. Jakarta: Salemba Four (2005)
3. Hoerl, R.W., Gardner, M.M.: Lean Six Sigma, creativity, and innovation. Int. J. Lean Six Sigma. **1**, 30–38 (2010). https://doi.org/10.1108/20401461011033149

4. de Oliveira, R.I., Sousa, S.O., de Campos, F.C.: Lean manufacturing implementation: bibliometric analysis 2007–2018. Int. J. Adv. Manuf. Technol. **101**, 979–988 (2019). https://doi.org/10.1007/s00170-018-2965-y
5. Laureani, A., Antony, J.: Standards for Lean Six Sigma certification. Int. J. Product. Perform. Manag. **61**, 110–120 (2012). https://doi.org/10.1108/17410401211188560
6. Thomas, M., Singh, N.: Design for lean six sigma (DFLSS): philosophy, tools, potential and deployment challenges in automotive product development. SAE International, Warrendale, PA (2006). https://doi.org/10.4271/2006-01-0503
7. Iyede, R., Fallon, E.F., Donnellan, P.: An exploration of the extent of Lean Six Sigma implementation in the West of Ireland. Int. J. Lean Six Sigma **9**, 444–462 (2018). https://doi.org/10.1108/IJLSS-02-2017-0018
8. McDermott, O., Antony, J., Sony, M., Healy, T.: Critical failure factors for continuous improvement methodologies in the Irish MedTech industry. TQM J. **34**, 18–38 (2022). https://doi.org/10.1108/TQM-10-2021-0289
9. Trubetskaya, A., Manto, D., McDermott, O.: A review of lean adoption in the Irish MedTech industry. Processes **10**, 391 (2022). https://doi.org/10.3390/pr10020391
10. McGrane, V., McDermott, O., Trubetskaya, A., Rosa, A., Sony, M.: The effect of medical device regulations on deploying a Lean Six Sigma project. Processes **10**, 2303 (2022)
11. McDermott, O., Antony, J., Sony, M., Healy, T.: Critical failure factors for continuous improvement methodologies in the Irish MedTech industry. TQM J. (2022)
12. Melvin, T.: The European medical device regulation-what biomedical engineers need to know. IEEE J. Transl. Eng. Health Med. **10**, 1–5 (2022). https://doi.org/10.1109/JTEHM.2022.3194415
13. Antony, J.: Design for six sigma: a breakthrough business improvement strategy for achieving competitive advantage. Work study (2002)
14. Avelar, W., Meiriño, M., Tortorella, G.L.: The practical relationship between continuous flow and lean construction in SMEs. TQM J. **32**, 362–380 (2020). https://doi.org/10.1108/TQM-05-2019-0129
15. Sundar, R., Balaji, A.N., Kumar, R.M.S.: A review on lean manufacturing implementation techniques. Procedia Eng. **97**, 1875–1885 (2014). https://doi.org/10.1016/j.proeng.2014.12.341
16. Kumar, S., Dhingra, A.K., Singh, B.: Process improvement through Lean-Kaizen using value stream map: a case study in India. Int. J. Adv. Manuf. Technol. **96**, 2687–2698 (2018). https://doi.org/10.1007/s00170-018-1684-8
17. Kikuchi, T., Suzuki, M.: Kaizen and standardization. In: Otsuka, K., Jin, K., Sonobe, T. (eds.) Applying theKaizen in Africa, pp. 111–149. Springer, Cham (2018). https://doi.org/10.1007/978-3-319-91400-8_4
18. Sharma, P., Kulkarni, M.S.: Framework for a dynamic and responsive. Int. J. Product. Perform. Manag. **65**, 207–222 (2016). https://doi.org/10.1108/IJPPM-07-2014-0113
19. Hopp, W.J., Spearman, M.L.: To pull or not to pull: what is the question? M&SOM **6**, 133–148 (2004). https://doi.org/10.1287/msom.1030.0028
20. Kumar, C.S., Panneerselvam, R.: Literature review of JIT-KANBAN system. Int. J. Adv. Manuf. Technol. **32**, 393–408 (2007). https://doi.org/10.1007/s00170-005-0340-2
21. Matzka, J., Di Mascolo, M., Furmans, K.: Buffer sizing of a Heijunka Kanban system. J. Intell. Manuf. **23**, 49–60 (2012). https://doi.org/10.1007/s10845-009-0317-3
22. Tortorella, G.L., Vergara, L.G.L., Ferreira, E.P.: Lean manufacturing implementation: an assessment method with regards to socio-technical and ergonomics practices adoption. Int. J. Adv. Manuf. Technol. **89**, 3407–3418 (2017). https://doi.org/10.1007/s00170-016-9227-7
23. Byrne, B., McDermott, O., Noonan, J.: Applying Lean Six Sigma methodology to a pharmaceutical manufacturing facility: a case study. Processes **9**, 550 (2021). https://doi.org/10.3390/pr9030550

24. Gurumurthy, A., Kodali, R.: Design of lean manufacturing systems using value stream mapping with simulation. J. Manuf. Technol. Manag. **22**, 444–473 (2011). https://doi.org/10.1108/17410381111126409
25. Vamsi Krishna Jasti, N., Sharma, A.: Lean manufacturing implementation using value stream mapping as a tool. Int. J. Lean Six Sigma **5**, 89–116 (2014). https://doi.org/10.1108/IJLSS-04-2012-0002
26. Rother, M., Shook, J.: Learning to see: value stream mapping to add value and eliminate muda. Lean Enterprise Institute (2003)
27. Fullerton, R.R., McWatters, C.S.: The production performance benefits from JIT implementation. J. Oper. Manag. **19**, 81–96 (2001). https://doi.org/10.1016/S0272-6963(00)00051-6
28. Forno, A.J.D., Pereira, F.A., Forcellini, F.A., Kipper, L.M.: Value stream mapping: a study about the problems and challenges found in the literature from the past 15 years about application of Lean tools. Int. J. Adv. Manuf. Technol. **72**, 779–790 (2014). https://doi.org/10.1007/s00170-014-5712-z
29. Mann, D.: Creating a Lean Culture: Tools to Sustain Lean Conversions. Productivity Press, New York (2015)
30. Psomas, E., Antony, J.: Research gaps in Lean manufacturing: a systematic literature review. Int. J. Qual. Reliab. Manag. **36**, 815–839 (2019). https://doi.org/10.1108/IJQRM-12-2017-0260
31. Laureani, A., Brady, M., Antony, J.: Applications of Lean Six Sigma in an Irish hospital. Leadersh. Health Serv. **26**, 322–337 (2013). https://doi.org/10.1108/LHS-01-2012-0002
32. Ahmed, W.: Understanding alignment between lean and agile strategies using Triple-A model. Int. J. Prod. Perform. Manag. **71**, 1810–1828 (2021)
33. Slattery, O., Trubetskaya, A., Moore, S., McDermott, O.: A review of Lean methodology application and its integration in medical device new product introduction processes. Processes **10**, 2005 (2022). https://doi.org/10.3390/pr10102005
34. Cronemyr, P.: DMAIC and DMADV - differences, similarities and synergies. Int. J. Six Sigma Comp. Adv. **3**, 193–209 (2007). https://doi.org/10.1504/IJSSCA.2007.015065
35. Johnson, J., Gitlow, H., Widener, S., Popovich, E.: Designing new housing at the University of Miami: a "Six Sigma" DMADV/DFSS case study. Qual. Eng. **18**, 299–323 (2006)
36. Huang, C.-T., Chen, K.-S., Chang, T.-C.: An application of DMADV methodology for increasing the yield rate of surveillance cameras. Microelectron. Reliab. **50**, 266–272 (2010)
37. Pun, K.F., Chin, K.S., Lau, H.: A QFD/hoshin approach for service quality deployment: a case study. Manag. Serv. Qual. Int. J. **10**, 156–170 (2000). https://doi.org/10.1108/09604520010336687
38. Yin, R.K.: Qualitative Research from Start to Finish. The Guilford Press, New York (2011)
39. Brown, A., Eatock, J., Dixon, D., Meenan, B.J., Anderson, J.: Quality and continuous improvement in medical device manufacturing. TQM J. **20**, 541–555 (2008). https://doi.org/10.1108/17542730810909329
40. McDermott, O., Antony, J., Sony, M., Looby, E.: A critical evaluation and measurement of organisational readiness and adoption for continuous improvement within a medical device manufacturer. Null. 1–11 (2022). https://doi.org/10.1080/17509653.2022.2073917
41. Yin, R.: Case Study Research Design and Methods. Sage, Thousand Oaks (2016)
42. Eisenhardt, K.M., Graebner, M.E.: Theory building from cases: opportunities and challenges. AMJ **50**, 25–32 (2007). https://doi.org/10.5465/amj.2007.24160888
43. Agyeman, N.E.S.: The impacts of lean principles on the production of civil aircraft in Boeing. Aircr. Eng. Aerosp. Technol. **93**, 212–217 (2021). https://doi.org/10.1108/AEAT-05-2020-0107

44. Antony, J., Lancastle, J., McDermott, O., Bhat, S., Parida, R., Cudney, E.: An evaluation of Lean and Six Sigma methodologies in the UK national health services. Int. J. Qual. Reliab. Manag. **40**, 25–52 (2021)
45. Fowler, J.W., Kim, S.-H., Shunk, D.L.: Design for customer responsiveness: decision support system for push–pull supply chains with multiple demand fulfillment points. Decis. Support Syst. **123**, 113071 (2019). https://doi.org/10.1016/j.dss.2019.113071
46. Bonnett, C.J., et al.: Surge capacity: a proposed conceptual framework. Am. J. Emerg. Med. **25**, 297–306 (2007). https://doi.org/10.1016/j.ajem.2006.08.011
47. Magnan, G.M., Fawcett, S.E., Birou, L.M.: Benchmarking manufacturing practice using the product life cycle. Benchmarking Int. J. **6**, 239–253 (1999). https://doi.org/10.1108/14635779910288523
48. Zou, B., Guo, F., Guo, J.: Absorptive capacity, technological innovation, and product life cycle: a system dynamics model. Springerplus **5**, 1662 (2016). https://doi.org/10.1186/s40064-016-3328-5
49. Carnerud, D.: 25 years of quality management research - outlines and trends. Int. J. Qual. Reliab. Manag. **35**, 208–231 (2018). https://doi.org/10.1108/IJQRM-01-2017-0013
50. Ohno, T.: Toyota Production System: Beyond Large-Scale Production (1988)
51. Yan, H.: The optimal number of Kanbans in a manufacturing system with general machine breakdowns and stochastic demands. Int. J. Oper. Prod. Manag. **15**, 89–103 (1995). https://doi.org/10.1108/01443579510099670
52. Klankamsorn, S.: Determination of the number of Kanban for automotive axle production. In: 2021 The 8th International Conference on Industrial Engineering and Applications (Europe), pp. 115–120. Association for Computing Machinery, New York (2021). https://doi.org/10.1145/3463858.3463877
53. Suominen, M.: Implementing Kanban in the operational purchasing process of two-bin items: a case study in the metal industry (2020)
54. Sharma, H., Sohani, N., Yadav, A.: Structural modeling of lean supply chain enablers: a hybrid AHP and ISM-MICMAC based approach. J. Eng. Design Technol. **21**, 1658-1689 (2023). https://doi.org/10.1108/JEDT-08-2021-0419
55. Chen, K., Chen, J.C., Cox, R.A.: Real time facility performance monitoring system using RFID technology. Assem. Autom. **32**, 185–196 (2012). https://doi.org/10.1108/01445151211212334
56. Hassan, M.G., Akanmu, M.D., Ponniah, P., Mohd Sharif, K.I., Belal, H.M., Othman, A.: A framework for implementing a supplier Kanban system through an action research methodology. Benchmarking Int. J. ahead-of-print (2022). https://doi.org/10.1108/BIJ-12-2020-0656
57. Antony, J., McDermott, O., Powell, D.J., Sony, M.: Mapping the terrain for Lean Six Sigma 4.0. In: Powell, D.J., Alfnes, E., Holmemo, M.D.Q., Reke, E. (eds.) Learning in the Digital Era: 7th European Lean Educator Conference, ELEC 2021, Trondheim, Norway, October 25–27, 2021, Proceedings, pp. 193–204. Springer, Cham (2021). https://doi.org/10.1007/978-3-030-92934-3_20
58. Chiarini, A., Kumar, M.: Lean Six Sigma and Industry 4.0 integration for Operational Excellence: evidence from Italian manufacturing companies. Production Planning & Control. 0, 1–18 (2020). https://doi.org/10.1080/09537287.2020.1784485
59. Bortolini, M., Calabrese, F., Galizia, F., Mora, C.: A three-objective optimization model for mid-term sustainable supply chain network design. Comput. Ind. Eng. **168**, 108131 (2022). https://doi.org/10.1016/j.cie.2022.108131

60. Rahman, N.A.A., Sharif, S.M., Esa, M.M.: Lean manufacturing case study with Kanban system implementation. Procedia Econ. Finan. **7**, 174–180 (2013). https://doi.org/10.1016/S2212-5671(13)00232-3
61. Kharub, M., Gupta, H., Rana, S., McDermott, O.: Employee's performance and Kaizen events' success: does supervisor behaviour play a moderating role? TQM J. (2023, ahead-of-print). https://doi.org/10.1108/TQM-06-2022-0203

Challenges for Optimal Efficiency in Pull Production Within Complex Production Systems: A Literature Review

José Dinis-Carvalho(✉) and Helena Macedo

Department of Production and Systems, University of Minho, Guimarães, Portugal
{dinis,helena}@dps.uminho.pt

Abstract. One of the most relevant paradigms shifts that has happened in manufacturing in the last decades is the concept of pull production. This principle of operational excellence developed by Toyota in the 1950s has brought significant improvements in global productivity and delivery times. Several techniques have been developed to materialise pull production however, the enormity of challenges becomes evident as factors such as product variety, demand variability, and the need for batch and series size reduction escalate. The main difficulty is to achieve tight deadlines while maintaining productivity and machine utilization at high levels in complex production environments. Approaches such as Kanban, CONWIP, POLCA, or COBACABANA confront adaptation issues in complex production units with a wide range of articles, routes, and batch sizes. This study's literature review seeks to uncover the vulnerabilities of existing pull production techniques in dealing with complex environments. By carrying out a thorough examination and analysis of Kanban, CONWIP, POLCA and COBACABANA, the vulnerabilities of these pull production approaches will be revealed.

Keywords: Pull production · Complex production systems · Kanban · ConWIP · POLCA · COBACABANA

1 Introduction

Today's industrial organizations operate in a highly competitive context, where the demand for high-quality, high-productivity, and cost-effective products is relentless. The emergence of mass customization environments, driven by diverse customer demands and a need for efficiency comparable to mass production, necessitates the adoption of sophisticated and complex production systems [1, 2]. In some cases, highly personalized orders might not be repeated and hence cannot be maintained in stock, these businesses frequently have to juggle a variety of unique order specifications and need to answer to customers' demands at short notice. Effective flow control of materials plays a vital role in achieving optimal performance in these complex production systems [3]. In order to keep the shop floor and each station busy while simultaneously delivering confirmed orders in a timely manner, companies that operate in this complex environment must find a balance between the rate at which orders are received and their capacity [4].

Published by Springer Nature Switzerland AG 2024
T. van Kollenburg et al. (Eds.): ELEC 2023, IFIP AICT 681, pp. 327–343, 2024.
https://doi.org/10.1007/978-3-031-63265-5_24

Creating a continuous flow is lean production's ultimate objective [5] as clearly expressed in the Lean Principles [6] and in the Value Stream Mapping methodology [7, 8]. Through the limitation of work in progress (WIP), Pull production (pull for short) approaches offer a valuable strategy for inventory management and regulation of throughput times [9–11]. Despite the various methods and tools available for establishing a pull production system, they all share a common explicit feature: the limiting of WIP within the production system, which is the characteristic that distinguishes a pull system from a push one [12]. Pull systems manage WIP by restricting releases into the system, resulting in a reduced average WIP level. According to Little's Law, this also results in lower throughput times [13]. Pull Production is a very powerful concept that has been applied with very good results in terms of performance improvements in modern production organizations. This concept has revolutionized the way in which the progression of materials/parts/products through the various machines (or other process steps) is managed. It is one of the most impactful concepts of TPS (Toyota Production System) [9] and perhaps the most counterintuitive, since even today many managers do not understand it or its role in performance such as productivity and lead time. To emphasize the important role of this concept in the entire paradigm shift created by TPS, pull production, or Just-In-Time, as it is referred to in the same Taiichi Ohno's book, it is one of only two pillars of the entire philosophy associated with TPS. Importantly, the pull production concept was adopted as key principles by the most popular models of operational excellence such as Lean Thinking [6], Shingo Model [14] and obviously the TPS update, the Toyota Way [15].

Although there are some misinterpretations of this concept, and it may be somewhat difficult to explain, it would not be wrong to say that for pull production to be achieved, it is necessary to have a mechanism limiting WIP, i.e., limiting the number of jobs waiting to be processed in each step of the production process. This method of elucidating the concept is also shared by Christoph Roser in his fascinating book about pull production [16].

From a certain perspective the existing flow control mechanisms address two main problems: (i) whether a job should be released into the shop floor, and (ii) whether a station should be authorized to produce (15). Methods such as CONWIP and COBACABANA address the first concern, whether a job should be released into a production system, but ignore the second. These methods employ a backlog of production orders that precedes the manufacturing system, and orders are only released to the shop floor if particular system criteria, such as WIP levels, are met. Kanban and POLCA, on the other hand, are concerned with the issue of production authorization at shop floor stations. This means that they respond to the question of whether any job should be produced at a station, but lose sight of whether a job should be released to the shop floor. Jobs enter the shop floor directly and go to the line in front of the first station in their routing, where the production authorization decision is made. In both approaches, dispatching rules are applied to select the next job to be processed from a list of jobs awaiting servicing. In the case of order release, dispatching rules decide the backlog sequencing [17], and in the context of station authorization which job should be produced next [18].

While pull production has proven effective in simpler environments, with limited product variety, steady demand, and established process plans or routes, its application in complex settings can introduce unique challenges. POLCA and COBACABANA are techniques capable to deal with productions units with some complexity such as job shops even if the demand is variable although both methods do exhibit certain limitations.

Complex production systems, such as those involving a high-mix and low-volume environments, often involve numerous interdependencies, variable demand patterns, unpredictable material flow and a wide variety of products passing through different routes and sequences jobs, priorities, and different processing times [19]. These factors can lead to increased uncertainty, bottlenecks, and disruptions in the flow of work. As a result, companies with complex production system, often rely on traditional practices centred on push-type production systems, functional layouts, and the utilization of Material Resource Planning (MRP). The MRP system determines the order releases for a certain period according to existing capacity and the day-to-day shop floor decisions are left to local production manager and supervisors.

Understanding and acknowledging the vulnerabilities of pull production in complex contexts is crucial for effectively managing and optimizing production systems, ensuring smooth operations, and minimizing potential bottlenecks and inefficiencies. By identifying and addressing these vulnerabilities, practitioners and researchers can work towards enhancing the applicability and adaptability of pull production approaches in complex production environments.

2 Methodology

The methodology employed in this systematic literature review involved a structured approach to identify, select, and synthesize relevant studies addressing the topic of pull production in complex production systems. The steps showed in Fig. 1 were followed to ensure a comprehensive and unbiased analysis.

Firstly, specific research question is defined to guide the review process, aiming to uncover vulnerabilities and challenges in pull production approaches within complex production systems. The research question is:

- What are the vulnerabilities in current pull production approaches in dealing with complex production systems?
- The search criteria were then developed, including keywords, publication date range, and language, to conduct a systematic search across relevant academic databases.

The search strategy utilized the string [("Pull Production" OR "Pull" OR "Kanban" OR "CONWIP" OR "POLCA" OR "COBACABANA") AND ("Job Shop" OR "Complex Production Systems" OR "High Variety" OR "High-mix" OR "one-of-a-kind")] to capture the majority of studies that address pull production approaches in complex production environments. The result was a list of 183 documents.

Only papers published in English were considered to ensure accessibility and understanding of the content, with a time horizon ranging from 2000 to 2023. Additionally, to refine the scope of the review, certain subject areas were excluded from the search. Specifically, papers related to the fields of Social Sciences, Environmental Science, Medicine, Energy, Chemical Engineering, Arts and Humanities and Agriculture and Biological Sciences were excluded from the review. The result is a list of 128 documents (Link here). From the remaining papers, 36 were excluded since there was no

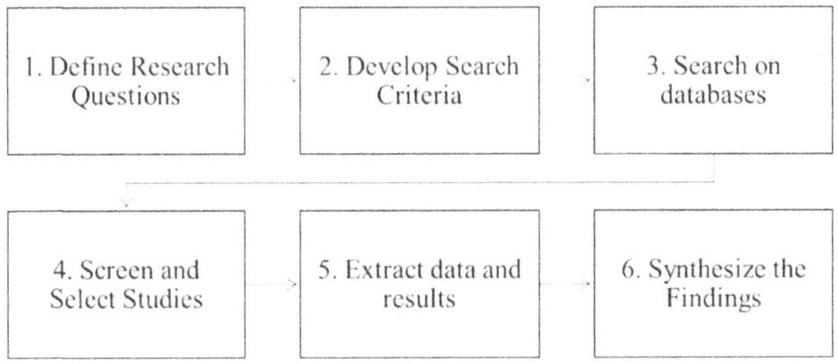

Fig. 1. Methodology applied.

access to full paper mainly because they were published in conferences. The selected studies were screened to assess their relevance to the study. In this stage, 28 publications were excluded.

The database search resulted in 64 papers relevant publications to be the ground for the study. The methodological approaches listed in Table 1 were used to categorize the chosen papers.

Table 1. Number of publications excluded in each stage.

Stage	Stage description	No. of Excluded Papers	No. of remaining Papers
1	Only papers in English	5	178
2	Time horizon 2000–2023	41	137
3	Subject Area	9	128
4	Full Text Available	36	92
5	Relevance	28	64

Subsequently, data and results were extracted from the selected studies, encompassing essential information such as authors, publication year, approach employed to control workflow (e.g., Kanban, CONWIP, POLCA, COBACABANA), their vulnerabilities and implementation context (e.g., real case implementation, simulation, mathematical modelling). This extraction process ensured the collection of pertinent details from each study, allowing for a comprehensive analysis of the findings and a deeper understanding of the vulnerabilities and corresponding mitigation approaches in the context of pull production within complex production systems. Lastly, a synthesis of the findings was performed, organizing and analysing the extracted data to identify common themes and patterns across the selected studies. By following this systematic methodology, we aimed to minimize bias, ensure reproducibility, and provide a comprehensive review of the existing literature on pull production in complex production systems.

3 Literature Review

The domain of production systems and manufacturing strategies is a dynamic landscape, continually molded by industrial demands and evolving consumer expectations. Within this context, pull production techniques have emerged as critical contributors, renowned for their capacity to minimize waste, improve flow, and optimize resources utilization. However, the application of pull production methods in complex manufacturing environments, characterized by high-mix low-volume production, one-of-a-kind manufacturing, and complex routing configurations, presents a unique set of challenges and opportunities.

Before embarking on an exploration of the vulnerabilities and limitations of pull production systems in these complex manufacturing environments, it is essential to understand the research landscape in which this work is placed. This chapter begins with bibliometric study of the current status of research in this topic. Some insights into the historical growth of pull production studies, the importance of each pull production approach, and the temporal evolution of research focus are given.

The pull techniques referred in the publications, considered in this study, are Kanban, CONWIP, POLCA, COBACABANA and Others. In the broader literature, additional techniques, such as "DRACO - Dispatching, Release, and Authorization to dynamically Control Order flow" [20], a "Deep reinforcement learning approach with CONWIP" [21], "LOOR - Load-Oriented Order Release DEWIP" [22], "MPBB - Modified Path-Base Bottleneck" [23], and "Capacity Slack CONWIP + PBB - Path Base Botleneck" [24] have emerged in the landscape of pull production methodologies. These diverse approaches collectively shape the dynamic field of pull production strategies, warranting comprehensive exploration in our literature review.

3.1 Bibliometric Analysis

Publications Over Time. To understand the trajectory of research on pull production systems in complex manufacturing environments, we studied the number of publications throughout the years. The graph Fig. 2 illustrates the growth of publications from 2000 to the present (July 2023). The vast majority of articles on the subject were published after 2013.

Distribution of Publications on Pull Production Techniques. The Venn diagram in Fig. 3 shows the distribution of the 64 studies on various pull production techniques within high mix manufacturing environments. Each circle represents one of the four pull production methods: CONWIP, POLCA, Kanban, and COBACABANA. The size of each circle corresponds to the number of studies dedicated to that technique. Additionally, the diagram highlights the overlaps between these categories, indicating studies that simultaneously investigate combinations or comparisons of these techniques.

The distribution of published studies within these categories is in more detail presented in Table 2. In that table are also included the publications referring more than one technique studies. Notably, there were no studies found that simultaneously explore COBACABANA and CONWIP.

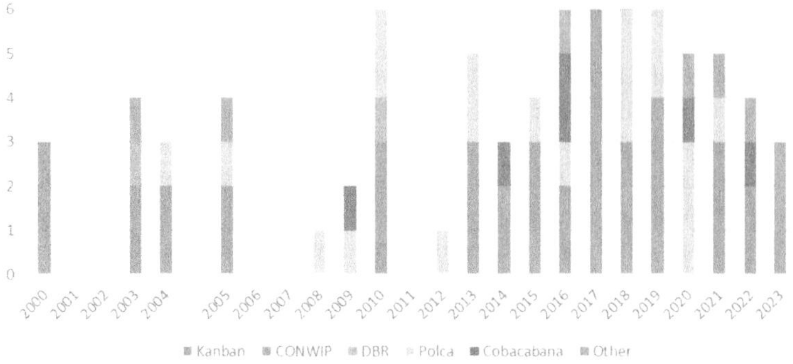

Fig. 2. Number of publications per year on each technique.

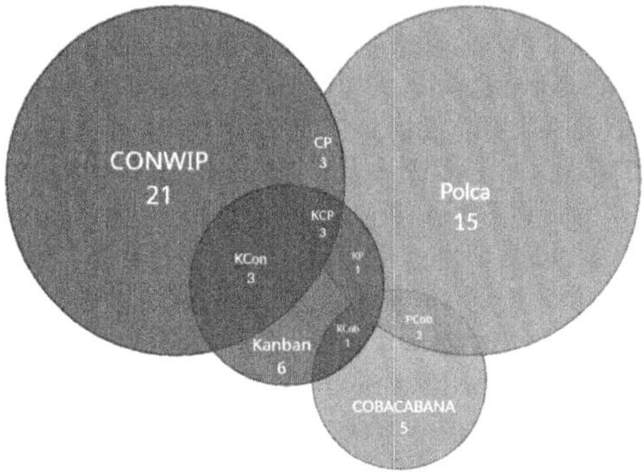

Fig. 3. Venn Diagram of Pull Production Techniques in High Mix Environments.

It is visually evident from the diagram that CONWIP and POLCA receive significant attention from researchers, with 21 and 15 studies respectively. Intriguingly, the relatively limited number of studies dedicated to Kanban (6) and COBACABANA (5) may be attributed to the historical context and unique characteristics of these pull production methods. Kanban, dating back to its inception in the 1950s [9], is the earliest and most well-established pull production technique. Its extensive use and successful application in traditional manufacturing settings have been extensively documented. However, its adaptation and resilience in high mix environments may have posed challenges, possibly leading to a lower volume of research in this context.

Conversely, COBACABANA, the most recent addition to the pull production methods, having been introduced only in 2009 [67] presents an intriguing and comparatively uncharted territory for research. Its novelty and innovative features may have limited its widespread adoption and exploration in the literature. Researchers may be cautiously approaching COBACABANA, given the need for a deeper understanding of its intricacies and suitability in high mix manufacturing environments. As such, the lower number of studies focusing on COBACABANA is indicative of its emerging status in the field and merits further investigation.

Table 2. Studies on pull production techniques.

Technique	Publications
CONWIP (21 studies)	[21, 24–26, 26–42]
POLCA (15 studies)	[43–47, 47–56]
Kanban (6 studies)	[57–62]
COBACABANA (5 studies)	[63–67]
Simultaneous investigation of Kanban and CONWIP (3 studies)	[68, 69, 69]
Comparing CONWIP and POLCA (3 studies)	[70–72]
Exploring POLCA and COBACABANA (2 studies)	[73, 74]
Examining Kanban and POLCA (1 study)	[75]
Comparing Kanban with COBACABANA (1 study)	[76]
Investigating Kanban, CONWIP, and POLCA (3 studies)	[77–79]

The presence of studies examining the combined use of Kanban-POLCA, POLCA-COBACABANA and the trio of Kanban, CONWIP, and POLCA implies a potential interest in hybrid systems or the comparative analysis of these pull methods. The absence of any studies on COBACABANA and CONWIP concurrently may suggest uncharted territory or a lack of research focus on this particular combination, possibly because it might not be a meaningful or effective pairing.

Another interesting fact in the studies is that the vast majority of the studies (41 of the 64 studies) were based on simulation while only 9 of the 64 studies were based on case studies or were real application on real shop floors [32, 50, 51, 53, 62, 63, 68, 74, 75]. The other studies were based either on mathematical modelling or just theoretical considerations.

3.2 Vulnerabilities of Pull Production Systems in High Mix Environments

In this section, an in-depth analysis of the vulnerabilities and constraints associated with various pull production systems when applied in high-mix low-volume manufacturing environments is provided. The following methodologies were examined: Kanban, CONWIP, POLCA, and COBACABANA, and the challenges and limitations faced by each of them were highlighted.

Kanban Systems. The first WIP limitation mechanism, pull production technique, or even flow control of materials, designed to materialize the pull production concept was the Kanban system, which started to be developed by Toyota in the 1950s [9]. Nevertheless, the first scientific publication in English on the subject was only in 1977 [80].

The Kanban system limits the number of specific products, components, or parts waiting in queues to be processed or to be transported to another location. When the product mix is higher and the demand for the family of products is stable a similar technique can be used, the generic Kanban [81]. While in the classic Kanban systems a set of kanbans is assigned to each specific part, in the generic Kanban mode a set of kanbans is assigned to a specific pair supplier-client, considering that each 'client' or 'supplier' could for example be a workstation or a supermarket. When a part, or a container of parts is processed in the client station, an equivalent space becomes available, or authorization (a Kanban) is given so another part or container of parts can be sent from that supplier to the client's queue. This alternative can work effectively if the processing times are similar. Although Kanban is only effective within flow shop type environments, its applicability can extend to job shop type environments through the imposition of specific restrictions or conditions [59].

Within the existing literature, notable constraints or vulnerabilities linked with Kanban materialize as follows:

- Struggles in variable mix production [22, 49, 51, 52, 61–63, 66, 68, 70, 77].
- Inadequate consideration of workload and order crossovers [77].
- Lack of load-balancing capabilities across different workstations or processes [68, 76].
- Challenges in managing multiple cards and workloads [22].
- It is only adequate to high-volume production environment with low variety of products [82].
- It is sluggish to respond to changes in demand [68, 83].
- Kanban systems require a minimum inventory of each product to be maintained at the output of each workstation resulting in a proliferation of work-in-progress (WIP) inventories at each stage of the process [51, 75].
- It is only applied when routing variability is low [84].
- It shows high sensitivity to processing time variability [84].
- It does not support other planning tasks, such as due date estimations during customer enquiry management [65].

CONWIP. Another popular WIP limitation mechanism is known as CONWIP (Constant Work In Process) [32, 85]. The authors claimed that this technique solved the problems of Kanban. Some author claim that this method is able to deal with job shop type production with high variety of products with multiple routes [35, 36].

The CONWIP technique limits the amount of work in progress between two defined points in a sequence of processes without specifying the products or parts. To clarify this concept a bit more, let's assume, for example, a production unit with several machines where, as soon as a product is shipped to another production section, an authorization is given for a new product to enter that production unit to be processed. In this way the WIP is maintained constant in a macro level point of view. WIP is kept constant (pull production) when looking at the production unit as a whole but the WIP in each machine (micro level) in that production unit is not limited by anything (push production). High inventories can appear in front of slow machines and when a machine, for instance, breaks down.

One technique that needs to be mentioned has having a CONWIP component is Drum-Buffer-Rope (DBR) [33, 86]. The principles of this technique were earlier referred in another famous book "The Goal" [87]. In this technique a CONWIP mechanism is applied between the bottleneck and the first process step for each route. From the bottleneck to downstream process steps the products are processed in a push production manner.

Correspondingly, in the realm of ConWIP, key constraints or susceptibilities found in the literature include:

- Difficulties in accommodating changing demand, varying process times and optimizing resource utilization across different routings [12, 26, 38, 72, 84].
- Need for multiple loops to handle different types of products effectively [42].
- Some standardization of products is needed because if the number of cards is to regulate the level of WIP, the workload represented by each card will have to be similar [31, 52, 77].
- It needs end items to be grouped into families of common routings restricting customization possibilities and applicability [77].
- Unfortunately real systems rarely fulfil the hypotheses of CONWIP (i.e. similar routings and processing times among jobs and no setup times) [26]. According to the same authors this technique also does not take into account the fact that the number of cards may change.
- Lack of load-balancing capabilities hinders its use for more complex shops [24, 28, 38, 49, 63, 66, 71, 73, 77].
- Requires the development of an independent sequencing rule and its application to establish the processing order of products during manufacturing stages [39, 40, 75].
- The simplified release procedure of CONWIP makes backlog-sequencing based on planned release dates dysfunctional. This negatively impacts the performance of modified capacity slack-based sequencing rules that were recently shown to be the best choice for Workload Control [28].

POLCA. In order to achieve pull production in micro level point of view in complex production environments, with high-mix and variable routing environments, Rajan Suri proposed the POLCA technique (Paired-cell Overlapping Loops of Cards with Authorization) [51, 88].

Complex production systems are understood to be production systems where a large variety of items are produced in small quantities with unstable demand and with a large variety of routes. POLCA allows you to limit WIP between pairs of machines or cells regardless of the products or parts. Each pair is composed of a supplier machine or cell and a customer machine or cell. There is a loop of cards in each supplier/costumer pair, limiting the WIP since products can only be in the loop if a card is attached to it. Since the number of POLCA cards is limited in each pair the WIP is also limited. The WIP is limited both from a macro and micro point of view, assuming that the machine or cell is the smallest unit within the production unit under consideration.

Likewise, as elucidated by literature, a comprehensive enumeration uncovers the critical shortcomings or vulnerabilities within POLCA:

- POLCA faces many challenges with high variety and unstable production mix [22, 49, 52, 54, 58, 63, 67, 74].
- It needs to be combined with a material requirements planning system to determine delivery dates [51, 63, 65, 73, 77, 84].

- Premature dispatching constraint due to immediate card allocation [43, 89].
- Insufficient synchronization of processes between manufacturing cells, resulting in waiting times between cells and unbalanced workloads [55].
- Needs to be incorporated with other methods if it is to address job entry and job release [43].
- More suited to the flow shop rather than the job shop [43]. To be useful in a job shop the system has to accommodate high routing variability, including upstream travel.
- The dispatching decision is constrained as soon as the POLCA card arrives from the downstream station, which may be long before the dispatching decision is actually executed [43]. It does not decide which job should be authorized. The decision concerning which job should be authorized is executed by the card-allocation and dispatching decisions.
- POLCA cards are job anonymous. POLCA cards do not indicate which job to work on – just that a job requires processing at two consecutive stations of the loop (e.g. A-B). As a consequence, there is still a need to choose between alternative jobs waiting in the queue of a station [48].
- In the original POLCA system, an order must be authorized, i.e., the earliest release date calculated for a particular order at a station must have been reached. But this condition is myopic since there could be a better sequence of jobs for processing at a station; better in terms of different performance objectives. Therefore, we argue that the highest priority should be given to the job that is likely to contribute the most to system performance regardless of whether the earliest release date calculated for this job has been reached or not [48].
- Weakness in the prioritization of orders and weakness in capacity control [48].
- The POLCA system may lead to blocking if there are feedback loops in the routing [22, 78, 84].
- It does not support other planning tasks, such as due date estimations during customer enquiry management [65].
- If a part may leave its mapped production routing, it may disrupts the POLCA system [52].

COBACABANA. Control of Balance by Card Based Navigation (COBACABANA) [67] is another WIP limitation mechanism or work load control system able to deal shop floor environments with high-mix and variable routing. This card-based method is slightly different method from POLCA method since the orders are only released to the shopfloor when all required capacity for each equipment in their routes is available. This method does not limit the amount of WIP in each machine but limits the amount processing time required in each machine according to its capacity.

According to the literature, a similar enumeration reveals the significant limitations or vulnerabilities inherent in COBACABANA.

- Difficulty in tracking the progress of orders due to the absence of a clear sequence of operations. Tracing the remaining operations of an order becomes time-consuming, leading to delays in monitoring production [63].
- When limits are tightened, large jobs may find it harder to fit within the workload limit. Resulting in the increase of the mean tardiness [73].

- COBACABANA's release method cannot be directly implemented to pure flow shops [64].
- Weaknesses in Original Due Date Estimation Procedure [64, 66].
- Uncertainty regarding work represented by each card [64, 67].
- Increased complexity with unstable production mix and routings [67, 74].
- Complexity in calculation of release card requirements. Errors, delays, and challenges in accurately managing the issuance of cards [67].

4 Conclusions

This study has provided a comprehensive examination of the vulnerabilities and limitations of various pull production techniques when applied in complex manufacturing environments including those characterized by high-mix low-volume production, one-of-a-kind manufacturing, and high variety of products with intricate routing configurations. The research question assumed in this study was "What are the vulnerabilities in current pull production approaches in dealing with complex production systems?". Through an extensive review of the literature and the analysis of a substantial number of research studies, several notable insights have emerged.

First and foremost, it is evident that CONWIP and POLCA have garnered substantial attention from researchers, with 21 and 15 studies, respectively. This attention is reflective of the recognized potential of these systems in addressing the challenges posed by high mix production. The research community's interest in these techniques signals their perceived adaptability and suitability for a wide range of manufacturing scenarios.

Intriguingly, the relatively limited number of studies dedicated to Kanban (6) and COBACABANA (5) requires further exploration. Kanban, the pioneering pull production technique dating back to its inception in the 1950s, has firmly established itself in low variety and single route environments. Its application in high mix environments may have presented unique challenges, contributing to the fewer research activities in this context. On the other hand, COBACABANA, introduced more recently in 2009, remains an emerging and relatively uncharted field of study. Researchers are understandably cautious, requiring a deeper understanding of its intricacies and its applicability in high mix manufacturing. As a result, the limited number of studies on COBACABANA underscores its nascent status, warranting further investigation.

Furthermore, the presence of studies examining the combined use of Kanban-POLCA, POLCA-COBACABANA, and the trio of Kanban, CONWIP, and POLCA indicates a growing interest in hybrid systems and the comparative analysis of these pull methods. These endeavors highlight the dynamic nature of research in this field, as scholars explore innovative combinations to address the complexities of high mix production.

Significantly, the absence of any studies concurrently exploring COBACABANA and CONWIP suggests that this particular combination may not hold substantial practical or research interest.

Several vulnerabilities have been identified in the existing literature for all the principal pull production techniques. Table 3 presents a possible comparison between these distinct techniques for controlling the flow of materials in production. It is important to note that this comparison, derived from the comprehensive literature analysis, remains subjective and may not achieve consensus, as it exclusively mirrors the interpretation and perspective of the authors of this paper. The criteria adopted for this comparison encompass the number of different products (mix of products), the multiplicity of routes, the variability of processing times and the variability of demand.

Table 3. Performance assessment of different pull techniques in dealing with complexity

	Product mix	Routing complexity	Variability of processing times	Variability of Demand
Kanban	Low	Low	Low	Low
CONWIP	Medium	Low	Low/Medium	Medium
POLCA	Medium	Medium	Medium	Medium
COBACABANA	Medium	Medium	Medium	Medium

Kanban is the technique less capable to be effective in controlling the flow of materials in complex production environments especially because it is product specific and does not work when products change often. Furthermore, Kanban does not easily accommodate variations on demand. POLCA and COBACABANA on the other hand, are the pull production techniques more capable of dealing with complex production environments. Nonetheless, those techniques still have many vulnerabilities in dealing with such demanding production environments.

The large majority of studies are based on simulation rather than real-world experimentation. This is one of the biggest flaws in existing public knowledge expressed on scientific investigations. Unfortunately, very few evidences of practical implementations in real context exist in order to validate some of the claimed advantages and vulnerabilities of POLCA and COBACABA.

In conclusion, this research offers a holistic understanding of the vulnerabilities and constraints of pull production systems in high-mix manufacturing environments. The findings not only shed light on the existing challenges but also highlighted the need for future investigations in the development of techniques able to deal with complex production systems as well as being effectively integrated with ERP systems.

Acknowledgments. This work has been supported by FCT – Fundação para a Ciência e Tecnologia within the R&D Units Project Scope: UIDB/00319/2020.

References

1. Zhang, X., Ming, X.: A Smart system in Manufacturing with Mass Personalization (S-MMP) for blueprint and scenario driven by industrial model transformation. J. Intell. Manuf. **34**(4), 1875–1893 (2023)
2. Bouchard, S., Gamache, S., Abdulnour, G.: Operationalizing mass customization in manufacturing SMEs—A systematic literature review. Sustainability (Switzerland) **15**, 3028 (2023)

3. Rossit, D.A., Tohmé, F., Frutos, M.: Industry 4.0: smart scheduling. Int. J. Prod. Res. **57**(12), 3802–3813 (2019)
4. Thürer, M., Fernandes, N.O., Stevenson, M., Qu, T., Li, C.D.: Centralised vs. decentralised control decision in card-based control systems: comparing kanban systems and COBACABANA. Int. J. Prod. Res. **57**(2), 322–337 (2019). [Internet] https://www.scopus.com/inward/record.uri?eid=2-s2.0-85041014215&doi=10.1080%2F00207543.2018.1425018&partnerID=40&md5=b702da98b786da3e86b1950032e64263
5. Rother, M., Harris, R.: Creating Continuous Flow. Lean Enterprise Institute, Boston (2001)
6. Womack, J., Jones, D.: Lean Thinking: Banish Waste and Create Wealth in Your Corporation. Free Press, New York (1996)
7. Womack, J.P.: Value stream mapping. Manuf. Eng. (2006)
8. Rother, M., Shook, J.: Learning to See: Value Stream Mapping to Add Value and Eliminate MUDA. The Lean Enterprise Institute, Boston (1999)
9. Ohno, T.: Toyota Production System: Beyond Large-Scale Production. Press C, editor. Productivity, Inc., New York (1988)
10. Zhou, B.: Lean principles, practices, and impacts: a study on small and medium-sized enterprises (SMEs). Ann. Oper. Res. **241**(1–2), 457–474 (2016)
11. Womack, J., Jones, D., Roos, D.: The Machine that Changed the World. Free Press, New York (1990)
12. Hopp, W.J., Spearman, M.L.: To pull or not to pull: what is the question? Manuf. Serv. Oper. Manag. **6**(2), 133–148 (2004)
13. Little, J.D.C.: A proof for the queuing formula: $L = \lambda$ W. Oper. Res. **9**(3), 383–387 (1961)
14. Miller, R.: The Shingo model for operational excellence. Jon M. Huntsman Sch. Bus. **45** (2016)
15. Krijnen, A.: The Toyota way: 14 management principles from the world's greatest manufacturer. Action Learn. Res. Pract. (2007)
16. Roser, C.: All About Pull Production: Designing, Implementing, and Maintaining Kanban, CONWIP, and other Pull Systems in Lean Production. AllAboutLean.com, Offenbach (2021)
17. Thürer, M., Land, M.J., Stevenson, M., Fredendall, L.D., Godinho Filho, M.: Concerning workload control and order release: the pre-shop pool sequencing decision. Prod. Oper. Manag. **24**(7), 1179–1192 (2015)
18. Blackstone, J.H., Phillips, D.T., Hogg, G.L.: A state-of-the-art survey of dispatching rules for manufacturing job shop operations. Int. J. Prod. Res. **20**(1), 27–45 (1982)
19. Peron, M., Alfnes, E., Sgarbossa, F.: Kanban System in Industry 4.0 Era: A Systematic Literature Review. In: Wang, Y., Martinsen, K., Yu, T., Wang, K. (eds.) IWAMA 2021. LNEE, vol. 880, pp. 12–19. Springer, Singapore (2022). https://doi.org/10.1007/978-981-19-0572-8_2
20. Kasper, T.A.A., Land, M.J., Teunter, R.H.: Non-hierarchical work-in-progress control in manufacturing. Int. J. Prod. Econ. **257**, 108768 (2023)
21. Tomé De Andrade e Silva, M., Azevedo, A.: Self-adapting WIP parameter setting using deep reinforcement learning. Comput. Oper. Res. **144**, 105854 (2022)
22. Lödding, H., Yu, K.W., Wiendahl, H.P.: Decentralized WIP-oriented manufacturing control (DEWIP). Prod. Plan. Control **14**(1), 42–54 (2003)
23. Huang, G., Khojasteh, Y.: Using an incentive-compatibility due-date quotation to improve the performance for one-of-a-kind production shop floors controlled by load-based pull systems. Int. J. Prod. Res. **62**, 1072–1091 (2023)
24. Huang, G., Chen, J., Khojasteh, Y.: A cyber-physical system deployment based on pull strategies for one-of-a-kind production with limited resources. J. Intell. Manuf. **32**(2), 579–596 (2021)
25. Vinci-Carlavan, G., Alejandro Rossit, D.: Personalized production in Industry 4.0: a CONWIP approach. In: 2022 International Conference on Decision Aid Sciences and Applications, DASA 2022, pp. 670–675 (2022)

26. Ragazzini, L., Negri, E., Macchi, M.: A digital twin-based predictive strategy for workload control. IFAC-PapersOnLine **54**(1), 743–748 (2021)
27. Huang, G., Chen, J., Wang, X., Shi, Y., Tian, H.: From loop structure to policy-making: a CONWIP design framework for hybrid flow shop control in one-of-a-kind production environment. Int. J. Prod. Res. **55**(12), 3374–3391 (2017)
28. Thürer, M., Fernandes, N.O., Stevenson, M., Qu, T.: On the backlog-sequencing decision for extending the applicability of ConWIP to high-variety contexts: an assessment by simulation. Int. J. Prod. Res. **55**(16), 4695–4711 (2017)
29. Romagnoli, G.: Design and simulation of CONWIP in the complex flexible job shop of a Make-To-Order manufacturing firm. Int. J. Ind. Eng. Comput. **6**(1), 117–134 (2015)
30. Fredendall, L.D., Ojha, D., Wayne Patterson, J.: Concerning the theory of workload control. Eur. J. Oper. Res. **201**(1), 99–111 (2010)
31. Li, J.W.: Simulation study of coordinating layout change and quality improvement for adapting job shop manufacturing to CONWIP control. Int. J. Prod. Res. **48**(3), 879–900 (2010)
32. Slomp, J., Bokhorst, J.A.C., Germs, R.: A lean production control system for high-variety/low-volume environments: a case study implementation. Prod. Plan. Control **20**(7), 586–595 (2009)
33. Kim, S., Roscoe Davis, K., Cox, J.F.: An investigation of output flow control, bottleneck flow control and dynamic flow control mechanisms in various simple lines scenarios. Prod. Plan. Control **14**(1), 15–32 (2003)
34. Ryan, S.M., Choobineh, F.F.: Total WIP and WIP mix for a CONWIP controlled job shop. IIE Trans. (Institute Ind. Eng.) **35**(5), 405–418 (2003)
35. Ryan, S.M., Baynat, B., Choobineh, F.: Determining inventory levels in a CONWIP controlled job shop. IIE Trans. (Institute Ind. Eng.) **32**(2), 105–114 (2000)
36. Luh, P.B., Zhou, X., Tomastik, R.N.: An effective method to reduce inventory in job shops. IEEE Trans. Robot. Autom. **16**(4), 420–424 (2000)
37. Khan, S., Standridge, C.: Aggregate simulation modeling with application to setting the CONWIP limit in a HMLV manufacturing cell. Int. J. Ind. Eng. Comput. **10**(2), 149–160 (2019)
38. Olaitan, O., Alfnes, E., Vatn, J., Strandhagen, J.O.: CONWIP implementation in a system with cross-trained teams. Int. J. Prod. Res. **57**(20), 6473–6486 (2019)
39. Olaitan, O., et al.: Achieving balanced workload distribution amongst. In: Moon, I., Lee, G., Park, J., Kiritsis, D., von Cieminski, G. (eds.) APMS 2018. IFIPAICT, vol. 535, pp. 355–363. Springer, Cham (2019). https://doi.org/10.1007/978-3-319-99704-9_44
40. Olaitan, O., Yu, Q., Alfnes, E.: Work in process control for a high product mix manufacturing system. Proc. CIRP **63**, 277–282 (2017)
41. Huang, G., Chen, J., Wang, X., Shi, Y.: An approach of designing CONWIP loop for assembly system in one-of-a-kind production environment. Int. J. Comput. Integr. Manuf. **29**(7), 805–820 (2016)
42. Huang, G., Chen, J., Wang, X., Shi, Y.: A simulation study of CONWIP assembly with multi-loop in mass production, multi-products and low volume and OKP environments. Int. J. Prod. Res. **53**(14), 4160–4175 (2015)
43. Fernandes, N.O., Thürer, M., Stevenson, M.: On the integration of card-allocation and dispatching decisions in POLCA systems: an assessment by simulation. Prod. Plan. Control **35**(13), 1–8 (2021)
44. Carmo-Silva, S., Fernandes, N., Thürer, M., Ferreira, L.P.: Extending the POLCA production control system with centralized job release. Production **30**, e20190159 (2020)
45. Abdolmaleki, S., Shokouhyar, S., Kasaee, M.: Simulation-based optimisation model for paired-cells overlapping loops of cards with authorisation system. Int. J. Ind. Syst. Eng. **33**(1), 58–74 (2019)

46. Thürer, M., Fernandes, N.O., Carmo-Silva, S., Stevenson, M.: Lot splitting under load-limiting order release in high-variety shops: an assessment by simulation. J. Manuf. Syst. **48**(June), 63–72 (2018)
47. Bong, C.S., Chong, K.E., How, W.C.: Job shop material control based on the principles of quick response manufacturing. J. Adv. Manuf. Technol. **12**(1 Special Issue 2), 15–30 (2018)
48. Thürer, M., Fernandes, N.O., Carmo-Silva, S., Stevenson, M.: Improving performance in POLCA controlled high variety shops: an assessment by simulation. J. Manuf. Syst. **44**, 143–153 (2017)
49. Eng, C.K., Ching, H.W., Siong, B.C.: Paired-cell overlapping loops of cards with authorization simulation in job shop environment. Int. J. Mech. Mechatronics Eng. **15**(3), 68–73 (2015)
50. Riezebos, J.: Design of POLCA material control systems. Int. J. Prod. Res. **48**(5), 1455–1477 (2010)
51. Krishnamurthy, A., Suri, R.: Planning and implementing POLCA: a card-based control system for high variety or custom engineered products. Prod. Plan. Control **20**(7), 596–610 (2009)
52. Vandaele, N., Van Nieuwenhuyse, I., Claerhout, D., Cremmery, R.: Load-based POLCA: an integrated material control system for multiproduct, multimachine job shops. Manuf. Serv. Oper. Manag. **10**(2), 181–197 (2008)
53. Wang, W., et al.: Implementation of POLCA integrated QRM framework for optimized production performance-a case study. Sustain. **13**(6), 3452 (2021)
54. Fernandes, N.O., Thürer, M., Mirzaei, N., Ferreira, L.P., Silva, F.J.G., Carmo-Silva, S.: POLCA control in two-stage production systems. Proc. Manuf. **51**(2019), 1491–1496 (2020)
55. Fernandes, N.O., Thürer, M., Ferreira, L.P., Carmo-Silva, S.: POLCA: centralised vs. decentralised job release. IFAC-PapersOnLine **52**(13), 1427–1431 (2019)
56. Luan, S.C., Jia, G.Z., Kong, W.: A mathematical programming formulation approach to the number of POLCA cards. In: International Conference on Management Science & Engineering - Annual Conference Proceedings, pp. 218–222 (2012)
57. Gonzalez-R, P.L., Calle, M., Andrade-Pineda, J.L.: Job shop management of products under internal lifespan and external due date. Int. J. Prod. Res. **56**(16), 5457–5474 (2018)
58. Müller, E., Tolujew, J., Kienzle, F.: Push-Kanban-a kanban-based production control concept for job shops. Prod. Plan. Control **25**(5), 401–413 (2014)
59. Li, J.W., Barnes, D.J.: Investigating the factors influencing the shop performance in a job shop environment with kanban-based production control. Int. J. Prod. Res. **38**(18), 4683–4699 (2000)
60. Nugroho, W.A., Suroso, J.S.: Optimizing kanban configuration in high mix, low volume environments by applying multi objective genetic algorithm. J. Theor. Appl. Inf. Technol. **101**(1), 293–300 (2023)
61. Lee, Q.: Kanban for the job shop—Adapting kanban for low volume & high variety. Abstract ID: 1582 Repl-, pp. 1985–1991 (2018)
62. Raghavan, V.A., Yoon, S., Srihari, K.: Lean transformation in a high mix low volume electronics assembly environment. Int. J. Lean Six Sigma **5**(4), 342–360 (2014)
63. Braglia, M., Marrazzini, L., Padellini, L.: COBACABANA: a real industrial application in a job shop system. Prod. Plan. Control. **33**(11), 1061–1077 (2022)
64. Thürer, M., Stevenson, M.: Card-based delivery date promising in pure flow shops with order release control. Int. J. Prod. Res. **54**(22), 6798–6811 (2016)
65. Thürer, M., Land, M.J., Stevenson, M., Fredendall, L.D.: Card-based delivery date promising in high-variety manufacturing with order release control. Int. J. Prod. Econ. **172**, 19–30 (2016)
66. Thürer, M., Land, M.J., Stevenson, M.: Card-based workload control for job shops: improving COBACABANA. Int. J. Prod. Econ. **147**(PART A), 180–188 (2014)
67. Land, M.J.: COBACABANA (Control of Balance by Card-Based Navigation): a card-based system for job shop control. Int. J. Prod. Econ. **117**(1), 97–103 (2009)

68. Leonardo, D.G., Sereno, B., Da Silva, D.S.A., Sampaio, M., Massote, A.A., Simões, J.C.: Implementation of hybrid Kanban-CONWIP system: a case study. J. Manuf. Technol. Manag. **28**(6), 714–736 (2017)
69. Arteaga, A.G., Calvo, R.: Experimental analysis of alternative production flow controls for high variety product manufacturing. Proc. Manuf. **41**, 82–89 (2019)
70. Farnoush, A., Wiktorsson, M.: POLCA and CONWIP performance in a divergent production line: an automotive case study. J. Manag. Control. **24**(2), 159–186 (2013)
71. Germs, R., Riezebos, J.: Workload balancing capability of pull systems in MTO production. Int. J. Prod. Res. **48**(8), 2345–2360 (2010)
72. Frazee, T., Standridge, C.: CONWIP versus POLCA: a comparative analysis in a high-mix, low-volume (HMLV) manufacturing environment with batch processing. J. Ind. Eng. Manag. **9**(2), 432–449 (2016)
73. Thürer, M., Fernandes, N.O., Stevenson, M.: Material flow control in high-variety make-to-order shops: combining COBACABANA and POLCA. Prod. Oper. Manag. **29**(9), 2138–2152 (2020)
74. Bertolini, M., Romagnoli, G., Zammori, F.: 2MTO, a new mapping tool to achieve lean benefits in high-variety low-volume job shops. Prod. Plan. Control. **28**(5), 444–458 (2017)
75. Olaitan, O., Fragapane, G., Alfnes, E., Strandhagen, J.O.: A nested configuration of POLCA and generic kanban in a high product mix manufacturing system. In: Lödding, H., Riedel, R., Thoben, KD., von Cieminski, G., Kiritsis, D. (eds.) APMS 2017. IFIPAICT, vol. 513, pp. 518–526. Springer, Cham (2017). https://doi.org/10.1007/978-3-319-66923-6_61
76. Thürer, M., Stevenson, M., Protzman, C.W.: COBACABANA (Control of Balance by Card Based Navigation): an alternative to kanban in the pure flow shop? Int. J. Prod. Econ. **166**, 143–151 (2015)
77. Stevenson, M., Hendry, L.C., Kingsman, B.G.: A review of production planning and control: the applicability of key concepts to the make-to-order industry. Int. J. Prod. Res. **43**(5), 869–898 (2005)
78. Harrod, S., Kanet, J.J.: Applying work flow control in make-to-order job shops. Int. J. Prod. Econ. **143**, 620–626 (2013)
79. Suri, R., Shinde, R.: Setting card levels for a multiproduct jobshop using mean value analysis. In: IIE Annual Conference Exhibition 2004, vol. 3, no. 1, p. 2323 (2004)
80. Sugimori, Y., Kusunoki, K., Cho, F., Uchikawa, S.: Toyota production system and kanban system: materialization of just-in-time and respect for human systems. Int. J. Prod. Res. **15**, 553–564 (1977)
81. Chang, T.M., Yih, Y.: Generic Kanban systems for dynamic environments. Int. J. Prod. Res. **32**, 889–902 (1994)
82. Bonvik, A.M., Couch, C.E., Gershwin, S.B.: A comparison of production-line control mechanisms. Int. J. Prod. Res. **35**(3), 789–804 (1997)
83. Sharma, S., Agrawal, N.: Selection of a pull production control policy under different demand situations for a manufacturing system by AHP-algorithm. Comput. Oper. Res. **36**(5), 1622–1632 (2009)
84. Thürer, M., Stevenson, M., Protzman, C.W.: Card-based production control: a review of the control mechanisms underpinning Kanban, ConWIP, POLCA and COBACABANA systems. Prod. Plan. Control **27**(14), 1143–1157 (2016)
85. Spearman, M.L., Woodruff, D.L., Hopp, W.J.: CONWIP: a pull alternative to kanban. Int. J. Prod. Res. **28**(5), 879–894 (1990)
86. Goldratt, E., Fox, R.: The Race. North River Press, Great Barrington (1986)
87. Goldratt, E., Cox, J.: The Goal: A Process of Ongoing Improvement. North River Press, Great Barrington (1984)

88. Suri, R.: Quick Response Manufacturing: A Companywide Approach to Reducing Lead Times. Productivity Press (1998). [Internet]. https://www.routledge.com/Quick-Response-Manufacturing-A-Companywide-Approach-to-Reducing-Lead-Times/Suri/p/book/9781563272011. Accessed 18 May 2021
89. Thürer, M., Fernandes, N.O., Carmo-Silva, S., Stevenson, M.: Improving performance in POLCA controlled high variety shops: an assessment by simulation. J. Manuf. Syst. **44**, 143–153 (2017). [Internet]. https://www.scopus.com/inward/record.uri?eid=2-s2.0-85019349246&doi=10.1016%2Fj.jmsy.2017.05.006&partnerID=40&md5=b56998a6a35fb01a207580d561150937

Author Index

Published by Springer Nature Switzerland AG 2024
T. van Kollenburg et al. (Eds.): ELEC 2023, IFIP AICT 681, pp. 345–346, 2024.
https://doi.org/10.1007/978-3-031-63265-5

GPSR Compliance

The European Union's (EU) General Product Safety Regulation (GPSR) is a set of rules that requires consumer products to be safe and our obligations to ensure this.

If you have any concerns about our products, you can contact us on ProductSafety@springernature.com

In case Publisher is established outside the EU, the EU authorized representative is:

Springer Nature Customer Service Center GmbH
Europaplatz 3
69115 Heidelberg, Germany

The manufacturer's authorised representative in the EU is Springer Nature Customer Service Centre GmbH, Europaplatz 3, 69115 Heidelberg, Germany. If you have any concerns regarding our products, please contact ProductSafety@springernature.com

Printed and bound by CPI Group (UK) Ltd, Croydon, CR0 4YY
30/09/2026
02225558-0013